The Heresy of Ham

REVISED EDITION

The Heresy of Ham

REVISED EDITION

· · · ·

What Every Evangelical Needs to Know About Young Earth Creationism, the Creation-Evolution Debate

…and what we all can learn about rigid ideology and "fighting the culture war"

JOEL EDMUND ANDERSON

FOREWORDS BY Sy Garte *and* Karl Giberson

RESOURCE *Publications* · Eugene, Oregon

THE HERESY OF HAM, REVISED EDITION
What Every Evangelical Needs to Know about Young Earth Creationism, the Creation-Evolution Controversy . . . and What We All Can Learn about Rigid Ideology and "Fighting the Culture War"

Copyright © 2024 Joel Edmund Anderson. All rights reserved. Except for brief quotations in critical publications or reviews, no part of this book may be reproduced in any manner without prior written permission from the publisher. Write: Permissions, Wipf and Stock Publishers, 199 W. 8th Ave., Suite 3, Eugene, OR 97401.

Resource Publications
An Imprint of Wipf and Stock Publishers
199 W. 8th Ave., Suite 3
Eugene, OR 97401

www.wipfandstock.com

PAPERBACK ISBN: 979-8-3852-2573-6
HARDCOVER ISBN: 979-8-3852-2574-3
EBOOK ISBN: 979-8-3852-2575-0

To Ian Panth, my good friend for the past 29 years

"Friendship is born at the moment when one man says to another 'What! You too? I thought that no one but myself...'"

C. S. Lewis

Contents

	Foreword by Sy Garte	xi
	Foreword by Karl Giberson	xv
	A Brief Response and Discussion	xxiii
	Preface (2016)	xxxiii
	Preface to the Second Edition	xxxvii
	Acknowledgments	xl
1	Walking the Plank on Noah's Ark	1
2	History and Heresy	23
3	Church Tradition and the Bible	34
4	Genesis 1–11: From the Early Church to Today	54
5	The Basics of Biblical Exegesis	76
6	Interpreting Genesis 1–11	90
7	She Blinded Me With Science!	128
8	The Enlightenment Heresy of Ham (Part 1)	147
9	Ham's Lie: It's Already Gone (Part 2)	160
10	The Heretical Bloggings of Ham (Part 3)	183
11	Taking a Cue from Irenaeus of Lyons	214
12	Hamming It Up	239
13	Ark Encounters	258
14	The Historical Adam Debate Today	278
	Epilogue: An Ever-Evolving Personal Story	285
	Book Recommendations	291
	Bibliography	295

Foreword

By Sy Garte

IN THIS EXCELLENT BOOK, Joel Edmund Anderson presents us with a comprehensive treatment of the creation/evolution controversy within the Church. Sadly, this old controversy, instead of fading away, has become more heated and divisive with time, especially in our current era of confrontational culture wars. While it might seem to many that questions about *how* God created our universe and everything in it—not why or for what purpose—are ultimately scientific issues and should not be considered foundational for Christians, some voices are insisting that they absolutely are. One of the loudest such voices is that of Ken Ham, the founder and leader of Answers in Genesis, and—for many Americans—the leader of the young-earth creationist movement.

As the book's title makes clear, Anderson accuses Ham of heresy. But, as he describes it, this heresy is more consequential than most of the historical heresies we know about (which the author discusses in Chapter 2). Ken Ham is not simply advancing a theological narrative that conflicts with established teachings of the Church. The heresy that Anderson accuses Ham of (and provides all the necessary evidence for and more) is nothing less than deliberately causing an unresolvable and highly destructive division in the fabric of the Christian religion. He devotes three chapters (8-10) to explaining the details of Ham's heresy, in an utterly convincing way.

Diversity of theological opinion among Jesus' followers began even before his Crucifixion, as the arguments among the disciples recorded in the Gospels show. The Book of Acts also makes it clear that the first Christians were sharply divided over many issues, including the acceptance of Gentiles and the role of dietary laws. But, if we read carefully, we can also see in these debates, as well as in many of Paul's letters, that such differences in viewpoint were not weaknesses but strengths in the building of the new faith.

What we can take away from this history is that diversity of opinion on many topics within the church is natural, and ultimately healthy. In fact, the opposite—a rigid insistence on one strict and dogmatic way of thinking about the Bible and the message of Christ—has often been a detriment for spreading the good news. Jesus Himself encouraged some degree of openness and interpretation by teaching in parables, allowing (and sometimes correcting) interpretations of their meanings.

In Chapter 4, Anderson provides a comprehensive history of the interpretation of Genesis from the early Church Fathers on. He covers in detail the role of Seventh-Day Adventist writer George McCready Price and his book on *New Geology*, followed by the famous Scopes trial in 1925, and the origins of what became modern young-earth creationism—which, as Anderson clearly demonstrates, is not the traditional Christian view it claims to be.

But Anderson also makes it clear (right at the beginning of the book) that it's *not* Ham's insistence on what he calls a "literal" interpretation of Genesis and his young-earth and anti-evolutionary views that earn him the "heretical" label. The heresy comes in when Ham insists that *only* such an interpretation of Scripture allows a person to be considered a Christian. This is a view that cannot be attributed to the Bible, to the Church Fathers, or to any Christian authority. Even the original purveyors of these ideas never suggested that acceptance versus rejection of evolution or an old earth are salvation issues and fundamental to Christian faith. The heresy of Ham, in other words, is to label all who disagree with him as heretical to the point of exclusion from the faith.

Being a scientist, my favorite chapter is Chapter 7, where Anderson addresses the science behind the evolution debate. This is one of the most thorough and comprehensible discussions I have read on this topic. The author gives a good summary of the famous Ham/Nye debate and uses just the right amount of detail in explaining why the evidence from tree rings, ice cores, starlight, the fossil record, genetics, phylogeny, and other scientific sources refutes young-earth creationism. The material in this chapter alone makes it worth having this book as a resource.

In this second edition, Anderson includes new chapters on his personal story of being fired for teaching about evolution, and his subsequent struggles. He also adds an insightful chapter on the Adam and Eve story. These new chapters enhance and expand the message of the book in many ways. Altogether, *The Heresy of Ham* is a well-written, well-researched, and important contribution to the future success of the Christian faith in bringing new people to Christ, and in bringing the church together in love and harmony.

Foreword

By Karl Giberson

Ken Ham is a cultural cancer. He and his fellow anti-science biblical literalists have exerted a pernicious influence on American society in general and evangelical Christianity in particular. Kudos to my friend Joel Anderson for his work exposing Ham and his movement.

Ham's career started in Australia where he peddled imaginative conspiracies about how modern science was willfully blind to the truths of Genesis. Schoolchildren in an educationally backward part of the country would read Ham's tales about how scientists, literally inspired by Satan, were colluding to fool people into thinking that Darwin had successfully refuted the Genesis account of creation and replaced it with a scientific account. By suppressing evidence that supported the Bible, connecting invisible dots, and inventing imaginary natural processes, the scientific community, inspired by Darwin, was converting everyone to atheism.

Down under educational reform destroyed the demand for Ham's conspiracies but a timely summons from God called him to deeply religious America where a rich market for his ideas still flourished. Initially he joined Henry Morris, an actual scientist and the founder of the American creationism movement, at the Institute for Creation Research (ICR) in San Diego. ICR had an ambitious, expensive agenda—to do the scientific work necessary to show that the Genesis account was accurate. To this end they set up laboratories, hired scientists, and began the hard work of creating defensible empirically based models that aligned with a literal reading of Genesis. This expensive and challenging project was a complete disaster. Absolutely nothing of consequence came of it. Money, time, and credibility were squandered.

Meanwhile, Ham discovered that doing actual scientific work was not necessary to fight evolution. All you needed to do was trumpet the importance of reading Genesis literally as the only genuinely Christian approach. So, Ham elevated belief in a young earth, a literal Garden of Eden, and even a global flood during which the animal kingdom was preserved on an ark. And, with particular emphasis, Adam and Eve were literally the first humans, created on the 6th day of creation and, through their disobedience, responsible for all the imperfections in God's Creation. After all, no less an authority than St. Paul referred to Jesus as a "second" Adam, a claim that would be nonsensical if the "first" Adam was fictional. So, by writing books with titles like *D is for Dinosaur* and *Evolution: The Lie,* Ham converted the discussion about the age and history of the earth into a cosmic battle between the forces of good and evil. Straining credulity, Ham argued that evolution was responsible for all the ills of the contemporary world, from homosexuality and divorce to drug addiction and pornography. To accept Darwin's dangerous idea was to embrace the very mechanism by which Satan was destroying all that is good.

Ham abandoned ICR with its futile scientific pretensions and became the champion of "Biblical"—as opposed to "Scientific"—Creationism. His organization *Answers in Genesis* was a resounding success. He raised $27 million and built an impressive "Creation Museum" in Kentucky, where busloads of children from Christian schools learn that scientists have lied to them about the "true" history of the world. A few years later he built a giant $120 million theme park inside a full-scale replica of Noah's Ark—one of the largest wooden structures on the planet.

Ham's insistence of a literal reading of Genesis as central to genuine Christianity was convincing and profoundly influential. Over and over again, I heard his arguments coming from my students at Eastern Nazarene College, many of whom had visited his museum, read his book and watched his videos.

Despite continual scientific progress in understanding evolution and the ascendancy of genetics as a dramatic new way to understand the relatedness of all living things, 40% of Americans now reject what has become the central concept of the entire field of biology—the theory of evolution. This number has declined by only 10% over the past several decades. Virtually all evolution deniers are evangelical Christians.

If this were an in-house theological squabble, we could dismiss it as mere nonsense, like the lunatic ravings of the flat earth society or nut case politicians claiming wildfires are caused by Jewish space lasers. But the evolution-denying evangelical demographic comprises the bulk of the Republican voter base. Denying evolution is now, for many voters, part of being a Republican, much to the dismay of many—probably most—leaders of the GOP. In the 2012 GOP primary the seven candidates were asked if they believed in evolution. Only Jon Huntsman raised his hand. He was gone from the race a few days later, and widely criticized for being clueless about the beliefs of the GOP voter base.

The pernicious influence of Ham and his ilk can be seen in the present intellectual crisis afflicting much of America, and the GOP in particular. By continually claiming scientists are anti-Christian zealots, Ham et al have sowed seeds of widespread distrust of all sorts of authority, not merely those voices promoting evolution. Not long ago I had an energetic debate with a family member about vaccines. She was insistent that Jenny McCarthy—a former playboy bunny and notorious anti-vaxxer—was a more reliable source for information than Francis Collins, then head of the National Institutes of Health, and one of the world's leading scientists. It made no difference that Collins was an evangelical Christian and a personal friend of mine.

American evangelicalism—at least the white demographic—and the GOP with which it has become intertwined are now deeply mired in anti-intellectual quicksand. Respected news outlets are now "fake news;" leading universities promote ideological "woke brainwashing;" "alternative facts" are now a thing; medical advice should be view with suspicion; judicial decisions are now just politics by another name. Evangelicals readily dismiss knowledge claims if they originate in a progressive context and embrace nonsense from right wing propagandists like Alex Jones, Tucker Carlson, David Barton, Ken Ham, and the talking heads of Fox News. The attacks on science that have animated the anti-evolution movement are now embedded in a powerful flexible template that can be used to undermine any knowledge claim, regardless of its source.

I am painting with broad brush strokes here and there are, of course, many exceptions to the generalizations of the preceding paragraph. The author of this book is one such exception, as is Francis Collins, and many other intellectuals who have fought in these trenches. I was an exception before I abandoned evangelicalism, after three decades of writing, speaking, and teaching alongside Christian thinkers like Joel. I concluded, unhappily, that the task that Joel has heroically embraced in this book is hopeless. Devotees of Ken Ham have an armor-plated ignorance that protects them from unwanted revelations about the nature of reality—whether that relates to the age of the earth, vaccines, the complexity of gender, the origins of life and humans, climate change, free market economics, or the LGBT community.

My conviction that evangelicals are unpersuadable on evolution grew as I came to appreciate the central theological role played by Adam. I had long understood that a historically real Adam as the source of sin in the perfect world God had created was the single greatest challenge posed by evolution. My sharpest students at Eastern Nazarene College, suspicious of the anti-evolution fervor in their churches, uneasy about Christians' wholesale rejection of so much science, but protective of their faith, would inevitably zero in on the challenge of reframing the theology of original sin without a historical Adam. To make matters worse, St. Paul had given Adam a central role as the door through which the fallenness of creation had entered the world. My friend and fellow traveler Pete Enns once commented that "evangelicals will never make peace with evolution until they can accept that St. Paul believed in a historical Adam—but he was wrong."

Here's the problem: virtually all Christian theology—from the most conservative to the most liberal—is built on a foundation of "Creation-Fall-Redemption," which is vague enough to admit of various constructions. Christ, however he is understood in these constructions, is first and foremost a "redeemer." He enters and embraces a fallen world and redeems it from sin and the consequent evils of death and suffering. But this sin, of course, cannot have been created by a sinless holy omniscient God. That mocks the concept of the perfect Creator. Sin had to come from somewhere—it cannot be simply a part of the created order, like the laws of nature, or the existence of moral beings. Finding an acceptable origin for sin without Adam is challenging.

This challenge came into sharp focus in the early days of BioLogos, Francis Collins' ambitious project to help evangelicals make peace with evolution. During a planning meeting at his home, when we were discussing strategies, formulating mission statements and reviewing CVs from fundraisers, public relations firms, and so on, I raised the subject of Adam and how we would handle that hot button topic. There were four of us in the meeting—all scientists. We were unanimous in our conviction that belief in a literal historical human named Adam had to be dislodged if evolution was ever to be accepted. We all understood that there simply was no place in natural history where the entire human race consisted of just two people, whose genes have since multiplied into the astonishing diversity we see today. Evangelical scholars had been hunting in vain ever since Darwin for an historical opening where Adam could be inserted, a hook on which to hang the Fall and the origin of sin. Such an opening simply does not exist, unless the Genesis account is replaced with another origins story that bears little resemblance to the one it is replacing.

Collins' relation to the story of Adam is telling. He became a Christian as an adult, having been raised in a strongly pro-science, secular family. He describes his fascinating conversion in the book that launched the Biologos project—*The Language of God: A Scientist Presents Evidence for Belief.* I asked Collins how, as a new, scientifically informed, Christian putting it all together for the first time, he dealt with the question of Adam. He told me it never even occurred to him that anyone reading Genesis would think that the story of Adam and Eve in the Garden with the talking snake was literally true. The beautiful diorama of Adam handing fruit to Eve in Ken Ham's creation museum was a profound myth brought to life, not a retelling of history.

In agreement that Adam was not historical, the BioLogos team rode enthusiastically off into territories where Charles Darwin was regularly compared to Hitler. We were eager to spread the good news that evolution was not the enemy of Christianity, that God created everything through evolutionary processes, that the earth was billions—not thousands—of years old, that the biblical story of creation could be reconciled with scientific accounts of natural history, and, of course, that none of this required that Adam be a historical character.

Little did we know how naïve we were. Helmed by a marquis celebrity with a great conversion story like Francis Collins, and generously funded by The Templeton Foundation, BioLogos was well-received, even welcomed, by many evangelical groups. Of course, Ken Ham and his merry band of young-earthers castigated us as "wolves in sheep's clothing" but more thoughtful evangelicals embraced the message of BioLogos. Donors lined up. InterVarsity Press invited us to submit book manuscripts and we soon had two books in print.

I ran BioLogos in the early days out of offices at Eastern Nazarene College near Boston (Francis had gone to work at the National Institutes of Health). I hired various support personnel, including a webmaster, and we launched an ambitious website. We hired Pete Enns, a respected Old Testament scholar, unafraid of controversy and solidly in the "Adam is not historical" camp. We were publishing all over the place and forging alliances with evangelical luminaries like Rick Warren and the late Tim Keller.

But something seemed to be wrong. Serious conversations with donors would run out of steam. One promising donor even started a competing project—a sort of "BioLogos lite." Our funders at Templeton created a team to "review" us and delivered a hostile verdict that we were on the wrong track. Pete Enns and I—the leading champions of the "Adam is not a historical figure" argument— were soon gone. The BioLogos conversation changed from "How do we reformulate theology without a historical Adam" to the far more saccharine "What version of the Adam story do you prefer?"

The BioLogos site now, contrary to the vision of its founders, suggests that Christians can just agree to disagree on Adam; we can choose from a menu of "multiple views," all of which are "consistent with both sound biblical interpretation and current scientific evidence."[1]

While "consistency" sounds respectable, in practice it represents an abandonment of scholarship and intellectual integrity. Our approach to the Bible, as Enns stressed consistently, should be guided by a respect for the Biblical authors and a commitment to understand what they meant when they wrote and compiled the texts. We should not ignore the original message and replace it with one that is merely "not contradicted" by the text. Is it plausible that the authors of Genesis intended the seven days of creation to refer to geological epochs, when they had no knowledge of such epochs and nobody suggested this reading until the 18th century? Is it plausible that the first verse of Genesis refers to a cosmological Big Bang, that nobody had any idea about until the 20th century? Such ideas are "consistent" with a literal, albeit creative, reading of Genesis but they are certainly not what the original authors were intending to communicate.

Similar problems emerge on the scientific side. Neither the fossil record nor the genetic evidence suggests in any way that all of humanity has descended from two humans who lived in the Middle East a few thousand years ago. Not one scientist has suggested that this is where the evidence leads. On the other hand, with a sufficiently imaginative reading of the data, one can conjure a "consistent" model of origins that does not rule out the possibility that we are all descended from a single couple.

1. https://biologos.org/common-questions/were-adam-and-eve-historical-figures (Accessed April 21, 2024)

But again, "consistency" means only "not excluded by the evidence;" it does not mean "supported by the evidence."

To make progress on questions like this, Christians need to raise the intellectual bar from "consistency" to "evidentiary." We should hold positions resting on evidence, not on imaginative constructions that are merely "consistent" with evidence.

The conversation at BioLogos is probably the most intellectually significant one on origins within American evangelicalism; there is plenty of intellectual firepower, generous funding, and Francis Collins as a celebrity mascot. But if the Gallup Polls are to be believed—and there is no reason to reject them—the needle is simply not moving. Acceptance of the BioLogos view that "Humans evolved, with God guiding" remains stuck around 33%, below where it was 40 years ago. Meanwhile, acceptance of "God created humans in present form" – the view on display in Ken Ham's Creation Museum—continues as the preferred option for Americans.

My years on the front lines of this controversy have eroded all of my youthful optimism and I have given up on this battle, passing the torch to younger crusaders like Joel. I cannot see a future evangelical theology built on anything other than the traditional "Creation-Fall-Redemption" paradigm, and a historical Adam seems to be a central part of that understanding.

As I write these words Ukraine is struggling to hold back a Russian invasion of their country. There is little chance they can eliminate the challenge from Russia and drive the invaders from their territory. But they can hold the line, perhaps, and not lose further ground. Perhaps this is how the battle against Ken Ham and the young earth creationists should be construed. Joel and his brothers-in-arms cannot eliminate the intellectual scourge led by Ken Ham and the larger anti-science movement of which he is a part. But perhaps they can prevent it from becoming more influential.

A Brief Response and Discussion

I WANT TO THANK both Sy Garte and Karl Giberson for taking the time to write such thoughtful forewords for this revised edition of *The Heresy of Ham*. I wanted to write a brief response to both men's comments because I think it would be interesting to highlight the uniqueness of each of our stories, particularly when it comes to science, faith, and the creation/evolution debate.

As I discuss in the book, I grew up within Evangelical Christianity and eventually found my way to the Orthodox Church. Still, I taught both English and Bible in Evangelical schools for sixteen years and was still very much in the Evangelical world, even after becoming Orthodox. By the time I ever looked into the creation/evolution debate, I had already gotten two master's degrees (OT, NT) and a PhD (OT) in Biblical Studies, and it was my own study of Genesis 1-11—a good twelve years before I even began to investigate the creation/evolution debate—that convinced me that Genesis 1-11 was not trying to "do history." So, by the time I look into the creation/evolution debate, the traditional Evangelical objections to the theory of evolution that are rooted in an assumption in the historicity of Genesis 1-11 to some extent were not an issue for me. Therefore, I was able to investigate and seriously consider the basic claims of evolution without that misguided fear that evolution was the same as atheism, and that it was a threat to Christianity and the Bible. Simply put, my story is one of someone who grew up in Evangelicalism, whose spiritual journey led him to the Orthodox Church but who still harbored no ill-will to Evangelicalism, and whose background in Biblical Studies led him to understand Genesis 1-11 wasn't meant to be understood as history. Because of all of that, I came to be convinced of basic evolutionary theory, precisely because I understood that it was not a threat to the Bible.

SY GARTE'S STORY

Sy Garte's story is rather different. You can read Sy's own story in his book, *The Works of His Hands: A Scientist's Journey from Atheism to Faith*. The book title pretty much says it. Sy grew up as a self-described militant atheist, and as a scientist he studied and investigated evolutionary theory and knew it to be true. Still, in his scientific studies, he came to question his own materialist assumptions. Eventually, his study of the natural sciences led him to see there was something more than just the material world. In the end, Sy became an Evangelical Christian. He has written books about science and faith, is a contributor to BioLogos, and has become a well-known figure in within the Evangelical world.

I got to know Sy through an online creation/evolution group on Facebook back around 2015. We interacted quite a bit in that group. He read *The Heresy of Ham*, as well as another book of mine, *Christianity and the (R)evolution in Worldviews in Western Culture*, while I read his books as well. He even asked me to write an article for *God and Nature Magazine* in 2019. Ironically, a couple of years ago, roughly at the same time, we both decided to leave that creation/evolution group on Facebook for pretty much the same reason. Although the group officially focused on the creation/evolution debate, members began to inject divisive political and social opinions into the discussions that had nothing to do with evolution, the age of the earth, or the interpretation of Genesis 1-11. Both Sy and I saw that when it comes to both scientific and biblical issues, when the political and cultural ideologies of political correctness get a foothold into the discussions, things get vicious pretty quickly.

We've kept in touch and now Sy has graciously written a foreword for the revised edition of *The Heresy of Ham*. It is amazing how Sy's story (one of a militant atheist and scientist who, precisely because of his study of science, eventually came to accept Christ) and my story (one of an Evangelical-turned-Orthodox biblical scholar whose study of Genesis 1-11 allowed me to be open to the idea of evolution) have intersected the why they have.

KARL GIBERSON'S STORY

Karl Giberson's story is rather different still. As he shares in his foreword, he spent most of his professional life within Evangelicalism, teaching at Eastern Nazarene College. He also was one of the founders of BioLogos, serving as both vice-president and president in the early days of the organization, reaching out to the Evangelical world in attempt to show Evangelicals that Christianity and evolutionary theory are not at odds. Eventually, though, Karl left Evangelicalism and has lost hope that the Evangelical world will ever come around to accept the theory of evolution. He now views Evangelicals largely as anti-science, ignorant, right-wing MAGA cultists.

I first came across Karl Giberson in 2009 when I was still the Biblical Worldview teacher at the small Evangelical Christian school I mention in this book. Part of my Senior Worldview curriculum included a unit on Darwin, where I laid out the various views in the creation/evolution debate, had the students discuss the strong and weak points in each position, and then write a short paper on their own views on the topic. Now, my areas of expertise were in literature and Biblical Studies, so when it came to the creation/evolution debate, I knew I had to read up on the issues myself.

It was around that time that BioLogos was getting started, and I found their material to be very helpful. It was also around that time that I read Karl's book, *Saving Darwin*. I found it extremely enlightening. Later on, in 2015, I found his next book, *Saving the Original Sinner*, to be incredible. By that time, of course, the painful drama I talk about in this book, where the new headmaster at my school forced me out when he found out I didn't agree with Ken Ham, had played out, and I was in the midst of writing what would become *The Heresy of Ham*.

I decided to contact Karl and ask him for some feedback and advice on my book. I was elated that such a "big name" in the creation/evolution debate, and the former president of BioLogos nonetheless, took the time to read my manuscript and give me some advice on it. He was the one who advised me to start the book off with a personal story that engages the reader. So, the opening story about the intense initial interactions with "Pastor Clark" and "Mr. Spencer," as well as the entire story about my final year at the school that I've added in this revised edition of *The Heresy of Ham* can ultimately be credited to Karl's advice to include my personal story.

Karl and I have been Facebook friends since 2015, and we have had numerous discussions and debates on a wide range of issues over the course of these past nine years. Other than our shared concern about Ken Ham and YECism, though, when it comes to politics and modern cultural issues, we disagree on just about everything else. And we don't just disagree, we vehemently disagree.

When I asked Karl to write a foreword for *The Heresy of Ham*, he was up front with me and said he was probably going to say some things I was not going to agree with, but that I could always write a response to his foreword, and that might generate more interest and discussion about my book. Well, I have to say, he did not disappoint. To the point, the tone and focus of Karl's comments pretty much runs contrary to everything I write in the book. In light of that, there are three points I want to make.

First of all, my intended audience for *The Heresy of Ham* is primarily American Evangelicals, and my purpose is not to attack Evangelicals, but rather to warn them about what I feel is the toxic and divisive teaching of Ken Ham and YECism. It's not that he just engages in bad biblical interpretation and makes absurd scientific claims. The main problem I have with Ken Ham is that he elevates his YECist claims as being fundamental to the Christian faith and then attacks everyone—Christians included—who doesn't accept his claims. The reason he does this, and I know this from firsthand experience, is that his real concern is *fighting the culture war*: if you don't accept YECism, you must be an enemy who is promoting "liberalism," and will be attacked. I lost my job over it, even though I am not by any stretch of the imagination a "liberal."

I grew up in Evangelicalism and taught in Evangelical schools for sixteen years. Even though I am now Orthodox, I still don't hate Evangelicalism. It has had a tremendous impact on my life. Now, it's true that Evangelicals reject evolution because they think it is the same as atheism (it isn't). And it's true that most are politically and socially conservative (for the most part, so am I). But most Evangelicals I know are not as rigidly ideological as Ken Ham. The creation/evolution debate simply doesn't not play a major role in their lives, and I don't think most Evangelicals really know what Ken Ham and the folks at AiG actually teach. My book, therefore, sheds light on that very thing. Simply put, *The Heresy of Ham* is a warning to Evangelical Christians, not an attack on them.

As is obvious from his foreword, though, Karl has written off Evangelicals. He not only says he has given up and has no hope for them, but he attacks them an anti-intellectual, anti-science idiots who, because they are so ignorant, are MAGA cultist Republicans. Sadly, I find that mindset to be eerily similar to the mindset of many YECists, just with the political affiliations reversed.

As I discuss in the book, when the YECist pastor and YECist headmaster at my former school found out I didn't agree with the YECism of Ken Ham, and that my views on creation/evolution and Genesis 1–11 didn't line up exactly with theirs, they immediately assumed I must be some sort of "godless liberal," even though I'm not. They effectively shoehorned a scientific issue (creation/evolution) and an exegetical issue (how to interpret Genesis 1–11) and into their larger political "culture war," and then projected onto me every negative caricature one could have of "liberals" or "the left." They weren't interested in honestly discussing the complexities of the scientific issue regarding evolution or the biblical issue regarding the proper interpretation of Genesis 1–11. As far as they were concerned, since I had a different view on those two issues than them, that was justification enough to label me and dismiss me as dangerous.

That mindset is far more concerning to me than someone's opinion regarding evolution or Genesis 1–11. The scientific question of evolution is *a scientific question, not a political issue*. The exegetical question of how to interpret Genesis 1–11 is *a biblical question, not a political issue*. If you're not convinced of evolutionary theory, or if you are not convinced by my argument regarding how to interpret Genesis 1–11, that's fine. We can disagree. But what neither of us should do is link those two issues to the larger "culture war." It is just as wrong to label someone who accepts evolutionary theory as being a godless liberal who wants to kill babies and push the LGBTQ agenda as it is to label someone who doesn't accept evolutionary theory as being an ignorant, unintelligent anti-vaxxer, climate denier MAGA cultist.

Simply put, I don't feel Karl's broad-brushed condemnation of Evangelicals en masse really does any good. It strikes me as the mirror image of the divisive rhetoric I've experienced from many YECists. Yes, there are some Evangelicals who can be quite crazy. But to characterize the entire Evangelical community that way seems disingenuous to me. Karl threw a lot of labels out there in his attack on Evangelicals but let me just focus on one of them—his insinuation that Evangelicals are "anti-vaxx." Most Evangelicals I know have no problems with vaccines. But since 2020, what they (and many others) were concerned about were the potential dangers with the COVID-19 mRNA vaccines that were, admittedly, fast-tracked, and they didn't think that particular shot should have been mandated.

Whether you agree with that concern or not, it does not deserve the label "anti-vaxx." Incidentally, those concerns with the mRNA vaccines have proven to be warranted. Recently, former CDC Director Robert Redfield testified at a congressional hearing and said, "I think there was not appropriate transparency from the beginning about the potential side effects of these vaccines. And I do think there was inappropriate decisions by some to try to under report any side effects because they argued that would make the public less likely to get vaccinated. I do think one of the greatest mistakes, of course, was mandating these vaccines. They should have never been mandated. It should have been open to personal choice. They don't prevent infection. They do have side effects."

In any case, *The Heresy of Ham* is a book that addresses the creation/evolution debate and the issue of how to interpret Genesis 1–11 and warns people about how dangerous and divisive it is to shoehorn those two issues into a larger perceived political culture war. It is just as dangerous and divisive when Karl does it as it is when Ken Ham does it.

Secondly, Karl raises the issue of "the historical Adam," particularly the way Paul uses the figure of Adam in Romans 5. That is a topic I specifically address in the book. Karl echoes the sentiment of biblical scholar Pete Enns, when Enns said, "evangelicals will never make peace with evolution until they can accept that St. Paul believed in a historical Adam—but he was wrong." He also expresses his frustration with BioLogos for letting him and Pete Enns go when the organization decided to not push as zealously regarding certain claims (like the historical Adam) as Karl would have liked. Karl now sees BioLogos as abandoning scholarship and intellectual integrity, using Francis Collins as a "celebrity mascot," and essentially selling out to try to gain acceptance from the Evangelical world. As far as Karl is concerned, Evangelical theology is built on the traditional "Creation-Fall-Redemption" paradigm, and you need a historical Adam for that. Therefore, since science has shown that a historical Adam is an impossibility, that whole "Creation-Fall-Redemption" paradigm has to go, too.

Now, I have appreciated much of Pete Enns' work, and I too do not believe there was a historical Adam. Yet I came to that conclusion long before I ever got into the creation/evolution debate. It was based on my own study of the biblical text, and evolution had absolutely nothing to do with my understanding of it. I explain my understanding of Genesis 1–11 more in depth in the book, but what I want to touch upon here is the claim by Karl and Pete Enns that Paul believed in a historical Adam but was wrong.

Karl says, along with Enns, that we should be "guided by a respect for the Biblical authors," that we should be committed to try to "understand what they meant when they wrote and compiled the texts," and that we should not "ignore the original message and replace it with one that is merely 'not contradicted' by the text." All that is true. The ironic thing, though, is that when it comes to Romans 5, Karl and Enns throw all those commitments out the window. Much like Ken Ham, they argue that since Paul mentions Adam in Romans 5, therefore he must have believed in a historical Adam—as if merely mentioning the figure from Genesis 2–3 automatically entails a historical claim.

When I was in my first graduate program at Regent College in Vancouver, I took a class on Romans from Dr. Gordon Fee. I clearly remember that on the day we covered Romans 5, Gordon Fee was emphatic that Paul was not talking about "original sin" and wasn't commenting on the historicity of Adam at all. The entire point of Romans 5 is that the work of Christ supersedes the effects of sin and death, of which the story of Adam in Genesis 2–3 clearly represents. Paul simply wasn't addressing the question of the historicity of Adam. Therefore, to claim that Paul believed in a historical Adam is to go way beyond what the actual text of Romans 5 addresses. It ignores Paul's argument (i.e. the original meaning) and it replaces it with pure speculation as to what Paul was thinking about the issue of the historicity of Adam while he was making his argument in Romans 5. Sure, it is possible that Paul believed in a historical Adam—that doesn't "contradict the text" of Romans 5—but there is absolutely no way one can discern that by what he says in Romans 5.

Furthermore, to add irony onto irony, in Karl's book *Saving the Original Sinner*, he acknowledges that before Augustine, when it came to the historicity of Adam and the notion of original sin, "no such consensus existed and many Christians viewed Adam simply as Everyman...."[2] He points out that it was Augustine's doctrine of original sin that established *for the Western Church*, the figure of Adam as a historical figure who was the historical origin of sin and evil in the world. Because of that, "Adam could never again be Everyman for Christians in the Western tradition."[3] Furthermore, he notes that Eastern Orthodoxy never embraced Augustine's view on this topic.

So, in Karl's own book, which I would unequivocally recommend by the way, he acknowledges that many Christians before Augustine saw

---

2. Giberson, *Saving the Original Sinner*, 29.
3. Giberson, *Saving the Original Sinner*, 71.

Adam more of an Everyman, that it was Augustine's doctrine of original sin that established the view in Western Christianity of Adam as a historical figure, and that to this day Eastern Orthodoxy doesn't fully embrace Augustine's teaching on this topic. Therefore, how in the world could he and Pete Enns, with any certainty, claim that Paul believed in a historical Adam, but was wrong? Sure, most Evangelicals assume Adam was a historical figure, but Karl and Pete Enns make the claim that *Paul* believed Adam was a historical figure. That claim isn't supported by the text of Romans 5, and it flies in the face of the historical reality of how Adam was viewed, not only in the first three centuries of the Church, but also in Eastern Orthodoxy to this day.

Finally, and this is admittedly more of a minor point, I couldn't help but notice how much Karl characterized the creation/evolution debate, particularly with YECists like Ken Ham, as a battle and a war. He equates Ken Ham and YECists like him to Russia invading Ukraine, calls me a "young crusader," and laments that although there is no hope that anyone could stop the YECist "invasion," maybe I and my "brothers-in-arms" can at least hold the line.

I want to be quite clear that I do not see myself as a "crusader." I am just a teacher. I taught both English and Biblical Worldview in Evangelical schools for 16 years, had the opportunity to teach Biblical Studies for a time at the university level, and am now just a single parent, teaching English again at the high school level. I'm not interested in fighting any wars. All I am doing in this book is sharing what happened to me ten years ago when an overzealous YECist headmaster viewed me as an "enemy" in the culture war and trying to help those struggling with what has become a very controversial and heated issue.

I'm not interested in "fighting back" or "taking up arms" against anyone, even though there is no doubt that YECists like Ken Ham do, in fact, see themselves as "fighting the culture war," and have hurt many people in the process. All I am interested in doing is bringing the truth to light—the truth about how Genesis 1–11 has been viewed throughout Church history, the truth about how to interpret Genesis 1–11, the truth about what evolution actually is, and the truth that science and faith are not "at war," despite what actual YECist crusaders like Ken Ham say. If I can do that—if I can make the truth about those things be clearly seen, well then, the truth can take care of itself, thank you very much.

Preface (2016)

LET'S CUT TO THE chase and state the obvious: the creation/evolution debate is controversial . . . *really controversial.* Therefore, writing an entire book on the controversy, and having it titled *The Heresy of Ham*, is bound to evoke intense reactions from people, depending on where they stand in the debate. If you've spent any time looking into the creation/evolution debate, you know what I'm talking about.

On one side there are militant atheists who rail against religion and insist that science, reason, and evolution have proven Christianity to be "mythical nonsense" that was forced onto people during the Middle Ages by means of threats of torture and death. Anyone who has any knowledge of actual history, science, or the Bible, though, knows such an accusation to be absurd. Nevertheless, those militant atheists are still out there.

On the other side you have young earth creationists who insist that society is going to hell in a secular handbasket and claim that evolution is to blame. They call it an "anti-God religion," and claim that if the universe isn't 6,000 years old, if Adam and Eve weren't created on the same day as dinosaurs, and if Noah's Flood didn't happen 4,000 years ago, then Christ died for nothing, and the Bible cannot be trusted. Anyone who has any knowledge of actual history, science or the Bible knows such claims are absurd. Nevertheless, those militant young earth creationists are out there.

Then there is a third group that doesn't know much about the creation/evolution debate. Most Evangelical Christians fall into this third group. Many may say something like, "I don't believe in evolution, I believe God created everything," but in reality, they don't know what evolutionary theory really says, and they don't know what exactly young earth creationists (like Ken Ham) really claim. They just go about living their lives, trying to follow Christ and share His love with those around them. And that is ultimately what is most important.

With that in mind, I want to confess a bit of trepidation in putting this work out there, for I pull no punches: I believe young earth creationism is not only unscientific but is actually a dangerous heresy that is gaining influence within Evangelicalism. Now, I know many Evangelicals will think that I am attacking the Bible, attacking God, and attacking *them*. Some will automatically assume that I am a liberal, a leftist, and a secularist. Simply put, there are some who think that anyone who questions or challenges young earth creationism is questioning Christianity itself and subverting biblical authority. Nothing could be further from the truth. By using the term *heresy*, I am not engaging in name-calling. I am arguing that young earth creationism is, in fact, a distortion of the traditional Christian faith that has existed for 2,000 years. This book is a *defense* of Christianity, not an attack on it.

The reason why the creation/evolution debate has become so heated and controversial is because it can get really complicated and confusing. What I try to do in this book is to clearly lay out some of the basic issues concerning the proper role of science and the proper interpretation of the Bible. Along the way, I look at the way Genesis 1–11 has been interpreted throughout Church history. Hopefully, this will put the creation/evolution debate in a clearer light, enabling one to make better sense of it all.

This book is written primarily for Christians, particularly those within Evangelicalism. However, I think anyone with questions regarding the creation/evolution debate will profit from this book. With that in mind, I want to make a few things clear.

First, the Christian faith and the reliability and truthfulness of the Bible do not depend on the outcome of the creation/evolution debate. Evolution is a scientific theory that does not threaten Christianity, even though many people think it does. If you allow me a bit of hyperbole, the theory of evolution is no more a threat to the Bible than photosynthesis. It only is seen as a threat when certain people (both atheists and young earth creationists alike) try to claim that evolution is more than it actually is.

Imagine if for 150 years both atheists and a certain segment of Christians managed to capture the public interest by arguing over whether or not photosynthesis proved or disproved the truthfulness of the Bible and the existence of God—and imagine you didn't care all that much for science, and the only thing you knew about photosynthesis was what you had heard in that controversy. What would your view of photosynthesis be? I'm guessing you'd probably be perplexed and fearful of it.

As crazy as that example may sound, I am convinced the exact thing applies to the theory of evolution. Ultimately, it is irrelevant to the Christian faith. Whether or not you believe it, or whether or not you even care about it, it is not a threat to Christianity.

Secondly, in regard to Genesis 1–11, the fact is there have been a *range of interpretations* of it throughout Church history, and at no time was anyone's faith called into question based on whether or not they interpreted Genesis 1–11 as history, allegory, or anything else. Now, I have my views regarding Genesis 1–11 and discuss them in this book. But I would never accuse anyone of being a "compromised Christian" who "undermines the Scripture," just because they don't agree with me. Yes, someone is going to be right and someone wrong, but that doesn't mean the person who is wrong is a "undermining biblical authority."

Thirdly, I am not saying merely believing the earth is young is "heretical," and I'm obviously not saying believing in a historical Adam and Eve or a literal worldwide Flood is "heretical." These are issues that Christians need to seriously investigate and wrestle with. Christians have always had differing opinions on how to interpret Genesis 1–11…and that's okay. What's not okay is the heretical claim that many young earth creationists like Ken Ham make, namely that a literal/historical interpretation of Genesis 1–11 is *the foundation to the Gospel itself.*

Therefore, what I am calling the "heresy of Ham" is the taking of what has always been a secondary issue within the Church and claiming it is now the foundational cornerstone to the entire Christian faith. That is the warning I wish to convey in this book. Young earth creationists like Ken Ham are not merely saying, "We believe the earth is 6,000 years old, we believe there was a worldwide Flood, and here's why." They are saying, "If you disagree with our conclusions, then you are mocking God and undermining the authority of the Bible." If you are a Christian who disagrees with them, they will hold you in suspicion, consider you a wolf in sheep's clothing, and accuse you of leading young people astray.

And if you happen to be a teacher in a Christian school, be it at the college or secondary level, they will do their best to put you out of a job. I know this firsthand. (Here in this second edition, I tell more about my story than I did in the first edition. When *The Heresy of Ham* first came out in 2016, the wounds were still too fresh for me to share my story. It's been almost ten years now, though, and I've gained enough distance from those events to where I feel I can finally share a bit more.)

I haven't written this book out of spite or anger. I've written it out of deep concern over what I see happening within the Evangelical world. I don't use the word "heresy" lightly, and if you don't like the use of the word, that's fine. But I want one thing to be clear: the modern young earth creationist movement, of which Ken Ham is the most well-known figure, is not scientific, is not biblical, and makes claims that have never been held in Church history. It is time to shed some much-needed light on what I consider a very dangerous movement.

Preface to the Second Edition

WHEN I FIRST CAME out with *The Heresy of Ham* back in 2016, the reason for my writing the book was simple. It was my attempt to make sense of what had happened to me. My contract at a small Evangelical high school was not renewed because the young earth creationist (YEC) headmaster did not want someone who didn't accept YECism to be the school's Biblical Worldview teacher. I wasn't actually taking any stance on the debate in my classroom, but I had written a critique of the Bill Nye-Ken Ham debate in 2014 on my blog. In it, I said that Ken Ham's arguments were not convincing to me and that we should interpret Genesis 1–11 in light of the historical and literary contexts of the ancient Near East (ANE), in consideration of 2,000 years of Church history, and not through the lens of modern science.

Over the course of my final year at the school, as I began to research Ken Ham and YECism, I realized two key things: (1) most Evangelical Christians don't really know what the proponents of YECism actually are claiming, and (2) the YECist arguments about Genesis 1–11 and the creation/evolution debate are not ends in and of themselves. In actuality, they are just weapons in the "culture war." Over these past eight years, as I've interacted with countless YECists, I am convinced of that more than ever. That being said, I've also come to realize that this obsession with "fighting the culture war" isn't the sole domain of Fundamentalist-Evangelical and YECist groups. It's everywhere, not only throughout modern American Christianity, but throughout our culture as a whole.

Consequently, Genesis 1–11 and the creation/evolution debate often get shoehorned into a toxic culture war that is largely driven by divisive political agendas. When it comes to modern Evangelicalism, this political/culture war has driven a wedge between politically conservative Evangelicals and politically progressive ex-Evangelicals, with both sides using exegetical, scientific, and political issues as litmus tests to decide who the "true Christians" are. Depending what one's stance is on Genesis 1–11 and evolution, each group immediately assumes what one's political views probably are, and that is what determines if you're a real Christian. Over these past eight years or so, this phenomenon has shifted into high gear.

Surely, you know what I'm talking about. How many times have you heard a liberal ex-Evangelical say something like, "Evangelicals are science-deniers, no wonder they worship Trump! They're all misogynists, racists, MAGA white supremacists!" And how many times have you heard a conservative YECist Evangelical say something like, "Any so-called Christian who accepts evolution undermines biblical authority, and that opens the door to gay marriage, abortion, and the LGBTQ+ agenda!"

Sadly, just as many conservative Evangelicals have wrongly conflated the Kingdom of God with the GOP party platform, many progressive Christians and ex-Evangelicals have wrongly conflated the Kingdom of God with the Democrat party platform as well. Both camps are guilty of cherry-picking certain Bible verses in an attempt to justify their particular political agendas, and both camps are guilty of claiming to "follow the science" only when it suits their political goals. When it doesn't, let's just say we all can be "science-deniers" at times.

Ironically, Ken Ham is right about one thing. There really is a culture war going on. Unfortunately, within conservative Evangelicalism and progressive ex-Evangelicalism alike, too many Christians are fighting it in the wrong way. There is nothing wrong with lively discussion and debate over issues of biblical interpretation and evolutionary theory. That's how we learn. But too often the discussion quickly takes a sharp turn over the cliff, with both sides devolving into insults and attacks involving political candidates, social issues, and broad-brushed accusations of what "that person" *is really trying to do*. When that happens, when both conservative and liberal combatants are convinced that God is on *their side* and that the *other guy* is the one who is the spiritual threat to both the Christian faith and the nation, there's something else going on.

That is something that all Christians who get into debates over Genesis 1–11 or creation/evolution need to take to heart. Such debates easily veer from debating the actual topics of science and biblical interpretation, to devolving into full-out attacks and counter attacks in the culture war. I've seen this firsthand over the past eight years since the publication of *The Heresy of Ham*, and it is something that I've tried to address, albeit in a roundabout way, in the additional chapters to this revised edition.

In addition to the main chapters of this revised edition of *The Heresy of Ham* are the same as in the first edition. What I've added to this edition are four additional chapters at the end that contain a few personal stories, as well as my take on the creation/evolution and historical Adam debates since the publication of *The Heresy of Ham*.

In Chapter 12, "Hamming It Up," I tell the story of my final year at the small Evangelical school from which I was unceremoniously let go over the issue of YECism. It is an absurd and infuriating story, but I think it is important to shine a light on how YECist ideology can lead to decidedly unchristian behavior.

In Chapter 13, "Ark Encounters," I tell two other stories. The first is about my attending an *Answers in Genesis* conference in my hometown, and the second is about my visit to Ken Ham's *Ark Encounter* and *Creation Museum*. What I hope to convey in these stories is just how absurd, funny, and oddly entertaining my "encounters" with AiG up close really were.

The purpose of my stories in Chapters 12-13 are crystallized in Chapter 14, "An Ever-Evolving Personal Story." In the chapter, I share my thoughts and reflections on what I have come to realize about both YECism and the culture war. The bottom line is this: YECists ideology is, indeed, divisive and corrosive to the Christian faith, but at the same time, as large as YECists like Ken Ham loom in the Evangelical world, they have little to no influence outside of that Evangelical bubble and pose no threat to the larger culture. The best way to "combat" them is to simply shine a light on what they claim, and then laugh at it. Ultimately, there is no reason to take them seriously.

It becomes a problem and a threat only if we take it seriously and think that YECism has more power and influence than it really does. If we do that, we get sucked into that culture war fight and end up being just as divisive and reactionary as YECists like Ken Ham.

Finally, in Chapter 15, "The Historical Adam Debate Today," I tell of what led me to my own understanding of the figure of Adam, as well as my assessment of where the debate within Evangelicalism over evolution and the historical Adam stands today.

Ultimately, what I hope comes across in these additional chapters is my vivid, infuriating, and comical account of my experience with the absurdities of the YECist movement.

Acknowledgments

Up until around 2009, I never had much interest at all in the creation/evolution debate. It was a controversy that essentially snuck up on me and hit me from behind. Or better yet, it was more like a trap into which I unwittingly stumbled. Due to circumstances that will be briefly discussed in this book, I ended up doing quite a bit of research on my own on the topic, just to make sense of it all. The result has been *The Heresy of Ham*.

That being said, no published work is ever purely a solo effort. In the course of writing this, there have been a number of people who have helped me tremendously. First of all, I'd like to thank my good friend Ian Panth. Over the past few years, we have had countless hours of discussion on this topic, and he has encouraged me in countless ways.

I'd also like to thank my father, Egil Anderson, my uncle, Dr. Edmund Anderson, and my friends, Alvin Rapien and Randy Finch, for reading through my rough drafts and not only offering corrections on typos and spelling errors, but also giving me valuable advice on how to make the book more readable and clearer.

In the course of the initial publication of *The Heresy of Ham* in 2016, I was able to make some acquaintances with a number of scholars who are far more versed and informed on the topic of the creation/evolution debate than I am. I thank them for providing me with their insights and encouragement: Joel Duff, Greg Laughery, and Karl Giberson.

Since then, I have gotten to know many other scholars who have taken interest in my book and have offered further encouragement and support: John Schneider, Sy Garte, Greg Davidson, Ken Wolgemuth, and Dustin Burlet.

1

Walking the Plank on Noah's Ark

I don't believe in evolution, I know creation's true
I believe that God above created me and you

Buddy Davis

PASTOR CLARK, A LOCAL Southern Baptist pastor whose children I had taught at the small Evangelical high school in town, wanted to meet with me. He came in during my free period right before lunch to talk to me about what I was teaching in Biblical Worldview. Pastor Clark was a rather large man with a thick Mississippi drawl and could easily pass for the big brother of Al Mohler, the president of the Southern Baptist Convention. As soon as he came in and sat down, I had a sinking feeling in the pit of my stomach.

Pastor Clark began in the following manner: "You know, Joel, let me just say up front that you are a brilliant man. I have read a number of posts on your blog, and you clearly have a sharp mind. Now, I probably should have come to you a few years earlier over some of my concerns, so for that I apologize. But last week, my son told me that you mentioned in class that you thought the book of Jonah was a parable. When you said that, you were telling my son that I was a liar."

What?!?

I certainly didn't see *that* coming. "No," I stammered out, "I wasn't saying you were a liar. I simply mentioned in passing that Christians interpret Jonah differently, and that I personally thought it read more like a parable."

"But when you told my son that, you were telling him to doubt that the Bible is true. Now that's just the most recent concern that I've had."

Thus began a 90-minute inquisition that lasted through lunch, in which Pastor Clark grilled me on topics that ranged from Jonah to Genesis 1–11, biblical inspiration, biblical inerrancy, the atonement, the resurrection of Christ, salvation by grace, and, of course, hell. Let me tell you, inquisitions are no fun at all, especially when they cause you to miss your lunch!

Be that as it may, I was forced to discuss the historicity of Genesis 1–11 with a Southern Baptist pastor on an empty stomach. Even my attempts at finding common ground seemed to fall on deaf ears. Yes, I said, I didn't believe Genesis 1–11 was meant to be read as straightforward history, but this was a topic that Christians have had different opinions on for 2,000 years. One's salvation didn't depend on it, and it certainly shouldn't be something that divides the Church. He responded by saying, "Well, there are some things that I'm willing to divide the church over."

Lunch ended and students began to trickle into my classroom. The 90-minute inquisition had to come to a close. As he got up from his chair, Pastor Clark said, "I have deep concerns over your qualifications to teach Worldview here at the school, and I don't know what I'm supposed to do about it." He then walked out. Needless to say, I wasn't exactly in top form for my afternoon classes. I had been a teacher in Evangelical schools for 15 years, I had two master's degrees and a PhD in the Bible, yet I knew that when a local pastor of a large church in the area issues a veiled threat that he was going to try to get you fired, you had better be concerned.

So, that night at the school football game, I made it a point to talk to Mr. Spencer, the new headmaster. I figured the best thing I could do was be open and honest, and make sure the headmaster had confidence in me. After all, I had been at the school for seven years, was one of the students' favorite teachers, had never had any problems my entire time there, and had even been told by Mr. Spencer himself that when he took the job at the school, he considered my Biblical Worldview classes to be one of the selling points of the school. Surely my job wouldn't be in jeopardy, right?

When I told Mr. Spencer about the conversation I had with Pastor Clark that afternoon, I actually broke down and teared up. At one point I said, "Now, I'm not a young earth creationist, but I don't see that as a fundamental issue of the Christian faith. I'm okay with Christians having different opinions on that topic." Mr. Spencer's response struck me as odd. He said, "Well, I am, but if the Board doesn't agree with me, I'll back off."

What? What kind of answer was that? What did that even mean? Back off from what? Needless to say, that was one odd answer.

A week later, Pastor Clark sent me an email with a list of questions he wanted me to answer. Apparently, his lunchtime inquisition of me had caused him to question whether or not I was even a Christian, so he wanted some clarification on a few theological issues. To be honest, I was quite hurt by that insinuation. My Christian faith is the most important thing in the world to me and I have dedicated my life to the study of the Bible and the teaching of the Christian faith to others. Nevertheless, I decided to take the time to answer his questions as thoughtfully as I could. I ended up writing twelve pages.

Pastor Clark asked if I believed in the bodily resurrection of Christ, the second coming of Christ, and that salvation is by grace through faith. Obviously yes. The next question seemed to come out of left field. He asked if I believed the "gender distinctions" in reference to God were accurate. Pastor Clark must have figured that since I thought the book of Jonah was a parable, I must be one of those liberals who thought God was a woman. I'm not. I replied, yes, God is the Father and Jesus is a man.

He then wanted to know if I believed the Bible was the *inerrant* Word of God and if I believed in the *verbal inspiration* of Scripture. I told him I believed the Bible was divinely inspired, that it taught the truth about God, and that it gave us historically reliable accounts of God's dealing with ancient Israel, as well as the life of Christ and the early Church. If that is what he meant by "inerrant," then yes. But I didn't take "inerrancy" to mean that it was giving scientifically accurate information. I also didn't hold to the "verbal plenary" understanding of inspiration that claimed God basically dictated Scripture to the writers of the Bible (cf. 1 Cor 1:14–16).

He then had specific questions about Christ: Did I believe in the virgin birth? Did I believe Jesus lived a sinless life and that he never erred? Did I believe in the substitutionary atoning death of Christ? I told him yes, I believe in the virgin birth—it is in the creeds, and I affirm it. Ultimately, though, it's a mystery, and it's something that is never elaborated upon in the New Testament. Yes, I believed Jesus lived a sinless life, but what did Pastor Clark mean by "never erred"? I'm sure the toddler

Jesus mispronounced words, maybe he occasionally got James and John mixed up (see Luke 2:52). Although he was divine, he still had human limitations like everyone else. Yes, I believed in the substitutionary atoning death of Christ. Still, that "legal language" isn't the only way that the New Testament explains the significance of Jesus' death. It uses "temple language" by describing Christ as the sacrificial lamb who restores fellowship and community with God. It also uses "physician language" that speaks of Christ as the one who heals us through his own sufferings and death. Christians need to recognize all three.

Pastor Clark then asked if I believed in a literal heaven and hell. I said the Christian hope is that believers will be resurrected with transformed, physical bodies and will live with Christ in the new creation. As for hell, I didn't buy the medieval Catholic description of hell as being a place of literal fiery pits and devils with pitchforks. I said ultimately the real question concerning hell is whether it is a place of *eternal torment* for souls who haven't accepted Christ or is it a place where those unsaved souls are *annihilated and cease to exist*. Either way, I believed in the existence of hell.

Finally, Pastor Clark asked if I believed Genesis 1–11 was actual, historical fact. I told him that the point of Genesis 1–11 was that God is the Creator, human beings are made in His image, but human beings sin and are estranged from God and are in need of salvation. It was speaking to the questions and concerns of the ancient Israelites in the ancient Near East (ANE), and wasn't, thus, trying to address modern scientific and historical questions. If it was, then it would have meant nothing to ancient Israel.

With that, I touched upon the creation/evolution debate and said that regardless of one's view of evolutionary theory, I didn't see how it threatened the truth and reliability of the Bible. I said even though I appreciated the goal that young earth creationists like Ken Ham often state, namely, to combat atheism, secular humanism, and moral relativity in our society today, I felt that trying to tie all that directly to the biological theory of evolution was misguided. The problem with the human race isn't the theory of evolution; *it is sin, pride, and rebellion against God.*

Pastor Clark didn't respond back. At the time, I wanted to think that while he probably didn't agree with every specific detail of my responses, he likely realized that when it came to the essential basics of the Christian faith, we really, truly were in agreement. As it turned out, I had unwittingly begun to provide the rope that would eventually get me hanged. That was November 2013.

Fast forward to March 2014. Bill Nye and Ken Ham had their debate the previous month, and I had decided to share my thoughts on it on my blog. After I had written a few posts about it, I received an email from Pastor Clark. Now, in one particular post, I had actually criticized the atheist Richard Dawkins for trying to claim that evolution "proved" atheism. I had made the point that what he was, in fact, doing was trying to smuggle his philosophical atheism into the biological theory of evolution. Therefore, what he was doing was fundamentally dishonest.

Pastor Clark felt impelled to write to me and tell me that my argument against Dawkins, in fact, destroyed my own claim that Genesis 1–11 wasn't historical. Pastor Clark actually said that the only reason I didn't accept Genesis 1–11 as historical *was because there was no evidence for it*. But that just meant there was no evidence *to my knowledge*. Therefore, according to him, my conclusion was just a "mere philosophical claim."

He concluded his email with, "Honestly Joel, wouldn't it be easier and more intellectually honest to just believe what is written in the Scriptures that you say you believe God inspired or admit that you don't believe it? Unfortunately, you seem to have chosen to make something else (literary genre, science, reason) a higher authority than the Word or the God who inspired it. That breaks my heart for you."

What???

Mystified, I read his email again. For a moment, I actually felt sorry for him. He was a pastor, a staunch young earth creationist/biblical literalist, yet he didn't understand a thing I had written. He evidently thought it was a virtue to believe something was historical, despite the fact *there was no evidence for it*. And did he insinuate I wasn't being honest, and that I should just admit I really didn't believe the Bible was true? Yes, I think he did. Wow…

Once again, though, nothing seemed to come of it. I never heard from Pastor Clark again.

Fast forward to June 2014. School had been out for a couple weeks, and I got a call from Mr. Spencer, the headmaster. He asked to meet me at Panera Bread to talk about the upcoming school year. Halfway through our chat, Mr. Spencer turned an abrupt corner and began to tell me that he had some concerns over some of my posts about the Bill Nye/Ken Ham debate. In one post, I had briefly written about how the early second century Church Father Irenaeus had written in his book *Against Heresies*, that Christians viewed Adam and Eve as being symbolic of childish humanity.

Mr. Spencer was extremely concerned by this. He asked, "Aren't you putting man's fallible word and the traditions of men over the infallible Word of God? If Adam and Eve weren't two historical people, then you are saying that God lied, and you are undermining biblical authority."

What??? (Again with the whole "lying" accusation!)

I said, "I'm not putting man's fallible word over the Bible. I'm just pointing out that that was how the early Christians interpreted the Adam and Eve story. The fact that Irenaeus was a student of Polycarp, who was a student of John, who was a disciple of Jesus himself, tells me that we should take what Irenaeus says seriously. After all, what he was teaching could very well have come from Jesus himself. We want to make sure we're interpreting Genesis 2—3 correctly. I think what Irenaeus says makes sense."

Mr. Spencer smiled and said, "Yes, that's the problem. It makes sense *to you*. You're letting your own reason have authority over God's Word."

WHAT?

I saw this conversation was on the verge of spiraling down into the abyss very quickly, so I decided to hit upon what I thought was an undisputed fact about the Bible that every Christian would surely agree. I said, "Listen, since we believe the Bible is inspired, whenever we read anything in the Bible, we need to make sure that we understand the original message, right? Because the original message is the inspired message, right?"

"Right."

"Okay, so for example, when we read Romans, we need to realize that Paul was writing to real people living in Rome around AD 60. Therefore, since the Bible is inspired, and since Paul was writing to those people back then, the original, inspired message had to make sense to them, first and foremost, right?"

"Oh no. I disagree with that."

WHAT???

"What do you mean you disagree with that?"

"God's Word is God's message to humanity for all time."

At that point, I felt like Mugato in the movie *Zoolander*, and thought, "I feel like I'm taking crazy pills!" One moment, Mr. Spencer had agreed that original context was important in interpreting the Bible *in general*, and within seconds he was disagreeing with that idea when it came to *any specific example*. I was mystified.

In any case, Mr. Spencer then told me that not only did he have concerns over how I read Genesis 2—3, but he was also concerned with the fact that I was Orthodox. To be clear, even though I had joined the Orthodox Church in 2005, there wasn't an Orthodox church within 80 miles of where I now lived, and I had been attending a Baptist church for the past six years. That didn't matter to Mr. Spencer. Orthodoxy was suspicious to him.

By the end of what I call, "The Inquisition: The Headmaster Strikes Back," Mr. Spencer told me even though my job was safe for the upcoming year, he had deep concerns about me staying at the school after that. He didn't feel I was "a good fit" for the Biblical Worldview program… *the Biblical Worldview program that I had built up from scratch*. It wasn't because there had been problems with parents, or any complaints from students. In fact, it was quite the opposite. I was a favorite teacher of the students, and I had, in fact, been told by Mr. Spencer himself that when he was interviewing for the job, he heard only great things about my Worldview classes. No, that wasn't the issue. Now that he knew of my personal stance on Genesis 1–11, it was a matter of *biblical authority*, and he had deep concerns about having the Biblical Worldview teacher who *found Orthodoxy appealing* and who, according to him, *undermined biblical authority*.

Mr. Spencer then, in very Pastor Clark type fashion, asked for more answers to be submitted to him in writing. He wanted me to write out my understanding of Orthodoxy and then email it to him within two weeks. So, over the course of the next two weeks, I wrote a concise explanation of Orthodoxy, although I knew full well that his real beef wasn't with Orthodoxy. It was with my take on the creation/evolution debate.

Thus began an exchange of emails and discussions in which I tried to keep my job. It ended up being a summer-long debate with Mr. Spencer over a number of issues ranging from the Bible, Church tradition, salvation, social issues, to what his real concern was all along: the creation/evolution debate. At every opportunity, I tried to give open and honest answers to his questions and explain the intricacies to the issues he brought up. Most importantly, I went out of my way to reassure him that we shared the same core Christian beliefs that Christians for the past 2,000 years have held in common.

In the end, it would not matter. Deep down, from the moment Mr. Spencer first brought up my critique of the Nye-Ham debate, I saw the handwriting on the wall. I just wasn't able to actually read it right away.

Throughout the course of that year, though, it became abundantly clear to me that not only did Mr. Spencer not want me there, but he saw me as a dangerous enemy, *a liberal enemy* who was a wolf in sheep's clothing. Needless to say, my last year at that school was a hard one. The long and short of it was that when that school year ended, my sixteen-year career in Evangelical schools was over because I disagreed with the standard YECist claims that the universe was 6,000 years old.

What I had thought in to be simply a secondary issue that Christians tended to have differing opinions on, turned out to be a fundamental plank in the theology and culture war of a growing segment of Evangelicalism that I had no idea really existed. I had taught Bible for sixteen years, and never dreamed that I would one day be forced to walk the plank on a young earth creationist version of Noah's Ark.

Looking back, I should have seen it coming.

THE FIRING OF AN OLD TESTAMENT SCHOLAR

In 2010, the well-known Old Testament professor Bruce K. Waltke lost his job at Reformed Theological Seminary (RTS) over a few comments he made about evolution for the BioLogos Foundation, a Christian organization that argues for evolutionary creationism. He said:

> "...if the data is overwhelmingly in favor of evolution, to deny that reality will make us a cult...some odd group that is not really interacting with the world. And rightly so, because we are not using our gifts and trusting God's Providence that brought us to this point of our awareness."[1]

Even though he is considered to be one of the preeminent Evangelical Old Testament scholars of today, his comments were too much for the folks at RTS. He lost his job...*over that*.

I was fortunate to have Dr. Waltke as a professor at Regent College back in the 1990s. The fact that this well-known Old Testament professor was let go over *that comment* shocked me. Granted, at the time I thought his comment was a bit over the top—I mean, a cult? Really? Surely, just because a Christian might not be convinced of evolution, doesn't make him/her a cult member. Isn't that making the theory of evolution into a bigger deal than it really is? Mere denial of evolution doesn't make you into a cult member. But then again, Dr. Waltke actually got fired over that

---

1. Jaschik, "The Video that Ended a Career," para. 2.

comment. And, as I have come to learn, many other Christian scholars, scientists, and theologians have suffered a similar fate over the past few years. I am now one of them.

I am afraid that Dr. Waltke was not only right, but also prophetic. Modern American Evangelicalism (or at least certain segments of it) *does* seem to be in danger of devolving into a cult, and it is due in large part to the growing influence of YEC that is creating nothing but division and strife among Christians.

Ultimately, the issue for YEC really is not over the age of the earth or the possible common ancestry of human beings and apes. For them, the issue is ultimately one of *biblical authority*: they think if you read Genesis 1–11 in any way other than it being a literal, straightforward historical and scientific account of origins that happened about 6,000 years ago, then you are rejecting biblical authority. Dr. Waltke left the door open for the possibility that evolution might be true, but that would mean the universe had been in existence for millions of years, and the Bible says creation happened 6,000 years ago—therefore, Dr. Waltke is subverting biblical authority and putting "man's fallible word" over "God's infallible Word." Therefore, Dr. Waltke must either repent or go.

What happened to Dr. Waltke was not an isolated incident. Within Evangelicalism, many teachers, professors, and scholars have suffered the same fate. Regardless of what one might personally believe about the age of the earth or evolution, ask yourself if you have ever thought that was a fundamentally crucial issue within Christianity. I certainly didn't, and I certainly didn't think anyone ever really felt that way.

But young earth creationists do. I mean, they *really* do. In fact, I think most people would be shocked at what young earth creationism actually claims. If now you're now beginning to ask, "So, what do they believe?" hold on to your hat.

THEY BELIEVE WHAT?

Ever since Charles Darwin published *Origin of the Species* in 1859, there has been controversy over the issue of evolution and how it may or may not affect the Christian faith and the Bible. It is a debate that continues to spark both interest and vitriol in many segments of our modern society. The reason for such hostility is due in no small part to publications like Richard Dawkins' *The God Delusion*, as well as increasingly influential young earth creationist organizations like Ken Ham's *Answers in Genesis*. There's no better way than to keep the fires of fear and paranoia stoked than to convince people that "the other side" is out to get them.

Despite such fearmongering, my personal experience has convinced me that, in reality, the majority of Evangelical Christians don't spend all that much time thinking about the creation/evolution debate. They go on with their lives and are content to hold to the simple idea that since God made the world, then evolution can't true because evolution says there is no God and all this happened by chance. In practical terms, the creation/evolution debate itself doesn't affect their lives all that much.

On one hand, this is a good thing. Christians know deep down that, despite what one thinks about the age of the earth or about precisely how God created the world, it simply is not a vital issue when it comes to following Christ. On the other hand, though, this is a bad thing. Since most Christians who don't think too much about it end up being ignorant of it, and such ignorance has left them susceptible to being manipulated by certain people who are using the creation/evolution issue to promote their own agendas. And as I have learned, the young earth creationist movement has an agenda.

Ever since Henry Morris' *The Genesis Flood*, was published in 1961, the young earth creationist movement has steadily gained a considerable amount of influence and power within certain segments of the American Evangelical church—the most well-known YEC organization being that of Ken Ham's *Answers in Genesis*. The reason why it has grown in influence is because it takes advantage of people's ignorance of history, science, and the Bible, and has convinced a significant portion of Evangelicalism that evolution is the front-line issue in the battle between Christianity and atheism/secular humanism.

Therefore, it really shouldn't come as a surprise to find that recent polls[2] have shown that 46% of Americans, and 69% of people who regularly attend church weekly, believe God created human beings in their present form at one time in the last 10,000 years or so. Within the Evangelical world, 64% of white Evangelical Protestants reject the idea that humans evolved at all. I doubt those poll numbers are the result of people having actually investigated the issue. It is rather because Evangelicals simply assume evolution is the same thing as atheism. They assume that

---

2. "Public Views on Evolution." *Pew Research Center: Religion and Public Life*. 30 Dec 2013.

because it is what they have been told by the various young earth creationists groups for decades.

The problem, though, is that not only is that claim demonstrably wrong, but it is also purposely deceitful. No, it's not because men like Ken Ham are trying to pull a fast one on well-meaning, but unsuspecting Christians. Ken Ham says what he says because he has an agenda, and that agenda is to win the culture war. He is so horrified at what he perceives to be the moral decline in our society, that he believes it is his duty to restore a sense of moral order. He is so convinced that the reason for American society's moral decline is directly linked to the theory of evolution, that he believes that if he can discredit the theory of evolution and convince people that Genesis 1–11 is scientifically and historically accurate, then this will convince people that the Bible is true, and thus lead to the restoration of Christian morality in our society.

In his attempt to prove Genesis 1–11 is scientifically and historically accurate, though, Ken Ham and *Answers in Genesis* have given some truly bizarre "answers" that, ironically, are not found in Genesis, or anywhere else in the Bible, for that matter. Among other things, he has claimed:

- Adam and Eve possessed a perfect genome,[3] stood anywhere from 12-16 feet tall, and had super-intelligence.[4]
- There was no death of any kind before the fall, except for plants and insects; they didn't have the "breath of life," so therefore they weren't technically "alive" in the first place.[5]
- As soon as Adam and Eve ate the forbidden fruit, their perfect genomes started to mutate, the second law of thermodynamics was ushered into existence.[6] Thus, hurricanes, cancer, and untold diseases and natural disasters burst into God's perfect creation.[7]
- Even though the human genome was no longer perfect after Adam and Eve's fall, the genetic mutations were still rare and so minor that it was okay for their children to marry each other and have incestuous relationships without it being detrimental to the normal functioning of human life. It was only thousands of years later, when

3. Mitchell, "Evaluating Giberson's Book *Saving the Original Sinner*," para. 10.
4. Ham and Lovett, "Was there Really a Noah's Ark and Flood?" paras. 4, 8.
5. Foley, "Did Adam Step on an Ant Before the Fall?" para. 2.
6. Danny Faulkner, "The Second Law of Thermodynamics and the Curse."
7. Ken Ham, "Was There Death Before Adam Sinned?" para. 9.

Moses led the children of Israel out of Egypt, that the genome become so mutated that God declared incest to be a sin.[8]

- The pre-flood civilization was highly intelligent and had access to advanced technology that dwarfed our modern technology.[9] This is what made it possible for Noah to build the Ark—he hired these intelligent people to help him build it. All of the pre-flood advanced technology, though, was entirely blotted out by the waters of the Flood, and we thus have no evidence of it today.[10]
- Dinosaurs were on the Ark, but only the small newborns (babies). That is how they were able to fit on the Ark.[11]
- Animals like the kangaroo were able to float to Australia on the pre-flood trees that had been ripped up by the Flood.[12]
- Even after the Flood, though, Noah's descendants became just as sinful as ever, and rebelled against God's command to be "fruitful and multiply" by refusing to have a lot of sex.[13]

So much for providing "answers in Genesis" (or anywhere else in the Bible, for that matter). And believe me, that is just the tip of the iceberg.

Nevertheless, Ken Ham is so convinced that his "battle plan" will save our society, and he is so convinced that God has called him to this fight, he feels that anything or anyone who questions him or doubts his claims is the enemy, not only to him, but to God and the Bible as well. It doesn't matter to him that the vast majority of the scientific community rejects his claims of a young earth—*they are in rebellion against God*. It doesn't matter to him that the most preeminent Evangelical biblical scholars of our day disagree with his interpretation of Genesis 1–11—*they are compromised Christians who are undermining biblical authority*. The culture war must be won, and the proper moral order must be reestablished. There can be no compromise. If Adam and Eve didn't possess perfect genomes, then Christ died for nothing.

---

8. "Who Was Cain's Wife?" paras. 4-5.
9. Ham and Lovett, "Was There Really a Noah's Ark and Flood?" para. 9.
10. Ken Ham, "Answering Claims About the Ark Project." paras. 15-16.
11. Davis, "Dinosaurs on the Ark." para. 4.
12. Taylor, "How did Animals Spread all Over the World from Where the Ark Landed? para. 16.
13. Hodge, "Why Don't We Find Human and Dinosaur Fossils Together?" para. 20.

The fact is, though, that the claims of Ken Ham and a number of other young earth creationists are not only unscientific, but they are also unbiblical and have never been universally held in the history of the Church. Let me repeat that, for it is what lies at the heart of this book: *the claims young earth creationism makes regarding Genesis 1–11 are provably unscientific, provably unbiblical, and provably without any basis in the history of the Church.*

Most Evangelicals, though, don't know this. Therefore, they go along with the young earth creationists party line and simply assume that Ken Ham's *Answers in Genesis* organization is just another Christian ministry dedicated to spreading the Gospel and standing up against atheism.

Yet, as has happened countless times, any Christian who ends up learning more about science, proper biblical interpretation, or the facts of Church history, and then starts to raise questions about some of the things that young earth creationism is claiming, will soon find that there is target on his back. His faith will be questioned, and, if that person happens to be either a teacher at an Evangelical high school or college, or a pastor of a church, chances are his career will be in jeopardy, not for questioning the Bible, but for questioning YEC dogma.

This book is an attempt to provide clarity for anyone confused by the creation/evolution debate, and reassurance for those people who've been frustrated, hurt, and have had their faith shaken because of what can be characterized as nothing else than young earth creationist zealots. Trying to understand the whole creation/evolution debate and wrestling with how to properly interpret Genesis 1–11 is hard enough. It takes a great amount of courage and faith to ask the hard questions and to seek the truth in both tasks. It therefore is tremendously disheartening and devastating to find certain Christians calling your faith into question, simply because you don't blindly parrot the party line of young earth creationism.

I believe the paranoia, divisiveness, and frustration the YEC movement fosters should serve as an indication that there is something fundamentally wrong with it. This is not simply a case of Christians having a difference of opinion on a certain topic. This is a case of a movement willing to declare war on everyone, Christian and non-Christian alike, who does not capitulate to what they have unilaterally declared to be true.

I have learned quite a lot about young earth creationism since I was informed by Mr. Spencer that I would not be rehired at the end of that school year. This book is the culmination of my attempt to make sense of something that, as you will see, is at its roots, nonsensical. What is one to make of the claims of young earth creationists? Are they right? Are they raising legitimate questions? Are they simply wrong or mistaken? Or does what they are teaching present a very real danger to the historical Christian faith? In a word, is it actually heretical? Now, I know that "heresy" is a loaded term, but it is a question this book will try to answer.

Before we get too far ahead of ourselves, though, let me give a bit more personal background and how I even got involved in this issue.

GROWING UP IN EVANGELICALISM

I never cared much for science, not in high school, in college, or for my first 38 years of life on this earth. For that matter, having grown up in Wheaton, Illinois, the virtual heart of Evangelicalism, I never cared much for Church history either. Who needed it? All I needed was Jesus in my heart and a Bible in my hand. That's what my Evangelical heritage had taught me.

There were a few other things that my Evangelical heritage taught me: secular rock music was ultimately of the devil, Christian rock music was suspect (especially that group "Stryper"), Catholics weren't *really* Christians, Jesus was coming back at any moment, the rapture was imminent, the tribulation would be hell on earth, abortion was murder, the gays were pedophiles, and, of course, evolution was an attack on biblical Christianity.

Now, it wasn't like anyone in my church or Christian high school actually *knew anything* about evolution—we didn't have to. We already *knew* what it was: man came from monkeys, blind chance, God doesn't exist. That was it—reject it. Go witness to your friends to keep them from hell, because the rapture might happen at any moment.

Despite what can be characterized as nothing short of a mild paranoia within Evangelicalism, though, my parents displayed an incredible amount of common sense in regard to some of the hot-button issues of the day. When I got into Christian rock music as a teenager, they were fine with it. They even let me play Stryper's rendition of "Winter Wonderland" in the house at Christmas! When I started to appreciate secular music, lo and behold, they liked some of it too. As for the whole dispensationalist thing promoted by Hal Lindsey (and later by Tim LaHaye) my parents' attitude was, "We don't really get that, but we believe Jesus rose again and will come again—that's what is most important."

Strangely enough, the whole creation/evolution debate never loomed large in my upbringing either. Don't get me wrong, everyone *said* they didn't believe in evolution because they believed God created everything, but nobody I knew ever obsessed over it. Besides, unlike Bill Nye, I was definitely *not* a "science guy." If the topic did come up in sophomore Biology, I tuned it out, as I did everything else in that class. Consequently, I was blissfully ignorant of any real controversy between evolution and creation for the simple reason that I didn't care about it at all. All I cared about was the Chicago Cubs...and a certain freshman girl I had a tremendous crush on.

Although I assumed Genesis 1–11 was historical, I had no problem believing dinosaurs lived millions of years ago. Did they live before mankind? Sure, but I didn't really know or care. Did Adam and Eve have a pet triceratops? That sounded dumb, but who knows? I didn't know and didn't care. Was the earth only 6,000 years old? I never gave it much thought. It didn't seem relevant anyway. As my dad said, "However the universe was made, the Bible tells us God ultimately did it." That was good enough for me. Besides, no one was going to come to Christ if it was proven Adam and Eve were the historical basis for *The Flintstones*. That was just silly. I never dreamed anyone would ever really think that.

TEACHING IN EVANGELICAL SCHOOLS

I made it through an English major, two master's degrees in Biblical Studies, and a PhD program in Old Testament without ever having to think about the creation/evolution debate. Sure, I had to wrestle with issues surrounding the proper interpretation of Genesis 1–11, but I never bothered about the creation/evolution debate. I was concerned with how the original audience of Israelites would have understood Genesis 1–11, not how it may or may not conflict with Darwin.

Over the course of the next twenty years, I taught Bible at three different Evangelical Christian high schools. I had decided early on in my graduate schooling that I wanted to take what I learned at the graduate level and build a solid Bible curriculum for Christian secondary schools.

In California, I taught a unit on Genesis 1–11 and focused on how, as inspired literature, it fits together, sets out the major themes of the

Bible, and relates to the book of Revelation. It never occurred to me that there really were some Christians who actually thought modern science had to coincide with Genesis 1–11. Being a good Evangelical, I just assumed evolution was a silly claim made by atheists who didn't want to admit there was a God. But that was science, and Genesis 1–11 wasn't doing science or trying to give a straightforward history of the creation of the universe and mankind. As a biblical scholar, that fact was obvious. I taught that course for three years, and it was one of the students' favorite classes.

At the second Evangelical school I taught, I got in trouble with a new administrator over the teaching of Genesis 1–11. It was the same material I had used at my previous school, but Arkansas wasn't California. The new administrator was alarmed I told students not all Christians took Genesis 1–11 as literal history, and that parts of Genesis 1–11 had some interesting connections with other ANE creation stories. It didn't matter that at no time did I even bring up evolution. It didn't matter that what I told them was true. Just trying to get students to understand the bigger interpretive issues in Genesis 1–11 was seen as dangerous by the fundamentalist administrator. I was fired at the end of my fourth year.

It wasn't until 2009, at my third Evangelical school, after the Ben Stein movie, *Expelled*, had come out, that I decided to actually address the creation/evolution debate in my Senior Worldview class. I figured, for better or worse, the fact is that Charles Darwin has made a considerable impact on the world. Since my Senior Worldview class tackled the cultural and philosophical issues in the modern world, I felt it was a topic that needed to be addressed. At that time, even though I still didn't believe evolutionary theory (because I never thought about it), I knew that Genesis 1–11 wasn't doing modern science or was literal history. Therefore, I didn't care how old the earth was, it had no bearing on the Bible.

Over the next few years, I learned a lot about what evolution actually is and came to the conclusion that evolution was the means by which God created and continues to create the world. I didn't share my personal view in class, though. I made it a point to cover all the views even-handedly in my class, have my students discuss what they felt the strengths and weaknesses of each view were, and then write a short essay on what view they most agreed with, and why. That, I felt, was what I as a teacher should do: challenge the students to critically think through the issue themselves.

At the end of my seventh year at the school, déjà vu happened all over again. Just like in Arkansas, a new headmaster who had come in was threatened by what I was teaching. I ended up losing my job because I was seen as a threat to the students' view of biblical authority. Mr. Spencer felt not holding to a belief in a young earth meant that I was calling God a liar, undermining biblical authority, and opening the door to "liberalism."

My experiences have not caused me to lose my faith in God, but they have opened my eyes regarding a shocking development within Evangelicalism. When YECists get in positions of power, heads start to roll. That kind of abuse of power should be alarming to anyone. I have come to know from firsthand experience how the YECist movement promotes an atmosphere of fear and paranoia within Evangelicalism in regard to science, scholarship, and the culture as a whole.[14]

THE CHALLENGE OF THIS BOOK

Writing this book presents a huge challenge. There is so much misinformation and ignorance surrounding the creation/evolution debate, one hardly knows where to begin to start trying to clean up such a mess. What makes it even harder is that most people, Christian and non-Christian alike, don't see how much of a muddled mess it is. In addition to the actual scientific questions in the creation/evolution debate, there are questions regarding biblical interpretation, biblical theology, Church history, and even philosophy. Consequently, addressing the creation/evolution debate is like walking into a house from the show *Hoarders*—the task of just getting some semblance of order, let alone actually getting the infernal place clean, is unbearably daunting. But you've got to start somewhere: start making piles, start hauling garbage out to the curb, and start with one small goal of getting at least a corner of the house clean.

But oh my, there's a lot of garbage. Just look at the poster-boys on both sides of the debate: Richard Dawkins and Ken Ham. Atheists like Dawkins routinely declare evolution proves there is no God and faith is the equivalent of clinical insanity. On the other hand, young earth creationists like Ham have built a small fiefdom within Evangelicalism by declaring that Genesis 1–11 is science, evolution is an "anti-god" religion,

---

14. Janet Kellog Ray alerts people to the same thing in her book, *The God of Monkey Science*.

and that if you don't believe the universe is 6,000 years old, then you are casting doubt on the resurrection of Christ.

None of that is accurate, honest, or true. Yet truth isn't valued in this debate. Both sides have a vested interest in stoking the fires and keeping the controversy alive and are all too happy to continue throwing out their pat-answers and clichés—they have agendas to push. We first must realize that most of the garbage comes from the camps these two men represent. We then need to identify what that garbage is so we can throw it out for good. Let's start by understanding what biblical literalism really is.

WHAT IS BIBLICAL LITERALISM? IS IT REALLY IDOLATRY?

The term *biblical literalism* is cat nip to two entirely different groups that, for different reasons, sends people into a tizzy. Say *biblical literalism* to secularists like Richard Dawkins and Bill Maher, and they will engage in a litany of condemnations of everything southern, conservative, evangelical, white, Republican, anti-science, homophobic, misogynistic and anti-intellectual. The irony, of course, is their view of the Bible is just as literalistic as that of the ultra-Fundamentalists they condemn.

Say *biblical literalism* to Fundamentalists like Ken Ham, and you'll see it is worn as a badge of honor. Although this group does not comprise the entirety of Evangelicalism, it is a very vocal and influential subset within the Evangelical world. To them, *biblical literalism* means you believe the Bible is literally true in all areas (except, of course, the parts you want to ignore). It means young earth creationism, "traditional marriage," and being against Barak Obama. Anyone who disagrees with this group is often put in the camp of the secular-atheistic, gay-marriage-loving, evolution-nihilistic-godless liberals of the Democratic party.

Name-calling is very big in both camps. The smugness of both groups is the same, but the words they use are obviously different. Either way, not only does one never really learn anything, but it is very likely that one will get caught in the crossfire if one ever tries to actually understand what's going on. In fact, the rhetoric from both sides will simply make one blind, deaf, and dumb to the real issues. This sort of thing is a hallmark of idolatry. The Old Testament prophets testify that those who worship idols will become just as blind, deaf, and dumb as those very idols. In that sense, biblical literalism is nothing short of biblical idolatry.

As human beings, we all yearn for purpose and meaning. Yet the fact is, purpose and meaning can only be attained by someone who does the hard work of trying to examine life in all its complexity. It requires contemplation, reflection, humility and determination. It doesn't come easy. This, though, presents a problem: far too many people don't do the hard work of searching for truth. It's too hard, too time-consuming, and sometimes uncomfortable—after all, when we search for truth, we will inevitably have to confront things about ourselves that we'd like to pretend aren't there, and sometimes we have to admit we are wrong. Herein lies the dilemma: how does one attain a sense of purpose, truth, and meaning if one is either too lazy, too busy, or too fearful to search for it?

The answer to that question can be seen in every society throughout human history: *idolatry*. In the ancient world there were literal temples people went to, and literal idols that people bowed down and worshiped, and to which they sacrificed. Although such actions may have given them a sense of purpose, truth, and meaning, the fact is that they simply promulgated an illusion—an illusion promoted and fed by the countless number of pagan priests who sought to hold ancient pagan societies together on a foundation of over-simplistic answers and convoluted rituals.

The pagan priests were the ones who manipulated the so-called oracles. The priests would crawl into the hollowed-out heads of the huge idols in the temples and shout out from them, making it seem like the god had actually spoken through the image. The priests were the ones who kept the people of the ancient world cowering in fear of the gods: "Don't make the gods angry! Offer your sacrifice! Don't question the fates!" Life in the ancient world was kept simple and tidy, in a fearful sort of way.

In today's world we often encounter different forms of idolatry. It may be a particular political ideology or cult of personality. Oftentimes, within Evangelical Christianity, idolatry comes in the form of obsessing over "right doctrine," which of course, often means the obsession over precisely *wrong doctrine*. My favorite professor from graduate school, Dr. Gordon Fee, often said that "right doctrine" has become the theological idol of Evangelicalism.

He was right. From the dawn of the Reformation, Protestants have been really good at destroying one another over the smallest of theological points. Obviously, Christians need to strive for correct doctrine and a right understanding of the Bible. But when one obsesses over trying to make the Bible spell out *everything*, when one tries to construct a theology that explains *everything* about God, leaving no room for mystery, we should be wary that such a theology, in much the same way the biblical writers described idolatry, has been "made of human hands." When a particular doctrinal system or view of the Bible is too simplistic, or too obsessive over one particular issue, chances are it has become an idol.

This is the challenge facing Evangelicalism today. Biblical literalism has divorced the Bible from the Church, put the Bible on a pedestal, and made it an idol that can be manipulated in order to promote some very dangerous teachings that have never been universally held in Church history. This can clearly be seen today in the current creation/evolution debate that is being promoted by young earth creationists like Ken Ham and *Answers in Genesis*.

WHO IS KEN HAM?

Ken Ham is a former high school science teacher from Australia who is at the forefront of the young earth creationist movement here in America. He came to the United States in 1986 to work for Henry Morris' organization *Institute for Creation Research* (ICR). Henry Morris, along with John Whitcomb, wrote the YEC manifesto, *The Genesis Flood*, in 1961, that, as Ken Ham has said, sparked the YEC movement.

Ham eventually broke away from ICR to start his own organization, *Answers in Genesis*, located in northern Kentucky, just outside of the Cincinnati area. In 1987, Ken Ham wrote *The Lie*, in which he essentially laid out his brand of young earth creationism. In it, he laid out his basic talking points that he has used up to this day:

1. Evolution is an atheistic philosophy/religion that is fundamentally rebellious against God.
2. There are two kinds of science. "Observational science" makes our technology, and can be tested, repeated, and observed; "Historical science" is simply beliefs about the past that cannot be tested, repeated, or observed.
3. Genesis 1–11 is God's eyewitness historical account of the creation of the physical universe and mankind, therefore the entire universe is only 6,000 years old, and there was a worldwide Flood 4,000 years ago that explains all geological phenomena.

4. The Bible is God's authoritative word on all matters of life, even science. Therefore, to doubt the historical and scientific accuracy of Genesis 1–11 amounts to undermining the Word of God.

5. Acceptance of evolution has led to the moral breakdown in society.

Since 1987, Ken Ham has slowly built up a considerable following in the Evangelical world. Back in 2009 he opened his Creation Museum and has now built a life-sized Noah's Ark near his Creation Museum, claiming that it will prove to the world that God's Word is true. In February of 2014 he debated Bill Nye "the science guy" over whether or not young earth creationism was a viable science.

Even though he is hardly known outside of Evangelicalism, within the Evangelical world Ken Ham is viewed as a champion of Christ, fighting the good fight against godless secularism and standing firm on biblical authority. He routinely condemns fellow Christians and Christian organizations for compromising the Bible (i.e. not subscribing to his modern-scientific interpretation of Genesis 1–11) and takes every opportunity to promote *Answers in Genesis* as the sole light of truth in a dark world and to call a compromising Christian church back to God.

That is unfortunate, because what Ken Ham teaches is neither biblical nor scientific. What is more, the fundamental claims he makes about the Bible and Christian faith simply have never been held in the history of the Church. Yet he has been able to wield considerable influence throughout Evangelicalism because he has convinced people that what is at stake in the creation/evolution debate is the authority of the Bible itself and the moral soul of the nation. That claim simply is not true. Whatever your opinion on the age of the earth and evolution is, the fact is that YEC has never been universally held in the history of the Church.

In order to understand the underlying problems with YEC, we first have to address and clarify a number of basic issues so we can be in a better position to analyze the claims of YEC and biblical literalism. Therefore, this book is not simply an apologetic against YEC, but it also serves as a primer to various other issues that Christians should be familiar with, including Church history, biblical exegesis and interpretation, the particular historical and literary contexts surrounding Genesis 1–11, science, and philosophy.

The name of this book is *The Heresy of Ham*. Yes, "heresy" is a loaded word, so we need to be careful not to level it at anyone in a careless fashion. In fact, it would be best if we first took the time to understand precisely what it really is. In order to do so, we need to journey back, long before there ever was a creation/evolution controversy, to a pivotal event in Church history: that of the Arian controversy of the fourth century.

You don't know what that is? You're in luck. I have a story to tell.

2

History and Heresy

"The whole world groaned and was astonished to find itself Arian."
—St. Jerome

THERE WAS A PRIEST NAMED ARIUS

IN ALEXANDRIA, EGYPT, AROUND the year AD 320, there was a priest named Arius. Based on his own reading and understanding of Scripture, Arius began to put forth a unique teaching about Jesus Christ, namely that the Son did not share full equality with God the Father. According to Arius, Jesus, as the Son of God and the second member of the Trinity, was not truly divine, at least not in the same way God the Father was. Rather, Jesus the Son was the greatest creation of God the Father. As great as the Son was, "there was a time when the Son was not."

Now let's face it, trying to understand how Jesus could be both God and man, or trying to understand the inner workings of the Trinity, is ultimately impossible. Given our limited human understanding, we simply cannot fathom the realities of God—we might get a few glimpses here and there, we might understand bits and pieces, but we would be fools to think that we've figured God out.

But apparently, Arius saw things differently. It didn't make logical sense to him that the *Son* of God could share full, equal divinity with the *Father*. Furthermore, there were certain verses that indicated that he was not, in fact, equal to the Father. Therefore, Arius reasoned, since the

Bible did not clearly spell out the nature of Christ, Jesus was ultimately a creation of God. After all, the Scriptures said things like:

- You heard me say to you, "I am going away, and I will come to you." If you loved me, you would have rejoiced, because I am going to the Father, for the Father is greater than I" (John 14:28)
- Jesus said to her, "Do not cling to me, for I have not yet ascended to the Father; go to my brothers and say to them, 'I am ascending to my Father and your Father, to my God and your God.'" (John 20:17)
- Jesus said to him, "Why do you call me good? No one is good except God alone" (Luke 18:19)
- The LORD created me at the beginning of His course as the first of His works of old (Proverbs 8:22)

Based on verses like these, the only reasonable thing to conclude was that the Son was not equal to the Father; there was a time when the Son was not; the Son was not fully divine. As it turned out, Arius' views found a following among a significant minority in the Alexandrian church. The way Arius was able to be successful was that he essentially came up with a slick marketing campaign…sort of: he wrote his new-found theological insights into catchy "pop-tunes" of the day. It is known today as Arius' *thalia*. He took songs sung down by the docks, and then put his own lyrics to the tunes, and voila! The catchy tunes were the vehicle through which Arius was able to get his theological ideas out to the public.

Such a tactic still works today. Think of the times you found yourself singing certain advertisement jingles, and then going to purchase that very product. Such is the nature of advertising—It is able to get certain ideas past your rationality and into your head. The difference, of course, is that while the modern-day advertising jingles might get you to be more inclined to buy a Big Mac, Arius' jingles were putting some very unbiblical and dangerous ideas about Christ into the minds of many unlearned Christians.

THE ORTHODOX RESPONSE TO ARIUS' TEACHINGS

When Alexander, the bishop of Alexandria, got wind of what Arius was teaching, he promptly called a local church council in Alexandria to condemn Arius: Arius' teaching was a novel teaching that had never been held in the previous 300 years of the Church. Even though Arius' teaching was condemned, Arius himself was not deterred. He simply moved to Nicomedia, where a number of sympathetic friends like Eusebius of Nicomedia lived, and together with Eusebius and others, he continued his "there was a time the Son was not" ad-campaign. Pretty soon, Arius' teaching was popping up in various places throughout the empire and creating quite a lot of division and conflict throughout the Church.

Arius' teaching thus prompted the calling of the first Ecumenical Church council. It took place in Nicaea, in AD 325. The emperor Constantine, a relatively new Christian, called for the council because the last thing he wanted to see was his newly found faith (and his empire) to be torn apart by schism. And so, he called upon church leaders from around the empire to address the validity of Arius' teachings.

Address them, the council did. There wasn't even that much of a debate. Athanasius, a young deacon of Alexandria who served under Alexander, was able to successfully argue that Arius' teaching was neither biblical, nor in line with what the Church had ever taught. After Arius quoted a number of Bible verses out of context to argue his position, Athanasius famously said to Arius: "What Church Fathers can you quote?" This appeal to the teachings of the early Church Fathers was the deciding factor in the condemnation of Arius. After all, heretics can quote the Bible too, but they can't claim the support of the historical Church teaching.

After condemning Arius' teachings again, and after drafting an official creed, now famously known as the Nicene Creed, that outlined the fundamental tenants of the Christian faith, the Church kicked Arius out because he refused to renounce his heretical teaching and sign the creed. Constantine then banished Arius. It was abundantly clear that Arius' teachings were divisive and heretical. Case closed.

ARIANISM MAKES A COMEBACK

Unfortunately, Arius proved to be too much like Count Dracula in Bram Stokers' novel. Like the Count's coffin, Arius was able to get his case reopened, and Arianism proceeded to suck the lifeblood out of the Church for the rest of the fourth century. Ironically, the way Arius was able to revive his condemned heresy was very much like the way in which Dracula was able to make his way to England: deception, smooth-talking, and flat-out violence.

Arius was able to get his influential friends like Eusebius of Nicomedia to manipulate Constantine and play upon Constantine's desire for unity within the empire. Since Constantine was not a theologian who was able to understand the theological nuances of the debate over the natures of Christ, Eusebius was able to convince Constantine that Arius had simply been misunderstood and had thus been treated poorly. Simply put, he portrayed himself as a victim.

And so, Constantine took pity on Arius. He lifted the ban and tried to let Arius go back to Alexandria to be reinstated in the Alexandrian church. By that time, though, Athanasius had become the bishop of Alexandria, and there was no way he was about to readmit Arius into the Alexandrian fold. The nature of Christ was a fundamental issue, and to get that wrong would inevitably have dire implications for other aspects of the Christian faith. Athanasius saw just how divisive and heretical Arius' teachings really were. Neither the people of Alexandria nor Athanasius wanted Arius back. So, Arius was not welcomed back.

Arius, though, was able to use the circumstances to his advantage. He continued to paint himself as the victim and Athanasius as a belligerent bully who was simply intolerant and hostile toward a Christian brother. Over time, Arius gained sympathy, both with Constantine and with a growing number of church leaders. By manipulating the compassion of Christians, Arius slowly made a comeback.

Over the course of the next few decades, Arianism was revived in a big way. On his deathbed, Constantine was actually baptized by Arius' friend, the Arian bishop Eusebius of Nicomedia. Arian bishops had been able to play upon the religious ignorance of Constantine to gain political advantage. Through political maneuvering, they were able to gain control of a number of influential churches. Once they did, though, they began to show their true colors. In fact, they used their political clout to actively persecute many Orthodox bishops and priests, and thereby destroy the Orthodox Christian faith that had been held since the time of the apostles.

It's shocking how quickly things changed. Jerome famously declared, "The whole world groaned, and was astonished to find itself Arian." Despite not being supported either by biblical interpretation or the traditional teaching of the Church, despite being clearly shown to be heretical at the Council of Nicaea, Arianism ended up almost destroying the historic Christian faith that it claimed to affirm. How did this happen?

ARIAN TACTICS

The first way Arius was able to get his teaching to the public was, as was already mentioned, by putting it in the form of "pop tunes," essentially slick-sounding advertisements. Second, Arius and his supporters were able to take advantage of the Christ-like sympathies of well-meaning Christians who were nevertheless not well-educated in the Christian faith. Third, Arius and his supporters preyed upon people's ignorance of the faith they claimed to uphold and kept people ignorant of historical Church teaching. And fourth, once the Arians gained positions of influence, they used their political power to utterly crush any dissent.

Like a perfect storm, when these four factors converge, the results can be rapid and devastating. Arianism was never the majority view of the Church, but for a time, that Arian minority was able to gain positions of power in the Church and then force its view on others. Arian church leaders effectively silenced any dissent through banishment, intimidation, and even murder. Arianism effectively attempted to make mental adherence to a limited and so-called logical human claim the litmus test that defined the Christian faith. If you didn't agree that "there was a time when the Son was not," you had no place in their church, and you might very well be killed.

The result of the Arian heresy was, quite obviously, a tremendous amount of conflict and strife throughout the Church. It was ripping the Church apart. The fighting became so hostile and venomous between Arians and Orthodox Christians that it opened the door to the potential destruction of the Christian faith entirely…but not by the Arians.

JULIAN THE APOSTATE

In AD 361, Julian the Apostate became the new emperor. Although he was a member of Constantine's family, and although he had been brought up in Christian circles (he actually was the schoolmate of Basil of Caesarea and Gregory of Nazianzus), Julian had become enamored with paganism. Part of paganism's appeal for Julian, no doubt, was that it seemed to be so religiously tolerant, quite unlike the ugly and divisive fighting within the Church between Arians and Orthodox Christians. And so, shortly after he became the emperor, he rejected Christianity and proved himself to be an apostate.

Unfortunately, this is nothing new in the Church. There are scores of people who, even though they were raised in the church, witnessed so much hatred and fighting among so-called Christian leaders that they were sickened by the whole thing and ended up throwing out the baby with the bathwater. Most people go on with their lives quietly, but many end up becoming anti-Christian zealots who actively try to destroy the faith. This is precisely what Julian the Apostate became, and this is precisely what he attempted to do. When he became emperor, he made it his personal mission to revive paganism on a massive scale and to destroy the Church.

Of course, he was not about to launch a full-out persecution of the Church. He was smart enough to realize that past persecutions of Christians actually united Christians and strengthened the Church. So, Julian devised a different tactic: *foster schism and division*. He purposely ordered that all the men who had been banned from the Church over the previous thirty years because they were spreading heretical teachings to be reinstated in the Church. By forcibly letting heretics back in, Julian figured that he'd stoke the fires of Arianism so that they would burn down the entire Church. He then would revive paganism from the ashes.

Unfortunately for Julian, he failed miserably. Christianity had simply been planted too deeply in the empire's soil to be uprooted. People were fleeing paganism, not because of any Christian persecution of paganism, but rather because Christianity had such a positive impact on the lives of everyday people that they clearly saw the utter moral bankruptcy of paganism. Julian would order pagan festivals in an attempt to revive the old pagan ways, but simply no one would show up. Two years into his reign, he died.

Despite the raging debates between Arian and Orthodox leaders, despite the vitriol that infected so many, the fact was that the simple and life-changing faith of thousands of everyday Christians sustained the Church. People saw that on a grassroots, day-to-day basis, the Christian faith was living, vibrant, and having a powerful impact on Roman society. Yes, the schism was bound to hurt many people, but it could not destroy the historic Christian faith. When Julian died, paganism in the empire effectively died with him. The controversy over Arianism, though, wouldn't definitively be over until the Council of Constantinople in AD 381, when

Arianism finally had a stake driven through its heart and was buried for good.

Over the course of the Arian heresy, from the Council of Nicaea in AD 325 to the Council of Constantinople in AD 381, no other Church leader suffered more than Athanasius of Alexandria. He was banished from his position as bishop of Alexandria five times and was falsely accused by Arian instigators of numerous crimes, from subverting the empire, to murder and treason. When hunted by imperial soldiers, he was hidden by desert monks.

In the long run, Athanasius' faithfulness to Christ and his commitment to the truth of the Christian faith won out. He dedicated his life to defending the truth of the Gospel from the divisive and hateful heresy of Arianism. If it wasn't for Athanasius, the traditional Orthodox Christian faith might have been stamped out by a slick-sounding, manipulative, and ruthless heresy.

WHAT IS HERESY, AND WHAT MAKES A HERETIC?

Heresy is easy to identify when you are reading history books. After all, the books spell it out for you: "Arianism was a heresy because…." Historical distance gives clarity and perspective. Yet when one is in the middle of a movement or controversy, lines are often blurred, and things get confusing. Therefore, heresy is a difficult thing to deal with in real time. It is difficult because at the beginning *it really isn't a heresy*. It is simply starts as an idea that a Christian might have as he tries to think through and understand his faith.

Arius wasn't a heretic for merely *thinking* that perhaps, on some level, the Son didn't share full equality with the Father. Just putting out the idea that perhaps "there was a time the Son was not," doesn't get you banished from the Church. Contemplating the relationship between the Father and the Son is the only way one can come to a better understanding of the Trinity. For the first 300 years of the early Church, Christians had wrestled with how to understand the relationship between Jesus the Son and God the Father. Therefore, Arius wasn't even a heretic for sharing his thoughts. The way the Church comes to a fuller understanding of God is when individual Christians share their thoughts within the Church, so that the Church, as a body, as a community, can grow up *together* in Christ.

What made Arius a heretic was that once the Church had debated his views, once it was clear he had no support from any of the Church Fathers for the first 300 years of Christianity, once it was abundantly clear that his idea subverted and undercut the very heart of the Gospel, *he refused to admit he was wrong.* After Nicaea, the Arians proceeded to fixate on Arius' novel doctrinal point, set up his idea as their own theological idol, and then went about, by means of manipulation, intimidation, and violence, forcing their heretical view on the Church as a whole, and making Christians bow down to Arius' theological idol that was made not by God, but by his own hands.

Arius and the heretical movement he started was not Christian. He effectively was a theological pagan. He might have used Christian terms and language, but he erected a theological idol and proceeded to rip apart the Church. And, in the midst of the turmoil he precipitated, it was only a matter of time until things got so ugly that someone like Julian the Apostate ended up trying to destroy the Church completely.

LET'S CLARIFY SOMETHING: I WAS NOT A TEENAGE HERETIC

That being said, simply holding a certain view or teaching does not necessarily make one a heretic. Case in point, let's consider 14-year-old Joel. Being a child of the 70s-80s, I grew up when Hal Lindsey and the *Thief in the Night* movies had convinced Evangelical America that the rapture was imminent and that Jesus was coming back, probably in 1988. Although I didn't know the word "dispensationalism," I unthinkingly assumed that Christians had always believed that.

Eventually, I came to see that many of the assumptions I held as a child were recent inventions by people who claimed they had a "new revelation" that, shockingly to me, had never been held or taught before in the entire history of the Church. Such a teaching is, by definition, a heresy. But that does not mean that I was a heretic in my early life. I was just a kid who had grown up within a certain Christian subculture, and who had unthinkingly imbibed certain theological beliefs that I had never taken the time to really think about until later. When I got older and critically thought through my faith, though, I realized there were a number of beliefs from the Evangelical subculture of my youth that simply were not true:

- II Thessalonians 4:16–17 is *not* about a "secret rapture"
- Matthew 24 is *not* about Jesus' second coming at the end of a seven-year tribulation period
- Daniel 9 is *not* a future blueprint for a seven-year tribulation period
- Revelation is *not* a divine script for the *Left Behind* books and movies

A basic knowledge of biblical history, exegesis, and Church history proves this quite easily. Now Christians who happen to grow up in churches that do, in fact, tend to believe such things, are not necessarily heretics. They are Christians who love and follow Christ who, although they might *say* they believe in something like "the rapture," in reality don't really give it much thought or concern, and it doesn't impinge on their daily lives as Christians.

The actual heretics are the speakers, authors, and pastors who promote it, peddle it, and ultimately profit from it, whether it be in terms of money, power, fame, or influence. This is where the danger lies—heresy starts from *within* the church. It may start off as a sincere speculative idea that deserves consideration. There isn't a Christian alive who has not held to a certain belief that, under further scrutiny, turned out to be wrong. Yet, heresy is born when a teaching is actively promoted, even though it is shown that there is very little biblical support for it, and that it has never been held in the history of the Church. The fruit of heresy is easily discernible: it is bitter, divisive, and an incoherent mess. The fruit of heresy shows it to be, ultimately, not merely *un*-Christian, but ultimately, *anti*-Christian.

Unfortunately, by the time the bitter fruit becomes obvious, the sad truth is that the heresy has already taken root within the soil of some parts of the Church. It therefore becomes really hard to uproot, for the peddlers of the heresy claim it is some "new revelation," some "secret knowledge of good and evil" that has been made known only to them. They are convinced that they are bearing the cross of Christ, and offering the fruit from the Tree of Life, when in reality they are offering false fruit from a forbidden tree, and then crucifying anyone who questions them.

RELIGIOUS AMNESIA AND HERESY WITHIN PROTESTANTISM

The reason why it is important to know the story of Arianism is that today in the Evangelical world, people simply do not know how to recognize heresy. For all the positive contributions of the Protestant Reformation, perhaps the most glaring problem within Protestantism is that there is simply no way to address heretical teachings. For that matter, within Protestant circles, the very idea of heresy is problematic.

Throughout Church history up to that point, "heresy" was understood as promoting a teaching within the Church that contradicted the historic Church teaching that was handed down by the apostles. Yet during the Reformation, "heresy" came to be used as a pejorative that any reformer would use to criticize anyone who didn't agree with his own view. Instead of heresy meaning, "That which went against the historic teaching of the Church," it came to mean, in the mouth of Luther (or any other Reformer), "Anything that goes against what I believe."

Consequently, *everyone* was called a "heretic" by *someone*, and thereby "heresy" was rendered meaningless: if *everyone* is a heretic, then *no one* is a heretic. Martin Luther, for example, didn't have a problem with just the Catholics. He had a problem with Ulrich Zwingli, the Anabaptists, the Jews…you name it. He despised anyone who didn't agree *with him*. So, for the past 500 years, the Protestantism has been characterized by schisms and divisions, to the point where there are actually more than 20,000 different Protestant denominations in the world today.

The result of all this is that within Protestantism there is simply no agreed upon understanding of the historical Christian faith as recorded in the New Testament and preserved by the early Church. The reason for there being no agreed upon understanding of the *historical Christian faith* is that there is no understanding of the *historical Church*. Consequently, American Evangelical Christians today are largely ignorant of the very faith they espouse and the Church of which they claim to be a part. Put those two factors together, and you have left the door wide open for any individual to plant heretical teachings and let them take root.

So how much Church history do you really know? As a kid who grew up in an Assemblies of God church, what I knew about Church history could be summed up as follows:

> "Baptists, Methodists, Presbyterians, Anglicans, a bunch of others? They're all Christians who came after Martin Luther started

the Protestant Reformation and broke away from the Catholic Church, because those Catholics teach that (a) you should pray to Mary, (b) communion is really Jesus' body and blood, (c) the Pope is infallible, and (d) you must do good works to get saved. Catholics also drink alcohol and are dead in their rituals and traditions. Before the Catholics corrupted the Church, the early Christians were part of the pure Church and were persecuted by Nero and the Romans. It was only after the Roman Emperor Constantine became a Christian that the Church became polluted with power and worldly desires. Martin Luther started to reform the Church, but it wasn't really until the Azusa Street Revival in 1906 that God started to pour out His Holy Spirit on the Church again, and we are now living in the last days."

Does that pretty much sum it up for you, too? If so, that means a mere 150 words comprise your understanding of Church history. Depending on your given denomination, the above summary will no doubt be altered a bit, but overall, if you are a Protestant, and especially if you are an Evangelical, chances are this encapsulates your knowledge of Church history.

But is it really possible to adequately summarize 2,000 years of worldwide Church history with 150 words? The obvious answer is "no." After all, the Gettysburg Address, which commemorated just one battle in the Civil War, was 268 words! Understanding Church history will certainly take more than just a Reader's Digest version of a Reader's Digest version of a Reader's Digest version.

The real danger of holding to such an anorexic view of Church history gives a shallow understanding of not only what the Church is, but who Christ is, what the Gospel is, and what God's purposes in history are. Furthermore, it leaves you open to being manipulated or misinformed on a whole number of levels, both from within and without the wall of your particular church.

That is how heresy takes root in Christian communities. It preys upon people's ignorance of Church history and traditional Church teaching, and the leaders who push a particular heresy do their best to keep people in the dark through manipulation, intimidation, and deception. That is why it is so important to have at least a general handle on the basics of Church history and Church Tradition.

Not sure what Church Tradition is? You're in luck…I've got another history lesson for you.

3

Church Tradition and the Bible

"The heretics follow neither Scripture nor Tradition"

—St. Irenaeus of Lyons

"Let us look at the very tradition, teaching, and faith of the catholic Church from the very beginning, which the Word gave, the Apostles preached, and the Fathers preserved. Upon this the Church is founded."

—St. Athanasius

THE IMPORTANCE OF CHURCH TRADITION

SINCE KNOWING YOUR HISTORY is important, in this chapter we are going to have a little bit of a history lesson on the concept of Church Tradition and how it has guarded the beliefs and claims the Church has held for the past 2,000 years. If you are a Christian, you are a part of the Church, and that Church has a history. It is in the course of that history that the fundamental beliefs and practices of Christianity have been developed, clarified, and taught. Therefore, one cannot fall into the trap of thinking, "It's just me, Jesus, and the Bible!" and completely ignore 2,000 years of the history of Christ working through the Church to save the world.

If you are a Christian, you need to realize that you have been saved to be a part of something, *the Church*—and that Church has *a history*. It is the *Body of Christ*, the *Temple of the Holy Spirit*, and the *Family of God*. And just like in any family, you gain wisdom and insight by talking to and learning from your aunts, uncles, parents and grandparents; so it is with the family of God. For 2,000 years, those family members have left us a legacy of their wisdom and insight regarding the Christian faith. So, we should listen to their advice and learn from their experiences, so that we can continue to grow in our faith.

By contrast, heretics don't want their followers to know the history of the Christian faith. They dismiss that history because they want to push their own teachings that have never been held in Church history. Heresy hammers home one and only one commandment: *to question the one in authority is to doubt God, and doubting God is a sin*. That is why it is important to know your Church history. It protects you from heresy.

Unfortunately, it is on this point most Evangelical Christians come up short. It is not really their fault. It is just an unintended consequence of the Reformation. The sad fact is that by and large, Evangelicalism has cut itself off from the historical roots of the Church, and therefore doesn't have a solid grasp of a historical understanding of the Church.

Let's just admit it is time to get a solid grasp on the history of the Church. Even a general knowledge of Church history will help us understand what the true fundamentals of the Christian faith have always been. This is why the Church councils were called: to help clarify and preserve the fundamentals of the Christian faith that have been held since the very beginning. This is what is known as *Church Tradition*. Now, most Protestants, and certainly most Evangelicals, don't know what to make of that phrase. It is a foreign concept to them—and that is precisely the problem.

That is why I eventually joined the Orthodox Church—not because I think the only true Christians are in the Orthodox Church, but rather because the Orthodox Church is committed to preserving those fundamentals of the Christian faith. In fact, *bearing witness* to that faith is the number one priority of the Orthodox Church. As I read and studied more about Orthodoxy, I found myself saying things like, "Yes! That is something I always thought! That's how I've always understood it!"

On my spiritual journey, I found a home in the Orthodox Church, for it was in Orthodoxy that I understood what the Church is, and because of that, I saw Christ more clearly and I understood salvation better.

In fact, once I joined the Orthodox Church, I actually started to feel more at home in other churches as well. Once I understood what the *Living Tradition* of the Church was (the foundational doctrines, beliefs, and practices that all Christians share) I was able to see aspects of it more clearly in every denomination. Every denomination has its shortcomings, but having a firm grasp of the faith of the historic Church helped me recognize that Living Tradition within all denominations, and thus differentiate that Living Tradition from the secondary issues that Christians often get hung up on.

Look at the statement of faith of your church, or any church organization or Christian institution. You'll see statements regarding God the Father, Christ's humanity and divinity, the Holy Spirit, the Trinity, and the Church. All that comes from Church Tradition and the Church councils. One might say, "No, that all comes from the Bible!" Really? What verse in the Bible clearly tells us about the Trinity? Where is it clearly stated that Christ is both man and God? You simply won't be able to find those verses in the Bible, because they're not there.

We might be able to pick out verses in the Bible to illustrate doctrines like the Trinity and the divine/human natures of Christ, but the reason we can do that is because the early Church and Church councils preserved the proper interpretation of those passages for us, and then clearly articulated the fundamentals of the faith in the creeds. They preserved the Living Tradition that gives us the context in which to faithfully interpret the Bible. That is why understanding the concept of Church Tradition is so important. Without it, our faith will be easily derailed or lost.

CHURCH TRADITION AND CHURCH COUNCILS

Before the Reformation, for the first 1500 years of the Church, there was a process by which heresy was addressed: the Church council. Whenever a particular teaching about a fundamental aspect of the Christian faith seemed to go against what had always been taught in the Church since its earliest days, Church leaders from around the world would convene a Church council, discuss the historic Christian faith, and debate the particular issue at hand. This is what happened at the first Church council in Nicaea in AD 325.

As I talked about in the previous chapter, Arius' teaching was causing division in the Church, and therefore it had to be addressed. When they addressed controversial teachings in the Church councils, what the Church Fathers really ended up doing was declaring what Christianity *wasn't*. Only then did they venture to clarify a certain Church teaching in response to the heretical claims. For example, when Arius declared that the Son was *of a similar substance* with the Father (*homoiousius*), the Nicene Council, in order to clarify the relationship between the Father and Son, stated that the Son was *of equal substance* with the Father (*homoousius*). Yes, the crux of this debate centered on a single letter's difference.

The Church Fathers knew that the description of *homoousius* was bound to be an imperfect description because, ultimately, the relationship between the Father and the Son is a mystery we can never fully comprehend. Still, it served as a necessary check against Arius' heretical teaching of *homoiousius*. Now, you might ask, "What's the big deal between 'being of similar substance' and 'being of equal substance'?" Theologically, it is a huge deal. Without going into all the details, Athanasius' main argument against Arius' *homoiousius* was that if Jesus is only *similar* to God the Father, and not *equal* to God the Father, then that is a denial of Jesus' divinity. If Jesus isn't divine, then he is unable to redeem us from our sins. His death was just the death of another man.

By trying to define Jesus as *homoiousius* with the Father, Arius' teaching undercut the entire Gospel. Yes, Arius kept things rather simple: the Father was here, the Son was there. That's easy to grasp with our limited reason. It takes away the mystery and doesn't challenge our intellect. But it also keeps God separate from mankind, and it destroys the Gospel. The Nicene Council realized the need to admit the limits of reason and the need to come up with a word, however imperfect, that would act as a placeholder that pointed to the mystery that made the Gospel possible.

The Church Fathers certainly were not infallible. They believed, though, that as flawed as each individual Church leader may be, the Holy Spirit was working through the Church council, through their own floundering attempts to understand the truth, and was moving them to bear witness to the truth. Indeed, they believed the Holy Spirit was "guiding them in all truth" (John 16:13), just as Jesus said he would.

Often, they would issue their findings (see Acts 15:28) beginning with, "It seems right to the Holy Spirit and to us…." Thereby, they were not making authoritative pronouncements *of what the truth was,* but were rather *bearing witness to the truth*—and by doing so, they were living out the authority that Christ had bestowed on the Church from the very beginning. That is why, despite all the failings and faults of individual Christians throughout Church history, the fundamental, historical Christian faith has been able to be preserved for the past 2,000 years.

THE CREEDAL FUNDAMENTALS OF THE CHRISTIAN FAITH

So, what are the essentials of the historic Christian faith, or what I like to call the *creedal fundamentals* of the faith? Fortunately, the early Church councils made it a point to articulate the true, bedrock fundamentals of the Christian faith by developing the early Church creeds. First there was the Apostles' Creed, then the Nicene Creed, and eventually the Chalcedon Creed. Let's briefly look at the Nicene Creed to see what was considered the "fundamentals" of the faith for the early Church.

> *I believe in one God, the Father Almighty, Maker of heaven and earth, and of all things visible and invisible.*

What is being emphasized here about God the Father? That there is one God, and that He is the creator of the universe. But what does "all things visible and invisible" mean? Basically, this was an acknowledgement that there is more to reality than just the physical, visible world. There are invisible realities that go beyond the natural world, and that God is the creator of them as well as the natural world.

> *And in one Lord Jesus Christ, the only-begotten Son of God, begotten of the Father before all worlds; God of God, Light of Light, very God of very God; begotten, not made, being of one substance with the Father, by whom all things were made.*

What the Nicene council wanted to emphasize about Jesus Christ was that, as the Son of God, he was the "only-begotten" of God, and that he wasn't "made." This meant that Jesus was not merely a creature God the Father made. He was, in fact, in some mysterious way that the term *homoousius* emphasizes, actually of "one substance" with the Father.

Think of it this way. While obviously *the body* of Jesus, being of biological and natural material, was a product of the creative biological processes of nature, *the very being* of Jesus was not created into existence along with his body (as is the case with each one of us). The very being of Jesus is eternal, because it is "of one substance with the Father."

> *Who, for us men for our salvation, came down from heaven, was incarnate by the Holy Spirit of the virgin Mary, and was made man. He was crucified also for us under Pontius Pilate. He suffered and was buried. The third day He rose again, according to the Scriptures. He*

ascended into heaven and sits on the right hand of the Father. He shall come again, with glory, to judge the quick and the dead. His kingdom shall have no end.

This section of the Nicene Creed is actually the easiest to understand. It basically states that Jesus, although he is God, still was very much a human being who lived in history, in the first century of Second Temple Judaism. He was really born, he really was crucified, he really suffered and was buried, and he really rose again—he defeated death, and now reigns over God's creation. His historical life has cosmic implications.

I believe in the Holy Ghost, the Lord and Giver of Life, who proceeds from the Father, who with the Father and the Son together is worshipped and glorified, and who spoke by the prophets.

As you can tell, even the early Church Fathers had a hard time articulating the Holy Spirit. Despite the mystery, they insisted that the Holy Spirit was to be worshipped along with the Father and the Son. This is what we understand to be the Trinity.

I believe in one holy catholic and apostolic Church. I acknowledge one baptism for the remission of sins. I look for the resurrection of the dead, and the life of the world to come.

Finally, the Nicene Council emphasized the unity of the Church, the future physical resurrection of the dead, and the future consummation of the new creation. So, if we were to make a list of the *creedal fundamentals* of the early Church, this is what they would be:

1. There is one God, the Father, the Creator of all of reality.

2. Reality is not limited to the natural world; there are realities that go beyond nature.

3. Jesus Christ is eternal and of the same substance as the Father.

4. Jesus Christ was still a real person with a real material body, who lived a real life; he was really crucified and really physically raised from the dead, and thus overcame the power of death.

5. Jesus Christ, by defeating death, has authority to rule over God's creation. He is in the process of bringing about the New Creation, which will be consummated at the future resurrection of the dead.

6. The Holy Spirit is also to be worshipped along with the Father and the Son; he is the one who "speaks through the prophets." It is through the Holy Spirit that God interacts with his people.

7. There is one Church, and believers work toward unity in the faith.

There it is: the fundamentals of the faith as expressed in the Nicene Creed. These were explanations and clarifications of what was rooted in Scripture and what had been taught and believed in the early Church. It also should be noted that along with clarifying these creedal fundamentals, the Council of Nicaea also clarified what the canon of the New Testament was. In other words, the Council of Nicaea exercised the authority that Jesus Christ bestowed on the Church to not only articulate the creedal fundamentals of the Christian faith, but to also bear witness to what the authoritative Scriptural canon for the Church was to be.

As history progressed, later Church councils were called to further clarify Church teachings, but I don't think one can go wrong by looking to the Nicene Creed to get a handle on the fundamentals of the Christian faith. Notice, though, that although there are some clear facts stated (i.e. Jesus' crucifixion and resurrection), most of the Nicene Creed consists of tremendous *metaphysical* and *philosophical* statements. These statements, if one takes the time to really consider them, significantly affects one's worldview and shapes the way one understands God, the natural world, the life of Christ, mankind, and the future and purpose of God's creation.

SOME OBSERVATIONS REGARDING THE CREEDAL FUNDAMENTALS

The early Church Fathers were not uneducated rubes. Many were some of the most learned, sophisticated philosophers and thinkers of their day who understood that the Christian faith wasn't simply a matter of mental assent to a laundry list of historical facts. Now, of course, the historical facts regarding the life of Jesus Christ, particularly the resurrection, were crucial. Without them there would have been no Christian faith in the first place. Those historical facts revealed a deeper knowledge and understanding about who God is, what the purpose of creation was, and what the role of the Church was to be as the Body of Christ who bears witness to Christ's saving activity in the world.

That being said, notice what sort of things were never mentioned as fundamental to the Christian faith. Baptism was essential, but the manner by which baptism was administered didn't really matter, be it immersion or sprinkling, adult baptism or infant baptism. Notice too that the whole "predestination vs. free will" controversy that Protestants have argued for 500 years wasn't seen as a fundamental issue either. It's fine to debate that issue, but it is not a fundamental tenant of the Christian faith.

Given the topic of this book, please note that there is absolutely no insistence *anywhere*—not in any creed, Church council, or pronouncement *ever*—that the early chapters of Genesis were to be understood as a point-by-point historical and scientific account of the creation of the material universe in general, and of the first human beings in particular. The historical fact is that early Church Fathers, as well as Christian leaders throughout Church history, held to a variety of interpretations of the early chapters of Genesis. Although there were different ways Christian leaders might interpret Genesis 1–11, no one questioned the inspiration or truthfulness of these chapters, and no one saw any particular interpretation of Genesis 1–11 as a fundamental teaching of the Church.

This is an important point to make, for heresy is not limited to simply wrong teaching about something. It also can involve undue emphasis of a particular theological point or view, and actually elevate a secondary or non-essential issue to a level of primacy, equal to the resurrection of Christ.

THE "CAPITAL-T" TRADITION OF THE CHURCH

This leads us to a vital point to make regarding Church Tradition. When the early Church councils came together to articulate those creedal fundamentals of the faith, they also made clear what traditions in the Church weren't fundamental to the faith. Therefore, if you are going to get a firm grasp on Church Tradition, you will need to make a distinction between what we can call *"Capital-T" Tradition* and *"small-t" traditions*.

The "Capital-T" Tradition of Christianity is the teachings and practices of the early Church that Christ handed down to the apostles. We see the result of this "Capital-T" Tradition in both the New Testament and the early Church creeds. Remember, the New Testament did not drop out of Heaven, directly from the writing desk of God. It was the product of the early Church.

The apostles didn't just sit down and write their books after Jesus ascended to Heaven. They went out and proclaimed the Gospel and shared the "Capital-T" Tradition that the risen Jesus Christ had given to them. During that first century, as they proclaimed the Gospel, some of them also wrote letters and books. Over time, the next few generations of Christians collected these writings into what we now have as the New Testament. It, therefore, was written by the early Church, bore witness to the original Gospel of Jesus Christ, and was preserved by the Church.

This is important to realize, because nowhere did the apostles write down a clear doctrine that said, "Christ is both fully divine and fully human." Nowhere did they articulate a systematic doctrine of the Trinity. You can't find those things clearly articulated in the New Testament. That's okay, because the New Testament is part of the larger "Capital-T" Tradition of the Church. We know the apostles taught, and the first century Christians believed in, the divine and human natures of Christ, and we know they worshipped the Father, Son, and Holy Spirit as God because the teaching was preserved in the "Capital-T" Tradition of the Church.

Think back to the last chapter, when we learned about how Arius claimed that Jesus wasn't divine. The Church was able to come together at Nicaea and say, "Even though nowhere in the New Testament does it actually say, 'Christ is both fully divine and human,' not only are there passages all over the place that indicate this, but it is abundantly clear that Church teaching has always taught that Christ is fully divine and human." And so, that "Capital-T" Tradition of the early Church regarding the divinity and humanity of Christ helped provide the context to understand the Scriptures. Yes, the Scriptures teach that, but it was the early Church "Capital-T" Tradition that preserved it, explained it and rightly taught it.

THE SMALL "T" TRADITIONS WITHIN THE CHURCH

Somewhat different from the "Capital-T" Tradition of the Church is what we will call the "small-t" traditions of the Church. These are the non-essential traditions that can be found in every branch and denomination of Christianity. Baptists have their "small-t" traditions, as do Methodists, Presbyterians, Lutherans, Catholics, and the Orthodox. We are not going to articulate all the "small-t" traditions in all of these denominations, but since we are currently discussing the early Church, we should point out that within the Orthodox Church there are a number of "small-t" traditions that they still practice today that many Protestants find troubling: things like praying to the saints, praying to Mary, the belief that Mary was a virgin her entire life, and the belief that the flesh and blood of Jesus is "mystically present" in the bread and wine during communion.

Initially, these were the sorts of things that troubled me too. Did I have to believe that Mary never had sex, not even after she got married to Joseph? When I read in the Bible that Jesus had brothers and sisters, did I have to believe that it didn't really mean that? When I asked the local Orthodox priest about this, he explained to me the difference between the "Capital-T" Tradition and the "small-t" traditions of the Orthodox Church.

He told me that since the Orthodox Church is committed to preserving the teachings and practices of the early Church, and since by the time of the Council of Nicaea these "small-t" traditions were being taught and practiced, the Orthodox Church still teaches and practices them. Still, it fully realizes that the teaching of the perpetual virginity of Mary is clearly not on the same level as the teaching of the resurrection of Christ—hence the distinction between "Capital-T" Tradition and the "small-t" traditions of the Church.

The "Capital-T" Tradition is bedrock, foundational, and non-negotiable; the "small-t" traditions, while certainly historical, are not essential—it's okay to question them, and even not completely buy into them if you don't really get them. This is extremely important to realize because young earth creationists like Ken Ham are claiming that a modern historical/scientific reading of Genesis 1–11 is a fundamental issue of the faith and part of the "Capital-T" Tradition, on par with the Trinity, the divine/human natures of Christ, and the resurrection of Christ. Yet if you know your Church history, you will know that not only is young earth creationism not a "Capital-T" Tradition, it has not even been a "small-t" tradition anywhere in Church history, with the exception of 20th century Seven-Day Adventists and a small segment within 20th century Fundamentalism. What Ken Ham is claiming is verifiably false.

KEN HAM AND THE ISSUE OF AUTHORITY

This fact, though, means nothing to young earth creationists like Ken Ham, for he rejects anything in the history of the Church that doesn't agree with his YEC claims. By doing so, he ultimately rejects Church history and Tradition itself. Ken Ham will say that if you do not hold to the YEC view that Genesis 1–11 should be read as a modern historical and scientific account of the material origins of the universe that happened a mere 6,000 years ago, then you are undermining *biblical authority*.

Consequently, non-Christians who accept evolutionary theory are called adherents of the "secular religion of atheism," and Christians who accept evolutionary theory are accused of being unfaithful to Christ and going after the kinds of *traditions of men* that Christ himself condemned. This is truly an astounding and illogical claim, for in order to justify his YEC claims, Ken Ham has not only divorced the Bible from the history of Church Tradition, but he has also even gone so far as to dismiss that very Tradition that Christ handed down to his apostles as the "traditions of men" that Christ condemned.

The way Ken Ham gets away with it is by mixing up terms like "tradition," "authority," "the Bible," and "the traditions of men" in a giant theological blender without properly defining what he means by any of them. So let's clarify what these terms really mean by asking a very crucial three-pronged question: (1) what is meant by "tradition," (2) what is its relation to the Bible, and (3) where is authority in a Christian's life rooted? The answer to that question actually is going to vary, depending on what branch of Christianity you're talking about: Catholicism, Protestantism, or Orthodoxy. Let's do a quick run through each one. Get ready for another brief history lesson. Trust me, you'll thank me later.

Catholicism

Due largely to historical factors we will not discuss here, medieval Catholicism came to view Church Tradition as being *over the Bible*. What that meant is that since most people were illiterate, since the only literate people in Europe tended to be priests and bishops in the Catholic Church, and since there weren't copy machines that could mass produce the Bible into the common languages of Europe, the Catholic Church was very protective of the Bible. It was afraid that if the Bible was translated into the common languages, then commoners who had no knowledge or training of Church Tradition would come up with their own uneducated interpretations of the Bible. Let's face it, that's a valid concern.

Another factor to consider is that the Catholic Church came to be the main administrative engine of restoration to a Europe that had collapsed after the disintegration of the Roman Empire in the West. And like modern day businesses and organizations, there developed a very codified hierarchy of authority within the Catholic Church so it could essentially oversee the reorganization of Europe. The Pope acted as more or less as a CEO, the College of Cardinals acted as the board of directors, and then down to the priests, monks, nuns, and friars who worked at the local levels.

So, in medieval Europe, the Catholic Church and her institutional traditions largely shaped the culture of European society. In doing so, it also shaped the way people understood the Bible—after all, the Bible was in Latin, and the only people who could read Latin were priests and bishops. In the medieval Catholic Church, Church Tradition *had to be over* the Bible, because your typical peasant couldn't even get his hands on a Bible, let alone read it. Of course, as time proved, such power can corrupt, and corruption often was rampant throughout the ecclesiastical structure of the medieval Catholic Church. That's why the Reformation happened.

Protestantism

The Protestant Reformation changed things drastically. After Gutenberg made it possible to mass produce the Bible and Martin Luther translated it into German, suddenly, the commoners had access to the Bible. In addition, there was the growing political backlash throughout Europe to the corruption within the Catholic Church. The result wasn't just a *reformation*, but literally a Protestant *revolution* against Catholicism.

The end result was that Protestantism came to view the Bible as being *over Church Tradition*. In fact, due to papal abuses in medieval Europe, Protestants eventually rejected all Church Tradition, because they associated it with the Pope, and they viewed the Pope, quite frankly, as the anti-Christ. Of course, once that happened, the Reformers were faced with a crucial question: "What is to take their place as the sole source of authority for the Protestant Christian?" The battle cry of the Protestant Reformation was, *"Sola Scriptura!"* The Bible, and the Bible alone, was authoritative, and thus stood *over* the Church and, as far as the Reformers were concerned, *against* Church Tradition.

But let's tease out the implications of all this by looking more closely at the Reformation's slogan *"Sola Scriptura."* We have to remember that it was directed against the abuses of the Pope and the Catholic Church at the time. The Catholic Church essentially put the Pope's authority *over* Scripture, and essentially said, "You must obey the Pope and what he says Scripture is about. You are not allowed to read the Scriptures for yourself. You must believe what the Pope tells you Scripture means."

Such a view is clearly wrong, and the Reformers rightly rejected it. Yet we must remember that even though men like Martin Luther and John Calvin claimed, "Sola Scriptura," they still regularly consulted the works of the early Church Fathers as a vital part in their elaboration of Scripture. When they rejected "tradition," they were rejecting the abusive, authoritarian "tradition" of the medieval Catholic Church, not the very useful wisdom of Church Fathers who had gone before them.

What happened in the aftermath of the Reformation was people came to think they didn't have to consider the early Church Fathers, or traditional Church teaching *at all*. In a reaction against the Catholic Church putting the Pope on a pedestal, the Reformers ended up putting *the Bible itself on a pedestal and* started equating *all* the rich history of Church teaching for over 1500 years as "the traditions of men," and they thus rejected *all of it*.

We also must remember that the Reformation was happening roughly at the same time as the Enlightenment, which ironically called for the rejection of the Church and its traditions as well. In its place, the Enlightenment elevated autonomous human reason as the sole arbiter of truth. I bring this up to point out an extreme historical irony: the elevation of autonomous human reason as the sole arbiter of truth was not simply "an Enlightenment thing." It was ironically also "a Protestant thing," because that was what the Reformers were advocating as well! They said, "Reject Church tradition, get alone with your translation of the Bible, and you'll be able to come to the truth using your own reason." Martin Luther himself famously said at the Diet of Worms:

> "Unless I am convinced by *Scripture* and *plain reason*, I do not accept the *authority* of popes and councils, for they have contradicted each other. My conscience is captive to the Word of God. I cannot and will not recant anything, for to go against conscience is neither right nor safe."[1]

---

1. Griffiths, *From Calvin to Barth*, 5.

In face of the abusive and authoritarian Catholic Church at that time, Luther was right to stand against it. But (and here's the key) when it comes to understanding the Bible, it simply is not wise to reject all of Church Tradition and rely on your own, limited, autonomous reason, without any consideration of what countless Christians over the centuries have taught—and this is precisely what Luther was advocating. Such a view proved to be outright dangerous, as the violent religious wars that erupted in the wake of the Reformation proved. Protestants didn't just fight Catholics, they started fighting each other as well.

Let's be clear, though. On a practical everyday level, when I come to the Scriptures to try and understand them, of course I have to use my reason. At the same time, I have to remember that my view is inevitably going to be limited in a variety of ways. Therefore, I shouldn't blindly accept what some Pope tells me a certain passage means. But neither should I simply disregard traditional interpretations throughout Church history and set up my own, limited autonomous reason as the sole arbiter of understanding Scripture.

In order to come to a fuller understanding of Scripture, I must use my own reason, but I also must try to understand Scripture within the context of the Church. Now, obviously, the Holy Spirit can and does speak to individuals in their personal study of the Scriptures. But when it comes to elaborating and explaining the teachings and doctrines that the Church has always held to, it is very dangerous to just "go it alone," without reading and interpreting Scripture with an eye to what Christians throughout Church history have understood about it.

When people do that, it often leads to heretical and cultish doctrines. In the first five centuries of the Church there were heresies like Arianism, Apollinarianism, Pelagianism. In our modern world we have had examples like the Millerites, the Mormons (the Church of Jesus Christ of Latter-Day Saints), the Jehovah Witnesses, the "health and wealth gospel," as well as the more widely accepted heresies within Evangelicalism of dispensationalism and young earth creationism. What do they all have in common? They were started by people who claimed to have a "special insight" into the Scriptures, but ignored or rejected the traditional teachings of the Church, and thus went off in an exceptionally heretical directions.

As we've noted earlier, this has been a problem with Protestantism since its inception. By rejecting Church Tradition and claiming, "the Bible alone," Protestants were left with their own autonomous reason alone in order to interpret the Bible. If your interpretation differed from mine, then you must be a heretic, because I'm claiming "Sola Scriptura"—but then you'd say the same thing to me. Hence, within Protestantism, the very concept of heresy has been rendered meaningless, and is now simply used as a pejorative to denounce any teaching one doesn't happen to agree with.

In time, especially here in America, much of the early hostilities between denominations died down as a growing sense of religious amnesia and the emergence of a "feel good gospel" took root. Nowadays, it seems nobody really even cares enough about basic theology and the true essentials of the Christian faith to even argue. We are too busy following a new "gospel" that says, "Be a good boy, be positive, and believe that God wants to pat you on the head with blessings galore! To be a Christian means to be a nice guy! It means vanilla ice cream, no more 'rocky roads' to Calvary!"

When theology isn't valued, heretical teachings tend to take root, grow, and eventually hurt a lot of people and destroy the faith of many.

Eastern Orthodoxy

When it comes to Eastern Orthodoxy, the problems that racked Catholicism and Protestantism regarding Church Tradition or the Bible as the sole source of authority never have really come up, simply because Orthodoxy has never viewed either Church Tradition or the Bible as being "over" the other. Orthodoxy views them as complementary to each other and are thus inseparable—*the Bible is a part of Church Tradition.*

Think about it, who wrote the New Testament? The inspired writers of the early Church. Who compiled the New Testament that we have today? Church leaders at the Council of Nicaea. What is the determining canon and guide for the Church? The Bible. But who wrote the Bible? The inspired writers of the early Church!

You see? You simply cannot separate Church Tradition from the Bible. To separate them is a big mistake—you can't do it without doing irrevocable harm. The divisive history in both medieval Catholicism and the entire Protestant movement bears witness to this very fact. Now that is not to say that Eastern Orthodoxy hasn't had its share of problems—of course it has. But when it comes to this specific issue of authority, the whole "Tradition vs. the Bible" problem never has come up.

This history lesson should help us understand what the role of Church Tradition should be throughout Christianity as a whole. As we've said before, the reason why Church Tradition is considered so important in the Orthodox Church is because it is committed to preserving the teachings of Christ and the Tradition he handed down to the apostles.

CHURCH TRADITION, PAUL, AND JESUS

The word "tradition," though, has become somewhat of a boogeyman in Evangelical circles, particularly in the YEC camp. Ken Ham and his followers routinely accuse any Christian who doesn't agree with YEC of both rejecting the authority of the Bible and putting the "traditions of men" in a place of authority over the Bible. By doing this, Ham subtlety equates *his interpretation* of Genesis 1–11 with *biblical authority,* and therefore paints all other interpretations of Genesis 1–11 as being "traditions of men" that subvert biblical authority. This tactic is simply deceptive.

The Church is meant to bear witness to Christ, preserve Christ's teachings, and pass down to future generations the tradition that Christ himself handed down to his apostles. Paul himself talks about this very thing in II Thessalonians 3:6: *"Now we command you, beloved, in the name of our Lord Jesus Christ, to keep away from believers who are living in idleness and not according to the tradition that they received from us"* (NRSV). He also speaks of it in I Corinthians 11:2: *"I commend you because you remember me in everything and maintain the traditions just as I handed them on to you"* (NRSV).

What we see within the very pages of Scripture itself is testimony that Paul and the apostles were dedicated to handing down the Tradition that Christ passed down to them. We must remember that even after Jesus' death and resurrection, the disciples still didn't "get it." They had come face to face with the resurrected Christ and still did not understand what really had happened and what the implications of Jesus' resurrection really were. It was only after the resurrected Jesus opened the Scriptures to them and taught them that they came to understand (Luke 24:13–35).

By doing this, Jesus handed down to the apostles the "Capital-T" Tradition: the teaching and practices of the Church. Whenever the apostles would travel to a place and start a church, they would pass on the very teaching that Christ had handed down to them. They would train leaders so they could continue that teaching once the apostles left.

That Tradition is the original Tradition the resurrected Jesus taught the disciples, and the Tradition has been preserved in the life of the Orthodox Church. That Tradition is what led to the formation of the New Testament canon and what still serves as a guide as to how the Bible should be understood. That Tradition has articulated the creedal fundamentals of the Christian faith for the past 2,000 years and the core beliefs that all Christian branches and denominations have in common, whether or not they know exactly where the teachings really came from

Let's state the obvious: the Bible did not drop out of heaven. It was written and preserved under the inspiration of the Holy Spirit by the Church, and it has been taught by the Church and has guided Christians for 2,000 years. Paul himself commands Timothy that part of his calling as a Church leader is to "rightly explain the word of truth" (2 Timothy 2:15). That means even though the Bible is divinely inspired, it needs to be read, understood, and explained correctly—and it is the calling of the Church (particularly Church leaders) to make sure that it is being taught correctly, and that the teaching stays faithful to the original teaching that Christ gave to the apostles. That is what is meant by Tradition.

With all that in mind, we must clearly state that at no point in Church history have the claims of YEC ever been considered part of that living Church Tradition. The early Church Fathers, as well as Christian thinkers and theologians throughout Church history, interpreted Genesis 1-11 in many ways—and that was acceptable and good, because that issue was never seen as a vital, primary issue within the living Tradition of the Church. That is why, when seen against this backdrop of Church history, we can see that Ken Ham's dismissal of the early Church Fathers' treatment of Genesis 1–11 as the "traditions of men" is utterly deceptive.

CHURCH TRADITION, THE BIBLE, AND AUTHORITY

Having said that, it is important to clarify just what the relationship between the Church, the Bible, and the concept of authority actually is. As I said earlier, the Orthodox Church sees the Bible as part of Church Tradition. Obviously, it is the most important part, in that it is the collection of the earliest documents of the early Church, but it cannot be divorced from the Church Tradition and elevated on some pedestal. Since the Bible is a part of the larger life of the Church, the only way to truly understand the Bible is to read it in the larger context of the living Tradition of the Church.

Now, it's not like Church Tradition is some sort of authoritarian "believe this or else" dictator. It simply sets the boundaries as to what is and what is not the core, fundamental theology of historical Christianity. Simply put, it preserves biblical Christianity; it does not make up what Christianity is. For example, if someone reads John 20:17, when Jesus says to Mary, "I am ascending to my Father and your Father, to my God and your God," and starts preaching that Jesus wasn't divine, Church Tradition can step in and show that from the very beginning of the Church, Jesus' humanity *and* divinity have always been a core tenant of the Christian, and it will be able to show just what the early Church Fathers taught concerning that verse.

By the same token, if Christians start to disagree with each other over whether or not the story of the Rich Man and Lazarus in Luke 16:19–31 is a parable or an actual historical occurrence, Church Tradition can step in and show that the issue of whether or not Luke 16:19–31 is a parable or not was never considered to be a vital, core tenant of Christianity. The point of the story is that Jesus is condemning the rich hypocritical religious leaders of his day for ignoring the poor and for refusing to acknowledge him, even after he rises from the dead. As far as whether or not it is a parable, there is room with the Church to discuss and debate that issue, and even disagree on that issue. It is not a core tenant of the Christian faith.

When understood in this way, Church Tradition helps us keep a clear eye on what is vital in the Christian faith, and what is secondary and therefore open for discussion and even disagreement. This is actually very comforting, for Church Tradition itself shows us that Bible-believing Christians will interpret things differently and have different insights into particular passages, and that's okay, just so long as those things that are being interpreted differently are not the core theological truths that the Church has always held. Open and honest discussion about a host of things within the Christian faith is a good thing. It is the way in which the Church continues to learn and grow. As Christians read the Bible on their own, and as they talk about and discuss what they believe and understand with other Christians, within the community of the Church as a whole, that is the way that the Holy Spirit guides us in all truth (John 16:13).

When Christians take no account of Church Tradition, it is a recipe for disaster. Early Protestants killed each other over whether or not you should sprinkle or immerse in baptism. If they knew their Church tradition, they would have known that in *The Didache*, an early second century document, it discusses baptism and basically says, "If you can baptize in a river, do it; but if you can't, then a pool of some sort is fine; but if you can't do that, then sprinkling is fine as well." Case closed—it is clear, the way in which baptism was done wasn't a big deal. But after the Reformation, it became a big deal for some because people were ignorant of the traditional understanding of baptism the Church had always held. Because they didn't even consider Church Tradition regarding baptism, people ended up literally killing each other over this issue.

A proper understanding of Church Tradition helps Christians in three ways: (1) it guards against heretical teachings, (2) it tells us what the core theological issues are, and (3) it reassures us there is room for discussion and differing views on a variety of topics that are not core theological issues. Without being mindful of Church Tradition, you lay yourself open to (1) being led astray by heretical teachings, (2) forgetting what the core Christian beliefs are, and (3) mistaking secondary issues as primary issues of the faith. You simply cannot make things up on your own or be dogmatic about things the Church has never been dogmatic about. Unfortunately, this is precisely what Ken Ham does on a regular basis.

LET'S SUM UP

The Bible cannot be set up like an idol on a pedestal to impose its authority on the Church. The Bible is *a part* of the greater life of the Church, and it is *the Church* that has been given "all authority" by Jesus Christ, to go out and make disciples of all nations (Matthew 28:18–19). The Bible, as Paul says, is "inspired by God, and is useful for teaching, reproof, correction, and training in righteousness" (I Timothy 3:16). He does not say the Bible is an autocratic dictator that doles out commands to be blindly obeyed. He says the Bible is inspired and useful in making disciples and training in righteousness. The challenge, therefore, is to make sure one is using the inspired Scriptures correctly so that the Church can get on in the business of making disciples. So how does one make sure one is interpreting the Scriptures correctly? A good place to start is by focusing on the following two points:

1. Do your best to understand the historical and literary context of Scripture. Try to read Scripture through the eyes of the original audience, for God's inspired message was originally directed *to them*, therefore the inspired message had to make sense *to them*.
2. Do you best to be aware of how any biblical text has been interpreted throughout Church history. Such awareness will serve as a guardrail to prevent you from misinterpreting the Bible and falling into heresy when it comes to the fundamental teachings of Christianity.

In other words, interpret the Bible within the community of the historical Church. Consider what Jesus tells his disciples in John 16:13: "When the Spirit of truth comes, he will guide you into all the truth; for he will not speak on his own, but will speak whatever he hears, and he will declare to you the things that are to come." You should realize that in this verse, the "you" is plural, not singular. So, who is the "you" that Jesus is saying the Holy Spirit will guide in all truth? The Church—and that means the living Tradition of the Church.

So yes, as you strive to understand the Bible yourself, do your reading, think about what is being said, and pray about it. But then also go and consult others in the Church—from friends, to pastors, to great writers and theologians of the past—to make sure your particular interpretation does not fly in the face of the historical witness of the Church. Read and study the Bible within the context of Church Tradition—that is how the Holy Spirit guides you.

Unfortunately, this is precisely where Ken Ham and biblical literalists have gone wrong. Even though they claim they are just proclaiming the clear meaning of the Genesis 1–11, in reality they have rejected the "Capital-T" Tradition of the historic Christian faith that makes it clear that the YEC interpretation of Genesis 1–11 has never been universally held by the Church and has never been seen as a creedal fundamental of the Christian faith. Therefore, Ken Ham has absolutely no authority whatsoever to unilaterally declare that his YEC interpretation of Genesis 1–11 is a foundational issue for the Christian faith. No one has ever made this claim in the history of the Church up until the 20th Century.

This is, by definition, what heresy is: elevating a personal interpretation of Scripture above what the Church has always taught.

4

Genesis 1-11: From the Early Church to Today

"Who is so foolish as to think that God, just like a farmer, literally planted a paradise in Eden, somewhere in the east?"

—Origen of Alexandria

So, what does Ken Ham say about Genesis 1–11? As we will see in more detail later on, Ken Ham claims Christians have always interpreted Genesis 1–11 as being historically and scientifically accurate, have always believed that the universe was only 6,000 years old, and that it was only after Charles Darwin came up with his theory of evolution that Christians, particularly Church leaders, started to reinterpret Genesis 1–11 to fit in with science and "millions of years." Thus, in Ken Ham's eyes, they compromised the authority of the Word of God and submitted to man's fallible interpretation. That is Ken Ham's take on history. That take is historically wrong.

It is a simple fact that scores of early Church Fathers did not read Genesis 1–11 as historical. These were the same Church Fathers who were at the Church councils that helped put together the New Testament, who defined the doctrine of the Trinity, and who combated heresy in the early Church. Their writings on Genesis show that from the earliest days of the Church there were countless Christians who read and interpreted the early chapters of Genesis in a way that was not literal, young earth creationism.

For that matter, they couldn't have been young earth creationists, any more than they could have been Socialists, Capitalists, Democrats or Republicans. For YEC is a thoroughly modern movement that has come about as a reaction to the modern theory of evolution. In its attempt to "defend" the Bible, YEC actually imposes modern scientific concepts back onto the biblical texts. The problem is that our modern scientific questions were not being asked back in the time of the Bible and the early Church. The early Christians had an entirely different interpretive paradigm than our modern scientific one. Simply put, YEC's reading of Genesis 1–11 is the new interpretation in the history of the Church, not the other way around.

From the very beginning of the Church, Christians have interpreted Genesis 1–11 in many ways, even though they all agreed on the basic theological message of those chapters. An extremely good book on this very subject is titled, *Beginnings: Ancient Christian Readings of the Biblical Creation Narrative*, by Peter C. Bouteneff. In it, he discusses how many early Church Fathers in the first four centuries of Church history read, interpreted, and taught Genesis 1—3. It would be worthwhile to state upfront Bouteneff's conclusion regarding this very issue:

> "None of the fathers' strictly theological or moral conclusions—about creation, or about humanity and its redemption, and the coherence of everything in Christ—has anything to do with the datable chronology of the creation of the universe or with the physical existence of Adam and Eve. They read the creation narratives as Holy Scripture, and therefore as 'true.' But they did not see them as lessons in history, or science as such, even as they reveled in the overlaps they observed between the scriptural narrative and the observable world. Generally speaking, the fathers were free from a slavish deference to science."[1]

Bouteneff's conclusion directly contradicts Ken Ham's claims about Church history. Bouteneff takes the reader through what many early Church Fathers actually wrote about Genesis 1—3, it is absolutely clear they did not emphasize a straightforward historical reading of those chapters. Even if some presumed those chapters to be historical, Bouteneff notes that they considered it to be "scarcely consequential."[2]

---

1. Bouteneff, *Beginnings*, 183.
2. Bouteneff, *Beginnings*, 84.

Remember, the early Church was so intent on combating heresy that they convened seven councils to address specific heretical teachings and to articulate what the Church had always taught on those issues. The fact that the early Church never addressed the issue of whether or not Genesis 1–11 was literal or figurative should tell us that from the very beginning, the Church never viewed this issue as a core, fundamental issue of the Christian faith. No one was ever accused of subverting or questioning the authority of the Bible based on their interpretation of the first few chapters of Genesis.

READING OF GENESIS 1–11: FROM THE EARLY CHURCH TO THE REFORMATION

The problems with reading Genesis 1–11 as "God's historical science textbook," as Ken Ham likes to call it, are obvious as soon as you start reading Genesis 1–11: the history and chronology doesn't make sense. Let's just bring up two examples within the first two chapters. In Genesis 1, on the third day, we are told of the creation of vegetation and plants. Then, on the sixth day, we are told of the creation of man—both male and female. Yet then in Genesis 2:4–5 we are told two odd things.

First, we are told, "*on the day* God created the heavens and the earth…." In Genesis 1, though, we have just been told that it took *six days* for God to create the heavens and the earth, with 2:1 acting as a summary statement of the chapter 1. So, did God create the heavens and the earth in six days or on one day? Second, we are also told explicitly that God created man *before* any vegetation has sprouted from the ground—yet in Genesis 1 we have vegetation on day 3, and man created on day 6. In both instances, if you hold to a literal, chronological understanding of Genesis 1—2, you have two clear contradictions. You can't get around it. Of course, it wasn't like the ancient Jews and early Church Fathers didn't notice this. They were extremely well-educated men who were completely aware of these things.

Philo of Alexandria (25 BC–AD 50)

The first person to consider is the first century Jewish philosopher Philo of Alexandria. Since he didn't believe Genesis 1—2 was to be read 'literally' in the first place, he wasn't bothered about these apparent contradictions.

He argued they weren't contradictions at all, but rather were intentionally put in the text to alert the reader to look for a deeper meaning in the text. He argued that Genesis 1—2 wasn't a chronological account, but rather two different stories. Genesis 1 focused on the grandeur and orderliness of creation, whereas Genesis 2—3 focused on the nature and frailty of humanity. The "contradictions" were thus the author's way of alerting the reader, "Don't read these things literally! It's not about chronology! It's about deeper truths regarding nature and [hu]mankind!"

Origen of Alexandria (AD 185–255)

Origen of Alexandria, one of the most influential Christian theologians in Church history was one of the most important philosophers of his day. He was also probably the first Christian in history to do what is known today as "textual criticism." In order to discern the original text and meaning of any given book in the Old Testament, Origen did something amazing: he wrote the famous *Hexapla*. It was a hand-written copy of the Old Testament in six different versions, including the original Hebrew and various other Greek translations. It is impossible to underestimate the importance of Origen's work and the impact he had on the history of biblical translation and interpretation. Needless to say, when it comes to getting to the original meaning of biblical texts, Origen was the master. When it came to the creation account in Genesis 1—3, Origen wrote:

> "Who with any understanding would suppose that the first, second, and third day, along with the evening and the morning, existed without a sun, and moon, and stars, or that the first day was, as it were, also without a sky? And who is so foolish as to think that God, just like a farmer, literally planted a paradise in Eden, somewhere in the east, and placed a tree of life in it that was both visible and tangible, and that if one actually sank their teeth in and ate its fruit, that they would obtain life?"

> "Again, who would think that one was a partaker of good and evil by munching on what was taken from the other tree? And as far as God walking in the paradise in the evening, and Adam hiding himself under a tree, I do not think that anyone doubts that these things are to be taken figuratively, and that they indicate certain mysteries, the history having taken place in appearance, and not literally."[3]

3. Origen, *De Principiis*, 4, 16.

Origen, the first systematic theologian and textual critic in Church history, opposed a literal reading of Genesis 1–11, making it abundantly clear that to do so is utterly ridiculous, and calling anyone who does so "foolish." It was clear to him that the early chapters of Genesis were not to be read as literal history. Christians back then, just like today, were faced with the challenge of reconciling what they read in the early chapters of Genesis with the science of their day. As Bouteneff tells us:

> "Already by Origen's day, Christians versed in cosmology were faced with a choice: either suspend their belief in nature as they observed it, or suspend their insistence on the literal or scientific interpretation of Genesis 1—3. Origen seemed to opt for the latter, yet his understanding of Scripture had never been wedded to a scientific interpretation in the first place, so he never felt forced to suspend anything."[4]

Origen was not alone in his view. It was obvious to him and many other early Church Fathers that Genesis 1—3 wasn't concerned with science and wasn't primarily concerned with history.

Saint Augustine (AD 354–430)

Saint Augustine was another early Church Father who argued that an allegorical interpretation of these texts was to be preferred. He stated that Genesis 1—2 was written to address the concerns of the people at that time, and that when it comes to the world itself, God created it with the capacity to develop and change. When it comes to certain "hard to understand" passages, Augustine wrote:

> "In matters that are so obscure and far beyond our vision, we find passages in Holy Scripture that can be interpreted in very different ways without prejudice to the faith we have received. In such cases, we should not rush in headlong and so firmly take our stand on one side that, if further progress in the search of truth justly undermines this position, we too fall with it. That would be to battle not for the teaching of Holy Scripture but for our own, wishing its teaching to conform to ours, whereas we ought to wish ours to conform to that of Sacred Scripture."[5]

---

4. Bouteneff, *Beginnings*, 118.
5. Augustine, *The Literal Meaning of Genesis*, 41.

Basically, Augustine is saying that when it comes to certain passages in the Bible that are dealing with things ultimately beyond our understanding, it is best not to take any dogmatic, rigid view. It is best to say something like, "Well, I *think* it should be interpreted this way, but there's a lot we don't know yet, so I'm not going to set my limited opinion in stone." Augustine also said in the same work in regard to Genesis 1:

> "Some works belonged to the invisible days in which he created all things simultaneously, and others belong to the days in which he daily fashions whatever evolves in the course of time from what I call the primordial wrappers."[6]

Read that again. Yes, Augustine speculated that things in nature could evolve. No, Augustine didn't discover evolution 1500 years before Darwin. He was not talking about what we would today call the modern theory of evolution, but his comments reveal the way in which the early Church understood the early chapters of Genesis had very little to do with insisting they were "God's eyewitness historical account," as Ken Ham likes to say.

But Augustine didn't stop there. He went out of his way to warn against those who insisted on a literal reading of certain passages like Genesis 1-11, when it flew in the face of reason. He wrote:

> "In regard to things about the earth, the sky, other elements of this world, the motion and rotation or even the magnitude and distances of the stars, the definite eclipses of the sun and moon, the passage of years and seasons, the nature of animals, of fruits, of stones, and of other such things, it should not be surprising that such things can be known with the greatest certainty by reasoning or by experience, even by one who is not a Christian. Therefore, it is an utterly disgraceful and ruinous thing—and something that should be greatly avoided—if [a non-Christian] hears a Christian speaking like an idiot on these matters and trying to make them accord with Christian writings. When that happens, [the non-Christian] will say that he can't keep from laughing when he sees how totally in error they are. In view of this and in keeping it in mind constantly while dealing with the book of Genesis, I have, insofar as I was able, explained in detail and set forth for consideration the meanings of obscure

---

6. Augustine, *The Literal Meaning of Genesis*, 41.

passages, taking care not to affirm rashly some singular meaning to the prejudice of another and perhaps better explanation."[7]

Augustine warned Christians not to try to make the early chapters of Genesis out to be some sort of scientific textbook about the natural world. Such claims were *disgraceful, ruinous,* and *idiotic.* Augustine saw that such ignorant and foolish talk makes Christianity look stupid to non-Christians. Even when putting forth his take on "obscure passages," Augustine had the sense not to hold too dogmatically to his view, because a better explanation might come up later on. When discussing the relationship of Scripture to the physical realities of the natural world, Augustine also wrote:

> "With the scriptures it is a matter of treating about the faith. For that reason…if anyone, not understanding the mode of divine eloquence, should find something about these matters [the physical universe] in our books, or hear of the same from those books, of such a kind that it seems to be at variance with the perceptions of his own rational faculties, let him believe that these other things are in no way necessary to the admonitions or accounts or predictions of the scriptures. In short, it must be said that our authors knew the truth about the nature of the skies, but it was not the intention of the Spirit of God, who spoke through them, to teach men anything that would not be of use to them for their salvation."[8]

Augustine was saying that God's intention concerning the early chapters of Genesis *was not to give biological or historical facts about the world,* for such facts were simply irrelevant to what God was trying to convey. God wasn't intending to talk about biology; he was intending to explain the need for salvation. How ironic that 1700 years later, not only is Ken Ham insisting that the early chapters of Genesis are about biology, astronomy, and geology, but he is claiming that the very truthfulness and authority of the Bible is dependent on it. It's fair to say that Origen and Augustine would consider such a claim foolish, to say the least.

---

7. Augustine, *The Literal Meaning of Genesis,* 41.
8. Augustine, *The Literal Meaning of Genesis,* 41.

The Cappadocian Fathers: Gregory of Nyssa (AD 335-394), Gregory of Nazianzus (AD 329-390), and Basil of Caesarea (AD 330-379)

The Cappadocian Fathers were three highly influential early Church leaders in the fourth century who were at the forefront of developing vital Christian doctrines like the Trinity. Ironically, Basil of Caesarea and Gregory of Nazianzus went to school in Athens along with the man who would one day become the emperor, Julian the Apostate. While Julian decided to ultimately reject Christianity and embrace paganism, these Cappadocian Fathers devoted their lives to further building the Church and clarifying Christian doctrine. It just so happens that all three men had some very illuminating views regarding the early chapters of Genesis, including a concept of creation generally referred to as "the universal seed." This concept basically said that God created the natural world with the capacity to develop, grow, and adapt over time into the variety of species that we know today. For example, Gregory of Nyssa wrote:

> "What is the nature of things? The Creator of the elements did not endow them with constancy or permanence. That is, all things are subject to change. This change is unceasing among the elements and by necessity they pass into other things, undergo alteration, and change again."[9]

Gregory of Nyssa even wrote about people's relationship and connection with the natural world itself. Describing nature as "a sort of graduated and ordered advance to the creation of man," he wrote:

> "The creation of man is related as coming last, as of one who took up into himself every single form of life, both that of plants and that which is seen in brutes. His nourishment and growth he derives from vegetable life; for even in vegetables such processes are to be seen when aliment is being drawn in by their roots and given off in fruit and leaves. His sentient organization he derives from the brute creation. But his faculty of thought and reason is incommunicable, and a peculiar gift in our nature."[10]

Now, as with Origen and Augustine, Gregory of Nyssa was not speaking of the modern theory of evolution, but he certainly saw that not only did God create things with the ability to adapt and evolve to some

---

9. Bouteneff, *Beginnings*, 157.
10. Gregory of Nyssa, *On the Soul and Resurrection*, 5:441-442.

extent, but that there was an intimate connection at the natural level between mankind and the nature world around them. All three men show that they understood nature in a similar way: things in nature adapt, change, and evolve because that's how God set up nature to act.

What's more, when it came to Eden and the figure of Adam in Genesis 2-3, it is quite clear that Gregory of Nyssa didn't see things the way Ken Ham does. As Bouteneff maintains, "Gregory does not envisage a historic pre-fallen immortal state; although he posits Adam as the beginning of human genealogy...he alludes twice in *Catechetical Oration* to the fact that Moses is speaking through a story, or an allegory."[11]

What is also clear from the writings of Gregory of Nazianzus is that whenever he discussed Genesis 2—3, he focused on showing how the story of Adam is the story of us. He saw the paradise and Adam stories as fundamentally about our own sin. As Bouteneff points out, "He brings his ideas on Adam's significance together in *Orations* 33.9, enumerating what human beings share: 'We all have this in common: reason, the Law, the Prophets, [and] the very sufferings of Christ by which we were re-created. For all partake of the same Adam and were led astray by the serpent and slain by sin and are saved by the heavenly Adam and brought back by the tree of shame to the tree of life whence we had fallen.'"[12]

Then there is Basil of Caesarea. In his *Homilies on the Hexaemeron* 1.11, when Basil discussed Genesis 1, he made it abundantly clear that the six days were not telling us about science but rather about God:

> "'If we undertake now to talk about [the theories of scientists], we shall fall into the same idle chatter as they. Let us rather allow them to refute each other. Let us stop talking about the substance, since we have been persuaded by Moses that 'God created the heavens and the earth.' Let us glorify the Master, and from the beauty of visible things let us form an idea of Him who is more than beautiful.'"[13]

A brief look at these early Church Fathers leaves no doubt. Not only did they not read the early chapters of Genesis as scientific accounts, they made it a point to emphasize that they were not scientific accounts. It is also clear that even if they presumed the historicity of Adam and Eve, they

---

11. Bouteneff, *Beginnings*, 164.
12. Bouteneff, *Beginnings*, 144.
13. Bouteneff, *Beginnings*, 171.

did not see that even as that important. They were far more concerned with showing how the story of Adam and Eve is the story of humanity.

Thomas Aquinas (AD 1225–1274)

During the Middle Ages, the Catholic theologian Thomas Aquinas shared his thoughts on the creation of the natural world. He believed that God didn't create everything all at once, but rather He created nature with the potential to develop over time. He wrote: "All things were not distinguished and adorned together, not from a want of power on God's part, as requiring time in which to work, but that due order might be observed in the instituting of the world."[14]

Given the comments of these men, it is not much of a stretch to say that if they were told about the modern theory of evolution, none of them would be frightened by it. In fact, they'd probably start teaching how the theory actually further proves God's providence in the world. As should be obvious by now, reading Genesis 1–11 as a straightforward, literal, historical and scientific account was *never* the dominant view or teaching of the Church. Sure, there were some theologians who read Genesis 1–11 as actual history, and some who clearly said Adam and Eve were historical people. But even in those cases, no early Church Father ever came close to making the sort of claims modern YEC does.

The History of Reading of Genesis 1–11: From the Reformation to Today

The major paradigm shift in how people viewed the world happened with the coming of the Reformation, the Scientific Revolution, and the Enlightenment:

1. Since the early Reformers rejected the entirety of Church Tradition, this eventually led to later Reformers becoming ignorant of the way the Church had always read and understood the Bible in general, and Genesis 1–11 in particular.

2. The scientific discoveries regarding the natural world opened up a whole new field of inquiry, and the scientific method became the working paradigm to find out how the natural world worked.

14. Aquinas, *Summa Theologica,*: Volume 1, 357.

3. Even though the rise of modern science happened precisely because of the work of Christians like Copernicus, Kepler, and Galileo, later Enlightenment philosophers convinced the Western world that "religion" and "faith" were the enemies of science, and that the scientific method was the *only way* to discover truth.

With those three radical shifts in thinking, it wasn't long until people assumed that in order for anything to be "true," it had to be "scientific." Extend that thinking to the Bible, and what you have is people assuming that everything in the Bible, particularly Genesis 1–11, has to be scientifically and historically accurate in order to be true. Ever since that shift in worldview, people in the West, even Christians, have attempted to read Genesis 1–11 with Enlightenment assumptions. Thus, ignorance of historical Church's teaching on Genesis 1–11 has led to modern Christians assuming Genesis 1–11 was a modern scientific and historical account of material origins.

Perhaps an analogy will help. Imagine what would happen if Americans completely threw away and forgot most of the rules of football, but then found themselves left with helmets, pads, and footballs. What do you do with these things? Well, let's say someone said, "I know! These are obviously to be used in sports! Tennis is a great sport! These must be used in some form of *team tennis*!" And so, people started to suit up in football gear, and set eleven men on each side of the tennis court with tennis rackets, and try to serve and volley the football. They would think that they were honoring the game of George Halas, Vince Lombardi, and Jim Brown, but they would be doing no such thing. They might have the right equipment, but they would not be playing the right game.

This is the sort of thing that happened regarding the interpretation of Genesis 1–11 within the Protestant world during the time of the rise of modern science, and specifically ever since the time Charles Darwin proposed his theory of evolution. And just as it would seem odd to try to hit a football over a net with a tennis racket, a basic reading of Genesis 1–11 immediately reveals a number of odd things if one tries reading Genesis 1–11 as a modern scientific and historical account.

Martin Luther and John Calvin

This shift in thinking didn't happen all at once. A look at Martin Luther and John Calvin shows that although they thought Genesis 1–11 was a description of what historically happened, their views were still very different than that of the young earth creationism of today. In his commentary on Genesis 1–11, Luther stated he did not agree with Augustine's notion that God had created all at once, and not over a span of six days. He wrote: "With respect therefore to the opinion of Augustine, we conclude that Moses spoke literally and plainly and neither allegorically nor figuratively."[15] He believed that mankind was originally created perfect by God, and that when Adam and Eve sinned, they fell from that state of perfection.

Luther also believed the world to be no more than 6,000 years old. Of course, the focus of his argument when making this claim was not in opposition to modern scientific claims. It was to challenge philosophical assertions by the ancient Greeks that the universe was eternal. He wrote:

> "From Moses…we know that 6,000 years ago the world did not exist. But of this no philosopher can be persuaded; because, according to Aristotle, the first and last man cannot…be determined, although however Aristotle leaves the problem in doubt whether or not the world is eternal, yet he is inclined of the opinion that it is eternal."[16]

John Calvin, while sharing Luther's view of the historicity of Genesis 1–11, nevertheless did not insist that what we read in Genesis 1–11 was an exact description regarding the specifics of how God created the universe. When discussing the creation of the sun and moon in Genesis 1:16, Calvin acknowledged that what astronomers had discovered didn't line up perfectly with what Moses was saying in Genesis 1:14–16. He did not see this as a problem because Moses wasn't writing as a scientist attempting to give a scientific description of the cosmos. Calvin wrote:

> "Moses wrote in a popular style things which without instruction, all ordinary persons, endued with common sense, are able to understand; but astronomers investigate with great labor whatever the sagacity of the human mind can comprehend. Nevertheless, this study is not to be reprobated, nor this science to be condemned, because some frantic persons are wont boldly to reject whatever is unknown to them. For astronomy is not only pleasant, but also very useful to be known: it cannot be denied that this art unfolds the admirable wisdom of God.

---

15. Luther, *Luther on the Creation*, 41.
16. Luther, *Luther on the Creation*, 40.

> Nor did Moses wish to withdraw us from this pursuit in omitting such things as are peculiar to the art; but because he was ordained a teacher as well of the unlearned and rude as of the learned, he could not otherwise fulfill his office than by descending to this grosser method of instruction. Had he spoken of things generally unknown, the uneducated might have pleaded in excuse that such subjects were beyond their capacity."[17]

Calvin's point was simple: Moses wasn't doing science. If God had inspired Moses to do so, his original audience wouldn't have understood what he was talking about. Therefore, Moses spoke in a way that was based on what they saw when they looked up in the sky. Astronomy was a tremendous science and should not be rejected because it has discovered something that seemingly "contradicted" what the Bible said.

Luther and Calvin were brilliant men, but both were children of their time. When Copernicus put forth the idea that the earth went around the sun, Luther considered him to be a heretic, because Joshua 10:12 clearly implied the sun went around the earth.[18] Calvin, though not specifically mentioning Copernicus, considered any who suggested that the earth went around the sun to be "stark raving mad" and possessed by the devil.[19]

Like everyone, they struggled to understand the Bible in light of new scientific discoveries, because they were working from certain assumptions, namely that the Bible had to be scientifically accurate in order to be true. But then again, as seen in the above quote by Calvin, they didn't always think that. They were simply human beings trying to come to a better understanding about both the Bible and the natural world.

James Ussher and John Wesley

Even though some Christians in Church history had totaled up the genealogies in Genesis, it wasn't until after the Reformation and the rise of modern science that anyone claimed the earth *must* be only a few thousand years old, and if one didn't believe that then that would be the equivalent of saying that the Bible wasn't true. The man who popularized this notion was James Ussher in the sixteenth century. He calculated

---

17. Calvin, *Commentaries on Genesis*, 1:85.
18. Luther, *Luther's Works. Vol 54. Table Talk*, 358–59.
19. Young, *John Calvin and the Natural World*, 47.

that God had made the earth on October 22, 4004 BC. His view would have been seen as an odd anomaly, except that it made its way into the marginal notes of the King James Bible (KJV). Later on, modern day ultra-Fundamentalists who swore by the KJV went back, found these calculations and built their YEC theology off of it.

Although some Protestants argued Genesis 1–11 was a historical and scientific account, that wasn't true for everyone. John Wesley didn't read the opening chapters of Genesis literally. He said, "The inspired penman in this history... [wrote] for the Jews first and, calculating his narratives for the infant state of the church, describes things by their outward ... appearances, and leaves us, by further discoveries of the divine light, to be led into the understanding of the mysteries couched under them."[20]

The Nineteenth Century: Darwinism and Dinosaurs

This brings us to the big issue often attached to Genesis 1–11: Darwinian evolution. As mentioned before, Ken Ham would have you believe that up until Charles Darwin published *Origin of Species* in 1859, that all Christians for all time read Genesis 1–11 as literal history, and thought the earth was relatively young. We've already seen that Christians throughout history, in fact, did not read Genesis 1–11 as literal history. It is also a matter of historical fact that before Darwin, Christians were already concluding that the earth was a lot older than a few thousand years.

The reason why is that in the nineteenth century dinosaur fossils were discovered. As Victorian Era geologists calculated the age of these fossils, they realized that these dinosaurs (and subsequently the earth as well) were millions of years old. This may have contradicted Ussher's claims of a young earth, but it didn't contradict the Bible. It also must be noted that the geologists making these claims were not atheists. Quite the contrary, they were Anglican clergymen—they were, in fact, Christians ... just simply not disciples of James Ussher.

By the time Darwin wrote *Origin of the Species* in 1859, most geologists believed the earth was much older than 6,000 years, and no one saw that as a threat to Christianity or the Bible. Take for example Alfred Edersheim, the Christian biblical scholar of Jewish descent, who wrote extensively on biblical history and culture. In his book titled *Bible History*, he had this to say about the Genesis 1—2:

20. Wesley, *Wesley's Notes on the Bible*, 22.

> "...we must expect to find in the first chapter of Genesis simply the grand outlines of what took place, and not any details connected with creation. On these points there is ample room for such information as science may be able to supply, when once it shall have carefully selected and sifted all that can be learned from the study of earth and of nature. ...we ought, therefore, to be on guard against the rash and unwarranted statements which have sometimes been brought forward on these subjects."[21]

Edersheim wrote this in 1876, seventeen years after the publication of *The Origin of Species*. Other prominent Christians, like Catholic Cardinal John Henry Newman, said in 1868: "Mr. Darwin's theory *need* not then to be atheistical, be it true or not; it may simply be suggesting a larger idea of Divine Prescience and Skill. ...I do not [see] that 'the accidental evolution of organic beings' is inconsistent with divine design. It is accidental to *us*, not to *God*."[22]

Charles Kingsley, an Anglican priest, university professor, and friend of Charles Darwin, also stated evolution showed a noble concept of God.[23] Even B. B. Warfield, the nineteenth century conservative Calvinist, the man who came up with the modern concept of biblical inerrancy, not only *didn't* believe Genesis 1–11 taught a young earth, but he even believed that evolution gave the proper scientific account of human origins. He did not believe that Scripture and science were at odds at all. In fact, he said, "I do not think that there is any general statement in the Bible or any part of the account of creation...that need be opposed to evolution."[24]

Far from being frightened by Darwin's theory, many nineteenth century Christians actually came away with even more wonderment and praise for a God who was even more creative than they had thought.

William Paley and "Intelligent Design"

A group of nineteenth century Christians who *did* have a problem with Darwin's theory were followers of William Paley. His view of creation coming from the mechanization of the Industrial Revolution, described

---

21. Edersheim, *Bible History: Old Testament*, 11.
22. Newman, *Interdisciplinary Encyclopedia of Religion and Science*.
23. Darwin, *On the Origin of Species*, 481.
24. Coffman, "What is Darwinism?" 31.

God as the *Ultimate Designer*, and argued life was so complex that every creature had to be individually designed, and "hand-crafted" if you will.

One can almost see Paley as the godfather of the present-day Intelligent Design movement. Needless to say, Darwin's theory *was* a threat to Paley's description of God and his understanding as to how nature worked. But Paley's description of creation as a "giant watch" that God had put together had more in common with the Deistic notion of God and the mechanical worldview of the Industrial Revolution, than it had with the traditional understanding and teaching of the historical Church.

And Charles Darwin Himself?

Regarding Darwin himself, he was not even an atheist. He was actually born into a Christian home and was a Christian for much of his early life. Contrary to popular opinion, it wasn't his development of the theory of evolution that caused him to lose his faith. It was something much more personal: it was the death of his ten-year-old daughter. When she died of tuberculosis, Darwin simply could not reconcile a belief in a good God with the reality of suffering and injustice in the world.

Darwin didn't rebel against God. He was heartbroken. And he wasn't an atheist; he was an agnostic who believed there must be an intelligent mind behind everything. That's right: the man who developed the theory of evolution by natural selection said it was impossible for this universe to be conceived by blind chance. He wrote in a letter to John Fordyce, on May 7, 1879, "It seems to me absurd that a man cannot be an ardent theist and an evolutionist.... In my most extreme fluctuations, I have never been an atheist in the sense of denying the existence of a God."[25]

So what we see is that by the end of the nineteenth century, not only was it Anglican geologists who began to put forth the idea that the earth was older than what James Ussher claimed in the King James Bible, and not only did many of the leading Christian theologians and thinkers of the day not view Darwin's theory as a threat to the Christian faith, but Charles Darwin himself declared that he didn't see evolutionary theory as atheistic at all. Properly speaking, we could say that Darwin was a theistic evolutionist, though certainly not a Christian.

---

25. Darwin, *Interdisciplinary Encyclopedia of Religion and Science*.

The Seventh Day Adventists, and the Scopes Monkey Trial, 1925

It wasn't until the twentieth century that the modern "creation/evolution war" broke out. It erupted in the 1920s when two things happened. In 1923, the Seventh Day Adventist George McCready-Price published his book, *The New Geology*. Two years later, in 1925, the Scopes Monkey Trial in Dayton, Tennessee took place. McCready-Price was an amateur geologist who was heavily influenced by the Seventh Day Adventist, self-proclaimed prophetess Ellen G. White. She claimed God had shown her, by revelation, the creation of the world and Noah's Flood. Her visions and prophecies were largely limited to the Seventh Day Adventist community, but Price's book brought her teachings to a wider audience.

The Scopes Monkey Trial, though, was national news from day one. Tennessee had passed a law prohibiting the teaching of evolution, and certain people in Dayton, Tennessee wanted to put the law to the constitutional test. And so, they got John Scopes to claim that he had taught evolution at the local high school, so that they could have a trial. It was, from beginning to end, a show trial ultimately about the issues of politics and morality, and not really about science and religion.

How do we know this? Just look at the prosecutor, William Jennings Bryan, and the defense attorney, Clarence Darrow. Jennings, a devout Christian, was no country-bumpkin. He was a two-term congressman, a three-time Democrat candidate for President, and the Secretary of State under Woodrow Wilson. His point of contention with Darwin's theory of evolution wasn't so much the science itself, but rather how some people were imposing it on society in the form of *Social Darwinism* to justify horrible and inhumane behavior on "the least of these" throughout humanity. Many of the nineteenth century industrialists used Darwin's theory to justify their horrible treatment of the poor: "It's just survival of the fittest," they would say, "if our big companies put the smaller ones out of business and force those poor slouches to the curb!"

Let's face it, "survival of the fittest" leaves no room for Christian charity and mercy. Bryan saw this clearly and found it horrifying. Also, take into consideration other things that were going on in the 1920's: Eugenics, Communism in Russia, and the rise of Nazism in Germany. All of these movements applied Darwin's biological theory to human society to justify horrible, inhumane, and evil actions against humanity. Simply put, Bryan's concern was with *Social Darwinism*, not the biological theory itself. It was pretty clear that Bryan didn't even understand it.

On the opposite side of the court case was Clarence Darrow, an ardent atheist and ACLU lawyer who hated religion and wanted to prevent any kind of religious influence in public education. He *wanted* evolution taught in school because he thought it provided a better basis for morality. In any case, it was clear both Bryan and Darrow assumed evolution and the Bible were incompatible, because they both were working from the Enlightenment paradigm that assumed that Genesis 1–11 was trying to make historical/scientific claims, because after all, the only way for something to be "true" was for it to be historical and scientific!

It was also clear, though, that Bryan thought that the reason why evolution conflicted with the Bible was because it seemed to imply that man was just a primate and was not made in the image of God. Likewise, it was also clear that Darrow's antagonism toward religion sprung from his imbibing of the nineteenth century Enlightenment propaganda that tried to present Christianity as the age-old enemy of science and progress.

There is no need to give a full account of the Scopes trial itself. It should be noted, though, that when Bryan took the stand to be questioned by Darrow about the specifics of Genesis 1–11, it was clear that Bryan did not believe in a literal six-day creation only 6,000 years ago. Bryan was not a young earth creationist. When he was pressed to explain specifics from Genesis 1–11 (i.e. where did Cain's wife come from?), Bryan's answers made it quite clear that he didn't know because the Bible didn't address them. Nevertheless, Bryan felt that those unanswered questions did in no way diminish the truthfulness and authority of the Bible.

At the trial's end, Bryan issued a summation that was passed out in the courtroom but was not read in court. Far from being a wild-eyed YEC fundamentalist, Bryan's statements were poignant and thoughtful:

> "Science is a magnificent force, but it is not a teacher of morals. It can perfect machinery, but it adds no moral restraints to protect society from the misuse of the machine. It can also build gigantic intellectual ships, but it constructs no moral rudders for the control of storm-tossed human vessels. It not only fails to supply the spiritual element needed but some of its unproven hypotheses rob the ship of its compass and thus endanger its cargo.
>
> In war, science has proven itself an evil genius; it has made war more terrible than it ever was before. Man used to be content to slaughter his fellowmen on a single plane, the earth's surface. Science has taught him to go down into the water and shoot

up from below and to go up into the clouds and shoot down from above...making the battlefield three times as bloody as it was before; but science does not teach brotherly love. Science has made war so hellish that civilization was about to commit suicide; and now we are told that newly discovered instruments of destruction will make the cruelties of the late war seem trivial in comparison with the cruelties of wars that may come.... If civilization is to be saved from the wreckage threatened by intelligence not consecrated by love, it must be saved by the moral code of the meek and lowly Nazarene. His teachings, and His teachings alone, can solve the problems that vex the heart and perplex the world."[26]

Bryan's real concern was obvious, and it was an exceedingly important point. His problem was not so much in the actual theory of evolution itself, but rather the very real danger that science, when unchecked by a moral code, could bring great destruction upon human society. Bryan's summation is not only true, but his statement proved to be absolutely prophetic as the twentieth century witnessed the greatest atrocities known to man: it was advances in science, coupled with the tearing away of the Christian moral code that had governed Western society for almost 2,000 years, that made it possible for things like the gulag, Auschwitz, and the atomic bomb.

At the same time, there was a major flaw in Bryan's view that still is repeated to this day. As true as Bryan's summation was, it must also be pointed out that nothing in it really addressed the *scientific claims* of the biological theory of evolution at all. His concern was the effects of *Social Darwinism*, and the dangers of taking the biological theory of evolution and using it as a supposed "scientific justification" for *Social Darwinism*, and the subsequent atrocities that sprang from it.

But it must be clearly stated: *social Darwinism* and the *biological theory of evolution* are not the same thing. The failure to make that distinction has led to the so-called creation/evolution debate that is still going on today. Simply put, the battle that Ken Ham (and ironically Richard Dawkins too) is waging today is one that is based on the failure to make that important distinction.

The other important thing to note about the Scopes Monkey Trial is that at no time did Bryan insist Genesis 1–11 *had to be* a literal, historical account of creation. Bryan was not a young earth creationist. Not too

---

26. Bryan, "Summary Argument in Scopes Trial."

many people at that time were. As of 1925, the only people who were claiming the earth was only 6,000 years old was a small group of Seventh Day Adventists who had read McCready-Price's book, and who believed Ellen G. White had been given a firsthand look at the creation and Noah's Flood.

Henry Morris' The Genesis Flood, and the Emergence of YEC

So, if those "crazy fundamentalists" at the Scopes Monkey Trial weren't young earth creationists, and if the only people who thought the earth was 6,000 years old was a small fringe group on the outskirts of Christianity, how in the world did young earth creationism come to be so influential in Evangelicalism today? The answer to that question can be summed up with one book title: *The Genesis Flood*.

It wasn't until almost 40 years after the Scopes Trial, in 1961, that YECism emerged as a real movement. In that year, Henry Morris (a hydraulics engineer) and John Whitcomb (an Old Testament professor) co-wrote *The Genesis Flood*. In it, they argued a literal, world-wide, catastrophic Flood about 4,000 years ago could be proven on scientific grounds. The motivation for the book was their belief that the moral decay in Western society could only be restored if we returned to a literal reading of the Bible, most notably, Genesis 1–11. If you get people convinced that Noah built a physical, literal ark 4,000 years ago that survived a world-wide Flood, you'll advance the Christian faith and get more moral people!

Morris and Whitcomb helped launch the *Creation Research Society* in 1963, and then the *Institute for Creation Research* in 1972. Ken Ham credits the work of these two men with spear-heading the modern young earth creationist movement. Unfortunately, just like the propagandists of the Enlightenment, these men did their job well…at least in America. As of today, polls regularly show that 46% of Americans believe that human beings were created in their present form no more than 10,000 years ago.

At the same time, the same polls show that 32% of Americans believe that evolution over millions of years is a God-guided process—this is known as *theistic evolution*. And for all the press Richard Dawkins has gotten over the past decade, still only 15% of Americans believe in what can be described as *naturalistic evolution*—a completely atheistic understanding of life on earth. Nevertheless, the fact remains that YEC has never been taken seriously in academic and scientific circles. Ken Ham claims that the reason YEC isn't accepted in academia is because most scientists are God-hating atheists who don't want to admit that there is a God, because if they did, they would have to live according to God's Word. But perhaps the other reason lies in what YEC organizations like *Answers in Genesis* actually claim:

1. The universe was created in six literal 24-hour days;
2. The universe is only 6,000 years old;
3. Humans and dinosaurs were created on the same day, lived on the earth at the same time;
4. Noah's Flood was an account of a worldwide flood 4,000 years ago.

The reason why YEC isn't taken seriously in scientific circles is simple: *there's no scientific evidence to support those claims*. It's not a matter of rebellion against God. It's a matter of lack of evidence.

Nevertheless, young earth creationists continue to make their claims. On the *Answers in Genesis* website, one can find, in article after article, claims that the only reason why scientists claim that the earth and universe is millions of years old is that they are trying to push a naturalistic-atheistic agenda upon society, and to undermine the reliability of the Bible. Furthermore, there are routine accusations that Christians who subscribe to either theistic evolution or old earth creationism are "compromised Christians" who are simply trying to gain the 'approval of men' (i.e. the scientific community), and who are unwittingly subverting the authority of the Bible by not subscribing to a literal reading of Genesis 1–11.

CONCLUDING REMARKS

We have learned quite a lot in this chapter, and I haven't even dealt yet with any specific scientific claim or interpretive issue regarding Genesis 1–11! I have simply tried to lay out as clearly as possible a number of historical instances that have brought us to the modern creation/evolution debate. On a purely historical note, putting the actual science aside, the problem with the claims of young earth creationists like Ken Ham is that a historical/scientific reading of Genesis 1–11 was simply never the teaching of the historical Church to begin with. There are even clear warnings by Church Fathers about the dangers of insisting that the early chapters of Genesis be read literally and scientifically.

Ever since Charles Darwin came up with the theory of evolution, there has been debate over how it may or may not affect our understanding of the Bible and the Christian faith. That's to be expected. But it's one thing to wrestle with new discoveries and theories; it's quite another to utterly reject new discoveries and theories by making certain historical claims regarding biblical interpretation that are flat out wrong and, ironically, unhistorical.

This brings us to the next area we must look at: that of biblical interpretation. Get ready for an introductory crash course on the topic of biblical exegesis. Exa-what? Be patient, the answers are coming.

5

The Basics of Biblical Exegesis

"When people ask me 'do you take the Bible literally?' I reply, 'Well, I take it naturally—according to the type of literature.' Taking it naturally is what I mean by taking it literally."

—Ken Ham

"A text cannot mean what it never meant. The true meaning of the biblical text for us is what God originally intended it to mean when it was first spoken. That is the starting point."

—Gordon Fee

THE CHALLENGE OF INTERPRETING THE BIBLE

ALTHOUGH THE "SCIENTIFIC" CLAIMS of young earth creationist groups are in no way based in any actual science, that is not where their fundamental problem lies. It lies in their inability to properly read the Bible. They are simply wrong in their assumption that Genesis 1–11 is a scientifically accurate historical account. We've just seen in the previous chapter that they are wrong in their claim that such a view has been the way Christians throughout history have always understood Genesis 1–11. In this chapter we will see what entails proper biblical exegesis and interpretation. Once you know just the most basic, common-sense rules of biblical exegesis, you'll be able to see exactly where Ken Ham and young earth creationists go wrong in their interpretation of Genesis 1–11.

It goes without saying that the issue of how to interpret Genesis 1–11 is quite a controversial topic. It tends to spill over into a host of other issues like that of inerrancy and biblical authority, and it often is seen as a litmus test for determining whether one is deemed a "liberal" who compromises on evolution and undermines the Bible, or a "conservative" who stands firmly on God's Word and fights against "godless evolution."

The reason why so much of the Evangelical church in America is up in arms about the creation/evolution debate has little to do with any actual scientific claims regarding the natural world. The reason why it is such a big topic of concern is that there is a more fundamental issue at stake: the reliability and truthfulness of the Bible, or so they think. By and large, Evangelicals reject evolution because they think it is an attempt to discredit the Bible and force atheism on the culture. They think, "The Bible says the world was made *this way*, but evolution says the world was made *that way*, and since I believe the Bible is *true*, that means evolution must be *false*."

The problem with that line of reasoning, though, is it is based on an entire truckload of false assumptions about what the Bible actually is and what the Bible actually says. This is not an indictment on your everyday, average Evangelical. The fact is, most Evangelicals will never take college-level classes on either the Old or New Testament or in biblical exegesis (to prove my point, I'm guessing that some who are reading this are currently thinking, "What *is* biblical exegesis anyway?").

What that means is that it is the responsibility of church leaders and pastors to provide the people in their congregations with at least the basics of understanding what the Bible is and how it is to be read. But most churches don't do that. Consequently, most Christians are simply cannot fully articulate what they believe, why they believe it, or even how to really read and understand the Bible. Churches are really good at emphasizing that we should love God with all our heart, but that whole "loving God with all your mind" thing? Not so much.

So, what happens is every now and then someone like Ken Ham gets a platform and begins to expound what he thinks certain parts of the Bible are really about. And since many Evangelicals are not only ignorant of Church Tradition, but also are largely biblically illiterate (outside of a few stories in the Gospels, a handful of verses from Paul, and a few Psalms and Proverbs), people get taken in and deceived by new and novel teachings that have never been a part of the traditional Christian faith.

That is why it is not only important to know your Church Tradition, but also to *learn how to read your Bible*, not in the over-simplistic, Sunday school manner most of us tend to do, but in a focused and studious way. Don't worry, though. It's not as hard as you might think. That is what this chapter will attempt to do: give a very basic course on the fundamentals of biblical exegesis. You've got to start somewhere, so let this chapter be that first step.

THE BASICS OF BIBLICAL EXEGESIS

Yes, it's a crazy-sounding name: biblical *exegesis* (pronounced "exa-Jesus"). It is such an odd-sounding name, that when I first came across it in graduate school, I remember joking with a professor, and saying, "Exegesis? Is that the anti-Christ's cousin?" I just got a blank stare back from the professor. I don't think he found it funny. I did . . . I still do.

In any case, biblical exegesis actually is not that hard of a concept to grasp. Essentially, exegesis is the scholarly word used to describe the basic guidelines one should follow if one wants to understand the original intent of any given passage in the Bible. Take for example Ephesians 2:8–9, where Paul says, "*It is by grace you have been saved, through faith…not by works, so that no one could boast.*" That might seem like a straightforward verse, but there are a lot of questions to that verse that most people fail to grasp. Let's just take the most obvious one: what does Paul mean by "works"?

All throughout his letters, particularly in Romans, Paul talks a lot about how salvation comes through "faith," and not by "works." Ever since Martin Luther started the Protestant Reformation in 1517, the general way in which Protestants have understood these kinds of verses is the following: "You can't do enough good works to get saved. You have to believe that Jesus is God and that he rose from the dead."

Do you know what Paul would say to that? He'd say, "Well sure, but that's not what I'm talking about!" Neither Paul nor his fellow Jews ever thought they had to "do enough good works" in order for God to save them. They viewed themselves as already saved—*God had saved them from Egypt*. "Doing works" for them meant obeying the Torah out of a sense of gratitude for having been saved. Simply put, the Jews did the works of Torah *because they had been saved, not in order to get saved.*

Thus, clarifying what Paul meant by "works" changes your understanding as to what Paul was talking about.

In addition, what does Paul mean by "faith in Christ"? If you've grown up in an Evangelical church, chances are you tend to view "faith" as something akin to "I believe *a certain event happened* [the resurrection], even though I can't prove it." Then you use Hebrews 11:1 as justification for understanding faith in that way: "Faith is the assurance of things hoped for, the conviction of *things not seen*."

Well, that's not what Hebrews 11:1 is talking about. I can guarantee you, even though Paul undoubtedly proclaimed the actual physical resurrection of Jesus Christ, when he called people to "faith in Christ," he wasn't just saying, "You have to believe that it really happened, then you can be saved!" If that was the case, then Paul's call to faith is nothing more than mental assertion of a fact—and that, in fact, would be just another "work" that got you saved.

If that has your head spinning, good! You'll now be able to understand the importance and necessity of biblical exegesis. You need to realize that we are not living in the time of Paul, Jesus, David, Moses, or Abraham. We are separated from those times and cultures by thousands of years. Consequently, we are wholly unfamiliar with how people back then and there tended to think, view the world, and even write.

Therefore, if we are going to understand the Bible, we have to do our best to see the world as they saw it. We need to "get in that person's shoes" (or sandals) and understand what that person was saying within the historical context in which he lived. Biblical exegesis, therefore, is the attempt to understand any given biblical passage within that original context. But first, there are two other details that need to be addressed… and they're not controversial at all!

INSPIRATION AND THE BIBLICAL CANON

Christians should all strive to be somewhat competent in biblical exegesis, for we believe that the Bible is the inspired Word of God. Now, this concept of *inspiration*, along with the concept of *inerrancy*, is probably something that needs to be addressed. The two terms are not synonymous. The belief that the Bible is inspired basically comes from II Timothy 3:16: "All Scripture is inspired by God and is useful for teaching, reproof, correction, and for training in righteousness."

So, what does it mean that Scripture is "inspired" by God? Countless books have been written on this topic alone, and sometimes the discussion can get pretty tedious and speculative. We can cut through much of the speculation, though, and say this: *in the Bible we find God speaking the truth through human authors to people in particular situations of time and place.* This is true for both the way God spoke through the writers of the Old Testament and the New Testament. In fact, just as Jesus told his disciples that the Holy Spirit would guide them in all truth, what we see in the New Testament is product of the Holy Spirit's guidance in the early Church.

What we see in the Bible, therefore, are the writings of people who, under the guidance of the Holy Spirit, addressed specific situations and issues of their day. They spoke and wrote the truth that God was conveying to His people. And, as Paul says in II Timothy 3:16, that inspired Scripture is a *useful tool* for teaching, reproof, correction, and training subsequent generations in righteousness as they try to live as the people of God.

This is related to the concept of the *biblical canon*. It would be wrong to think that the only time the Holy Spirit inspired anything was the time when the biblical writers wrote, and that the only things that the Holy Spirit ever inspired were the Scriptures. The Holy Spirit continues to guide and inspire Christians up to the present day. What makes the biblical canon unique is that it is the collection of Holy Spirit-inspired writings from the early Church. Therefore, it acts as a "measuring stick" against which we are able to compare all other teaching regarding the Christian faith.

Simply put, the uniqueness of the Bible lies in its canonicity, not in its inspired status. The canon of Holy Spirit-inspired Scripture is the standard by which the Holy Spirit-inspired Church assesses all teachings and claims made by anyone regarding the truth about God, Christ, humanity, and the world. Therefore, we must see the Bible as the *product of the early Church* that was guided by the Holy Spirit in all truth, and the *Spirit-inspired testimony* of the Tradition that Jesus Christ handed down to the apostles that continues to be used in the Church today as the primary means (i.e. *canon*) by which the Holy Spirit continues to guide and inspire Christians today.

Yet we must remember that when God inspired the Scriptures, the truth He conveyed was given in the words of particular people, within particular cultures, at particular moments in history. As New Testament professor Gordon Fee said, "[God] chose to speak his eternal truths within the particular circumstances and events of human history.... In speaking through real persons, in a variety of circumstances, over a 1,500-year period, God's Word was expressed in the vocabulary and thought patterns of those persons and conditioned by the culture of those times and circumstances."[1]

This means that when God inspired His Word to be written, the truth He conveyed became bound in history. It has cultural texture and is bound up in the language, idioms, and worldviews of that particular culture in history. And since the meaning of words are constantly evolving within any given language, and since languages are vastly different, we need to do our best to make sure that what we're reading *here and now* is in fact what was being conveyed *back then and there*. So, if you believe the Bible is inspired by God, you need to do proper exegesis, because you want to make sure you are interpreting the Bible correctly and understanding the original intended message God inspired.

INERRANCY AND THE ENLIGHTENMENT

Inerrancy, though, is a concept quite different than inspiration. At the risk of being shocking, although inspiration is a completely biblical concept, inerrancy isn't. Inerrancy is a concept that is essentially an overreaction (and ironically a capitulation) to many false notions that stemmed from the Enlightenment. While certainly well-intentioned, it nevertheless has been an unintended accomplice to the current "Bible idolatry" within the Protestant (and particularly the Evangelical) church.

The nineteenth century saw the birth of what is known today as "historical criticism" of the Bible. Fueled by Enlightenment notions of achieving perfection and arriving at objective truth by means of the scientific method, many liberal theologians of the nineteenth century started to claim that the Bible wasn't so much inspired Scripture, as it was simply a collection of poorly written, haphazardly thrown together ancient documents of various ancient people that reflected their primitive (and ultimately wrong) understanding of God and the natural world.

And so, there was a push in the nineteenth century to deny any and all supernatural claims found within Scripture. Why? Because science supposedly "proved" that dead people do not rise from the dead, people

---

1. Fee and Stuart, *How to Read the Bible for All Its Worth*, 21.

could not walk on water, and miracles don't happen. After all, the prevalent worldview of the Enlightenment was to view the universe as a giant machine, constructed by a deistic god who wound it up like a clock and then left it to run on its own natural laws.

For Enlightenment thinkers, God was the creator, but that creation was now done and was running along all on its own, according to the laws of nature God put in place. So, God had no need to tinker with the finely tuned "machine" of nature. It was running perfectly on its own, thank you very much. That was why nineteenth century thinkers ruled out the possibility of miracles. God wouldn't dream of tinkering with his machine—it would violate the "laws of nature."

Now that is a whole different topic in and of itself. But I will say that no serious scientist or philosopher today accepts that deistic-Enlightenment concept of the universe running like a giant machine. We, though, have to understand that however much that view of the universe is rejected *today*, it nevertheless was the accepted view *back then*. And it was that view that led Enlightenment thinkers and liberal theologians to conclude that supernatural miracles don't happen, and therefore much of what is found in the Bible "isn't true." Ironically, their philosophical worldview that acted as the basis for their rejecting the Bible's historical claims is now a rejected philosophical worldview in and of itself.

Another problem with their rejection of the Bible was their deistic-Enlightenment assumption that the Bible was first and foremost a collection of scientific, historical claims. "Scientific facts" became the new Enlightenment measuring stick (i.e. canon) for truth, and it was assumed that all truth was simply provable scientific fact.

For example, the story of Jonah couldn't be "true" because science tells us that a man can't get swallowed by a fish and then survive after three days in the fish's digestive tract. Therefore, because the story of Jonah violated the known scientific laws, the story of Jonah was simply deemed "false," a fanciful story that only ancient, primitive idiots would ever believe, because after all, they weren't scientific. Again, there are a host of things wrong with the way nineteenth century theologians approached the Bible in the first place, but for now, I simply want to make a connection between what they concluded about the Bible and where the concept of inerrancy came from.

In light of the nineteenth century Enlightenment attack on the authority and truthfulness of Scripture, various Christian groups reacted in different ways. At that time the Catholic Church made papal infallibility official church dogma. In the face of these attacks on the truthfulness and historical reliability of the Bible, the Catholic Church responded, "Well, the Pope is infallible! He can't be wrong! What he says is right, no matter what you say!" Yes, that's over-simplistic, but hopefully you get the point.

Within Protestantism, this sparked the rise of Fundamentalism. One of the primary things Fundamentalism defended was the Bible… not just the inspiration of the Bible, but the inerrancy of the Bible. This concept, though, tended to slip into an Enlightenment-influenced understanding of inerrancy. Fundamentalists claimed the Bible was "perfect," and that there was no error *of any kind* in the original manuscripts.

Well, that claim posed a problem: we don't have any of the original manuscripts, and the manuscripts we do have are rife with variants, discrepancies, spelling errors, misplaced words, and omitted words. This should not be surprising, though. Think of a time when you copied by hand a page or two of writing, or a time when you were writing a letter. After finishing, you read back over it, only to discover minor spelling errors, word order errors, or places where you just accidentally left out a word.

Now, those kinds of errors are easily recognized and put right—and those kinds of errors are all over the biblical manuscripts we have. So technically, yes, there are errors in the biblical manuscripts we have. Fundamentalists would get around that by saying, "They weren't there in the *original manuscripts*, though." Okay, but we don't have the original manuscripts, so your claim is unprovable, purely speculative…and completely unnecessary.

Another problem with the Fundamentalist insistence on inerrancy was the tendency to assume everything in the Bible had to be factually true in the historical/scientific sense. The Fundamentalist logic ended up being, "If the Bible tells us something is a psalm, proverb, or parable, then we'll interpret it as a psalm, proverb, or parable. But if the Bible doesn't spell it out for us, we're going to assume that it then is a historical account. The genre of "history" was the default assumption for everything in the Bible, unless the Bible said something was specifically different.

Therefore, debates sprang up regarding stories like Jonah, Job, or the story of the rich man and Lazarus. Why? Because in none of those instances does the Bible indicate the genre of the literature. Fundamentalists would thus resort to their default position: if the Bible doesn't say otherwise, we'll assume it is a factual account of history. To this day, if anyone dares suggest that the story of Jonah has all the hallmarks of a parable, or points out that the book of Job is listed among the "Wisdom Literature" of the Old Testament and is not among the historical books, or that Jesus' story of the rich man and Lazarus is a parable, even though he doesn't start his story with, "By the way, this is a parable," the typical Fundamentalist response is, "You are denying the inerrancy of the Bible! You're saying the Bible isn't true!"

That's the problem with the notion of inerrancy. It makes a claim about the original manuscripts we don't have, and its very notion of inerrancy is based more on the false Enlightenment worldview that claims "truth" can only be expressed in scientific and historical facts. In that sense, the modern notion of inerrancy ends up viewing the Bible very much in the same way Islam views the Koran: a "perfect" book, essentially dropped out of heaven, without any kind of error whatsoever. But nowhere in the Bible is such an understanding of Scripture ever put forth. You can read claims of inspiration in the Bible, but you'll never find any claims of inerrancy in the sense that Fundamentalism understands inerrancy.

Most Evangelical Christians understand inerrancy as nothing more than saying the Bible is inspired by God, written by human authors, and speaks authoritative truth to the situations the authors were addressing. More simply, inerrancy and inspiration are seen as synonyms that are used to argue the Bible is true and speaks God's truth to the world. If that's the case, we would be much better off sticking to the words of Scripture itself: "All Scripture is inspired by God, and is useful for teaching, reproof, correction, and for training in righteousness" (II Timothy 3:16). Constructing a dogma of inerrancy rooted in false Enlightenment definitions of what constitutes "truth" just gets us into trouble.

GETTING BACK TO BASICS: BIBLICAL EXEGESIS 101

I allowed myself to get off track with that discussion of inspiration and inerrancy to show just how easily the claim of inerrancy distracts us from what we should be focused on: how to be good Bible readers who know how to get to the original, inspired message of any given biblical passage. Instead of wasting our time trying to defend the inerrancy of original manuscripts that we don't have and giving the field to the secular-Enlightenment definition of "truth" in our attempt to defend biblical inerrancy, we would be much better off doing everything we can to understand the original, inspired message in any given biblical text.

The fact is, everyone who picks up and reads the Bible is immediately involved in the exercise of *interpretation*. In order for us to arrive at the meaning of any given passage, we must interpret whatever we are reading. And since the goal of biblical exegesis is to make sure we are interpreting any given biblical text correctly, we must check all our assumptions and cultural presuppositions at the door and learn to read any given biblical text from the perspective of the original audience.

If we assume that *our understanding* of any given biblical passage is automatically the same as what the Holy Spirit *intended* as He inspired the human author, we are being quite foolish. As Gordon Fee and Douglas Stuart have stated: "We invariably bring to the text all that we are, with all of our experiences, culture, and prior understandings of words and ideas. Sometimes what we bring to the text, unintentionally to be sure, leads us astray, or else causes us to read all kinds of foreign ideas into the text."[2]

History is full of examples of individuals who started with their own assumptions and ended up developing countless heresies, from Arianism, to Mormonism, and Jehovah's Witnesses. I think we can add dispensationalism, and yes, young earth creationism. The lesson is simple: if you ignore the original context of any given biblical passage and the Tradition of Church teaching on the basics of the historical Christian faith, chances are you'll find yourself in a heresy.

The purpose of good biblical exegesis is to put us in a better position to relate the original inspired message to our lives today. As I've already said, we must first do everything we can to understand what God inspired the authors to say to their original audiences *back then and there*. Once we do that, we are in a better position, under the guidance of the Holy Spirit, both in our individual lives and within the life of the Church as a whole, to consider how what was said back then speaks to us in the *here and now*.

The Historical Context

The first thing to remember is that everything in the Bible has a *historical context*. When God inspired Moses to write the Torah, or when He inspired Paul to write his letters, He inspired them to address real issues

---

2. Fee and Stuart, *How to Read the Bible for All Its Worth*, 16–17.

to real people at that time. Therefore, since the Bible is inspired, I have a duty as a Christian to make sure I am doing everything I can to understand the inspired message God gave to the biblical writers that addressed those real world, historical concerns at that time. God inspired Paul to address specific problems in the Church at Rome (Romans), God inspired Moses to reveal who He is to ancient Hebrews who were coming out from 400 years of bondage in Egypt. If I don't take the time to understand the historical context in which those texts were written, I'm probably not going to understand them too well.

Take for example the Gettysburg Address or the Emancipation Proclamation. If I handed you those documents and you didn't know anything about the Civil War, Abraham Lincoln, or American slavery, you might understand them in a very general sense, but you simply wouldn't understand the majority of what is stated in those documents. That's why understanding the historical context is so important, especially when it comes to inspired Scripture.

So how do *you* understand how the *Christians in Rome* understood what Paul was writing to them in Romans? How do *you* understand how *the post-exilic Jewish community* understood the message of Jonah? How do *you* understand how *the ancient Israelites* would have understood the purpose of Genesis 1–11? The answer to those questions is simple in one respect, but somewhat of a challenge in another.

The simple answer is to make a commitment to understand the historical context of any time period the Bible addresses. Try to understand the time and culture of the author and the original audience. Try to get a grasp on what the occasion and purpose for each biblical book is. To put it in even simpler terms: get some good Bible commentaries and books on biblical history and read up on the history of any given biblical book.

The challenge to do this is to know where to start. We have essentially been trained to not care at all about the historical context of the Bible, and therefore we tend to read the Bible in a very self-centered way: "How does the Bible relate *to my life?*" We'll read Ephesians 2:8–9 and immediately try to "apply it to our own lives" without ever giving a thought as to what Paul was actually saying to the Ephesian believers back then. We say things like, "I read Ephesians 2:8–9, and I realized that there's nothing I can do to earn salvation. No matter how many soup kitchens I help out in, I have to remember that even good things like feeding the homeless won't mean I can earn my way to heaven."

Well, that is true, but Paul wasn't talking about that. Sure, the Holy Spirit may have spoken to you about working in soup kitchens through your reading of Ephesians 2:8–9. That doesn't mean you have understood the inspired message Paul had for the Ephesian believers. If you are a Christian who values the Bible, you must commit to understanding what that original inspired message to the original audience was.

Fortunately, understanding the historical context of any biblical book isn't hard to do. Scores of excellent, godly, Christian biblical scholars have already done the hard work, and have written Bible commentaries that explain to the reader that very historical context. In fact, you can get a solid study Bible, and the introductions written before each book in the Bible alone will help you. But the fact is, you're going to have to do some work.

The Literary Context

In addition to becoming familiar with the historical context, the other aspect of good biblical exegesis is to learn to read a given passage within its *literary context*. At the bare minimum, this means to be able to properly identify the kind of genre a particular biblical passage or book may be. The reason this is vitally important is because if you misunderstand what the genre of a particular passage or book in the Bible is, you are going to completely misinterpret that given passage or book.

A perfect example of this is the book of Revelation. Ever since Hal Lindsey's book, *The Late, Great Planet Earth* (1970), the typical Evangelical interpretation of Revelation (as well as random passages from Matthew 24, Mark 13, Luke 21, I Thessalonians, and Daniel) has been to read it as a prediction of the current "End Times" fears that have since been reinforced by books like the *Left Behind* series. The very term "apocalypse" has become synonymous with those "End Time" speculative scenarios.

The fundamental problem, though, as Inigo Mentoya of *The Princess Bride* fame once said, "That word…I don't think it means what you think it means!" The fact is "apocalypse" is a distinct literary genre that was quite popular among Jews from around the years of 200 BC to AD 200. It had distinctive literary features, and everyone knew how to read and interpret them. They were highly symbolic works of literature that contemplated how God would finally vindicate his people who were in the midst of persecution, and virtually all of the symbolic imagery in apocalypses directly correlated to something or someone who was known at the time.

What this means is that all of Lindsey and LaHaye's fanciful interpretations of Revelation, complete with Nicolae Carpathia, Blackhawk helicopters, a third temple being rebuilt, and people being whisked up into clouds during the rapture—all of it stems from a complete misunderstanding of the basic genre of Revelation. Revelation has never meant any of that, and it will never mean any of that. We know that because we know what kind of genre Revelation is, and apocalyptic literature never was meant to be taken as a prediction of future literal events. Not only would John's original hearers have not understood *The Left Behind* series, but no one in the first 1850 years of Church history read Revelation that way.

Making "Back Then and There" Relevant to the "Here and Now"

This gets us to the last, but immensely crucial, rule to remember when reading anything in the Bible. As the above example illustrates, the reason why you cannot automatically assume that a biblical passage is speaking *directly* to events in the here and now, and the reason why you cannot automatically assume that a biblical passage is using modern concepts and terminology, is because if you do, then you are completely ignoring, and in fact are rejecting, the fact that God inspired his Word to certain people at a certain time and place in history.

Whatever a biblical passage has to say to us today, it has to have its origins in the original meaning of the biblical text. Or as Gordon Fee has said, "The reason why one must *not begin* with the here and now is that *the only proper control for hermeneutics* [i.e. rules for interpretation] *is to be found in the original intent of the biblical text.*"[3] A biblical passage simply can never mean what it never meant. It is such a commonsense concept, that it is surprising to find how often it is completely ignored among so many Christians. That is why it must be emphasized right now: *the inspired message in any given biblical passage is what God originally intended to communicate to the original audience.*

Therefore, anyone who believes the Bible is the inspired Word of God cannot ignore this fundamental rule of biblical exegesis. To ignore it is to effectively, on a very practical level, reject the belief that the Bible

---

3. Fee and Stuart, *How to Read the Bible for All Its Worth*, 29.

is the inspired Word of God. But if you take time to learn a little biblical history and if you take the time to understand how to read literature, you'll be well on your way to understanding the Bible a whole lot better.

6

Interpreting Genesis 1—11

"Once you give up a literal Adam and Eve—and thus reject a literal Fall—then you may as well throw the Bible away."

—Ken Ham

GETTING A HANDLE ON GENESIS 1-11

WHEN IT COMES RIGHT down to it, the creation/evolution debate within Evangelical circles centers on the assertion promoted by young earth creationism that if evolution is true, then Genesis 1–11 can't be true, and if Genesis 1–11 isn't true, then how can anyone trust anything else in the Bible to be true? Such fear, though, stems from the YEC teaching that makes claims that have never been held in the history of the Church. It elevates a modern historical/scientific interpretation of Genesis 1–11—one that neither the original Israelites, the early Christians, nor Christians throughout most of Church history could have possibly understood—to the same level of importance as belief in the resurrection of Christ.

Young earth creationism claims that even though God inspired Genesis 1–11 to be written back then and there, it actually addresses and satisfies our modern criteria for what constitutes good history and science writing. Such a claim isn't only illogical, it is heretical. After all, if God had inspired Moses to write a modern historical and scientific account of material origins of the natural world, and address it to an ancient people coming out of a pagan, non-scientific culture who didn't even see a distinction between the "supernatural" and the "natural" worlds in the first place—they wouldn't have been able to understand it, would they?

That is why I have taken the time to tell the story of Arius and the first Church council at Nicaea. That is why I have taken the time to explain Church Tradition, how Christians leaders have interpreted Genesis 1–11 throughout history, and the basics of biblical exegesis. One needs to get a handle on all these more fundamental issues before one dives in and tries to tackle the specifics of Genesis 1–11. So, whether you feel you are ready for it or not, we're at the point in the book where we're going to take a concentrated look at Genesis 1–11. It's time we finally address the elephant in the room, and ask, "How *do* you interpret Genesis 1–11?"

As soon as you take the historical context of Genesis 1-11 seriously, you realize that God would not have inspired Moses to write a modern historical scientific account of the material origins of the natural world. Such a notion goes entirely against the very biblical notion regarding inspiration. God first and foremost inspired the writers of the Bible to address the culture of which they were a part. The text had to have made sense to them back then and there. It is only after we do our best to understand what the original, inspired message of a given text was, that we can put ourselves in position to properly apply that authoritative message to our lives today. So, the primary question remains: How are we to understand Genesis 1–11? What is its original, inspired message?

IT'S ABOUT THE BIBLE, STUPID!

As we will see in later chapters, one of the things Ken Ham consistently says is that the only reason why people have come to the conclusion that Genesis 1--11 isn't literal history is that they have put more faith in evolution than the Bible. In other words, they are convinced that evolution is true, and then try to justify their belief in evolution by re-interpreting Genesis 1–11 away from its "obvious meaning" (i.e. literal history), and to something else like poetry, myth, or whatever.

Speaking for myself, evolutionary theory had absolutely no influence on my understanding of Genesis 1–11. What pushed me to my current understanding of Genesis 1–11 was the graduate level education I received in Biblical Studies. It was my study of the Bible and my firm belief in the inspiration of Scripture that brought me to my conclusion about Genesis 1–11. When it comes to interpreting any given biblical passage, we must take the original context seriously. When God inspired an Old Testament or New Testament writer, that inspired message first and foremost was directed to those people at that time—it had to make sense to them.

So, when God inspired Genesis 1–11 to be written, it would have been something that was directly relevant to the ancient Israelites. Therefore, Genesis 1–11 isn't going to be *directly* relevant to me in the twenty-first century. I need to understand what it *originally* meant, and then seek to *apply* it to my life. If I assume Genesis 1–11 was written directly for me, then I am bound to miss the inspired message. Instead, I will probably read into Genesis 1–11 things that I want it to say, based on my twenty-first century cultural assumptions. If I do that, then I am, in effect, disregarding what God actually said, and setting up in its place my own preconceived notions, and potentially, my own theological idol.

When coming to Genesis 1–11, the first question we must ask is: "What was the original context in which these chapters were written?" Well, there are basically two views on this question. One view is that these chapters ultimately go back to Moses during the Exodus, when he taught the Israelites about how YHWH was the true God. The other view is that they were actually written during the Babylonian Exile, and then placed at the beginning of the Torah to act as sort of a prologue. I think they do ultimately go back to the time of the Exodus, but that they were written in the form we have it today during the Exile.

Either way, their situation would have been similar: they were living in a pagan culture. In fact, as anyone who has read the Old Testament will know, the ancient Israelites were fairly pagan for most of their history, having continually imbibed the pagan religions of the ANE. Yet in Genesis 1–11, we find God had chosen them anyway to reveal the truth about Himself, humanity, and the world itself. So, when the ancient Israelites would have read the inspired truth of Genesis 1–11, what would they have been confronted with?

They would have immediately recognized a lot of things that would have directly challenged the other ANE creation stories, like those from Egypt and Babylon. *Those* stories taught things like (A) creation was a horrible, disgusting carcass of a dead and defeated serpent-god, (B) humanity was created out of the excrement of defeated gods to be the slaves of violent conqueror gods, and (C) there were many gods who were part of nature itself and who were constantly warring with each other.

What would have been immediately apparent to the Israelites was that although the style of Genesis 1-11 was similar to the other creation stories of the ANE, the content was radically different. Genesis 1-11 teaches: (A) creation is good, (B) humanity was created in God's image, and therefore has inherent dignity and worth, and (C) there was only one God, and it was He who created the world and yet was distinct from it. Beyond that, (D) the reason why human beings were so screwed up and violent wasn't because "the gods were always messing with them," but because human beings, by their sinful actions, have made it that way. At the most basic level, those are the inspired truths that Genesis 1-11 is teaching. If that makes sense to you, great. Remember that as you read what comes next.

THE GENRE OF GENESIS 1-11: YES, IT'S ANCIENT MYTHOLOGY

The fundamental question concerning Genesis 1-11 that lies at the heart of the creation/evolution debate is this: "Is Genesis 1-11 to be read as straightforward chronological history of the origins of the material universe and humanity?" Ken Ham responds to that question by saying not only is Genesis 1-11 a historical narrative, but if you don't read it as such then you are throwing the authority and reliability of the entire Bible into question and are putting your faith in the man-made theory of evolution.

He's simply wrong. Far from being history, Genesis 1-11 falls into the literary genre of *myth*. Of course, given the modern misunderstanding of myth, a lot needs to be unpacked in order to fully understand what I'm talking about. In our modern world, we use the term "myth" as a pejorative to criticize something as historically false. Chances are, when you read the above sentence, you started thinking, "He's calling Genesis 1-11 a myth! He's saying it's not true! He's saying it's a fairy tale!" If you thought that, then you and Ken Ham have something in common. He has said, "When believers dismiss Genesis 1-11 as myth or as unreliable, on what foundation can biblical doctrines stand?"[1]

Get that thought out of your head—it's wrong. The problem with that comment is that it equates "myth" with something being scientifically or historically "untrue," and that idea betrays an Enlightenment assumption that the only kind of truth that exists is that of historical or

---

1. Ham, "What's the Core Message of the Answers in Genesis Ministry?" para. 4.

scientific facts. We need to put that Enlightenment definition out of our minds if we are going to fully grasp the concept of the ancient literary genre of myth.[2]

When scholars say Genesis 1–11 is a myth, they are not saying it is a "false story." They are referring to the genre of literature used in the ancient world to address issues of ultimate meaning regarding human beings, creation, and the gods. No one in the ancient world read myths as having literally happened in history. No ancient Greek thought all the evils in the world literally came from an actual box that Pandora opened at one point in history. They understood that the myth of Pandora's Box was attempting to explain a truth about reality, namely that evil is inevitable, and that human beings often bring evil about unknowingly.

Virtually every culture in the ancient world had some kind of mythological story of origins. But the purpose of those stories *was not* to give a historical, scientific description of the creation of the material universe. Rather, they expressed what that particular culture believed regarding the nature of the gods, human beings, and the natural world. Their purpose was to shape that particular culture's worldview by providing the *metaphysical glasses* by which a culture would interpret the natural world, the gods, mankind, and history in general. Creation myths essentially laid the groundwork for all the other teachings, doctrines, and interpretations of history within a given culture. That was their purpose. They were never intended to be read as chronological accounts of material origins of the universe.

What makes any mythological story true or false isn't whether or not it got its historical facts right, because myths weren't trying to give historical facts in the first place. For example, the reason why the 'Flood story' in the *Epic of Gilgamesh* isn't true *isn't* because "there really wasn't a man named Gilgamesh," or because "it didn't rain for just seven days." The reason why *Gilgamesh* isn't true is because it teaches that (A) there are many gods, (B) that they are vicious and destroy human beings for petty reasons, and (C) human beings are worthless and cower in darkness and fear of those violent gods.

2. Although he hesitates using the word "myth" for Genesis 1-11, in his book, *Friend of Science, Friend of Faith*, Gregg Davidson acknowledges that what we are reading in the early chapters of Genesis is something other than straightforward, literal history, and that there is a certain amount of literary artistry at play: "Note that literary license is not a veiled way of saying 'less true.' It is simply a recognition that writers of Scripture sometimes used words and descriptions in ways they never intended to be taken in an absolute literal sense" (58).

It's not that it got historical facts wrong, but rather because its *theology* and *metaphysical worldview* is utterly false. By contrast, the reason why Genesis 1–11 is true isn't because it got historical facts right, but rather because its *theology* and *metaphysical worldview* has been revealed by God.

SIDE NOTE: DARWIN'S ORIGIN OF SPECIES, GILGAMESH, AND ATRAHASIS

Incidentally, the reason we know so much about ANE myths like *Gilgamesh*, *Enuma Elish*, and *Atrahasis*, is because we found copies of these ancient stories in the nineteenth century. *Gilgamesh* was discovered in 1853, and it was dated back to 2100-1800 BC Babylon. *Atrahasis* was discovered in 1899 and dated back to the eighteenth-century BC. This is really important to realize, especially in light of the creation/evolution debate. Here's why...

Think about it, the rise of liberal theology in the nineteenth century was, for the most part, the result of a faulty Enlightenment worldview that assumed the only things that counts as "truth" are "facts." Therefore, some theologians started assuming everything in the Bible was intended to be a historical/factual claim. Yet since everything in the Bible *isn't* intended to be a historical/factual claim, their Enlightenment assumptions led them to start discounting everything in the Bible as "not true."

Therefore, when Darwin came out with *Origin of Species* in 1859, the knee-jerk reaction of many people in the nineteenth century was to assume that evolution was one scientific/historical claim regarding the origin of life on earth, whereas Genesis 1–11 was another scientific/historical claim regarding the origin of life on earth. As scientific evidence that validates evolution mounted, many ended up concluding that Genesis 1–11 must be false—that it was making a scientific/historical claim but was wrong. People still make that assumption today.

That assumption is simply wrong. For those who really want to understand the truth, the evidence was there all along. The discovery of *Gilgamesh* in 1853, and *Atrahasis* in 1899 gave us clear evidence as to the genre of that type of literature. For the past 150 years, scholars have read, discussed, and explained the characteristics of ancient creation myths like *Gilgamesh* and *Atrahasis*, and at no time did anyone suggest that ancient people thought these myths were somehow scientific and historical.

Everyone knew what kind of literature these stories were. No one wrote a paper about how Darwinism disproved *Gilgamesh*, because everyone knew that *Gilgamesh* wasn't intended to be read as history. To compare Darwinism to *Gilgamesh* would be a categorical mistake.

Therefore, it completely baffles me why people for the past 150 years have argued that Genesis 1–11 is a scientific/historical account of the origin of the universe. The discovery of *Gilgamesh* and *Atrahasis* should have been the evidence that helped us understand that Genesis 1–11 was written in the genre of ancient myth, and not in the genre of modern science and history. The evidence was there to properly understand Genesis 1–11 all along.

For some reason, it was ignored. Why? Because we in the West are children of the Enlightenment and have adopted a scientific methodology for investigating the natural, material world. Secondly, we in the West have also been influenced by the Judeo-Christian culture and have always revered the Bible as a holy and truthful book, inspired by God. However, being children of the Enlightenment that we are, we assumed that since the Bible was true, that meant it had to be scientifically and historically true in all parts. After all, the Enlightenment has told us that "truth" equals "facts." This assumption has to be put to bed. It is not true.

THE APPREHENSION OF USING "MYTH"

With all that in mind, let's turn specifically to understanding Genesis 1–11 as written in the genre of myth. Now Evangelical scholars shy away from describing Genesis 1-11 as myth for one obvious reason: the term freaks Christians out! John Walton, a professor at Wheaton College who has written an amazing book titled *The Lost World of Genesis 1*, does not like the term "myth" because he states, rather correctly, that although there certainly are some similarities between Genesis 1–11 and the other ANE creation myths, Genesis 1–11 is doing something drastically different. Therefore, it doesn't really "fit" in with those other ANE myths.

My response is, *of course Genesis 1–11 is doing something different*. Nevertheless, it is still written in the genre of myth that was common in the ancient world. *Genre* is simply the package in which a particular truth or teaching comes. If that teaching ends up being radically different from the regular teaching that comes out of the "genre package" of myth, that doesn't negate the reality that the "genre package" is still that of myth.

Another way of seeing Genesis 1–11 is that it is perhaps sort of an "anti-myth." It uses the genre of myth, then subverts virtually every pagan presupposition and worldview normally associated with myth. Essentially, Genesis 1–11 used the polytheistic genre of myth to obliterate the pagan worldview and introduce the concept of monotheism. That, in my opinion, is quite an ingenious revolution in worldview.

Let's use an analogy: briefcases normally hold folders and papers. If someone smuggles a bomb in a briefcase, and it ends up blowing up an entire office, you don't refuse to acknowledge the bomb was in a briefcase, on the grounds that normally briefcases don't hold bombs. You acknowledge that the very thing that made it possible to smuggle the bomb into the office *was the briefcase*. Genesis 1–11 completely blows up the worldview and presuppositions of the ancient pagan world, but it still is a bomb that was smuggled into that culture by the briefcase of myth.

Rather than shying away from the term, we should teach what the term actually means. This reminds me of U2's album *Rattle and Hum*. The first song on the album is an in-concert cover of "Helter Skelter" by the Beatles. Bono introduces it by saying, "This is a song that Charles Manson stole from The Beatles...we're stealing it back!" This is what we need to do with the term myth. We need to restore its original meaning so we can more properly understand Genesis 1–11. To avoid using it at all ultimately allows the wrong definition of myth to further be solidified in our society and makes any critical explanation of Genesis 1–11 almost impossible.

The genre of Genesis 1–11 is ancient myth but calling it myth does not mean it is not true. Genesis 1–11 is true *in what it reveals*, but what makes it true isn't that it got the historical facts of creation right, whereas the other stories got the facts wrong. What makes it true is the *revealed theological truth* regarding the nature of God, mankind, and creation.

We must remember that no ancient society, Israel included, had any interest in figuring out historical and scientific explanations for the origin of the natural world. The creation stories of ANE societies were concerned with explaining the nature of the gods, the nature of human existence, and the reason for suffering and evil in the world. They were not interested in an "objective/factual analysis" of the scientific/historical origins of the world. Therefore, to insist that Genesis 1–11 has to be historically true is to impose a modern/scientific reading on a text that the original audience would have had absolutely no concept of or interest in.

C. S. LEWIS, J. R. R. TOLKIEN, AND THE IMPORTANCE OF MYTH

There's more to understanding myth, though, than just stating it's not meant to address historical facts, or stating it is trying to explain the truth about God and mankind. The power of myth is that it is the door that opens to us to experience the reality of God Himself. It gives us a foothold and basic worldview through which we can make sense of the world and His unfolding redemption in history. Not only is myth *not* a threat to the truth of Christianity, but men like C. S. Lewis and J. R. R. Tolkien would argue that it is *outright essential* to Christianity. It is a glorious positive that helps bring us into the biblical world where we experience reality itself.

One of the things that got Lewis to accept Christianity was Tolkien's claim that myth and storytelling are crucial to the way God reveals Himself. Tolkien said that to the ancients, "the whole of creation was 'myth-woven and elf-patterned.'"[3] Since man's *imaginative inventions*, just as his capacity for abstract thought, find their origin in God, when men made myths, they were acting as "sub-creators" and were "fulfilling God's purpose and reflecting a splintered fragment of the true light."[4] Simply put, ancient pagan myths were creative stories about the deeper realities of existence, and however imperfect, they had elements of truth in them.

Those seeds of truth could then point the way to recognizing the truth regarding Christ—the story of Christ, Tolkien said, was essentially myth being realized in history. Therefore, far from blinding us to the truth of Christ, men like Lewis, Tolkien—and even early Christian philosophers like Justin Martyr—argued that myth paves the way for truly understanding God's truth revealed in Christ.

This is true not only for ancient myths, but it also helps us understand the purpose of Genesis 1–11. In contrast to the other pagan myths of its time, Genesis 1–11 gives a distinct mythical perspective on the nature of God, the nature of mankind, and the meaning and purpose of creation. It reveals the state of reality and the problems we as human beings face—and we then find the answers to those problems in the revelation of Christ.

The other thing to realize about the genre of myth is its purpose. As Humphrey Carpenter wrote in *The Inklings*, C. S. Lewis believed that

---

3. Carter, *The Inklings*, 43.
4. Carter, *The Inklings*, 43.

a story of a mythical type "gives us an experience of something not as an abstraction but as *a concrete reality*. We don't 'understand the meaning' when we read a myth, we actually encounter the thing itself. Once we try to grasp it with the discursive reason, it fades."[5]

Therefore, mythical literature isn't about "knowing facts;" it is about "tasting and experiencing." As Lewis believed, "What you [are] tasting turns out to be a universal principle. Of course, the moment we state the principle, we are admittedly back in the world of abstractions. It's only while receiving the myth *as a story* that you experience a principle concretely."[6] Now, you might right now be thinking, "What does that mean?" Let me explain, using Genesis 1–11 as the focus.

What we experience when we read the mythical creation account in Genesis 1—3 is the reality of the orderly and good creation itself. We experience the reality of the sovereignty and goodness of the God Himself. Genesis 1 reveals that creation itself is good and orderly, and we see that goodness and order every day—we "taste" the truth of Genesis 1 every day, every time we step outside. We "taste" the truth of the creation of Adam in Genesis 2 every time we take a breath. We experience and "taste" the truth and reality of "the fall" of Genesis 3 every time we reach out for something we're not ready for, or blame someone else for our sin, or experience shame for doing something we know we shouldn't have done.

Simply put, the truth of what is contained in Genesis 1—3 isn't "objectively proven" through historical/scientific analysis or the scientific method. Rather, it is experienced in our daily lives and tasted in our very experience as human beings. We don't "know" Genesis 1—3 is true as a historical fact; we experience the truth of Genesis 1—3 by virtue of being human. In that sense, on that existential level, we "know" it to be true.

This can be extended to all of Genesis 1-11. The purpose of the mythical account of Genesis 1-11 is not to speak to historical or scientific questions that can be proven or disproven. It serves as the mythical backdrop to the entirety of human experience to which we all relate. If "all the world is a stage," then Genesis 1-11 is the backdrop against which human history play out. It provides the existential context against which we can understand God's dealings in the history of Israel, culminating in the historical reality of Christ's ministry, death, and resurrection.

---

5. Carter, *The Inklings*, 143.
6. Carter, *The Inklings*, 143.

We see this in literature all the time. J. R. R. Tolkien's book *The Silmarillion* provided the mythical backdrop to the entire world of Middle-Earth, and thus is the setting for the stories in *The Hobbit* and *The Lord of the Rings*. The "history" of those stories only could be told once the "myth" of *The Silmarillion* was established. Sure, it is possible to enjoy *The Hobbit* and *LOTR* without having read *The Silmarillion*, but your understanding of those stories will be enhanced greatly if you go back and read *The Silmarillion*, for when you do, you will drink in and "taste" that highly symbolic and mythical world that is the backdrop to *The Hobbit* and *Lord of the Rings*.

That is the power and purpose of mythical literature. Far from being "not true" or "lies," mythical literature opens the door to the heart of reality that we experience. No, there is no literal ring of power that archeologists can dig up to "prove it is true," but there are many "rings of power" throughout human history—and they are very real, and they wreak havoc in our world. They might be in the form of kingly crowns and scepters, or they might be in the form of deals with lobbyists and lack of term limits. …but the truth of "the ring of power" is not tied to a literal ring that speaks to a Hobbit named Bilbo Baggins.

The same dynamic can be seen in the Bible. Genesis 1–11 is the founding myth inspired by God that provides the true Biblical Worldview, and the true understanding of the reality of creation: a good Creator God, a humanity created in God's image, but due to people's foolish choices, a humanity not fully in God's likeness, and thus lost and in need of redemption…and a creation itself, groaning in labor pains, longing for the revelation of the sons of God (Rom 8:19–22). Simply put, the myth of Genesis 1–11 is essential to understanding the historical facts and events of human history as elements within God's salvation story.

Men like Ken Ham are partly right when they insist that Genesis 1–11 is essential to the truth of Christ. But it is essential precisely because it is myth: it's the backdrop against which history is played out. Therefore, to deny Genesis 1–11 is mythological, and instead insist that it has to be historically factual in order to be true, would be like insisting that the backdrop on the stage has to be torn down and made into actual characters in the play. Without the backdrop, though, there can't be a play, and the characters cannot be fully understood.

That is the power and purpose of myth, and we see it at work in the opening chapters of Genesis. God is Creator and is therefore creative in His revelation. Myth is not the enemy to the Gospel; it is the backdrop to it. It sets the stage for the Gospel to be played out in history. Far from debasing the truth of the Bible and the Gospel itself, saying Genesis 1–11 is in the genre of myth is to elevate the truth of the Bible, and to open the doors to the much wider reality God's creation. With that in mind, let's briefly run through Genesis 1–11 to get our bearings in the mythical backdrop of the biblical story.

A BRIEF COMMENTARY ON GENESIS 1-11

Perhaps the best book I've read on Genesis 1 is *The Lost World of Genesis One* by John Walton. It should come as no surprise that Ken Ham hates it and has actually called Walton, unsurprisingly, a compromiser. In his book, Walton makes a convincing case that if you take historical context seriously, there is simply no way you can conclude that Genesis 1 (or Genesis 1–11 for that matter) is addressing modern, scientific concerns and questions. It was addressing the concerns and questions of an ancient pagan culture. If you want to understand what the original, inspired message God was conveying to the ancient Israelites, Walton's book will help immensely.

Genesis 1: Creation

As far as Genesis 1 is concerned, Walton argues it was never meant to be read as an account of the material origins of the natural world. Instead, Walton calls Genesis 1 an *ancient cosmology* that depicts God bestowing order and function on a chaotic and functionless universe. If that sounds odd, let me flesh out Walton's argument. Simply put, Genesis 1 is not describing the process of how creation came about—it is explaining the purpose for which creation exists.

The reason why it is unreasonable to assume that Genesis 1 is an account of the creation of the "natural world" is because in the ancient world, there was no concept of any kind of dichotomy between the "natural world" and the "supernatural world." They did not believe there was a "natural world" governed by "natural laws," and that God/the gods only intervened on special occasions. That is a thoroughly modern concept of the universe that came about with the rise of modern science and deism. And one thing is for certain: the people in the *ancient* world were not *modern deists*. As Walton said, "The idea that [God] got things running then just stood back or engaged himself elsewhere would have been laughable in the ancient world because it was not even conceivable."[7]

Instead, the ancient world believed that the entire "natural world" was in fact being constantly run by God/the gods. They never would have asked the question, "At what point in the past did God create the world?" as if creation was over and done with and is now simply being kept going by the laws of nature. Rather, they would have asked, "What function and purpose has God/the gods given creation?"

Those are two very different questions. The first is a question we in the modern world are concerned about. We want to know about the origin of matter, because we assume that the material world is the only reality. The ancient world, though, was concerned about the second question. They wanted to know about the origin of purpose and function in the world, for something didn't truly exist unless it had a function within an ordered system. For them, creation meant bringing order and function to nonfunctioning chaos. It was a *creation of purpose and function*, not a *creation of matter*.

This really should be obvious to anyone who reads the first few verses of Genesis 1, for what is presented before God's creation *isn't nothingness*. What does it say? "In the beginning, when God created the heavens and the earth, the earth was *tohu wabohu*, and darkness was on the face of the deep, while the Spirit of God was sweeping over the face of the waters." For those who want to argue that Genesis 1 is an account of the material origins of the universe, Genesis 1:2 poses a big problem: "the earth" and "the deep waters" were already there before God started creating. But if one reads Genesis 1 within its ANE context and sees that it is an account of the origins of function and purpose, there is no problem—everything makes perfect sense. Now, two things about Genesis 1:2.

First, the "deep" and the "waters" Genesis 1:2 were not references to some literal sea or primordial water resource. Every person in the ancient world would have known exactly what it was—the mythological abode of chaos, violence, and evil. Why depict it as a sea? Simple—the sea was literally chaotic and dangerous! What better image do you want? Furthermore, in many ANE cultures there was often a giant sea serpent that was associated with the Evil One—Mesopotamia had Tiamat, and even in the Old Testament there are references to Leviathan and Rahab. In any case, the picture that is painted in Genesis 1 isn't one of God creating the

---

7. Walton, *The Lost World of Genesis One*, 18.

material world out of nothing. It is one of God establishing order within a chaotic, uninhabitable universe. And that leads to point two…

We are told that the earth was *tohu wabohu*. Most translations, assuming Genesis 1 is an account of the material universe, translate this as something like "formless and void" (i.e. void of material stuff). But that's not what *tohu wabohu* means. "*Tohu*" means something more akin to "unproductive, non-functional, and useless," while "*Wabohu*" means something like *wilderness*, or *wasteland*. What Genesis 1:2 is actually saying is that the earth (which apparently was there before God started "creating") was an unproductive, non-functioning wilderness. Given that as a starting point, God begins to create order and function. And that is exactly what we see in Days 1—6.

Day 1: The Creation of Time

In Day 1 God said, "Let there be light," called it "good," and separated it from darkness. What's going on? If one reads this as an account of the material universe, there is an obvious problem: how can God create "light" *before* the creation of the sun, moon, and stars? But if one reads this as an account of God bringing order to chaos, one can see the significance of God separating the light from the darkness: he has created *time*, day to night, and night to day. Perhaps a better way to articulate this would be to say that God said, "Let there be a period of light," (i.e. day). Furthermore, his calling it "good" does not indicate some kind of "perfection," as it simply is a way of saying something like, "And God said it was good to go"—light was good because it was given a function within the universe.

Day 2: The Creation of Weather

In Day 2 God said, "Let there be a dome in the midst of the waters, and let it separate the waters from the waters." A materialist reading of Day 2 creates a problem. There is no literal "dome" in the sky holding up the clouds. But from the ancient world's perspective, since water would come from the sky, they surmised there must be a "dome" up there that held up the waters above the earth. So, what Day 2 is revealing isn't how God created clouds, but rather that He has not only opened up space for land (that's to come in Day 3), but that he has also created *weather*. The "holding up of the waters above" allows the possibility for things like rain to fall on the earth and ultimately produce vegetation. Hence, Day 2 creates another functional condition necessary to produce life.

Day 3: The Creation of the Basis for Food

In Day 3, with the bringing up of the land out of the sea, God establishes the basis for *food*. Combined with Day 2, the land is able to produce vegetation and food, yet another functional condition for life. As Walton notes, "We should not be surprised to find that the three major functions introduced in the first three days of Genesis 1 are also prominent in ANE texts."[8] Simply put, what we find in Days 1—3 follows the same pattern of creation function that is found in other ancient creation texts.

Day 4: The Establishment of the Heavens for Festival Celebrations

In Day 4, God sets the sun, moon, and stars in the heavens to (a) separate day from night, and (b) act as signs for "the seasons, days, and years." What is this talking about? Well, it's not talking about the four seasons of winter, spring, summer, and winter. Instead, what these are for is the establishment of *festival celebrations* often associated with things like harvest time. By the way, the very fact that ways to establish festival celebrations were created *before* human beings is yet another indication that Genesis 1 is not trying to give a chronological account of the creation of the material world. Furthermore, in contrast to other ANE stories that depicted the sun, moon, and stars as various gods in their own right, Genesis 1 declares something shocking: the sun, moon, and stars *aren't gods*. The true Creator God created them, and he uses them as a means to maintain order and functionality within his created order.

Day 5: God's Dominion over the Sea Creatures

In Day 5 we find the creation of the sea creatures and the commission to be "fruitful and multiply." In our modern world we will naturally think this is merely a description of aquatic life, and nothing more. But if we look at this from the point of view of the ancient world, there is a lot more going on. As Walton points out, in the ancient world, the cosmic

---

8. Walton, *The Lost World of Genesis One*, 58.

sea was believed to be filled with creatures that constantly warred against the ordered system. In some cases, a great mythological sea creature like Tiamat was seen as the embodiment of chaos itself, locked in an eternal struggle against the gods.

But here in Genesis 1, to everyone's shock, we are told that the Creator God created the sea creatures and exercises ultimate authority over them. Simply put, in contrast to other ANE stories, there is no "cosmic war" going on in Genesis 1; the sea creatures, however dangerous they may be, are nevertheless kept in check by the God who created them. To reduce Genesis 1 to nothing more than a chronological account of material origins, and thus Day 5 to the creation of fish, is to ignore a crucial theological truth that God revealed through Moses to the Israelites.

Day 6: Man Made in God's Image

In Day 6 we have the creation of land animals and mankind. The key theological truth in Day 6, of course, is that mankind was made *in God's image*. A lot of ink has been spilled trying to explain exactly what "being made in God's image" entails. Does it refer to our ability to reason? Is it a reference to our conscience, our ability for language, or something else? When understood from the vantage point of the ANE, it's really not that complicated. In the ancient world, to speak of things being made in the image of anything was to use *idol language*.

In the ANE, people worshipped pagan gods, and had images (i.e. idols) of those gods in their temples and in their homes. And it was believed that wherever an image/idol of a particular god was, that particular god was present in that image/idol. The same concept went for kings and rulers. Think about it—even in the modern world, look at your typical tyrannical dictator, be it Stalin, Hitler, or Saddam Hussein. Those men and their pictures up everywhere in their country. Why? It conveyed the message to every single citizen, "The Great Leader is watching you!"

If one is aware of this concept of images/idols in the ancient world, one is immediately struck at the revolutionary teaching regarding human beings that is coming out of Day 6. In the ANE, not only were human beings supposed to bow down to images/idols of various gods, they were also taught that they, human beings, were created out of the excrement or corpse of a defeated god, and were thus created to be lowly slaves to the victorious gods. In essence, ANE mythology taught that human beings were pieces of crap.

But here on Day 6, we find that human beings are made in the image of the Creator God. Not only are we *not* pieces of crap from a loser god, but we are created to be the representatives and "images" of the all-powerful and good God—we have inherent dignity and worth, and God is present wherever we are. Since that is the case, our job as image-bearers of God is to rule over and care for his creation as his god-like vice-regents. That is a far cry from being taught you are a slavish piece of excrement. To reduce Day 6 to simply be saying, "God created people on the sixth day," and then try to explain "image of God" in some psychological way (i.e. it means we have the ability to reason), completely misses the fundamental truth revealed in the Bible regarding human beings.

Day 7: The Sabbath: God's Rule, and the Cosmos as His Temple

Arguably, the most important part of the creation narrative is Day 7, the day on which God rests. If you are like me, chances are you tended to think that this simply was saying, "After God worked for six days, he took off his gloves, kicked off his shoes, and took a rest in his hammock on the seventh day!" Therefore, since God took a break, part of what it means to follow him is to make sure we "take a break" once a week too and imitate what he did. Well, it shouldn't come as a surprise by now, but that is definitely *not* how the people of the ANE would have read Day 7.

In actuality, Day 7 is the most important day of all. As Walton says, "In the ancient world, 'rest' is what results when a crisis has been resolved or when stability has been achieved, when things have 'settled down.' Consequently, normal routines can be established and enjoyed. For [God] this means that the normal operations of the cosmos can be undertaken."[9] Far from meaning, "kicking back in a hammock," "rest" actually meant something like sitting on the throne and proceeding to rule your kingdom. God has put his creation in order, and now begins to rule it.

But there's more. In the ancient world, gods only rested in one place: *a temple*. Such a view was no different in ancient Israel. Consider texts like Psalm 132, in which God "rests" in his dwelling place. Now, on one hand, it was believed that God dwelled in the temple in Jerusalem—that

---

9. Walton, *The Lost World of Genesis One*, 72.

was his house and his throne. But on the other hand, the people of Israel knew that the God of the universe was much bigger than that. At the dedication of the temple in Jerusalem, Solomon himself said, "But will God indeed dwell on the earth? Even heaven and the highest heaven cannot contain you, much less this house that I have built!" (1 Kings 8:27).

It should come as no surprise, therefore, to find the temple in Jerusalem was set up and decorated to be a "mini-cosmos." It was a representation of the entire created order. Therefore, the temple served as a symbol of God's real house—the entire cosmos itself. And that brings us back to Genesis 1 and Day 7: the entire created order is meant to serve as God's temple, the place of his dwelling—he is king, he has brought order and stability to the cosmos, and now he is 'at rest' and is actively ruling his good creation. And guess what, O person made in God's image? His intention is to rule his good creation *through you*! That's your job…but that gets spelled out in Genesis 2.

So, what is Genesis 1 about? It's not an account of the creation of the material universe. Rather, it is an account of God (A) bringing order, stability, and purpose to the created order, (B) establishing the entire cosmos as his dwelling place, and (C) reigning as king. This is not to say, of course, that God *didn't* create the material universe. It's just that Genesis 1 isn't attempting to give a blow-by-blow account of that.

When it comes to evolution, Christians don't have to fear that acceptance of the theory means the Bible isn't true or that one must reject the biblical account of Genesis 1. The theory does not contradict Genesis 1 for the sheer fact that it isn't attempting to tell us the origins of the material universe in the first place. To suggest evolution disproves or contradicts Genesis 1 would be like suggesting that a scientific explanation of the chemical reactions that go on in the body during sexual intercourse that make it possible for conception to occur somehow "disproves" or "contradicts" a Shakespearean love sonnet. The theory of evolution doesn't threaten Genesis 1—they're addressing two different things.

Genesis 2: Eden

Contrary to the image most people tend to have of the Garden of Eden (some sort of Amazon-like jungle), the Israelites would have interpreted the Garden of Eden as something akin to a walled-off royal garden upon the mountain of a great king. Eden was equated with the mountain of

God that stood against the waters of chaos, and the garden *in* Eden would have been God's royal palatial garden in which he communed with his vice-regent image-bearers, human beings. It was from Eden that the River of Life flowed through the garden, and eventually out to the rest of the earth. And it was in Eden where the Tree of Life was found, along with the Tree of the Knowledge of Good and Evil. The lesson? That life was to be found only with communion with God.

There is also the name "Adam." In Hebrew, "Adam" literally means *humanity*. Yes, in the story of Genesis 2—3, Adam and Eve are two individuals, but we must realize their story is also the story of mankind—you, me, everyone. What happens to Adam and Eve in Genesis 2—3 is what happens to every one of us: we are created in God's image, and because we reach out for what is forbidden in our attempt to become wise without God, we find ourselves exiled from Him and in need of salvation.

To focus only on whether they were two literal people misses the point of the story. We are "in Adam" because Genesis 3 is our story, not necessarily because our genetic code literally goes back to a real couple named Adam and Eve who sinned and contaminated the gene pool. Now, maybe there was a historical Adam and Eve, but "proving" it doesn't seem to be the purpose and intent of Genesis 2—3. In his book, *Saving the Original Sinner*, Karl Giberson notes that before Augustine in the fourth century, there was no clear consensus within Christianity regarding the question of the historicity of Adam and Eve, and that "many Christians viewed Adam simply as Everyman."[10]

In addition, Adam is formed "from the dust." From the very beginning of Genesis, the mortality of mankind is emphasized. John Walton has a very intriguing insight on this point. He pointed out that nowhere in Genesis 1—2 is it suggested that God created a "perfect and immortal" creation that was plunged into mortality and corruption by virtue of Adam and Eve's sin. Consider the following points:

- Genesis 1 tells us that what God created was *good* (not "perfect"), in the sense that it was made functional and useful.
- The death that came about with Adam's sin was physical death to human beings, but that was because Adam was exiled from Eden and had no access to the Tree of Life. His physical body was still natural and thus subject to decay (made from dust), so without access to the Tree of Life, his physical body would succumb to the

---

10. Giberson, *Saving the Original Sinner*, 29.

natural processes of death and decay (i.e. "dust you are, and to dust you will return").

- Genesis 2 also gives a clear description of Man's purpose in God's creation. We're told that God places the man in the garden to tend and keep it. The verb here translated as "to place" is the same verb used elsewhere to talk about the *appointing of priests*. Why is this significant? It tells us that human beings are to not only be *vice-regents* who help govern God's creation, but they are to be *priests* who tend to the creation, make it holy, and offer it up to God. Furthermore, they are to be *gardeners* and *custodians*. Simply put, human beings, being made in God's image, are to be *priestly-kings* who rule over God's creation by *serving* it.

As Genesis 3, the rest of the Old Testament, and our own experience shows, we haven't lived up to what God intended. But Christ has. That's why he is portrayed in these terms: our high priest, the king of kings, and the suffering servant. In Christ we see what human beings are meant to be.

Genesis 3: The Fall

When we come to Genesis 3 and discuss whether or not we should read it as a historical account of the first two human beings and their fall from perfection, there are a number of different interpretations. So, before we move on, let me briefly summarize the main differing views:

Ken Ham claims Adam and Eve were the first two human beings, created completely separate from any other thing in creation, a mere 6,000 years ago. They were perfect, as was creation itself, with no death anywhere. Then when they ate a literal piece of fruit from a literal tree, they sinned, became susceptible to death, and the entire world—and universe even—became tainted with sin, corruption and death.

Scholars like John Walton, N. T. Wright, and Bruce K. Waltke argue God brought about His creation through an evolutionary process that eventually produced people. God chose two of those people (Adam and Eve), bestowed on them His image, and placed them in a special place where they were to fulfill their vocation as priests and rulers of His creation, to care for it and to offer it up to Him in an act of worship. These two people failed in their vocation as God's image-bearers. The story of

Genesis 3, therefore, isn't meant to be read as a straightforward history, but more of an archetypal story explaining the human predicament.

My view is simply that Genesis 3 isn't about two literal people in history. It is a mythological story that explains the nature of human beings. In a sense, *we are Adam and Eve*; God created us, we sin, and we suffer consequences. Now to be clear, I'm not saying there *couldn't* have been a historical Adam and Eve, or Cain and Abel, or Noah. I just don't believe the purpose of those stories was to convey straightforward history.

At this point, let me reemphasize something about the use of the word *myth* and its relationship to history by giving an example from the world of British Literature. One of my favorite poems by Lord Byron is *The Destruction of Sennacherib*. As the name suggests, it is about the historical event of the Assyrian king Sennacherib besieging Jerusalem in 701 BC (II Kings 18—19; Isaiah 36—38). The entire poem is fantastic. It begins with:

> "The Assyrian came down like a wolf on the fold,
> And his cohorts were gleaming in purple and gold;
> And the sheen of their spears was like the stars on the sea,
> When the blue wave rolls nightly on deep Galilee."

Now obviously, this poem is about an actual historical event—*but it still is a poem*. Its genre is that of *poetry*. Granted, we know about the historicity of the event from other sources, but we wouldn't be able to confirm or deny that historicity based on the poem alone.

Now let's take another famous poem from Samuel Taylor Coleridge: *Kubla Khan*. It also contains some very famous lines: "In Xanadu did Kubla Khan/A stately pleasure-dome decree." In contrast to *The Destruction of Sennacherib*, *Kubla Khan* is not about any historical event—it was inspired by a dream Coleridge had. Nevertheless, it still is a poem, just like *The Destruction of Sennacherib*. Now, if all you had were these two poems, with no outside sources to confirm or deny the historicity of either one, there is simply no way you could definitively say one was historical and one was fanciful. And even with outside sources that confirm one is about a historical event and one is not, you'd still say that the genre of both was, in fact, *poetry*.

The same holds true for Genesis 1–11 in general, and here in Genesis 3 in particular. Its genre is *ancient myth*. If the original writer incorporated actual historical figures (Adam and Eve, Cain and Abel, Noah), Genesis 1–11 would still fall under the category of *ancient myth*. And since we have no outside sources to either confirm or deny the historical existence of Adam and Eve, Cain and Abel, or Noah, any speculation as to whether or not they were historical figures is just that—speculation.

Therefore, we must remember that the truth being conveyed in Genesis 1–11 *is not dependent on whether or not the stories refer to historical events*. We have no way of knowing if they do. That is why I see arguing over whether or not there was a historical Adam and Eve is ultimately pointless. There can be speculation about the historicity of two actual people, but there's simply no way to prove it. What is important is what the story is saying about us as human beings.

Therefore, I see Genesis 3 not as a "fall" of the original couple from perfection, but rather as the story of humanity: this is the state we are in. Let's face it, Adam and Eve certainly don't come across as too bright in the story. They appear to be quite naïve and gullible…hardly perfect. They get duped by a lie, foolishly eat from the Tree of Knowledge of Good and Evil, and only then realize, "Uh-oh! We're naked! Let's hide!" They, in fact, come across as gullible children. Therefore, to treat Genesis 3 as literal history is to be confronted with the apparent fact that, for being supposedly perfect, Adam and Eve certainly don't come across as intellectually perfect, much less even that mature. The early Church Father Irenaeus of Lyons pretty much said the same thing in the second century. (More on him later).

If we read Genesis 3 as a myth that reveals the truth about human beings, the story makes a lot more sense. Human beings are, after all, fallible, gullible, naïve. By the time we are old enough to begin to grasp knowledge of good and evil, it's already too late—we have already sinned, and find ourselves at odds with each other, with ourselves, and ultimately with God. This is the state every human being finds himself in. Thus Genesis 3 isn't so much an account of a "fall" *back then*, as it is a description of humanity *here and now*. If Genesis 2 describes God's intended purpose for mankind, Genesis 3 describes the tragic reality of mankind's failure to achieve it.

The good news in Genesis 3 is the Good News is already hinted at when God declares war on the serpent, curses him and subjects him to "eating dust" all the days of his life. That's significant because human beings are made out of dust—because of sin, they will succumb to death.

Furthermore, God promises that this war with the serpent will be waged through the woman, and it will involve the "serpent's offspring" and the "woman's offspring." What "war" is being talked about? Who exactly is the serpent's offspring? Who is the woman's offspring? Understanding this is the key to virtually everything else that comes later in the Bible. We see the first instance of this in Genesis 4: Cain, by virtue of his poor choices, shows himself to be the offspring of the serpent; and after Abel dies, Seth is thus depicted as the offspring of the woman (Genesis 4:25).

From there, there are two genealogies that trace the offspring of the serpent and the offspring of the woman. Take the sons of Noah, for example: Ham, by virtue of his poor choices, shows himself to be the offspring of the serpent, whereas Shem is seen as the offspring of the woman. In the later genealogies of Genesis 10—11, we find the peoples of Babylon, Assyria, Egypt, Philistia, Sodom, Gomorrah, etc. all come from the line of Ham, whereas the Hebrews come from the line of Shem.

This signifies that when God promised to wage war against evil and sin in the world, He would use a particular people (i.e. the offspring of the woman, the Hebrews, and eventually, the children of Abraham) through whom he would accomplish that goal. This concept of the war between the serpent and the woman plays out on every page of the Bible, and finds its conclusion in Revelation, where we find the Great Dragon trying to destroy the Woman Clothed with the Sun (i.e. Israel) and devour her offspring (i.e. Jesus). When he fails, he goes off to "wage war against the rest of her offspring" (i.e. Christians). And whom does he get to help him in this task? His own offspring—the beast from the sea. Eventually, Christ the Lamb and his followers will defeat the dragon and the beast, the war will be over, and there will be a new Heaven and new earth. Needless to say, Genesis 3 is crucial to understanding the current state of the world.

In regard to the penalties on the woman and the man in Genesis 3, the woman is told (A) she will have pain in childbearing, and (B) her husband will rule over her. Similarly, the man is told (A) he will have painful toil in his attempt to produce food, and (B) he will return to the dust (and be devoured by the serpent, if you will). In both cases, we see a similar result. Because of their sin, the process of bringing about new life, be it the fruit of the womb or the fruit of the field, is hampered, and will involve pain. Also, an element of slavery is introduced: the woman becomes subject to man (remember, male dominance is a result of sin, and is not what God intended for human beings), and mankind becomes subject to death.

The theological lessons of Genesis 2—3 are fairly well agreed upon by anyone who reads it. The question that must be wrestled with is this:

"Is the truth of those theological lessons dependent upon there being a literal, historical couple named Adam and Eve who were literally deceived by a talking serpent, and who literally ate from a literal Tree of Knowledge of Good and Evil?" I do not think so.

The thrust of the story is to reveal truths about the state of humanity and the reality of life we all experience. Simply put, we are Adam and Eve. Now, if we were to come across historical/scientific evidence that the first two human beings were, in fact, Adam and Eve, that would not really add anything to the revealed truth found in Genesis 2—3 regarding our nature. To put it another way, the fact that we don't have any historical/scientific evidence of Adam and Eve does not diminish the revealed truth of Genesis 2—3 in any way. The historicity of Adam and Eve is ultimately not essential to the truth about humanity revealed in Genesis 2—3.

Genesis 4—5: Cain and Abel, and More Genealogies

What we witness in the story of Cain and Abel is the continuation of the war between the serpent and the woman—and it even cuts right through family ties. What is interesting, therefore, about the story of Cain and Abel isn't that it is a factual account of the first murder in history—it is understanding the literary artistry in the story that elaborates on the effects of sin throughout humanity.

First, a couple of things about Cain should alert the reader to Genesis 3: (a) Cain is a worker of the ground—*the adamah*—the very ground that was cursed because of Adam's sin; and (b) God warns Cain that "sin is crouching at your door," and "its desire is for you, but you must master it"—this is the same language used of the woman when God tells her that her "desire" would be for her husband, but that he would rule over her.

Given these two things, the story of Cain and Abel comes into better view. Why doesn't God accept Cain's offering? Because it is the fruit of the cursed *adamah*. What's the significance of the "desire" language? It's basically "fighting language." Because the woman gave in to the serpent, there was now a battle of the sexes because of the animosity between men and women; and the end result is the oppression of women.

Here, Cain finds himself in the same position—will he give in to sin or not? Unfortunately, just as the woman listened to the serpent, Cain gives into his jealousy and ends up killing Abel. Thus, the effects of sin can already be seen: it begins with a fractured relationship between Man and God, and then extends to a fractured relationship between men and women. And now, the bonds of brotherly love are further fractured.

This leads to three more similarities with Genesis 3: (A) whereas in Genesis 3, where the *adamah* was cursed, now, because of Cain's murder, he is now *more cursed than the adamah*; and (B) whereas the man and woman were exiled from Eden, now Cain is a fugitive and exile from the very presence of God. Hence, the effects of the sin in Genesis 3 are being extended further. And this leads to one final similarity between Genesis 3 and 4: (C) in Genesis 3, God extends grace to the man and woman by giving them animals skins as garments to cover their nakedness. In Genesis 4, God also extends grace to Cain by giving him a mark. Most people think the "mark of Cain" is a curse, but it isn't. It signifies God's grace to Cain, to protect him from any who might try to harm him. Thus, the over-riding emphasis of Genesis 4 is to show both the further effects of sin and the further extension of God's grace.

The rest of Genesis 5 gives a genealogy from Cain to Lamech, who is so violent that if God took out 7-fold vengeance on anyone who hurt Cain, then He would have to take out 77-fold vengeance on anyone who hurt Lamech. What's the point of this? It's to illustrate that mankind is getting worse, and that Cain and his descendants are, in fact, the offspring of the serpent. Why? Because evil and sin had gained mastery over them.

By contrast, at the end of Genesis 4, we are told that Adam and Eve have another child, Seth, to replace Abel. It is through Seth that the woman's offspring—the people through whom God will work to bring salvation—will come. We see this in Genesis 5: the offspring that comes through Seth results in the birth of Noah, the one through whom God will work to deal with sin. We are even told Noah's name means "rest," and that he would be the one to give "rest from our deeds, the pain of our hands, and the *adamah* YHWH had cursed."

Incidentally...

If Cain and Abel were literally the third and fourth human beings in history, there are legitimate historical questions as to where did Cain's wife come from, who were the people out to kill Cain, and where did the people in the land of Nod come from? If Genesis 4 is a historical account, we have to be honest and admit that it doesn't do a good job answering all the obvious historical questions in the text. Any attempt to answer them must, therefore, come from somewhere other than the Biblical text itself—and that just throws up red flags in my book. If you say that Cain married his sister (as young earth creationists claim), I can unequivocally say that your claim, quite literally, is unbiblical. It's not there.

Now, if when we all get to Heaven, we learn that Adam, Eve, Cain and Abel were real people, that's fine. But we need to be responsible readers of the Bible and stay within the limits of what the Bible reveals. And, given what has been revealed in Scripture, and given that there are legitimate problematic historical gaps in the account, one should tread lightly before insisting that it has to be literal history, when revealed Scripture doesn't even attempt to give enough historical details to back the claim up. I think it is much safer to say, "Scripture here is doing something other than history. Even if there's a historical root to it, the Scripture doesn't attempt to push that point or prove it." We need to be okay with that.

Genesis 6:1-4: The Nephilim

There is perhaps no passage in the Bible that is as bizarre as Genesis 6:1-4: The "sons of God" look upon the "daughters of men" and take as many as they want? As if understanding that isn't hard enough, we are then told that the "Nephilim" were on the earth in those days, and that they were "heroes of old, men of renown?" What is going on here? Most translations make it very hard to understand this passage. With just a few clarifying comments, though, the story becomes very understandable.

First, what is translated as "sons of God" is actually "the sons of *elohim*." In Hebrew, *Elohim* can refer to either the singular God of Israel, or the various pagan "gods." Furthermore, the phrase "son of *elohim*" was also often used to describe kings, who were believed (in pagan cultures) to be descended from the gods, or (in Israelite culture) to be "adopted" as God's son to serve as his ruler over his people. Second, what is translated as "daughters of men" is actually "the daughters of *adam*." Although it simply means "mankind," it nevertheless makes the connection to Adam and Eve a bit stronger.

For the longest time, I thought that the "sons of *elohim*" looking upon the "daughters of *adam*" was simply pointing to the corruption of leaders who claim divinity yet who abuse of their power. History is filled with tyrants like this (Caligula, Uday Hussein, or ISIS for that matter) who use their political power to take, rape, and humiliate defenseless women. Therefore, what we find in Genesis 6:1–4 is a description of life that illustrates how sin leads to the corruption of all society.

I still think that interpretation is applicable, but the biblical scholar Michael Heiser has convinced me that there is something more to it than that. To understand Genesis 6:1–4 better, we need to see it as more or less a counter-narrative to a story in Mesopotamian mythology about certain divine beings called the *Apkallu* who were possessors of great knowledge, had sex with women, produced semi-divine offspring, and shared their supernatural knowledge with humanity. Even though they were punished into subterranean waters by the Babylonian god Marduk, they were nevertheless hailed as pre-flood cultural heroes in ancient Babylon. Furthermore, Babylonian kings claimed to be descended from them.

Simply put, in the ANE, the *Apkallu* were the divine beings who made it possible for Babylon to become great and powerful. What we see here in Genesis 6:1–4, though, is the exact opposite. The writer of Genesis is saying that these divine beings aren't responsible for humanity's culture and greatness, but rather for its corruption and destruction. Throughout the rest of the Old Testament and into the New Testament, this is from where the idea of fallen angels and demons comes from.

Secondly, this helps us understand who the Nephilim are. In Hebrew, the name literally means "fallen ones." What is often translated as "heroes of old, men of renown," actually means "mighty ones of old, men for a name." Simply put, these are not nice guys (certain Hebrew lexicons even connect the term to miscarriages). Remember, just as Cain's face "fell" before he murdered Abel, this group of people are called "fallen ones." Also, there is a huge difference in meaning between "heroes of old" and "mighty ones of old." "Heroes" denotes something positive, whereas "mighty ones" need not necessarily be positive. Hitler and Stalin were certainly "mighty," but they certainly weren't good. There is also a huge difference between being "men of renown" and being "men for a name." "Renown" suggests dignity and fame in a positive sense, whereas "being for a name" suggests someone who is just out to make a name for themselves—it is self-centered and narcissistic. Therefore, whereas Babylonian kings claimed to be the great and noble descendants of the *Apkallu*, here in Genesis 6:1–4, the writer is saying something quite the opposite—the descendants of these "sons of *elohim*" are horrible tyrants.

This can be seen in the way the Nephilim are connected to the giants in Canaan (Numbers 13:28–33; Joshua 15:13–14; I Samuel 17, II Samuel 21:19–22). In these passages, the evil Canaanites (some of whom were apparently quite big) were associated with these pre-flood mythological giants. Therefore, the Israelites interpreted the conquest of Canaan against the mythological backdrop of Genesis 2—6, namely a return to Eden and the vanquishing of the evil "serpent-offspring" of the Nephilim in the land.

Genesis 6—10: Noah and the Flood

There is no need to re-tell the story of Noah's Flood. I just want to focus on the verifiable connection Noah's Flood has to other ANE flood myths, most notably the Mesopotamian *Epic of Gilgamesh*, and the Akkadian story *Atrahasis*. What is interesting with *Gilgamesh* is that it parallels Noah's Flood at every turn. Sure, the dimensions of the boats are different, the names of the people and gods are different, and the time that it rained is different. But the entire plotline of both stories clearly follows the same basic script.

What makes things more interesting is that *Gilgamesh* was written before Genesis 6—9. Some have suggested the writer of Noah's Flood simply took his story from *Gilgamesh*. I think that is too simplistic an assertion. I think this type of mythological story was just common throughout the ANE. Whether or not it was inspired by a historical Flood is not really the issue. The issue here (as in all myths) is, "What truth is the story trying to convey?" The answer to this question comes into focus when one looks more closely at the differences between the two stories.

In *Gilgamesh*, the reason for the Flood is that people were being too loud, and the gods couldn't get any sleep. What better way to get things quiet than exterminate everyone? In Genesis 6—9, though, the reason for the Flood isn't just a little late-night rambunctiousness—it was the kind of sin and evil that we see in Genesis 6:1-4. This theological difference is of supreme importance. In reference to *Gilgamesh*, what would your opinion be of parents who murdered their children, simply because the kids were being too loud one night? That's right, you'd call those parents psychopaths—and that's exactly how the ancient world viewed their gods. By contrast, the picture you get of God in the Noah story isn't one of a murderous psychopath, but rather a God who is moral, just, and who is concerned with righteous behavior. Therefore, it's safe to say that *Gilgamesh* and Noah's Flood are completely contrasting in their theology right from the start.

Another thing to notice is how Noah's Flood has been shaped within the larger narrative of Genesis 1—11. It is a re-creation story: God casts the world back into the watery chaos of Genesis 1:1–2, only to then re-create it, with Noah essentially as the next Adam. The dove that goes out over the waters before dry land appears echoes the Spirit of God going back and forth over the waters before God begins to create and bring forth dry land. The raven that Noah first sends out over the waters in Genesis 8:9 is, in Hebrew, the same word used for "evening," another echo of the original creation story in Genesis 1 ("There was evening and morning").

Beyond the flood itself, the parallels really show up in Genesis 9, after Noah and his family come out of the Ark. First, in 9:1–7 God "re-blesses" humanity through Noah, in the very same terms as he did with Adam: (a) there is a blessing to be fruitful and multiply, (b) dominion is given to Noah, as it was to Adam, (c) there is a prohibition—the Tree of Knowledge for Adam, and the command not to eat flesh with blood in it for Noah, (d) a consequence for violating the prohibition is articulated: death, and (e) a statement of God's vengeance on anyone who harms a human being, and (f) the reassertion that humans are made in God's image.

Second, in 9:8–17 we find God's establishment of His covenant with Noah, and ultimately with all creation. The covenant promise is this: Noah's offspring, all flesh, and every living creature in the world (i.e., the whole earth), would never again be destroyed with the waters of a Flood. The reason why this is important is that, given what transpires throughout the rest of Genesis 1—11, one thing is clear: there is still evil in the world. And so, by the end of Genesis 11, the question thus becomes, "If God promised never to send a Flood again, and if there is still evil in the world, then what will God now do to combat evil?" The answer comes in the form of Abraham. But we are getting ahead of ourselves...back to Genesis 9.

Genesis 9:18–28 contains an odd story about how Noah planted a vineyard, got drunk, and passed out naked in his tent. We are told that his son Ham, *who is the father of Canaan*, went in, "looked upon his father's nakedness," and then went and told his brothers. Shem and Japheth walked backwards into the tent and covered Noah's nakedness. And then, when Noah woke up and realized *what Ham had done to him*, he proceeded to curse Ham/Canaan, bless Shem, and proclaim that Ham would be a slave to Shem. So, the obvious question is, "What is going on here?"

There are two things going on here. First, one must read this story against the backdrop of Genesis 3. Noah finds himself in the same position as Adam. Both start off in a garden/vineyard; both are tillers of the *adamah*; and both do something foolish which results in them being naked and helpless. The point is this: Noah, like Adam, was blessed by God but chose to do a sinful, foolish thing—sin is still in the world.

Secondly, one must read this story in its historical context. Remember, Genesis 1—11 contains the founding stories Moses taught the Israelites as they were leaving Egypt and going up to Canaan. One of the things they were told to do once they got to Canaan was to wipe out the Canaanite culture. An obvious question any Israelite might ask would be, "Why does YHWH want us to wipe out that culture?" The answer is found in this story of Ham, *the father of Canaan*.

Simply put, Ham is representative of the Canaanites. What he did wasn't an accidental "I happened to see my dad naked" thing. "To look upon someone's nakedness" indicates sexual activity. Here, the implication is some sort of sexual molestation. By contrast, Shem and Japheth show respect to Noah and act in a God-like way: just as God covered the nakedness of Adam and Eve, so too do Shem and Japheth cover their father's nakedness. The result is that Ham gets cursed, and Shem gets blessed. Why is this important? Because in the genealogy of Genesis 10 we find that the descendants of Ham are not only the Canaanites, but every "bad group" mentioned later in the Bible: Egypt, Babylon, Assyria, Sodom and Gomorrah, Philistia, etc. By contrast, one of the descendants of Shem are…the Hebrews.

This story, therefore, gives the justification for the Hebrews' conquest of Canaan: "The Canaanite culture is perverted and violent, just like Ham." And the truth is that Canaanite culture really was that bad—it was notorious in the ancient world for the worst kinds of violent perversions. Even among other pretty bad pagan cultures, the Canaanites were even worse.

Another thing the story shows is that the war between the serpent's offspring and the woman's offspring plays out throughout history. In effect, the rest of the Old Testament shows how this war is waged throughout the history of ancient Israel. Empires like Babylon and Assyria weren't just "bad empires"—they were the serpent's offspring. If you fail to read the Old Testament against the worldview backdrop of Genesis 1—11, you will miss a lot. You might understand the facts, but you will fail to interpret them correctly against the backdrop of Genesis 1—11.

So, Was There a Worldwide Flood?

With all this said, the question as to whether or not there was a literal worldwide Flood fades to irrelevancy. Was there a literal worldwide Flood? Probably not. There is no scientific proof for a worldwide Flood. Sure, there are certain things that may point to the possibility of a worldwide Flood. For instance, the mere fact that every culture in the world seems to have a 'Flood' story certainly seems to suggest something. But there's more to the story of Noah's Flood than merely the relaying of historical facts of a global, catastrophic Flood. What the story is saying about God's righteousness and justice, about humanity's wickedness, and God's unrelenting mercy is what is being emphasized.[11]

It's a story of re-creation, where God starts over with Noah. It sets Noah up as another type of Adam, only to end with the sad realization that there is still sin in the world: Noah gets drunk, and Ham violates Noah. Thus, it acts as justification for the conquest of Canaan. With all that clearly in the Flood story, there simply isn't much within the story itself that is trying to convince the reader of it being actual history. Whether or not there is a historical root to the story is ultimately irrelevant. Proving the historicity of the Flood simply is not the intent of the story.

Genesis 11: The Tower of Babel

The final episode in Genesis 1—11 is the Tower of Babel. We know the story, so I will just point out a few key things to note. First, there is a clear connection between Babel here in Genesis 11 and the Nephilim in 6:1–4. The Nephilim episode concludes the progression from Eden to so much evil in the world that YHWH must act (he does so with the Flood). In a parallel way, the Babel episode concludes the progression from God's "re-creation" with Noah to so much evil in the world that YHWH must once again act. The catch is this: now that God has sworn never to destroy the earth with a Flood, how will he deal with sin and evil *now*? The answer comes in chapter 12, with the covenant with Abraham—and that launches into the great historical narrative of God's actions in history.

Secondly, there is another connection between Babel and the Nephilim. The Nephilim were called "men for a name," meaning they were arrogantly trying to "make a name for themselves." In Genesis 11:4,

---

11. See also Dustin G. Burlet's book, *Judgment and Salvation*.

the reason why the men of Babel want to build the tower is *to make a name for themselves*. Thus, the result of both the Nephilim episode and the Babel episode is that God decides to act to curtail the spread of such wickedness: first with Noah and the Flood, but now here with a covenant with Abraham, who turns out to be in the genealogy that goes back to the woman—the woman's offspring through whom God will fight against evil and the serpent's offspring.

CONCLUSION REGARDING GENESIS 1—11

Genesis 1—11 fits together as a well-crafted literary work that lays out the fundamental theological framework and worldview by which the rest of the Biblical story is to be interpreted. It provides the metaphysical lens through which we can make sense of the world around us, and it serves as the backdrop against which we can interpret human history.

Genesis 1—11 isn't trying to give history or explain things scientifically. It is meant to reveal the truth about God, creation, humanity, and His determination to redeem His creation. So when it comes to the question, "Did Genesis 1—11 really happen?" let me ask, "Does it matter?" If an archeologist dug up the remains of Adam and Eve, and we were able to verify their existence, would that add anything to the truth of the story of Adam and Eve's sin, and how we all sin like they do? If we were to find Noah's Ark, would that add to our belief that God is determined to deal with sin and evil? I don't think so. The truth revealed in Genesis 1—11 simply is not dependent upon its historicity, because Genesis 1—11 isn't trying to do history in the first place.

To the point, if one is to claim something is historical, there must be some sort of historical indication that it is, in fact, historical. With Genesis 12, for example, we are told about Haran, Ur of the Chaldeans—historical places that we know for certain existed. We know where they are. And from Genesis 12 onward, we consistently see this in the Bible.

If one moves backwards into Genesis 1—11, though, none of that exists: in Genesis 11 we have the land of Shinar—that's ancient Babylon, so okay. In Genesis 6—9, we have the Ark resting on the "mountains of Ararat"—no one knows where that is. It certainly isn't Mt. Ararat in eastern Turkey. That mountain was only named "Ararat" at some point in the 1500s; in Genesis 4 we have "the land of Nod"—again, no clue; in

Genesis 2—3 we have Eden—I think ancient Israel associated it with the Promised Land, but as far as any "historical proof," it is non-existent.

To insist that Genesis 1–11 has to be historical is to insist on something the Bible itself does not go out of its way to prove and that cannot be historically verified. Furthermore, to *insist* that Genesis 1–11 has to be historical in order to be "true," is actually to mistake "facts" for "truth." Any serious look at the entire Bible shows that the primary way God reveals truth to us is through things like parables, metaphors, literary allusions, and poetry. Even the historical parts of the Bible are so overlaid with literary artistry, we simply have to acknowledge that it is the *Creative Word* that reveals truth and imparts life, and not just "cold, hard facts."

We are creative beings, made in the image of a creative God, and God reveals truth through the creativity found in all types of literature. To reduce His revelation to the conveying of supposed scientific facts is to, in fact, render it impotent and unable to speak to the heart of humanity.

We should stick to what the Bible teaches in these stories: the purpose of creation, the nature and goodness of the creator God, that humanity is made in God's image but is nevertheless sinful, that God is devoted to the destruction of death and sin and promises to do it through the sinful image-bearers He created. Those are revolutionary teachings that can change the world with their truth and power. We rob them of that transformative power by getting side-tracked into trying to "prove" the text's historical veracity, or things like there really was a talking serpent.

THE NEW TESTAMENT'S USE OF GENESIS 1—11

One more thing needs to be addressed concerning Genesis 1—11. What do you do with the fact that Adam and Noah are all mentioned by Luke, Paul, Peter, and Jesus in the New Testament? If Paul was inspired and referred to Adam, and if Jesus was God and talked about Adam and Noah, doesn't that prove Adam and Noah were historical figures?

Such a question actually betrays a modern assumption that only historical facts are indeed "true." That's a rather odd assumption, for most of what Jesus taught came in the form of *parables*. There was no historical prodigal son—that story didn't have to literally happen in history for it to be true. Therefore, to insist that because Jesus referred to Adam and Noah, that is somehow proof that they were historical figures is just illogical, because Jesus conveyed most of his teachings by means of parables, metaphors, and allegories. Given that, if you were to assume anything, you might have to assume they *aren't historical*.

Adam

Let's now look at the places in the New Testament where Adam and Noah are mentioned. If you were to do a word search on "Adam" in the New Testament, you would find the following passages:

1. *Luke 3:36–38*: Luke traces Jesus' ancestry back to Adam.

2. *Romans 5:12–21*: Paul contrasts Adam and Christ.

3. *I Cor. 15:21–22*: For since death came through a human being, the resurrection of the dead has also come through a human being; for as all die in Adam, so all will be made alive in Christ.

4. *I Cor. 15:45–49*: Thus it is written, "The first man, Adam, became a living being"; the last Adam became a life-giving spirit. But it is not the spiritual that is first, but the physical, and then the spiritual. The first man was from the earth, a man of dust; the second man is from heaven. As was the man of dust, so are those who are of the dust; and as is the man of heaven, so are those who are of heaven. Just as we have borne the image of the man of dust, we will also bear the image of the man of heaven.

5. *I Tim 2:11–15*: Let a wife learn in silence with full submission. I permit no wife to teach or to have authority over her husband; she is to keep silent. For Adam was formed first, then Eve; and Adam was not deceived, but the woman was deceived and became a transgressor. Yet she will be saved through childbearing, provided they continue in faith and love and holiness, with modesty.

As far as I Timothy 2:11–15 goes, regardless of Paul's controversial comments regarding women, I don't think anyone would think Paul was attempting to make a historical claim about Adam and Eve. He's clearly drawing a parallel between Eve being deceived in the Genesis 3 story and the tendency for uneducated wives to be deceived. I think the proper translation here in I Timothy 2:11–15 is not "woman," but rather "wife." The Greek word in question is γυνή (pronounced "goo-nay"), which can mean either "woman" or "wife," depending on the context. And the context here is specifically uneducated wives relying on their husbands for learning about the Christian faith, and not someone else.

Paul is not talking about women in general, and he's not saying women have a second-class role in the Church. He's saying wives are to be taught by their husbands, not someone else. In that culture, there weren't public schools in our modern sense of the word. Education was often done in the home, so in regard to wives receiving an education, particularly about the Christian faith, Paul is simply saying, "Let wives learn at home, and don't let them be asking questions during church."

In both Romans 5 and I Corinthians 15, Paul is really driving the same point home. Contrary to what some might think, Paul is not talking about "original sin" in Romans 5. He is not saying, "Because a historical Adam ate a piece of forbidden fruit, that sin came in through that historical act and then somehow that 'sin nature' was literally passed down from Adam to the rest of humanity." In actuality, the original doctrine of "original sin," as put forth by Augustine, stated that sin was transferred from parents to children because when children are conceived, their parents are in the throes of passion, and passion is a consequence of sin. Children are then literally conceived in the midst of a sinful act (cf. John 1:11–13).

As odd as it may sound, it points to a critical problem with reading Romans 5 as Paul teaching there was a historical personage named Adam who sinned, and through whom a "sin nature" was passed down somehow to every single human being in history. It ultimately requires you to somehow explain sin biologically. But that's completely missing the point as to what Paul is saying in Romans 5. Paul has essentially three points in Romans 5:12–21: (1) every human being in history has sinned, and thus deserves death, (2) sin was in the world before the giving of Torah at Mount Sinai, and (3) the work of Christ not only "balances out the ledger" in regard to sin, so to speak, but it actually supersedes the effects of sin and death. Or to put it more in the vernacular: the righteousness found in Christ kicks the butt of the sin and redeems the humanity of Adam.

Read what Romans 5:12 actually says: "Therefore, just as sin came into the world through one man, and death came through sin, and so death spread to all *because all have sinned*." Paul's point is simple: death comes to all people, because in our natural state, we sin. It is in that sense that we are all "in Adam." If you limit Paul's teaching here to simply, "He's saying Adam was a historical person," you're missing the larger picture, namely, his correlation of Adam in Genesis 2—3 to the entirety of humanity. Paul's point isn't so much to locate the *origin of sin* in history, as it is to state the *universality of sin*. We shouldn't read into Paul's statements something that he wasn't saying. Did Paul believe there was a historical Adam? Maybe, but we just don't get that answer from Romans 5.

Someone might say, though, "But Paul references Christ, and clearly he believed Christ to be a historical person, so it is a logical assumption to think that Paul viewed Adam as a historical person as well." Yes, that certainly is possible, but such an assumption is nevertheless reading into Romans 5 something that Paul isn't directly addressing. Remember, for Paul, believers (i.e. the Church) *are Christ's body*. In that sense, redeemed humanity *is Christ*—we are the *Temple of the Holy Spirit*, Christ is the *cornerstone*—just as God dwells within Christ, so too does God dwell within the Church. Why? Because the Church is Christ's body.

One sees a similar dynamic going on in I Corinthians 15. First, there is a clear connection between the figure of Adam and humanity on one hand, and the figure of Christ and redeemed humanity on the other hand. "Natural Adam"—the man of the dust, a mere living being, the humanity that we all share—dies: the natural body runs down and returns to the dust. By contrast, "Heavenly Christ"—the man of heaven, the life-giving Spirit, the humanity we share in Christ—will experience resurrection and triumph over death in a transformative way. Thus, in both Romans 5 and I Corinthians 15, the focus is not simply on the historical person of Adam being contrasted with the historical person of Christ. The focus is on the state of humanity in "Adam" as opposed to the state of humanity in Christ.

What about Luke's genealogy, where he traces the lineage of Christ back to Adam? Isn't that pretty clear cut that Adam is in the historical genealogy of Christ? You might think that but take a closer look at the genealogies in both Luke (which traces Christ's lineage through Joseph back to Adam) and in Matthew (which traces Christ's lineage through Joseph back to Abraham), and you're going to have second thoughts.

Simply put, the genealogies do not, and I mean do not, add up. Line them up, side by side, and it becomes obvious. It's not merely one or two discrepancies—the majority of both genealogies simply do not coincide. As odd as this sounds to modern ears, if Matthew and Luke were trying to give detailed, historical, factual genealogies, then the Bible clearly has contradictions and errors. There's no getting around it. Was Jesus' grandfather Jacob or Heli? How can Matthew have 10 generations between Jesus and Zerubbabel, whereas Luke has 19? How can Matthew have Jesus' genealogy going through Solomon and the royal line of David, whereas Luke has Jesus' genealogy going through another son of David's, Nathan, and therefore not in the line of Davidic kings at all?

It seems we are given two choices: (1) either we insist that Luke's genealogy is completely historical (and thus Adam was a historical person), and then admit we have a host of other insurmountable historical contradictions and errors regarding the genealogy of Jesus in Matthew; or (2) we acknowledge that the purpose of the genealogies in both Matthew and Luke are different than what we in the modern world assume.

It may sound odd, but Matthew and Luke weren't trying to be historically accurate with their genealogies. Matthew's purpose was to link Jesus to the royal Davidic line and present Jesus as the true king of Israel. Luke's purpose was to link Jesus to all of humanity. Simply put, Matthew and Luke weren't "doing history" with their genealogies; they were doing Christology. Their purposes were *theological*, not *chronological*. If that's the case, then our modern insistence that their genealogies have to be historically accurate simply has to be set aside.

Noah

The references to Noah in the New Testament are found here:

1. *Matthew 24:37–38/Luke 17:26–27*: Jesus says the "coming of the Son of Man" will be as in days of Noah—disaster will come suddenly upon those whom God judges.
2. *Hebrews 11:7*: "By faith Noah, warned by God about events as yet unseen, respected the warning and built an Ark to save his household; by this he condemned the world and became an heir to the righteousness that is in accordance with faith."
3. *I Peter 3:20*: Peter references those who perished by water in "the days of Noah," and relates the Ark that saved eight people through the waters with the baptism that saves those in Christ.
4. *II Peter 2:5*: Peter again references the eight people saved in the Ark while the rest of the ancient world perished in the Flood.

In none of the examples is the historicity of an actual Flood demanded to make the point in each passage: (1) In the Matthew and Luke passages, Jesus is talking about the coming judgment that would fall upon Jerusalem because they rejected the salvation that he, the Messiah, offered them. The sudden disaster that would come upon Jerusalem (in the form of Rome's destruction of the city and the temple in AD 70) would be like the sudden disaster that came upon the world in the story of Noah's Flood.

(2) In Hebrews, Noah's faith is held up as a model, along with the other heroes of the faith in Hebrews 11.

(3) In I and II Peter, Peter is drawing an analogy between (A) the Ark's "journey" in the waters of the Flood to salvation with the believer's "journey" through the waters of baptism for salvation, and (B) the Flood that destroyed the unrighteous with the "flood" of debauchery (see I Peter 4:4) that still destroys the unrighteous world.

Granted, these passages *could be* referencing an actual historical event, but one has to also admit the point being made in each passage does not necessitate there being an actual historical Flood. Many times, in an attempt to drive home a point about a present historical event, people will draw an analogy with a famous story. When I discuss the transformation that happened to Jesus at the resurrection, I sometimes reference the climactic scene in *The Matrix*, where Neo gets killed in the matrix, but is then "resurrected" by the love of Trinity and finds that he has new powers with which he can fight the evil Agent Smith. My analogy helps my students understand the importance of the historical resurrection of Jesus, but no one thinks for a minute that I am saying Neo was an actual man and the matrix is a real thing. The same principle holds here. *Even if* there was a historical Flood of Noah, these passages do not demand or prove it.

So, what does all this tell us? There is nothing in the New Testament that demands we read Genesis 1—11 as literal history. If anything, it suggests the opposite. We have to let the writers themselves, writing in their particular setting and culture, determine how we read certain texts, even genealogies.

7

She Blinded Me with Science!

"It's poetry in motion, she turned her tender eyes to me
Deep as any ocean, as sweet as any harmony
But she blinded me with science, and failed me in biology"

—Thomas Dolby

IT'S TAKEN SIX CHAPTERS, but now, here in chapter seven, we're finally going to address some actual scientific questions: What is science? What does the science actually say about evolution and the age of the earth? What are the limits to science? How does young earth creationism explain the scientific claims of evolution and an old earth? Is there any evidence to support young earth creationism?

SCIENCE IN THE MEDIEVAL AND THE MODERN WORLDS

The first question that needs to be addressed is this: "What is science and what are its limits?" Most would say that science is the study of the natural, material world, and therefore its scope of knowledge is limited to the natural, material world. For the most part, I agree. A brief look at history, though, throws us a curve ball, for in the Middle Ages, theology was called the *Queen of the Sciences*. But quite obviously, the study of theology is considerably different than the study of the natural world, so how can both be called "science"?

The simple answer is that in the Middle Ages there was a different definition of science. "Science" was seen more in terms of using logic and reason to understand the nature of existence…but here's the thing, *existence was not seen as limited to the natural, material world.* "Science" wasn't just about understanding *physical realities*; it was also applied to understanding *metaphysical realities*. That is why theology was considered to be the queen of the sciences: it was believed that anything that could be observed and understood in the physical universe only found its ultimate meaning and purpose within the larger metaphysical framework of theology.

One can study the physical properties of something, but one didn't truly understand it until one understood its purpose. This attempt to understand a thing's purpose is called *teleology* (from the Greek word *telos*, which means "goal," "end" or "purpose.") Now teleology and the search for purpose is not a *physical* study of something; it is decidedly a metaphysical undertaking.

The scholars of the Middle Ages were very wise to realize that the mere physical properties of something could not yield ultimate understanding of that thing. Meaning and purpose were purely metaphysical concepts—very real, but certainly not physical objects. Indeed, it was the metaphysical presuppositions found within Christian theology that opened the door to the study of the physical sciences. Medieval scholars held to the theological conviction that God was a God of order, and that conviction prompted them to do further scientific investigation of the natural world—they expected to find evidence of order and purpose within the creation that God had made. And indeed, they did.

With the rise of modern science, though, a distinction slowly arose between the physical sciences (like biology, geology, and astronomy) and the metaphysical sciences (like theology). Eventually, the word "science" came to be applied only to the physical sciences, and the metaphysical sciences were relabeled as "philosophy" or "theology." The ultimate effect of this distinction has been quite significant.

Now, medieval scholastics knew full well the difference between the physical sciences and the metaphysical sciences. They weren't idiots. In fact, they were a lot more insightful and wiser than probably many modern scholars, for they clearly understood that reality could not be so easily compartmentalized or confined to the material world. They saw that there was an inevitable overlap between the physical and metaphysical sciences—that's why they kept the two studies under the same heading of "science." Both studies required logic and well-ordered rational thinking about the reality of life. And here's the thing to remember: they were firmly (and rightly) convinced that the reality of life could not be limited to the natural forces of the physical world. To limit reality to solely what was physical was, in fact, to have an incomplete understanding of reality.

Given that, we should refine our initial question. What we want to know is this: "What is *physical* science, and what are its *limits*?" The answer is quite easy. The physical sciences study the physical, natural world, and their scope of knowledge is limited to the physical, natural world. This is something that modern scientists, medieval scholastics, and virtually everyone can easily agree on. The controversy does not lie on this level. The controversy lies in the question, "Can all of reality be reduced to the study of the physical sciences?" Or to put it another way, "Can something be true if it is not historically or scientifically factual?" If your answer is, "No, if something isn't factual, then it's not true," then congratulations, your worldview is shaped more by the Enlightenment and by philosophical materialism than by Christianity.

The upshot of this preliminary discussion of "What is science?" is this: we can all agree on what the scope and limitations of the natural sciences are. The controversy and confusion arises when we assume that the study of the physical sciences consists of the study of all reality. Or to put it another way, if you claim that the ultimate determiner of truth and reality is the physical sciences, and if you think that the only way for something to be true is to be historically or scientifically factual, then you need to be aware that your claim is not a scientific claim—*it is a philosophical claim that cannot be scientifically proven.*

THE HEART OF THE CREATION/EVOLUTION DEBATE

The reason why I wanted to clarify those things about science is because when it comes to the creation/evolution debate, the two most extreme groups who tend to dominate the headlines in the debate (Ken Ham's young earth creationism and Richard Dawkins' ultra-Darwinism), are ironically making the same presuppositional mistake—and that is what has led to such heated controversy. Let's be crystal clear: evolution is nothing more than a biological theory, it is not a worldview…despite what both Richard Dawkins and Ken Ham say.

When Richard Dawkins tries to claim that evolution "proves" God doesn't exist, he's not telling the truth. He's taking his presuppositional atheistic worldview and trying to smuggle it into the biological theory of evolution. He's trying to hijack a legitimate scientific enterprise in order to validate his particular worldview. That is fundamentally dishonest.

Ironically, though, Ken Ham looks at the theory of evolution and concludes the exact same thing as Dawkins: *if evolutionary theory is true, then there is no God.* Therefore, he thinks that if he can prove the earth is 6,000 years old that it was a literal six days of creation, or that Noah could have gotten all the animals on the Ark, that somehow he can prove the Bible and Christianity are true, and that evolution is false. In an ironic twist of fate, we find that Ken Ham and Richard Dawkins are both thorough Enlightenment thinkers who share the same fundamental worldview. *Both have determined that the physical sciences are the ultimate determiner of truth and reality, and the trustworthiness of the Bible is dependent on whether or not Genesis 1–11 is scientifically accurate.*

Such thinking turns the medieval notion of theology being the "queen of the sciences" on its head. It actually puts theology and biblical studies in a subservient position to the physical sciences, and then states, "The scientific method is the queen of all truth and reality." Therefore, what lies at the heart of the creation/evolution debate is, ironically, the acceptance of presuppositional philosophical materialism on both sides. Obviously, Richard Dawkins does not advocate a Christian worldview… but the fact is, neither does Ken Ham. In the course of the next few chapters that will become obvious. So, let's begin our analysis of Ken Ham and young earth creationism by going back to the Bill Nye/Ken Ham debate.

BILL NYE VS. KEN HAM: THE DEBATE

In February of 2014, Bill Nye debated Ken Ham on the question, "Is creation science a viable scientific theory?" Implied in that question was the "science" in question was that of the physical sciences. Thus, the question could be expanded to ask, *"Do the physical sciences—biology, astronomy, geology, genetics—support the proposition that the universe is 6,000 years old, and that there was a global Flood 4,000 years ago?"* Throughout the debate Ken Ham made the following points:

1. You can be a scientist who works on satellites, invents things like the MRI machine, and still believe in a young earth (that's true).
2. Since you can't observe the past, you can't prove anything in the past; you have to interpret evidence through a worldview.

3. The biblical worldview is based on a modern-historical reading of Genesis 1–11 (what he calls "God's authority"), as opposed to evolution (what he calls "man's authority" that is an attempt to establish an "anti-God religion").
4. All known variations in life stem from the people and animals that came out of Noah's Ark 4,000 years ago.
5. His ultimate motivation for promoting a young earth theory is to combat the moral relativism of today.

Look closely at those five points. They reveal the fundamental problem with Ham's case. Simply put, *none of it is actually based on the physical sciences*—and that was the focus of the debate: do the physical sciences support the claims of young earth creationism? Over and over again Ham would say, "You can't observe the past or prove it conclusively, so therefore I believe Genesis 1–11 to be literal history," and thus he sidestepped the entire topic of the debate. Right from the start Ham ironically admitted that the physical sciences *do not*, in fact, support young earth creationism. He spent the entirety of the debate simply denying evolutionary theory is valid science. But a mere denial of one theory doesn't validate your own theory. You still need to prove it scientifically if you want your theory to be accepted as science.

On the other side, Bill Nye brought up scientific evidence that points to the fact that the earth is a lot older than 6,000 years and all known varieties of species could not have come from Noah's Ark a mere 4,000 years ago. Ken Ham never responded to Nye's evidence. If you go to Ken Ham's *Answers in Genesis* website, though, there are countless online articles that do address Bill Nye's proposed evidence. In what follows, I will proceed to give my analysis of the proposed answers of *Answers in Genesis* to the evidence put forth by modern science. Since Ham's claim is that Genesis 1–11 is a scientific and historical account of material origins, we have to ask, "Are his arguments convincing?" If they're not, that doesn't make the Bible untrue; that means he is wrong. Disagreeing with Ken Ham does not equate doubting the Bible.

Tree Rings

Bill Nye pointed out that there are trees that have 9,500 rings, and are hence 9,500 years old, based on the observed phenomenon that trees get a new ring every year. How is that possible, if the earth is only 6,000 years old, and the Flood in particular happened only 4,000 years ago?

Ken Ham didn't address that in the debate, but in an article from the *Institute for Creation Research* posted on the AiG website titled, "Tree Rings and Biblical Chronology,"[1] Frank Lorey argues that there *could have been* multiple tree rings during wet years, and the "pre-flood greenhouse environment" *could have been* a factor in multiple tree rings every year. He then quoted John Whitcomb's book, *The Early Earth*, in which he said, *"Trees were likely created with tree-rings already in place. Rocks would likely have yielded old dates by the faulty radio-isotope methods in use today. Even man and animals did not appear as infants. This is known as the 'Appearance of Age Theory.'"*[2]

The answer AiG gives boils down to this: "Trees before Noah's Flood *could have* gotten more than one ring a year, and God *probably* created things with the appearance of age." Is that answer observable, testable, or scientific in any way? No. Even if that were true, there is nothing in the physical sciences that can verify it. The standard scientific assumption regarding tree rings is that (A) *since* from what we observe, trees grow one ring per year, and (B) *since* there are 9,500 rings on this particular tree, (C) *then* it is safe to assume that this particular tree is 9,500 years old. Can we go back in time and actually count the rings as they are formed? Of course not. But the scientific assumption of the past is based on something that can be observed here and now. That's what the physical sciences do.

By contrast, the YEC assumption regarding tree rings is that (A) *since* we're beginning with the assumption that Genesis 1–11 is literal history, and (B) *since* the genealogies in Genesis 1–11 total 6,000 years, (C) *then* despite the known, observable fact that trees grow one ring per year, we're going to claim that at some point in the past (although we have nothing to base it on in natural world) trees were able to grow more than one ring per year. That is problematic, to say the least. For the sake of argument, let's say it turns out that is true. It's still not a *scientific* claim, for it simply isn't based on observable, scientific occurrences in the natural world.

---

1. Lorey, "Tree Rings and Biblical Chronology," para. 11.
2. Whitcomb, *The Early Earth*, 40-48.

Ice Cores

Another point Bill Nye made was the fact that we have ice cores that show there are 680,000 snow layers in Antarctica (and each snow layer represents one winter-summer cycle). The AiG website claims that it is the secular scientists who are beholden to their assumptions: they are assuming that the bottom and middle portion of the ice sheet contain the same measured layers as the top portion. They say, "The main assumption is that the earth is very old — billions of years old. They *assume* that the Greenland and Antarctica ice sheets have existed for many millions of years. Furthermore, they believe these ice sheets have more or less maintained their present height in a state of *equilibrium* during all this time."[3] By contrast, AiG claims that if there was a post-flood rapid Ice Age, then the bottom and middle portions of the ice sheet *could have been* laid down very rapidly.

It's clear that AiG rejects the scientific claims regarding 680,000 layers because they claim secular scientists are assuming that the bottom and middle portions of the ice sheet was laid down in a similar fashion to the top portion (and this AiG article says they have no dispute about the layering of the top portion of the ice sheet). Yet then AiG posits their own assumption that is not based in any fact anywhere, other than their further assumption that Genesis 1–11 is literal history. They are rejecting an assumption based on an observable fact, in favor of another assumption based on yet another assumption, with no basis in observable fact. Such a proposal simply is not science…there's no scientific basis for it at all.

The Fossil Record

The third piece of evidence Bill Nye gave concerned two things about the fossil record that point to an old earth is the fossil record. First, human fossils throughout the world have *always* been found in the very top layer of the earth, with older, extinct animals (mammoths, dinosaurs, all the way down to prehistoric marine life) all being found in successive layers, deeper within the earth. Simply put, there has never once been a human fossil found in the same sedimentary layer as a dinosaur. Secondly, based on various dating methods and the time calculated to fossilized remains and the laying down of sedimentary layers, it has been determined that

---

3. Oard, "Do Ice Cores Show Many of Tens of Thousands of Years?" para. 5.

not only did human beings not live at the same time as dinosaurs, but that the time between human beings and dinosaurs was a really, really long time.

The AiG response to this is that when the Flood happened, the fountains of the 'great deep' surged so rapidly that large amounts of sediment from the ocean floor would have been picked up and thrown onto various lagoons and shallow seas, thus immediately burying the strange animals that lived in them, deep in the lowermost regions of the earth. That's why we don't have fossils mixing between the various sedimentary layers.

But what about the fact that human fossils and dinosaur fossils are in completely different layers? To this, Bodie Hodge of AiG responded in an article, "Why Don't We Find Human & Dinosaur Fossils Together?":

> "Biblical creationists believe that man and dinosaurs lived at the same time because God, a perfect eyewitness to history, said that He created man and land animals on Day 6 (Genesis 1:24–31). Dinosaurs are land animals, so logically they were created on Day 6. In contrast, those who do not believe the plain reading of Genesis, such as many non-Christians and compromised Christians, believe the rock and fossil layers on earth represent millions of years of earth history and that man and dinosaurs did not live at the same time."[4]

That is how they see the issue: they start with the assumption that Genesis 1 is literal history, and then claim the only people who don't agree with their assumption are either non-Christians or compromised Christians. They make reading Genesis 1 as literal history the determining factor in whether or not a Christian's faith is genuine or compromised. That mentality should be troubling to any Christian. But as to the question as to why human and dinosaur fossils aren't found together, Hodge proposed a few possibilities in the course of his article:

1. Humans who perished in Noah's Flood *probably* found boats or debris and were able to get to higher elevations before they died.
2. Most of their remains *probably* weren't fossilized—they were *probably* eaten by sea life.

---

4. Hodge, "Human and Dinosaur Fossils Together?" 55.

3. There was *probably* a small population of humans to begin with because rebelled against God's command to be fruitful and multiply. That's why they didn't leave traces of their existence.

4. Since 2/3 of humanity today amass around coastlines, it is *probable* that the pre-flood civilization wasn't spread out over the earth either; therefore, it is *possible* that we simply haven't yet found the places where the pre-flood people were buried.

5. Even though humans and dinosaurs lived at the same time, humans *probably* didn't settle anywhere near where the dinosaurs were, because they were so dangerous.

To my astonishment, Hodge concluded with statements like:

> "As biblical creationists, we don't require that human and dinosaur fossils be found in the same layers. Whether they are found or not, does not affect the biblical view of history."

> "God has filled the world with clear evidences that confirm the truth of His Word and the certainty of the Christian faith. The fossil record itself is an incredible testimony to the truth of God's Word and His promise to 'blot out' all land dwelling, air-breathing animals and humans in a worldwide catastrophe."[5]

Even if you give the benefit of the doubt to AiG's reasons why human and dinosaur fossils aren't found in the same layers, it just strains logic that there has never been even one instance of human fossils and dinosaur fossils to be anywhere close to each other in the fossil record. If there was a world-wide Flood, the fossil record would show all types of fossils, from human to dinosaur to marine life, all jumbled up together. Instead, on a worldwide scale, there is absolutely no evidence for this *anywhere*.

To reply to the glaring lack of any evidence whatsoever with, "We don't need evidence of the fossil record to believe Noah's Flood was true history," is to essentially say, "We don't care about historical evidence when we formulate what we believe about history." It is saying, "Even though we believe God brought about a world-wide Flood in history, we're okay with the fact that there is no evidence for it."

That's what makes the article's final statement even more shocking. After the entire article attempts to explain away the lack of evidence for

---

5. Hodge, "Human and Dinosaur Fossils Together?" 61–62.

Noah's Flood in the fossil record, it then claims that that very same fossil record is an incredible testimony to the truth of God's Word! I'm sorry, but how can you point to the very fossil record that provides no evidence for your claim of a world-wide Flood 4,000 years ago, and hold it up as "an incredible testimony" for your claim? That does not make any sense.

Starlight

Bill Nye also pointed to the scientific claim, based on the measured light from stars across the universe, that the universe is almost 14 billion years old. As said before, it is a scientific fact that light travels 186,000 miles per second in a vacuum. Based on that observable fact, scientists have been able to measure the distance of stars from the earth and conclude that there are stars literally millions, if not billions of light years away from the earth, and that the universe is approximately 14 billion years old.

YEC, though, claims that the entire universe is only around 6,000 years old. So how does it account for the scientific fact regarding starlight? In an article titled, "Distant Starlight," Jason Lisle of AiG says, "... if the light really took billions of years to get here, then the universe (or at least those galaxies) would therefore be billions of years old. But this interpretation clashes with a straightforward reading of the Bible, which indicates that God created the universe only a few thousand years ago."[6]

As someone who has a PhD in the Old Testament and whose undergraduate work was in literature, it is blindingly obvious to me that reading Genesis 1–11 as science and history is not a "straightforward reading" of Genesis 1–11. To interpret it as science and history is to, in fact, misinterpret it. In any case, given AiG's position, the natural question is, "How do they explain the distance of the stars from the earth?" The three responses I found on the AiG website were unbelievable.

Response #1: It was a miracle. God caused the light from the distant stars created on Day 4 to reach the earth simultaneously. If it was a miracle, then it is not relying on the constant laws of nature. If that's the case, then there simply is no scientific evidence for it—there can't be, but that's fine—*it was a miracle!* But the fact remains, if there isn't any scientific evidence for it, then you simply cannot claim this proposal is "scientific." Why would you feel the need to try to legitimize it scientifically anyway?

---

6. Lisle, "Distant Starlight," para. 4.

Response #2: It is a matter of playing with Einstein's theory of relativity. Lisle writes, "We may choose to regard the speed of light as being instantaneous when traveling toward us, providing the round-trip speed (in empty space) is always 186,000 miles per second. In this case, the light from distant stars takes no time at all to reach the earth since the light is traveling toward us. So distant starlight is not an issue."[7]

To simplify this, let's give an example: you shine a flashlight in a (very large!) dark room with a mirror on the other end of the room, and it takes 2 seconds for the light to leave the flashlight, hit the mirror and make its way back to the person with the flashlight. AiG states that Einstein's theory of relativity doesn't demand that the light *had to take* one second to get to the mirror, and then one second to get back. For all we know, it could have taken 1.8 seconds to get to the mirror, and 0.2 seconds to return.

Simply put, AiG rejects Einstein's theory of relativity regarding the consistency of the natural law of light traveling at a constant rate of 186,000 miles per second, and it is claiming, without any scientific evidence whatsoever, that light in a vacuum can speed up or slow down at will. This theory is called "anisotropic synchrony convention," for it claims that light can travel at different speeds in different directions. Let's be clear: if you do away with the natural law regarding the speed of light, then you are doing away with the known scientific fact and are replacing it with a proposal that is not based in anything known in the natural world—that is, by definition, the complete antithesis of science.

What is even more astounding about this is that AiG claims that not only did the biblical writer use this ASC convention in Genesis 1, but that this ASC convention was used in other ancient cultures as well. I'm sorry, I can guarantee you that no ancient culture ever used the ASC convention in their writings. They had no idea that the speed of light was 186,000 miles per second in the first place, let alone Einstein's theory. And they certainly didn't even know what the ASC convention was. They had no knowledge of scientific theory in the first place, so they couldn't have used a convention that didn't even exist at the time. To claim that ancient, pre-scientific cultures used modern scientific theory in their writing is nothing short of mystifying. Yet such claims are just par for the course with AiG.

---

7. Lisle, "Distant Starlight," para. 21.

Response #3: There might be time zones in space.[8] Just like you might get on a plane in Washington D.C. at 6:00 am, fly to Denver, and get off the plane at 6:00 am (due to the change in time zones), the same might hold true for outer space. Stars could be created on Day 4, and then, due to time zones in space, the light could travel through these time zones and arrive at the earth on Day 4 still. But why would God need time zones in space? Is there any scientific basis for this proposal? Is there any proof that time zones in space exist? No, of course not. There's nothing more to say on this point because time zones in space do not exist.

What we see from AiG regarding the issue of distant starlight is basically variations of the argument, "Well, maybe something different happened that does not in any way correspond to what we know about the natural universe. We have no evidence to prove this, but something like this must have happened because we have already concluded that Genesis 1–11 is literal history, and the genealogies total 6,000 years." That argument is not a scientific argument; it is not rooted in anything that has ever been observed or known in the world of nature.

Kinds, Species, and Noah's Ark

In addition to arguing that the universe is a lot older than 6,000 years, Bill Nye also addressed Ken Ham's claim that all the life forms we have today can be traced back to Noah's Ark. By just doing simple math, Nye showed Ham's claims to be impossible.

Now, according to Ken Ham, there were about 7,000 "kinds" of animals on Noah's Ark. In the debate, he claimed that when Genesis 1:21–25 talks about God creating animals "according to their kinds," that the word *kind* is to be understood, according to the modern scientific classification system, as on the level of *family*. To be clear, the modern categorization of animals goes like this: *kingdom-phylum-class-order-family-genus-species*. Therefore, what Ham claimed was that Noah didn't need all the different *species* of cats, dogs, and elephants—he only needed one pair of "cat kind," "dog kind," and "elephant kind." After the Flood, these "kinds" then branched out into the various species we now have today. That might seem like a nice and tidy answer, but we shouldn't forget that, in reality, *kind* is not a scientific categorization of animals. It's a made-up category that doesn't exist.

---

8. Lisle, "Straight Answers to Common Questions," para. 18.

On top of that, Ham and AiG don't even stick to idea that *kind* is the equivalent of *family*. He claims that there was an "elephant kind," but the category of Elephant is not that of *family*, but rather of *order*. So, which is it? Is *kind* the equivalent of a *family* or *order*? Well, thankfully AiG's Bodie Hodge and Georgia Purdom, in *The New Answers Book 3*, clears up the confusion.[9] In chapter 4 of the book, they make the following clarifications:

- A *kind* refers to animals that have the ability to breed together.
- A *kind* can refer to a *family* or *order*, but sometimes a *genus* or *species*.
- Today, the words *genus* and *species* are associated with the Linnean taxonomy system, but that is a modern invention that effectively changed the original meaning of the word *species* and has led to compromise in the church.
- In the Latin Vulgate, the words *genus* and *species* were used to translate the Hebrew word *min* (kind), so the Latin word *species* really meant *kind*.
- But in the 1700s, they changed the meaning of *species* from meaning *kind* to meaning something more specific: "the definition had changed so that, instead of there being a dog *species* (or dog kind), there were many dog *species*."
- It was a bait-and-switch fallacy, so that when Christian theologians would speak of a "fixity of species," they meant *kinds*, but with the new, modern definition of *species*, they sounded ignorant because clearly there is a variety within *species* (according to the new definition), as Darwin clearly showed.
- That is when churches started to compromise and accept things like theistic evolution.

That is quite an answer, isn't it? *Kind* can mean *family, order, genus,* or *species;* modern science used the ole bait-and-switch to make Christians look stupid; and now many churches compromised the Bible by accepting theistic evolution. Basically, "*Kind* can mean anything we want it to mean, and if you disagree, you're a compromiser who has been fooled by secular science!" That is what AiG is teaching in their books geared to children.

9. Hodge and Purdom, "What are 'Kinds' in Genesis?"

For the sake of argument, though, let's ignore all that and go with Ken Ham's claim in the debate that *kind* is equivalent to *family*, with all the variety of *species* (using that secular category of modern science!) came from those *kinds* that came off Noah's Ark, about 4,000 years ago. In the debate, Bill Nye pointed out there are 16,000,000 known species today. If you do the math, that would mean, in order to get from 7,000 *kinds* to 16,000,000 *species* in the span of 4,000 years, there would have to be eleven new species coming into existence every day for 4,000 years. I'm sorry, that is just impossible.

After the debate, Ken Ham took issue with Nye's numbers and pointed out that Noah took only *land animals* into the Ark. This would negate aquatic creatures and insects and would take the number of *kinds* on the Ark down to about 1,000. Given that, the variety of *species* of land animals today are only about 500,000. Therefore, instead of 7,000 *kinds* to 16,000,000 *species* over the past 4,000 years, the numbers are closer to 1,000 kinds to 500,000 species.

If you crunch those numbers, it still comes out to the fact that an entirely new species would have to come into existence every eight years. Sure, that's nowhere close to eleven new species every day, but that's a pretty extraordinary claim in and of itself. That would mean an original "dog kind" would have had to breed so much and gone through so many generations within the span of eight years, that there would have been enough genetic mutations to have produced an entirely new species of dog.

Or let's put it another way. Do you think your two pet beagles could breed so much, and produce so many generations within eight years, that by the eighth year you'd have a litter of Siberian huskies? If that happened, then Ken Ham's claim would be correct. But if you're still getting beagles, don't be upset. All that means is that evolutionary changes don't happen that quickly. Ken Ham likes to say that the only reason evolutionists claim the universe is millions of years old is because they need that long amount of time to make a case for evolution. Well, the facts are in: Ken Ham needs a lot longer than 4,000 years for his claims to be true too… unless you really believe that it is possible for two beagles to produce a Siberian huskie within eight years.

Humans, Primates, and Chromosome #2

In addition to the issue regarding the age of the universe, the other obvious issue young earth creationists have a problem with is the claim that all life on earth evolved, not from 1,000 fictitious "kinds" of animals on Noah's Ark, but from a common primal ancestor. Now I will be honest, I have my doubts that *all life* came from a common ancestor. But let's face it, who hasn't looked at a chimpanzee and thought, "Wow, that chimp's face looks almost human!"? There are obvious similarities, and you don't even need Darwin's theory of evolution to point that out, do you? Therefore, when I read that evolutionary theory proposes that human beings and chimpanzees evolved from the same primitive ancestor, I'll admit it, part of me says, "Yeah, I can see that as a possibility."

The recent genetic discovery regarding the chromosomes of the great apes and human beings further solidifies this evolutionary claim. Basically, there are 24 sets of chromosomes in chimpanzees, gorillas, and orangutans, but only 23 sets of chromosomes in human beings. If human beings and these apes shared a common ancestor, we would expect that human beings have 24 sets of chromosomes as well. But we don't. So why is that? Modern genetics has discovered the answer.

Picture each pair of chromosomes as something like those wooden tongue-depressors doctors use when they tell you to stick out your tongue and say, "ah." Now picture both ends of those tongue-depressors as being painted blue, with the middle of the tongue-depressors marked with a red band. Those blue ends on a chromosome are genetic markers called *telomeres*, and the red bands in the middle are genetic markers called *centromeres*. Each pair of chromosomes contains these genetic markers. Well, when comparing the chromosomes of the great apes and human beings, we find that 22 pairs of chromosomes are identical.

Yet what is found in human chromosome #2 is amazing. Imagine if two of those colored tongue-depressors were taped together, end to end, to where what you have as a result is an extra-long tongue-depressor with blue markings on both ends, as well as a thick blue marking in the middle, and then two red markings in between the blue markings. That is what was found with human chromosome #2. Despite having 22 identical chromosomes, the "extra-big" human chromosome #2 (which is basically the result of two chromosomes from the great apes being fused together) accounts for the vast differences between human beings and the great apes.

Granted, one can say that when God created apes and humans, He just created them that way from the start, with the only genetic difference being that one chromosome. In an ultimate sense, I would agree—human beings are not just a genetic mistake; the process that fused those chromosomes together is ultimately God's doing. But whether he did it instantaneously on Day 6, or whether he did it gradually through evolution over millions of years, isn't a huge issue with me. At the very least, human chromosome #2 proves that there is an undeniably strong relationship on the genetic level between human beings and the great apes.

Personally, I've never understood the charge that if human beings and apes descended from a common ancestor, that somehow "demeaned" the dignity of human beings. If God brought about human beings in that way, then how is His chosen act of creating human beings demeaning? Is literally being formed out of dirt somehow more ennobling and less demeaning than descent from a common ancestor? Or more simply put, is it the way God has created human beings that determines the worth of human beings, or is it the fact that God created us in his image that determines the worth of human beings? I think it's the latter.

If human beings share a common ancestor with apes, it wouldn't shake my faith in God, the resurrection of Christ, or the inspiration of the Bible, because the Bible doesn't address that issue at all in Genesis 1—2. The Bible addresses the "Who created?" question, not the "How did creation come about in a scientific sense?" question. So, however God created and continues to create, I have no problem with it, because Genesis 1–11 isn't trying to tell us the scientific details in the first place.

With the "Who created?" question firmly answered in Genesis 1—2, the "How does God create?" question opens the door for the study of the natural sciences. When seen in that light, any discovery in the natural sciences, far from "disproving God," actually further gives glory to God. This is what Ken Ham is missing. By insisting on a literalistic interpretation of Genesis 1–11, he fails to see that all the wonder that science (including evolutionary theory) has discovered actually makes a stronger case that there is a God.

A few years ago, I took my class to the Gibson guitar factory in Memphis. We've all seen guitars, and those of us who play them get a little more excited when we see them, because we know how to play them. But when you visit the Gibson guitar factory, and they walk you through the process by which they construct the guitars, your appreciation for the end product is not diminished in any way. Rather, understanding the process heightens your appreciation for the guitar, it doesn't diminish it.

Similarly, when we realize that the natural sciences discover the natural processes through which creation continues to unfold, these discoveries should *heighten* our appreciation for God's creation and impel us to further glorify and praise Him, for the discoveries in the natural sciences simply are revealing to us that God is infinitely more powerful, more creative, and more artistic than we previously could have imagined.

CONCLUDING REMARKS

Earlier in this book we saw that at no time in Church history had anyone up to the twentieth century ever advocated for YEC. It was, in fact, a movement that splintered off from early twentieth century Fundamentalism. Many early Fundamentalists took a stand against modern theological liberalism but found nothing insidious about the scientific theory of evolution, or the idea that the universe was much older than 6,000 years old.

And so, the witness of Church history testifies against YEC.

We also learned that the basic rules of biblical exegesis demand that in order for us to come to a true understanding of any biblical passage, we need to read that passage within its historical and literary contexts. When we apply the rules of biblical exegesis to Genesis 1–11, we realize that it is not addressing modern scientific questions that we in the twenty-first century have. Rather, it was addressed to the ancient Israelites who lived in a pagan culture, and who therefore were asking very different questions.

And so, the proper biblical exegesis of Genesis 1–11 testifies against YEC.

In this chapter we have looked at the findings of modern science itself to see that modern astronomy, geology, biology, and genetics show the universe is much older than 6,000 years old and there is a fundamental genetic connection between human beings and other living things. On top of that, the claims and responses of YEC are wholly unconvincing.

And so, modern science testifies against YEC.

What should we conclude? The answer is obvious. The ironic thing about AiG is that, despite their name being *Answers in Genesis*, the reality is the answers and explanations they give in their presentations, their museum, and on their website are not found in Genesis. Nowhere in Genesis is there any mention of "appearance of age," trees getting more than one ring a year, starlight being able to travel at a different rate than the known speed of light, "kinds" being a modern category of animals… the list can go on. Suffice it to say, not only are the attempted scientific answers at AiG not scientific, they aren't even in Genesis.

Since AiG claims YECism is scientific, it is valid to subject it to scientific questioning. If it can't give convincing scientific explanations, then we must discard those claims. That's what the scientific enterprise does: it challenges scientific proposals to see if they hold water. If AiG's claims don't stand up to scientific questioning, it is wrong to claim that rejection of YECism is a rejection of the Christian faith. It is not.

Christianity *is* true, the Bible *is* inspired, authoritative, and reliable, and Jesus *is* the way, the truth, and the life. But AiG's interpretation of Genesis 1–11 is just wrong. If God inspired Genesis 1–11 to be a scientific and historical account of the material origins of the universe, then the study of the material universe would bear that out. But it doesn't. And it's no good saying, "Are you going to believe 'God's Word' or 'man's word?'" Creation is *God's creation*. As Psalm 19:1–2 says, "The heavens declare the glory of God, and the sky above proclaims his handiwork. Day to day pours out speech, and night to night reveals knowledge" (ESV).

That very creation bears witness that it has been around a lot longer than 6,000 years: there are trees that have been around 9,500 years, the furthest stars are 14 billion light years away. When AiG insists that the universe is only 6,000 years old, contrary to everything that modern science has discovered, it is basically saying that God set His creation up to lie to us.

MY SUGGESTIONS

I realize that these are complex issues and many Christians struggle with the whole creation/evolution debate and how to read Genesis 1–11. So, as you continue to work through all these issues surrounding the creation/evolution debate, let me suggest a few things:

1. Come to terms with the fact that Genesis 1–11, in fact, *does not* insist that the universe is only 6,000 years old, and that science tells us that it is probably billions of years old.

2. Accept evolutionary theory as true *at least to a certain extent*. There is a clear genetic relationship between most life forms; change and adaptation certainly does happen *to an extent* in the natural world.

3. At the same time, it is perfectly okay to remain skeptical regarding the finer points of evolutionary theory. That being said, even if it turns out that God created human beings over time through evolutionary means, that's okay. He's God—He can create any way He wants.

4. Regarding Genesis 1–11 itself, accept the *genre* in which it was written is ANE myth. Even if there is a historical root to it all, God obviously did not find it important enough to preserve any historical evidence regarding Genesis 1–11. So don't insist that it has to be historical, and do not make a literalistic reading of Genesis 1–11 the basis for the Christian faith.

At this point you might be saying, "Okay fine, you've convinced me that YEC is a new phenomenon in Church history. Sure, you might have a point that Genesis 1–11, when read in its historical and literary contexts, isn't doing modern history and science. Yes, it sure seems that the scientific claims of YEC don't stand up to scientific questioning. But don't you think that calling Ken Ham a *heretic* goes a bit overboard?"

No, I don't. In the next three chapters you will see why.

8

The Enlightenment Heresy of Ham

"To believe in millions of years is a gospel issue."

—Ken Ham

"Error, indeed, is never set forth in its naked deformity, lest, being thus exposed, it should at once be detected. But it is craftily decked out in an attractive dress, so as, by its outward form, to make it appear to the inexperienced (ridiculous as the expression may seem) more true than the truth itself."

—St. Irenaeus of Lyons

MY FIRST EXTENDED LOOK into Ken Ham and *Answers in Genesis* was the debate between Ken Ham and Bill Nye in February 2014. After the debate, I ended up writing a series of posts about the creation/evolution debate on my blog. As it turned out, those blog posts led to my getting fired. Daring to say that Ken Ham's claims aren't convincing gets you into hot water with young earth creationists who think questioning Ken Ham is the equivalent of undermining biblical authority.

It was after I was told I was not going to be rehired that I started to read up more on Ken Ham and the claims of *Answers of Genesis*. I came to see the fundamental problem with Ken Ham's organization, and YEC as a whole, is not just the claims that the universe is 6,000 years old and that Genesis 1–11 is a "historical science textbook," or even the rejection of modern science, although I think they are wrong on all three counts.

The fundamental problem with Ken Ham and YEC is the utter deception in the way in which historical, biblical, and scientific issues are presented. On top of that, as we will see in these next two chapters, there is the very disturbing fact that Ken Ham routinely savages any other Christian who disagrees with his claims. That kind of rhetoric effectively brainwashes his followers into thinking it is part of their Christian calling to root out compromisers who don't stand on biblical authority. That is why college presidents fire credentialed Evangelical biblical scholars and why headmasters at small Evangelical schools fire their Bible teachers—not because they have denied any creedal fundamental of the historical Christian faith, but rather because they don't believe Ken Ham. His followers really think that to question *him* is to question the authority of the Bible. That is why I have become convinced Ken Ham and *Answers in Genesis* is, in fact, promoting nothing short of heresy.

WHAT EXACTLY IS HERESY?

To understand what I mean by "heresy," let's look at Alister McGrath's definition in *Heresy: A History of Defending the Truth*. Heresy is "best seen as a form of Christian belief that, more by accident than design, ultimately ends up subverting, destabilizing or even destroying the core of the Christian faith"[1] Thus, it is not Ken Ham's specific claims about science or Genesis 1–11 that are heretical—they are simply wrong.

The heresy of Ham that is actively "subverting, destabilizing, and destroying" the core of the Christian faith is the claim that a modern, scientific interpretation of Genesis 1–11 as literal history is fundamental prerequisite for the trustworthiness of the Gospel of Christ. It is the claim that if the universe is not 6,000 years old, if there was no historical Adam and Eve, and if there was no worldwide Flood 4,000 years ago, then that would make God a liar, that would mean there is no such thing as sin, and that would mean Christ died for nothing. Such a message is heresy, and that message has subverted, destabilized, and destroyed the Christian faith of many people, has destroyed careers, and unfortunately, has taken root within a significant portion of Evangelical Christianity.

Some people have questioned my calling of Ken Ham a "heretic" because they think I'm using it in the same way so many Christians have simply condemned the beliefs of anyone with whom they disagree, such

---

1. McGrath, *Heresy*, 11–12.

as when Luther denounced Zwingli over their differing views on communion. That is not what I am doing. I am using it as a way of defining a specific teaching that goes against and subverts the "creedal fundamentals" that the Church has always held. There are a host of things Christians can and will disagree over; there are a host of theological teachings and biblical texts that Christians can and will interpret differently—all that is okay, for they concern secondary issues of the faith.

What the early Church Fathers wisely did in those Church councils was to articulate the creedal fundamentals of the Christian faith, so the *primary beliefs* of Christianity could be distinguished from the *secondary issues* Christians can disagree on. If something subverts those primary issues as expressed in the "creedal fundamentals," we need to call it for what it is—heresy: either a denial of a primary belief of Christianity, or the elevation of a secondary issue to the level of primary belief.

This is what Ken Ham is guilty of doing. When he asserts that a modern historical/scientific interpretation of Genesis 1–11 is foundational to the Gospel, when he establishes an entire organization to promote that idea, and when he proceeds to condemn any and all Christians who don't agree with him as "compromised Christians," he is, in fact, elevating a secondary issue within the Christian faith to not only a primary tenet of the faith, but as the foundational belief on which rests belief in the resurrection of Christ. Such teaching is outside the historic teaching of the Church. What he teaches is not the Traditional Christian faith.

THE TALKING POINTS OF HAM

Nazi propaganda minister Joseph Goebbels said, "If you tell a lie big enough and keep repeating it, people will eventually come to believe it." He was referring to the use of propaganda, and in that respect, what he said can be applied to the tactics of Ken Ham and AiG. If you've ever been at one of their conferences or heard a speaker from AiG, you'll notice how they repeat themselves endlessly and fly through loads of material without giving you a moment to breathe and actually think about what they're saying. Why do they do this? If they repeat themselves enough, eventually you'll believe them without ever critically examining what they're saying. In any case, it is actually quite easy to sum up the talking points of Ken Ham and AiG, for they repeat themselves *ad nauseam*. If you want to know what Ken Ham is about, just look for these five talking points:

Claim #1: There are Two Kinds of Science

Ham claims there are two different kinds of science: "Observational science," the kind done with experiments and that builds our technology, and "Historical science," which Ham defines as beliefs about the past that cannot be tested or observed and are based on one's worldview.[2]

Contrary to what Ham claims, no scientist thinks there are two kinds of science. Yes, some science makes claims about the past, but those claims are based on actual observable evidence from today. Why do astronomers think the universe is 14 billion years old? Because they've measured the rate at which stars are moving away from each other. Since light travels at a constant rate throughout the universe, they can "turn the clock back" so to speak, and using basic math, determine at what point in the past all the material in the universe was concentrated in one place. This takes us to the "Big Bang Theory" (the theory, not the television show).

Ham makes up this fictitious category of "historical science," though, so he can define it as "belief without evidence." He has to define it this way for one basic reason: he wants to argue that Genesis 1–11 is scientific. But he has a problem: nothing that science has discovered about the past agrees with his "scientific" interpretation of Genesis 1–11. Since Ham insists that Genesis 1–11 is God's eyewitness historical/scientific account of the creation of the universe, since science doesn't support his claims, and since he is at heart an Enlightenment thinker who thinks the only kind of truth is scientific fact, he has to make up a new category of science, define it as "belief without evidence" and voila! Genesis 1–11 is science—*historical science*. It is a pure shell game. If you catch him on this, you destroy his entire argument.

Claim #2: Evolution is the Anti-God Religion of Atheism

Ham also defines the scientific theory of evolution as an anti-God, atheistic religion, and therefore mischaracterizes science as a philosophical worldview. The two are not the same. The theory of evolution is limited

---

2. Lacey, "Deceitful or Distinguishable Terms," para. 3.

to explaining phenomena in the natural world. It does not say there is no God. It is too limited and too powerless to even address that question. Ironically, both Ken Ham and Richard Dawkins are putting forth the same basic lie that the scientific theory of evolution and philosophical naturalism are one and the same.

Claim #3: All Geology/Biology Can Be Traced Back to Noah's Ark

Ken Ham claims everything in the natural world, from the fossil record to the variety of species we have today, can be explained by going back to Noah's Flood, 4,000 years ago. We've already touched upon this earlier in the book, so there is no need to elaborate on this claim any further. It is clear that the scientific evidence did not back up his claims.

Claim #4: If You Doubt Ken Ham, You're a Compromised Christian

A fourth talking point of Ken Ham is his continual warning about "compromised Christians." Ham routinely disparages, criticizes, and condemns any Christian or Christian organization that doesn't agree with his young earth creationist claims. He accuses them of undermining the authority of God's Word and actually helping the devil lead children away from God. Some of the people and groups he has criticized are Timothy Keller, N. T. Wright, Peter Enns, Karl Giberson, the BioLogos Foundation, Calvin College, Wheaton College, the Christian singer Michael Gungor, conservative theologian Millard Erickson, the Pope…and yes, even some of the original Fundamentalists who came out with the "Five Fundamentals" in the early 20th Century. Who would have thought that the original Fundamentalists were too liberal for Ken Ham?

Claim #5: It's Ultimately a Biblical Authority Issue

The final talking point of Ken Ham, as we've already seen, is the mantra, "It's not really an evolution issue; it's a biblical authority issue." We've touched on this issue of authority earlier in the book, and it is an issue that will come up again. What they call "biblical authority" leads them to not only reject all the findings of modern science when it comes to understanding the past, but also make some rather questionable, and dare I say outrageous, scientific claims. In addition, it is their take on "biblical authority" that forms the basis of their deeply flawed hermeneutic for reading Scripture, as we will now see.

THE HISTORICAL-GRAMMATICAL METHOD, BIBLICAL AUTHORITY, AND ENLIGHTENMENT THINKING

Ken Ham claims what is really at stake in the creation/evolution debate is the authority of the Bible. For him, that means that Genesis 1–11 has to be about historical and scientific facts. If it's not, then it cannot be authoritative. That mindset forms the basis of Ham's hermeneutic and shapes the way he not only reads the Bible, but also the way he assesses modern science. He believes if the Bible says God created the universe in six days, and if you can total up the genealogies in the Bible and get 6,000 years, then that must be taken literally—case closed. Consequently, if you "put your faith" in things like the constant speed of light, radiometric and carbon-dating, the results of the Human Genome project—then you are putting "man's fallible word" in authority over "God's infallible Word."

The guiding hermeneutic that YECists like Ken Ham says he uses is what is called the "historical-grammatical" method of exegesis. In an AiG article from February 22, 2011, titled "How Should We Interpret the Bible?" Tim Chaffey explains that the historical-grammatical method is how they "try to find the plain (literal) meaning of the words based on an understanding of the historical and cultural settings in which the book was written."[3] The distinguishing features of this method are (A) the insistence that God is the author of the Bible, (B) there is one single, intended message for each passage, (C) there cannot be any contradictions in Scripture, and (D) the Scripture must be its own interpreter.

The historical-grammatical method is right to insist there is an original, inspired message to any given text, and it is right when it says you must read any given passage within its historical and literary contexts. The problem, though, is that even though AiG says historical context is important, in reality they don't take historical context seriously at all.

So, when John Walton wrote his book, *The Lost World of Adam and Eve*, in which he explained how Genesis 2—3 would have been interpreted within its original ANE historical and literary contexts, Steve Ham of AiG savaged the book in his review. His main criticism of Walton's book was it "provided an example of what happens when one gives extra-biblical

---

3. Chaffey, "How Should We Interpret the Bible?" para. 16.

texts magisterial authority over the text of Scripture."[4] Translation? AiG criticized Walton for trying to understand Genesis 2—3 within its historical and literary contexts, because it conflicted with what they "already knew" Genesis 2—3 was about.

But how do they "already know" Genesis 1-11 is a modern scientific eyewitness account of the creation of the material universe? They respond with, "That's the natural reading of the text, based on biblical authority!" But that isn't really an answer, is it? If I ask, "How do you know what Genesis 1-11 means?" and you respond, "It means what it obviously says it means!" you haven't answered my question.

If I then press you and say, "Wait, I'm not sure your interpretation of Genesis 1-11 is right. Are you sure it's trying to do modern science? It reads a lot like *Gilgamesh* in parts," and you respond with, "You're undermining the authority of the Bible!" what you are doing is not defending the *authority of the Bible*, but rather *your own particular assumption* about what the Bible means. You're defending your own autonomous authority, not the Bible's.

For that matter, you're not exercising the proper authority Christ gave to the Church. In Matthew 28:18, Jesus declared all authority in heaven and on earth had been given to him, and that he in turn bestowed that authority on his followers, the Church. That authority was for proclaiming the Kingdom of God and for bearing witness to the Lordship of Christ. In time, the Church compiled the early writings of the first Christians and established the New Testament canon of Scripture. That, along with the accepted canon of the Old Testament, formed what we call today the Bible.

As we've discussed earlier, all Scripture is inspired by God (II Timothy 3:16). Thus, it is *useful* for teaching, correction, reproof, and training in righteousness. Yes, Scripture acts as the *canon* of belief and teaching. But the Bible can never "stand alone" as an authority unto itself. Heretics and false teachers quote and distort Scripture—so how do you know the correct interpretation and meaning of Scripture? You look to the authority of the Church as it bears witness to the Lordship of Christ.

Authority doesn't lie solely in the Bible as it is put on a pedestal. It lies in the life of the Church, in the life of Christians in community, reading, wrestling with, and applying the truth revealed in the Bible to the world around them. It is a living and breathing authority, empowered

---

4. Ham, "The Lost World of Adam and Eve—A Response," para. 3.

by the Holy Spirit in the life of the Church, and the Bible is a vital part of the life of the Church. As soon as you separate the Bible from the Church and put it on a pedestal, though, you are, in fact, turning the Bible into an idol that can be manipulated by the powers of any given age.

As I've said before, the problem of the modern age rests in the Enlightenment worldview that reduces "truth" to "facts" and "objective claims" about the natural world and history. Thus, the fundamental problem with Ken Ham's approach to Scripture, particularly Genesis 1–11, is that his presuppositional starting point is the modern-Enlightenment assumption that Genesis 1–11 is addressing modern scientific questions. For him, in order for Genesis 1–11 to be "true," it must be "true" in our modern understanding of "truth"—that being "the only kind of truth is scientific/historical facts." So, when someone says, "I don't think Genesis 1 is talking about a literal six days, I think it looks a lot more like Hebrew poetry," Ham responds with, "You are undermining the authority of the Bible, because what the Bible says *is true*,"—"truth" meaning, "scientifically and historically accurate facts."

This is crucial when it comes to understanding Ken Ham's take on the Bible. He *says* the goal is to get to the original, intended meaning of a passage; he *says* the way you do that is through studying the original language, the idioms, the figures of speech, the literary genre of a given passage, and the historical context of a given passage—all that is completely true. That's how you strive to get to the original, intended, inspired meaning of a passage.

...*but in actual practice, he does no such thing.*

In reality—as odd as this may sound—Ken Ham's supposed "biblical worldview" is not based on the Bible. His worldview is rooted in modern Enlightenment thinking, and he is imposing those Enlightenment presuppositions onto his reading of the Bible.

...*and he can't see he is doing it.*

Why? Because he has put the Bible on a pedestal and idolized it. He has mistakenly taken the authority Christ has given to *the Church* and has put that authority onto the pages of Bible that he has completely divorced from the life of the Church.

Don't get me wrong, *the Bible is fully inspired*. But it is the Church, the Christian community, that exercises Christ's authority as it reads, studies, and applies the Bible. The Bible is a part of the Church—to divorce the two, to put the Bible on a pedestal, and to assume that it speaks "authoritatively" on modern scientific questions is to, in fact, turn the Bible into an Enlightenment idol.

KEN HAM: THE CONSUMMATE ENLIGHTENMENT/ EPICUREAN THINKER

For all his insistence on biblical authority, Ken Ham's actual presuppositional worldview is that of the Enlightenment. In fact, most people today unthinkingly hold to an Enlightenment worldview. This is why the entire creation/evolution debate is so confusing. Far from being a debate regarding either actual science or the Bible, it is really a debate between—no, not two opposing worldviews, as Ken Ham likes to suggest—but rather between variations of the same worldview.

Those like Ken Ham who are supposedly "fighting for creation" from a "biblical worldview," are, in fact, doing no such thing. They have unthinkingly accepted the fundamental premises of the Enlightenment worldview, while at the same time have rejected actual modern science. In its place, they have tried to argue for a very modern Enlightenment misinterpretation of Genesis 1–11, and ironically have tried to pass that misinterpretation off as...you guessed it, *science*!

We have to realize that the modern Enlightenment worldview goes back to the ancient Greek philosopher Epicurus. The philosophy he started, quite obviously, was *Epicureanism*. Epicureanism taught that "the gods" had nothing to do with our world. Life in the material world is life in the material world, and when you die, you're done. The gods don't interfere in any way, so go ahead and enjoy your life while you can. Epicureanism essentially split the world into two, at least philosophically: the material world, and the spiritual (or immaterial) world.

With the rise of Christianity and the proclamation that God is immensely involved with this world, so much so that he sent his Son to redeem and transform the world, Epicureanism ended up falling by the wayside throughout most of Church history. But then three things happened in the sixteenth to eighteenth centuries.

First, there was the theological revolution of the Reformation. Protestants rebelled against the Catholic notion of authority and the perception that God was a bully in the sky who longed to interfere with your life by means of having to obey the Catholic Church. Second, there was the scientific revolution. The rise of modern science, from the discoveries of Copernicus, Kepler, Galileo, and Newton, caused people to abandon much of what was previously believed about the natural world.

Third, there was the philosophical revolution of the Enlightenment. Philosophers latched on the recent scientific discoveries, and then spun those discoveries to revive the long-abandoned Epicurean philosophy. They basically said, "Science shows that the universe runs on 'natural laws,' therefore, even if there is a God, he clearly doesn't have anything to do with the material world." *And voila! Deism was born!*

Deism was Epicureanism with the language of modern science, spurred on by the revolutionary spirit of the age...but it still was Epicureanism. It relegated "God" to another corner of the universe and insisted there was no room for intervention in the natural world by a supernatural figure. Put that all together, and you get an over-arching mentality that said, "Forget the old way of thinking and doing things! We can build a completely new world order!" This view essentially said, "The natural world, which can be objectively studied through science, is completely different than the supernatural world, which is not based on any evidence, and is just a matter of private belief." The natural world was deemed as reality, and the supernatural was considered, well...not reality.

What ended up happening in America, then, was that there essentially became an ever-widening divide between science and religion. On one hand there were the *secular Enlightenment thinkers* who thought that science held the key to an ever-progressing better world, and that since "faith" didn't really deal with the "real world" and couldn't be "proven," that it was best to forget the notion of "God" altogether. On the other hand, there were the *"old-timey religion" Christians* who viewed science with suspicion, and advocated instead that we needed to get back to the "B-I-B-L-E, because that's the book *for me*, I stand *alone* on the Word of God...the B-I-B-L-E."

Unfortunately, these simplistic notions persist today. Secularists like Richard Dawkins assume the Bible is just a book of factual, scientific distortions that "science" has proven wrong. Biblical literalists like Ken Ham insist everything in the Bible is scientifically and factually accurate, and "those scientists" who say otherwise are just working for the devil.

In any case, this Epicurean worldview eventually produced the rise of theological liberalism and modern biblical criticism. It *claimed* to be an objective scholarship of the Bible, but in reality, it was no such thing. Its starting assumption was that the "supernatural claims" in the Bible were obviously false, so we need to "objectively" find "what really happened." Sadly, such an assumption (or at least part of it) still dominates much of *Christian* thinking: the very assumption of "miracles" betrays an Epicurean worldview. The assumption that God occasionally intervenes in the form of miracles into what is normally a world run by "natural laws" is a "Christianized" and "bastardized" take on a fundamentally Enlightenment-Epicurean assumption regarding the natural world.

This Enlightenment-Epicurean worldview is so embedded in our modern world, that even well-meaning Christians have adopted it, not realizing just how unbiblical it is. The very use of the word "miracle" betrays this Enlightenment worldview. The traditional definition of "miracle" goes something like this: "God set the world up to run according to 'natural laws,' but every now and then He decides to 'intervene' and thus temporarily suspend those 'natural laws'—that's how Jesus healed lepers, walked on water, and rose from the dead."

A truly biblical worldview rejects that way of depicting Jesus' deeds, though. Of course he did those things, but to call them "miracles" is to unthinkingly accept the modern-Enlightenment depiction of a mechanical universe in which God occasionally meddles. The word translated into English as "miracle" is often one of two words in Greek, which more properly mean either "sign" or "dynamic deed." The reason why that is important is because neither of those words carry with them the false Enlightenment presupposition that the natural world is "here," that God is "over there," and that in order for "God over there" to affect the "natural world here," he has to violate some sort of natural law.

The biblical, and proper Christian, worldview does not view God as only occasionally intervening into the natural world via some sort of "miracle." The biblical worldview sees God as intimately involved with His creation at all times. There never is a time when He isn't involved. Therefore, what we have come to describe as "natural laws" are God's consistent way of doing things that we can understand. But Christians do not limit God's actions to "natural laws." We admit that there are other things God does that we can't understand. Enlightenment thinkers call those things "miracles," and eventually regulate them to non-existence. Biblical writers called them "signs" and "dynamic deeds" that further testify to the power and mystery of God and his dealing with the natural world.

Ken Ham doesn't get that though. That's why his presuppositional worldview is not the Christian worldview. Being the Enlightenment thinker that he is, he doesn't really seem to believe that God is directly involved in his creation. Being the Enlightenment thinker that he is, his entire focus is that Genesis 1–11 is a scientific/historical "eyewitness account" of what God created "back then and there." Being the Enlightenment thinker that he is, he views the universe as running all on its own, like a clock, unless God chooses to intervene and do something "miraculous."

Sure, that is where he also differs from other Enlightenment thinkers—he at least affirms God occasionally is involved in His creation, but his belief in miracles is still not part of a Christian worldview, because that belief presupposes an understanding that for most of the time, God is elsewhere, and not involved in his creation. Simply put, the view that God occasionally intervenes is, in fact, based on the Enlightenment understanding of the cosmos. Ham has essentially accepted the Enlightenment premise of a deistic God detached from his creation, but then tries to resuscitate him by insisting that he still occasionally intervenes.

This explains Ken Ham's obsession with trying to defend the Bible, and trying to prove that it is "true." His understanding of "truth" comes from the Enlightenment definition that equates "truth" with mere facts. That explains why so many of his claims make no sense. He's desperately trying to prove the Bible is true by showing that Genesis 1–11 is scientific history, but there is no scientific or historical evidence to support that claim. So he ends up inventing a new field of science, calls it "historical science," and then defines it as "unprovable beliefs about the past." It defies logic on every level: in order to prove Genesis 1–11 is scientific, he has to redefine science as something that has to be accepted on faith *without any proof*.

Sadly, many American Evangelical Christians have taken the biblical story, reduced the Bible as merely a collection of "facts and laws," and have tried to defend the Bible from the very Enlightenment worldview they have unwittingly adopted. Think about it: most churches, when they talk about the resurrection of Jesus, portray it as simply proof that Jesus is God. I'm sorry. To reduce the message of the Bible to that is to give a bizarre interpretation of the resurrection from an Enlightenment assumption of reality.

LET'S RECAP...

That is quite a bit of information. So, before we take a look at a number of specific examples from Ken Ham's own writing, let's recap the basic points from this chapter:

1. Ken Ham's YECism is fundamentally a heresy, in that it is "best seen as a form of Christian belief that, more by accident than design, ultimately ends up subverting, destabilizing or even destroying the core of the Christian faith."[5]

2. Ken Ham routinely repeats a number of "talking points": (A) The fictional distinction between *observational science* and *historical science;* (B) The description of the biological theory of evolution as an "anti-God religion"; (C) The claim that all the geological phenomena we see today can be traced back to Noah's Flood; (D) The condemnation of Christians who don't hold to his young earth creationist view as "compromised Christians"; (E) The insistence that the real issue is one of biblical authority, which requires one to make a choice between putting your faith in "man's fallible word," or "God's infallible Word."

3. The fundamental basis for Ken Ham's very approach to the Bible is that of a twisted view of biblical authority. This has led him to reject any extra-biblical sources, any ancient documents that give historical context to the Bible, and any teaching within the tradition of the Church if they, in his opinion, *go against the plain reading of the Bible*. This is problematic, given the fact that in order to get to the "plain reading of the Bible," one needs to read it in its historical context.

4. Ken Ham's real presuppositional worldview isn't the Christian worldview, but rather the modern Enlightenment worldview that he imposes on his reading and interpretation of the Bible. [/NL 1-4]

In the next chapter, we will look at the specifics of what Ken Ham has actually written in both his books and his blog. We will hear from the man himself.

---

5. McGrath, *Heresy*, 11-12.

9

Ham's Lie: It's Already Gone

"Whoever captures the hearts and minds of the children will rule the culture!"

—Ken Ham

"The surest way to corrupt a youth is to instruct him to hold in higher esteem those who think alike than those who think differently."

—Friedrich Nietzsche

IT IS NOW TIME to take a look at Ken Ham's actual writings, for it is in the reading of the man's own words that one is able to see his heresy in action. In order to shed light on the Heresy of Ham, I will focus on two of Ken Ham's books, *The Lie*, and *Already Gone*, and then analyze a number of blog posts he has written in 2014–2015 alone.

THE REAL ISSUE: IT'S NOT REALLY ABOUT GENESIS!

Back in 1987, when Ken Ham wrote *The Lie*, the initial cover was that of an evil-looking serpent coiled around a green apple with the word "Evolution" written on it. Ham has called the book "the textbook of the AiG ministry," and has said that *The Lie* is the "core message" of the AiG ministry. *The Lie* is essentially the "genesis" of Ken Ham's movement and the AiG organization. In it, Ken Ham laid out the rationale and talking points he has now used for the past 25 years. As we will see, all the main arguments he uses in blog posts today, as well as his books over the years, can all be traced back to Ken Ham's book, *The Lie*.

The driving force behind *The Lie* is not a desire to make sure we're reading the Bible correctly. In actuality, the driving force of Hamite theology is that Ken Ham sees himself as a crusader in a culture war. For him, the Bible is just his chief weapon to defeat the forces of liberalism, secularism and the Democrats. The real issues for Ken Ham are articulated on every page: homosexuality, abortion, unwillingness to obey those in authority, unwillingness to work, the abandonment of traditional marriage, pornography, "aggressive marketing campaigns by atheists promoting their religion," and yes, even the abandonment of clothing.[1]

Now it is true, many of these are very controversial societal issues that need to be addressed. I, too, am alarmed at the moral decay in our society. Where Ken Ham goes wrong, though, is that he insists the *reason* why these have become issues in our society is *because* people don't accept Genesis 1-11 as a scientific and historical account of the origin of the material universe.

As far back as 1987, Ken Ham's battle plan was clear: "Whoever captures the hearts and minds of the children will rule the culture!"[2] This explains why so much of the AiG material, both in their publications and presentations, is directly aimed at children and comes in the form of cartoons. His logic is simple: (A) indoctrinate children to believe young earth creationism is true and evolution is evil, (B) they will grow up to be moral people, who will thus (C) be able to get in positions of influence and power so they can rule the culture.

Ironically, Ken Ham seems to think that the goal of Christianity is to "rule over the nations," much in the same way the Jews of Jesus' day were hoping the Messiah would crush the nations and rule from Jerusalem. Yet Jesus' words to his disciples turn all that dominion thinking on its head: *don't* dominate and be tyrannical like the Gentiles. If you want to be great in the Kingdom of God, you must become a servant, you much become like a little child, not indoctrinate them so they can "rule the culture."

1. Ham, *The Lie*, 27–29.
2. Ham, *The Lie*, 31.

The Lie's Disregard for the Truth: a la Nietzsche and Goebbels

The Lie is also shocking in its apparent disregard for actual truth. Ham states: "It is not a matter of whether one is biased or not. It is really a question of which bias is the best bias with which to be biased."[3] Simply put, Ham believes it is one's biases (or what he often calls, "starting points") that should shape interpretation of the evidence. The evidence is just there, waiting for the right bias to interpret it. This is a tremendously shocking statement, for it obliterates the very notion of truth.

Ham's statement actually echoes the worldview and philosophy of Friedrich Nietzsche, who believed that there was no such thing as actual "truth." Instead, Nietzsche saw all claims of "truth" as simply masked attempts to gain power. Claims of truth were nothing short of power-plays. Likewise, it was Joseph Goebbels who said that eventually, if you keep repeating a lie long enough, eventually people come to believe it is true.

What we see with Ken Ham are the philosophies of these two men at work. Even though he claims he is proclaiming the truth, he openly admits his biases are driving his agenda, and that fidelity to his bias is more important than actual truth. In addition, he has used a number of specific talking points over and over again for the past 30 years that his followers just unthinkingly take as truth. He does this to gain influence and power so he can exercise dominion over the culture to shape it in the way he thinks best. It is essentially a "Christianized" version of Nazi propaganda tactics, with a dash of nihilism to make it go down smoothly.

The Lie: An Exercise in Humean Skepticism

Another man Ken Ham resembles is the eighteenth-century philosopher and skeptic David Hume. This can be most clearly seen in his claims that you can't know anything in the past for certain, his rejection of the claims of modern science, and his attempt to declare Genesis 1–11 as "historical science." The reason why Ham rejects the claims of the theory of evolution is, as he says, scientists weren't there when the world was created, so how could they know how it happened? He states:

> "The only way anyone could always be sure of arriving at the right conclusion about anything, including origins, depends upon his knowing everything there is to know. Unless he knew

---

3. Ham, *The Lie*, 37.

that every bit of evidence was available, he would never really be sure that any of his conclusions were right."[4]

Ken Ham believes there's no way to be sure that the claims of evolution are true because the scientists who make those claims never have actually observed the creation of the universe or the evolution of one creature into another in real time. Their claims are nothing more than the beliefs, biases, and, what Ham calls, the "historical science" of fallible men. Therefore, he rejects it in favor of the "historical science" of Genesis 1–11, which is, he claims, more reliable because it is God's eyewitness account of the creation of the universe, and God doesn't lie.

Note that Ken Ham has completely rejected all of scientific inquiry. After all, if he rejects evolution because scientists weren't there *back then* to observe the initial creation of the universe, then to be consistent he would have to admit that *every* scientific observation is technically something that has happened *in the past*. As soon as scientists observe something in the present, the phenomenon they are theorizing about has already happened. The stars we see in the night sky—the way we are seeing them in the present—is what they were like in the past, because of the time it takes starlight to travel from the distant star to us here on earth.

The fact is, scientists speculate on what happened *in the past* based on the natural phenomena they observe *in the present*. That's how science works—it's called "cause and effect." It is what makes it possible for scientists to make predictions and validate their hypotheses. But in the case of evolution, Ham rejects all of it because we can't see "an ape evolve into a human" in real time. When you point to actual, real-time observations of evolution in action, Ken Ham will say, "Oh, that little change may occur, but that monkey is still a monkey, not a man. You're pointing out a small step, but that's not a big step from monkey to man." But evolution claims that enough "small steps" over time eventually make big changes.

Ken Ham will never accept that, though, because he fundamentally rejects the notion of cause and effect. This is the kind of hyper-skepticism that David Hume advocated. If you threw a ball through a window and the window shattered, Hume would say, "Well, it certainly *looks as if* your throwing of the ball caused the window to shatter, but for all you know, there could have been something else that happened at the precise moment the ball was about to hit the window that really caused the window

---

4. Ham, *The Lie*, 49.

to shatter. You can't even really trust your sensory perception. Therefore, you can never be certain of anything in the natural world."

Such is Ken Ham's attitude toward science: a thorough rejection of any claims that have to do with the past, and a complete distrust of the ability of human beings to use their senses to understand the world.

The Lie: About the Genome

This leads us to a truly astounding claim made by Ken Ham in regard to the Human Genome Project, quite possibly the most significant scientific breakthrough in history. It has opened the door to the study of the very building blocks of life itself. Francis Collins, an Evangelical Christian and the former director of the National Institutes of Health, was able to map out the entire human genome, as well as the genome of countless other species. The significance of this is that it makes it possible for us to understand more about the evolution of life here on earth.

Francis Collins also started the BioLogos Foundation, an organization that seeks to reconcile science and the Christian faith. Collins is a theistic evolutionist who believes evolution is the process by which God has created, and continues to create, the world. Ham rages against BioLogos routinely on his blog. That is why it is so astounding to find that he makes a most jaw-dropping claim about the human genome project in his book, *The Lie*. He says, "The results of the Human Genome Project are an example of observational science confirming the Bible's history."[5] What makes this astounding is that is precisely what it doesn't claim.

The reason Collins holds to the theory of theistic evolution is partly because of his work in the Human Genome Project. He has conclusively proven that it is impossible that the 7 billion people who live on the earth today could have all descended from a single couple a mere 6,000 years ago. Instead, Collins argues that the genetic evidence indicates that the entire human race could "trace its roots" back to an original group of about 10,000 humans who lived about 100,000 years ago. If that is the case, then how in the world can Ken Ham hold up the findings of the Human Genome Project as "proof" of young earth creationism, all the while accusing the man who spear-headed the project as a "compromised Christian"?

---

5. Ham, *The Lie*, 61.

Here's the answer. Ham starts by stating that evolutionary theory claimed that there were many different races and is inherently racist. Then, after pointing out that the Human Genome Project conclusively proves all human beings are genetically related and are therefore one race, Ham confidently proclaims that proves evolutionary theory is racist and the Bible is true: we're all one race, descended from Adam and Eve!

There are two major problems with Ham's claim. First, evolution doesn't claim human beings were of different races. Those claims were made long before Darwin came onto the scene. Ironically, many of those claims were made by people who tried to use the Bible to justify such claims. Darwin grew up in a rather racist culture. Therefore, when evolution was put forth, an already racist European culture tried to use it (as it had done with the Bible) to justify its racist views.

Second, although the Human Genome Project shows how genetically related all human beings are, it most certainly does not prove all human beings descended from a solitary couple a mere 6,000 years ago. Ken Ham has simply not only lied about the actual claims of evolution, he has also mischaracterized the actual findings of the Human Genome Project in an attempt to claim that it really proves the claims of young earth creationism. It is deception, pure and simple.

The Lie: About the Flood Account

Another issue Ham deals with in *The Lie* is the account of Noah's Flood and the fact that there are similar 'Flood' stories in the ANE, like *The Epic of Gilgamesh*. His explanation for the existence of these 'Flood' stories is thoroughly unsubstantiated and provably false. He first claims that the people at the Tower of Babel had the "original account" of the Flood, but that as the people dispersed from Babel, "they changed the accounts, resulting in elements similar to the biblical account but with all sorts of embellishments and fictions that were not part of the original account. The original record, which has not changed, is in the Bible."[6]

How does he know this? The simple answer is, he doesn't. He has made it up. He starts with the assumption that the Flood account in Genesis was some sort of pure, undefiled account of a historical event they had perfectly preserved at Babel. He then imagines that somehow, the ancestors of Abraham, who would have been purely pagan, were able

---

6. Ham, *The Lie*, 61.

to "perfectly preserve" the original text, whereas the other pagans who dispersed from Babel altered and embellished copies of it. But there is no evidence for any of that anywhere. What Ken Ham says in order to back up his claim Genesis 6—9 is historical is something thoroughly unhistorical and imaginary.

The facts regarding the different ANE flood accounts are that stories like *Gilgamesh* are actually older than the Flood story of Genesis 6—8. Now, if you understand that the material in Genesis 1-11 falls under the genre category of myth, this makes sense. God inspired Moses to convey the truth about Himself, mankind, and creation, using the concepts, symbolism, ideas, and literary genre of myth to convey that truth. It would make perfect sense for God to do that—it was the genre they would have been familiar with.

That provides a problem for Ken Ham, though. For him, myth means "untruth." He insists Genesis 1-11 is actual history, and that Genesis 6—8 is the "original undefiled flood account," in contrast to other ones like *The Epic of Gilgamesh*. So how does he explain the similarities between Noah's flood and ANE myths? He says: "When this idea is closely investigated, we find that the Babylonian stories are rather grotesque and quite unbelievable in almost every aspect. When we read the biblical account of the Flood, it is certainly the believable account because it is the original one."[7]

I just have to ask: how is Gilgamesh's getting all the animals in a boat "grotesque and unbelievable," but Noah's doing the exact same thing not? And what are we to make of Ham's claim that Genesis 6—8 "is certainly the believable account because it is the original one"? It is believable because it is the original, and it is the original because…the other ANE myths are unbelievable, and this one isn't? This is circular logic, plain and simple.

Ham concludes his assessment of the other ANE flood stories with a host of unsubstantiated claims that further show his ignorance of basic biblical knowledge. He states:

> "When one thinks about it, stories handed down generation after generation that are not carefully preserved—particularly if they are handed down by word of mouth—do not improve with age. The truth is lost, and the stories degenerate markedly. The biblical records have been handed down in written form, carefully preserved by the superintendency of God, and have

7. Ham, *The Lie*, 62.

not been corrupted. The Babylonian stories, which only reflect the true record of the Bible, are the ones that have become corrupted, due to the limitations of human fallibility."[8]

First off, Ham's comments betray a complete ignorance of ancient culture. Ancient culture was largely an oral culture. They didn't have computers or copy machines that made mass production of written texts available. Being an oral culture, they were able to pass down their traditions and their stories orally with tremendous accuracy and precision, and because these stories were so well known in communities, if anyone radically changed something, the entire community (who knew the story as well) would be able to call him on it and correct him.

The difference between the Flood story in Genesis and the story in Gilgamesh isn't that Genesis 6—9 was perfectly preserved in written form, whereas Gilgamesh was a hopelessly altered oral story, and thus ended up getting the facts wrong. Both were originally passed down orally, and later written down. The reason why they're different is because they were teaching different things about the nature of God/the gods and the state of human beings. Different theology accounts for the differences in story, not a mishandling of historical facts.

In addition, Ham is flat out wrong when he says the biblical records have been handed down in written form. Ancient Israel was part of the ancient world that was an oral culture. His claim that they had the "original written account" at the Tower of Babel is entirely unsubstantiated and unverifiable. There is no evidence whatsoever for his claim. In actuality, even though the Torah has its origin in Moses during the Exodus (circa 1500-1200 BC), the evidence is that the Torah, along with much of the narrative sections of the Old Testament, was written down in its present form around the time of the Babylonian exile, during the 6th century BC. There was no pristinely written document of Genesis 1–11 from the time of the Tower of Babel that the ancestors of Abraham, and later the people of Israel, were able to preserve "perfectly." That is pure fiction.

Ham eventually finds time to address scientific evidence regarding whether there was a world-wide catastrophic Flood. What he says in order to support his young earth view, though, is not only illogical, it also subverts his own fictitious categories of "observational" and "historical" science. He states: "Observational science in regard to geology confirms the Bible's account of the Flood because it is obvious that massive

8. Ham, *The Lie*, 62.

fossil-bearing sedimentary layers (found in different continents) had to be laid down catastrophically, not slowly over millions of years."[9]

First, notice what Ham is claiming. He points to the fact fossils are found throughout the world, but then concludes the only way these fossils could have been laid down was to be by means of one catastrophic Flood 4,000 years ago. Ham has never considered there could have been local floods throughout the world that could lay down fossils as well. A world-wide Flood is not the only kind of flood that can lay down fossils.

Secondly, Ham claims *observational science* confirms the biblical account of the flood. Yet Ham routinely says Genesis 1–11 is *historical science* based on biased presuppositions about the past that cannot be tested and...*observed*. So, he rejects modern geology, biology, and astronomy when it comes to the age of the earth, on the grounds there is a difference between "observational" and "historical" science, but then turns around, points to observed fossils in sedimentary layers, and claims those "observed things" somehow confirm historical science. But by his own definition of "historical science," that is an impossibility.

The Presuppositional Apologetics of The Lie

One of the catch phrases at AiG is *presuppositional apologetics*. It is Ken Ham's own brand of apologetics that AiG wants churches and Christian schools to employ in order to indoctrinate their children in YEC. It simply is a way to do an end run around actually having to think through and interact with any actual scientific evidence. And let's be clear, "presuppositional apologetics" is aimed at dealing with Genesis 1–11, nothing else. What it boils down to is simple: "Don't bother me with science, Genesis 1–11 is God's eyewitness account of origins. God said it, so I believe it has to be history!" That's it. If you don't believe me, here's Ken Ham's own words about how the "presuppositional apologetics" method could be used in science class:

> "When using an evidential approach, the questions and comments from students would be something like, 'What about carbon-14 dating?' 'Haven't scientists proven fossils are millions of years old?' 'Surely given enough time anything can happen.' However, using the presuppositional approach (which brings the issues to the fundamental belief level), it was exciting to see

---

9. Ham, *The Lie*, 64.

a dramatic change in the nature of the questions asked: 'Where did God come from?' 'How do you know the Bible can be trusted and is true?' 'Who wrote the Bible?' 'Why is Christianity better than Buddhism?' The students started to see the real issue."[10]

There you have it from Ham's own pen: the problem with science is if you look at evidence, *you have to deal with the evidence,* and that just won't do because the evidence clearly points to millions of years. Ken Ham therefore suggests turning science class into "belief class." Who wouldn't want their children in Sophomore Biology class to have a lesson on why Christianity is better than Buddhism? The "presuppositional apologetics" approach turns not only Christianity, but science as well, into a matter of blind faith.

What is so astounding is that he is so blatant about it, and still part of the Evangelical world just accepts what he says. Consider Ham's response to a certain science textbook that attempted to explain precisely what science is. The textbook said the following:

> "Science requires repeatable observations and testable hypotheses. These standards restrict science to a search for natural causes for natural phenomena. For example, science can neither prove nor disprove that unobservable or supernatural forces cause storms, rainbows, illnesses, or cures of disease. Supernatural explanations of natural events are simply outside the bounds of science."[11]

A rational person understands this. Science deals with natural phenomena, and therefore is incapable of even addressing the issue of whether or not there is a God. It cannot prove or disprove the supernatural, therefore science is not a threat to belief in God. Ken Ham doesn't see it that way, though. He takes issue with the very definition of science and says: "Who decided that science could be defined this way? Those who do not believe in God and who arbitrarily defined science to eliminate the supernatural. . . .This is pure atheism. . . . these schools have become, by and large, temples of atheism."[12]

Wow! Ken Ham rejects modern science *because it doesn't include supernatural explanations.* He actually takes a quote that states science is unable to prove or disprove God and interprets it as an attempt to

---

10. Ham, *The Lie,* 67.
11. Ham, *The Lie,* 70.
12. Ham, *The Lie,* 70.

"eliminate the supernatural." He equates modern science with atheism and rebellion against God. He actually claims that the only reason why people even came up with the theory of evolution is that it is "a religion that enables people to justify writing their own rules."[13] And that leads us to his next topic: Ken Ham's real agenda.

The Lie's Focus: Societal Rebellion and the Culture War

Such a description of science and a characterization of the "rebellious motives" for the "religion of evolution/atheism" feeds right into Ken Ham's real concern: the culture war. As he sees it, the "origins issue" and the rejection of understanding Genesis 1–11 as God's eyewitness historical account is directly connected to why our society is going to hell in a handbasket: divorce, gay marriage, "abortion, sexual deviancy, parental authority, and so on."[14] That is why he sees the creation/evolution debate as the front lines of the culture war. That is why he clearly makes his battle cry in *The Lie*: "An all-out attack on evolutionary thinking is possibly the only real hope our nations have of rescuing themselves from an inevitable social and moral catastrophe."[15]

Ken Ham is convinced that the motive for coming up with the theory of evolution and the claim that the universe is millions of years old *is not* wanting to learn more about the natural world. The real motive, according to Ken Ham, is nothing short of man's rebellion against God:

> "They want evolution and millions of years taught as fact and the belief in creation banished because they…want to be a law unto themselves. They want to maintain the rebellious nature they have inherited from Adam, and they will not accept the authority of the One who, as Creator and lawgiver, has the right to tell them exactly what to do."[16]

That's right. The person who says, "Based on the fact that light moves at a constant speed throughout the universe, we can calculate that the universe is about 14 billion years old," that person is really saying, "I hate God, and want to live a life of debauchery!" In the world of Ken Ham, that makes complete sense, just as much sense as insisting that it is

---

13. Ham, *The Lie*, 69.
14. Ham, *The Lie*, 80.
15. Ham, *The Lie*, 110.
16. Ham, *The Lie*, 108.

a matter of salvation to mentally assert that an original couple lived at the same time as dinosaurs, that Cain married his sister, and that Noah built a big boat and put all the animals in creation on it.

Aside from that bizarre notion, Ken Ham has an equally bizarre take on the issue of women's fashion: "Many Christian women wear clothes that really accentuate their sexuality. And many a roving eye follows every movement. But what is happening? Men are committing adultery in their hearts—adultery for which they and the women will have to answer."[17]

Now, I agree that what we see in pop culture today, from Miley Cyrus, Lady Gaga, to Nikki Minaj, is the oversexualization of women. Sex is displayed everywhere in our society, and that further encourages people to just give into their "natural urges" and not practice self-control. But look what Ken Ham is doing here. He is taking Jesus' words about "if a man lusts after a woman he is committing adultery in his heart," and he is using it as a way to *blame women* for when men lust.

Jesus wasn't trying to make it harder for men not to sin by adding a tougher law. He was addressing self-righteous Pharisees who thought because they were *outwardly* moral and doing the right thing, that they were somehow sinless and righteous. Jesus was simply calling them to account: every man lusts after women at some point, so just because you don't actually sleep around, don't deceive yourself into thinking you're sinless.

Ken Ham doesn't seem to get that, though. Because he interprets Jesus' words through an entirely pharisaic and legalistic lens, he concludes, "That's another sin we have to watch out for! We must obey and not do that!" The result is that there is a clear implication (whether or not Ham intends to say this) that ultimately the one responsible for men lusting is *the woman*. In a touch of extreme irony, we can almost hear Adam in Ham's comments: *"The woman made me do it."*

The Lie Has Kissed Dating Methods Goodbye

In *The Lie*, after rejecting all scientific dating methods that indicate the earth is very old (which would be all of them), Ham then makes a very peculiar comment: "Every single dating method (outside of Scripture) is based on fallible assumptions."[18] This is peculiar for two reasons. First,

---

17. Ham, *The Lie*, 104.
18. Ham, *The Lie*, 127.

I was unaware that there were any scientific, geological dating methods proposed in Scripture! Yet Ham throws it in there, and just moves on. Second, what are the "fallible assumptions" in regard to carbon-14 dating? This mantra is commonplace for AiG. Ham says:

> "Why would any Christian want to take man's fallible dating methods and use them to impose an idea on the infallible Word of God? Christians who accept billions of years are…saying that man's word is infallible but God's Word is fallible! Once you have told people to accept man's dating methods and thus not to take the first chapters of Genesis as they are written, you have effectively undermined the Bible's authority!"[19]

Ask yourself, "What 'fallible word' is Ham talking about?" That the speed of light is consistent in a vacuum? That the half-life of elements like carbon-14 is constant? That there is a consistency to natural laws that makes it possible to do science in the first place? Should we consider gravity "man's fallible word" because Jesus ascended into Heaven? Should we consider heliocentricity "man's fallible word" because the Bible says the sun goes around the earth?

If Ham really believed what he was saying, he would have to deny gravity and the heliocentric universe. But the fact is, he only applies such a claim to Genesis 1–11. Why? Because *he is the one who is holding on to a fallible assumption*—and no amount of scientific evidence, solid biblical exegesis, or historical facts of Church history is ever going to change his mind. His only chance to keep you beholden to what he is claiming is to scare you by saying, "If you don't believe what I'm saying about Genesis 1–11, then you've undermined the authority of the Bible!"

Now Ham correctly points out that evolution is not found in the Bible: "Let's be honest. Take out your Bible and look through it. You will not be able to find any hint at all of millions or billions of years."[20] That is true. The Bible doesn't mention evolution. But if we are going to make it a habit to refuse to believe anything if it isn't explicitly mentioned in the Bible, then there is going to be a host of things that have to go: no DNA, no theory of gravity, no heliocentric universe, and no genome. If we insisted on biblical authority in regard to reproduction, we would have to reject the existence of sperm and eggs. We'd have to insist that a man literally plants his "seed" in the woman's "soil," and that she contributes

---

19. Ham, *The Lie*, 128.
20. Ham, *The Lie*, 126.

nothing to conception. She just provides the fertile field. That's what the ancients believed.

Law and Authority of The Lie

In *The Lie*, Ham at one point addresses the charge leveled at him by Christian academics, that "creation ministries" like his are divisive. In response, Ham said something that caused my jaw to drop: "In that claim they certainly are correct; the truth always divides. …Compromise is too often made with the Christian giving ground for the sake of peace and harmony."[21] Translation? "Of course we're being divisive! We're right!"

So what can be the cause of such divisiveness and pride over being so divisive? Reading Ken Ham's material makes it pretty clear: *authority and law*. He is obsessed with this idea of authority, and it is clear that such an obsession stems from a militantly legalistic understanding of God—the very kind of understanding that Jesus himself condemned in the Pharisees. Perhaps no better quote can illustrate this mentality than the following:

> "If you accept a belief in God as Creator, then you accept that there are laws, since He is the lawgiver. God's law is the reflection of His holy character. He is the absolute authority, and we are under total obligation to Him. Laws are not a matter of our opinions but are rules given by the One who has the right to impose them upon us for our good and for His own glory."[22]

For Ken Ham, being a Christian means to *obey God's rules*. He owns you. You are nothing, so you had better submit. If you don't, God is going to punish you. This kind of fear that drives Ken Ham is the same fear that drove the Pharisees in Jesus' day. They obsessed over the Torah so much so that they developed their own oral tradition to add to the Torah. They believed God was angry with them for not keeping *all the rules*. That's why they were under subjection to Rome. To the Pharisees, other Jews were compromisers and "sinners," and the only remedy was to double-down on the submission, not just to the Torah, but to their own oral tradition as well. They believed once they proved to God that they were good boys, then God would return, bless them, and set them up to "rule

---

21. Ham, *The Lie*, 134.
22. Ham, *The Lie*, 137.

the culture," while He let all the other compromised Jews have it for not being as good as the Pharisees.

But what was Jesus' response to the Pharisees? He condemned their oral tradition, and even called them "broods of vipers" (Matthew 3:7).

The Lie's Take on Evolution: The Root of All Evil

Despite the fact that in *The Lie* and throughout AiG's ministry, Ken Ham is dedicated to push the idea that the theory of evolution is the foundation of all of society's evils, he ironically goes out of his way to say, "It is important to understand that evolutionary beliefs and millions of years are not the direct cause of social issues like gay marriage, abortion, and so on."[23]

Ironically though, on the very next page, Ham displays a cartoon (one that is constantly used in AiG presentations) that depicts two castles, one labeled "humanism" and the other labeled "Christianity." The foundation of the castle of humanism is clearly labeled "Evolution/Millions of Years: Man Decides 'Truth,'" whereas the foundation to the castle of Christianity is clearly labeled "Creation/Thousands of Years: God's Word is Truth."

Above the castle of humanism are six balloons: pornography, family break-up, gay marriage, abortion, removal of Ten Commandments, and racism. While the cannons of the Christian castle are aimed at the balloons, the cannons of humanism's castle are pulverizing the foundation of the Christian castle, which is the YECist interpretation of Genesis 1–11.

So what does the cartoon show? Despite what Ham says, the cartoon picture clearly shows that Ham feels that evolution is the direct cause of social issues like gay marriage. That is what is so amazing: Ham denies something, and then, on the very next page, displays a picture that illustrates the very thing he has denied. Then, to top it off, Ham states, "People ask, 'Are you blaming evolution for all the evils in society?' My answer is, 'Yes and no.'"[24] Ham's cartoon is clear. As Ham says, "…we have to re-aim the cannons at the foundation of man's word. It is only when the foundation is destroyed that the structure will collapse."[25]

I guess evolution is the foundation after all.

23. Ham, *The Lie*, 139.
24. Ham, *The Lie*, 149.
25. Ham, *The Lie*, 152.

ALREADY GONE: THE STEPS

A more recent book Ken Ham has written is *Already Gone*. It argues that by the time children who have grown up in church have gotten to college, they are "already gone"—meaning they have already started to abandon the faith. The book, quite simply, is an alarmist piece of writing to convince people to buy AiG's curriculum. The message of the book is simple: ever since Charles Darwin, the church has gone to hell in a compromising handbasket, and the only way to save the church is to submit to biblical authority, stand firm on the historicity of Genesis 1–11, and buy Ken Ham's material for your church and home school. Here's how he makes his case.

Step One

Ham begins his book by lamenting the fact that churches are empty in England. The reason why, he says, is Charles Darwin is buried in Westminster Abbey. What in the world is that pro-evolution atheist doing in Westminster Abbey, alongside the likes of Isaac Newton? Ken Ham tells us: the Church of England has compromised the Word of God.

According to Ham, Charles Darwin came up with the theory, no, excuse me, the *worldview* of evolution in order to get rid of God from society, and the Church of England allowed this man's fallible "science" to trump the infallible Word of God. Therefore, Ken Ham laments, "A man who popularized a philosophy that hit at the very foundation of the Church (the Word of God) is honored by the Church and buried in the foundation of the Church. It is symbolic indeed."[26] According to Ken Ham, as soon as the Church of England started compromising on the age of the earth and evolution, people immediately started walking out the church doors: who is going to stay in a church that compromises the Word of God?

Step Two

Ham then claims that the same trend is happening here in America: scores of young people leave the church by the time they attend college. This mass exodus of young people from the church does not happen *after*

---

26. Ham, *Already Gone*, 73.

they start attending college. No—by the time they get to college, many church-going young people are "already gone." What can be done?

Given this alarming trend, Ham conducted a survey of 1,000 people who no longer regularly attend church. The main question, obviously, is, "What was the reason you have stopped going to church?" The answers might shock you…namely because they *don't support his premise* that belief in evolution is the reason why people are leaving the church.

1. Boring Service (12%)
2. Legalism (12%)
3. Hypocrisy of Leaders (11%)
4. Too Political (10%)
5. Self-Righteous People (9%)
6. Distance from Home (7%)
7. Irrelevant to Personal Growth (6%)
8. God wouldn't condemn to hell (6%)
9. Bible isn't relevant/practical (5%)
10. No preferred denomination (5%)

None of these answers mention evolution at all. It would seem Ham's own survey has put a big dent in his theory that evolution is the reason why so many young people are "already gone." But Ham won't be deterred by the facts in his own survey! The problem with many researchers is that they accept the "simple, superficial answers" people give in their surveys! And so, Ham brought in a "numbers expert" to do a follow up survey to really "dig deep" into those superficial answers until they found the "real reasons" why people are leaving the church. And wouldn't you know it? Ham triumphantly declared, "We found the real reasons, though some of them will shake many churches to their very core."[27]

Red Flags

What is your reaction to someone who says, "I gave a survey, got the answers, and didn't like the answers, so I gave out follow-up questions and manipulated the data in order to arrive at the conclusions that I wanted to find"? I'll tell you what my reaction is. *It's not an honest survey*. It is nothing more than someone pushing a particular agenda and masking sheer propaganda in pseudo-scientific garb.

Ironically, even after Ham did his follow-up survey, he essentially admitted that the numbers *still don't justify his foregone conclusions*! Ham noted that of those surveyed, only 10% said their pastor and Sunday school teachers ever said Christians could believe in evolution, and only

27. Ham, *Already Gone*, 30.

25% said it was okay to believe the earth is millions of years old. Furthermore, a whopping 80% said their pastor and Sunday school teachers actually taught that God created the earth in six 24 days, and only 6% said Genesis 1–11 wasn't historical. Simply put, most Evangelical churches *don't* teach evolution, they *don't* teach that the earth is billions of years old—if anything, they teach the very thing Ken Ham is pushing.

Amazingly, it's at this point in the book where Ken Ham completely changes his argument. The problem now isn't that American churches have accepted evolution and millions of years; the problem is that American churches *aren't pushing six-day creationism enough*! Ham laments that even though churches say the Bible is true, they teach the early chapters of Genesis only as a story, and when they say that parts of the Bible are "only a story," they are guilty of elevating man's fallible word over God's infallible Word—and their compromising of the Word of God is causing young people to doubt, and lose trust in the Bible…or so Ken Ham says.

The problem with that is that his re-vamped claim *is contradicted by his own survey*. Remember, his own survey showed that 94% of pastors and Sunday school teachers taught Genesis 1–11 was historical. Therefore, it simply doesn't make sense for Ham to turn around and accuse pastors and Sunday school teachers of saying that parts of the Bible are "only a story." Amazingly, none of his followers seem to notice this.

Let the Agenda Rear Its Head

After setting up his problematic argument that is not borne out from his own surveys, Ham then proceeded in the second half of his book to argue that evolution is a concerted attempt to destroy Christianity, and how churches need to start teaching "creation science" from the pulpit and in their Sunday School classes. Yes—*he wants churches to teach science.*

> "In America today, where do you go to learn about the geological, biological, anthropological, or astronomical history of the universe? School. That's where our kids learn what they perceive is the real stuff, the relevant stuff. In Sunday school they learn 'Bible stories.' (By the way, if you look at the definition of 'story,' it means 'fairy tale.' The Bible has become so irrelevant in our culture today that that's what most people think it is – just a spiritual 'fairy tale.')"[28]

28. Ham, *Already Gone*, 77.

> "Churches today in America are not a place where one talks about geology, dinosaurs, fossils, or the age of the earth – that is left up to the schools and colleges. Effectively, the Church basically hands over the history of the universe to the secular educational institutions and concentrates on the spiritual and moral aspects of Christianity."[29]

> "The Church and the Bible are no longer the places we go to learn historical science. The Church gave up that responsibility and relegated it to the world. We kept the spiritual things, the moral things, and the relationships things."[30]

Those are remarkable statements. Yes, church is often seen as irrelevant, and our modern worldview is beholden to the Enlightenment notion that only scientific facts are real. Ever since the Enlightenment, we have philosophically split reality into two: the "real world" of science and the "spiritual world" of religion. But instead of calling the Church to reject the Enlightenment worldview, Ham calls on the Church to reject the natural sciences themselves and replace them with his own fictional, "creation science" that is rooted in Enlightenment assumptions but bears no semblance to reality.

The problem is not the natural sciences, but the philosophical worldview of the Enlightenment. Ken Ham, though, misrepresents the findings of the natural sciences as being a philosophical worldview, rejects God's good creation that the natural sciences allow us to investigate, and then tries to replace it with idolatrous fiction of "creation science." He even wants pastors with no training in the sciences to teach science from the pulpit. In addition, Ham reveals his contempt for the major way in which God has revealed Himself in the Scriptures: *stories*. He falsely labels "stories" as "fairytales," and then says, "Of course young people are leaving the church! They're being told the Bible is full of fairytales!"

But the majority of the Bible comes to us in genres other than "history." It's not just the parables of Jesus, or the Psalms and Proverbs. Even the Gospels, as well as the Old Testament books that relate the history of ancient Israel are not "modern histories." They are conveying historical events to be sure, but they are conveying them in the literary form of narrative and story. That is why it is so troubling to find Ham disparaging the primary way God has chosen to reveal Himself in the Bible. Being

---

29. Ham, *Already Gone*, 78.
30. Ham, *Already Gone*, 84.

the Enlightenment thinker he is, Ham has swallowed the lie that the only things that can be true are scientific and historical facts. When he hears someone say, "That's a Bible *story*," he hears, "I don't believe the Bible is true!" and ends up dismissing the predominant method of revelation in the Bible as an "untrue fairytale."

Attack the Christian Colleges and Universities!

After criticizing churches for not teaching science from the pulpit, Ham then sets his aim on Christian colleges and well-known Christian leaders. Ham is no fan of the majority of Christian universities. He views them as compromised because they don't teach the universe is 6,000 years old. And so, Ham does his best to warn you not to send your children to such institutions. The way in which he does this, though, is an alarming display of manipulative double-speak. He praises and condemns at the same time:

> "Many well-known Christian scholars, professors, evangelists, and the like have compromised the Bible with an old (millions-of-years) earth. You would probably be shocked if we placed a list of names here. Some of these Christian leaders have led many to Christ and have done a tremendous work in the spread of the gospel. Unquestionably, the ministry of these men has had a profound positive effect on multitudes of individual lives. Eternity has been changed because of their commitment and devotion to the gospel. However...they have been part of a vicious attack on biblical authority."[31]

> "Whether we like to admit it or not, many of our contemporary champions of the faith are actually undermining the authority of the Bible (and thus the foundations of the Church) when they fail to defend what the Bible says about the age of the earth and the universe."[32]

Let me ask, how can a Christian do a tremendous work in the spread of the Gospel, and yet be a part of a vicious attack on biblical authority? James 3:9–11 speaks to the very thing Ham is doing here: "*With [our mouth] we bless the Lord and Father, and with it we curse those who are made in the likeness of God. From the same mouth come blessing and*

---

31. Ham, *Already Gone*, 80–81.
32. Ham, *Already Gone*, 82.

cursing. My brothers and sisters, this ought not to be so. Does a spring pour forth from the same opening both fresh and salt water?"

Of course not, yet Ken Ham is trying to do this very thing. What are we to make of that? When one looks at the bulk of his work and his vitriol against other Christians, it becomes clear that his work leaves a bitter taste in the mouth and causes bitterness and hurt throughout the Church.

There is one thing in the above quote that cannot be overlooked: Ken Ham clearly states that belief in a young universe is the *foundation of the Church*. That has never been claimed in Church history, *ever*. It is precisely that claim that makes Ken Ham's teachings heretical, for his claim is undermining historic Church teaching. Not only has the Church never claimed that the Bible teaches the universe came into being a mere 4,000 years before Christ, it has never claimed that such a position was a foundational issue to the faith.

Hissss…Did God Really Say?

One of Ham's favorite ways to attack those who disagree with him is to accuse them of speaking with the voice of the serpent. Not surprisingly, he accuses modern science of being that very serpent:

> "In the last 100 years, the attacks have begun to sound more and more scientific:
>
> - Did God really say that He created everything? Surely science has proven that the big bang happened spontaneously, without any outside force.
> - Did God really say that He created the earth in six days? Surely science has proven that life evolved over millions and billions of years.
> - Did God really say that He created life? Surely science has proven that the right chemicals in the right place over a long enough period of time will spontaneously generate living forms.
> - Did God really say that He created humanity? Surely science has proven that the human race is really just a highly evolved life form that is the product of time and random chance.
> - Did God really send a worldwide Flood in the time of Noah? Surely science has shown there never was a global Flood, and that the fossil layers were laid down over millions of

years – not by a Flood. The youth of today are wrestling with such."[33]

Such a tactic is powerfully effective. Not only does it completely shut down any possibility of dialogue at all, it also insinuates that anyone who dares to question Ken Ham's view is, in fact, *working for the devil*. As soon as you say, "Hey, is that really what that verse means?" Ken Ham will shoot back, "Did God really say that? I think I hear the voice of the serpent! It's the 'Genesis 3 deception'!" Of course, what you're asking really is, "Is Ken Ham correct in the way he interprets this?" Of course, Ken Ham will take that to mean that you're questioning God.

A Historical Genesis 1–11 Makes the Resurrection True

As Ham reasserts his claim that if you don't think Genesis 1–11 is literal history, then you have no basis for believing the Bible when it tells us about the resurrection of Christ, he employs some subtly deceptive rhetoric:

> "We accept that the Bible is the revealed Word of God – it is inerrant, inspired, the 'God-breathed' revelation from our Creator. And as such, we let God's word speak to us through this written Word. If it is history, we take it as history. We don't try to force our ideas onto God's Word; we let it speak to us in the language and context in which it is written. How about Jesus actually walking on water? Or that Jesus fed thousands of people from just a few loaves and fishes? Or that Jonah was swallowed by a great fish? We know, because it's in the Bible."[34]

Notice what he says: "We don't try to force our ideas onto God's Word; we let it speak to us in the language and context in which it is written." I'm sorry, that's not true. He's not reading Genesis 1–11 in Hebrew, and he's not considering it within the historical and literary context of the ancient world. What he is doing is forcing a twenty-first century/modern scientific reading onto an ancient text and forcing an Enlightenment worldview that equates "facts" as the only criteria for determining truth.

Despite his claims that a modern scientific reading of Genesis 1–11 is the foundation of the Gospel, we must remember that the Bible clearly states that Jesus Christ—the one who was crucified, dead, and buried,

---

33. Ham, *Already Gone*, 100.
34. Ham, *Already Gone*, 101–2.

and who was resurrected from the grave, never to die again—is the foundation of the Church, the cornerstone of God's temple, and the Lord of all creation. We need to realize that Ken Ham is literally saying that there is a different cornerstone and foundation. Whatever Ken Ham is building, it is *not* the Christian faith; it is *not* the Church. It is, in fact, a pagan temple, and its idol is the YEC heretical teaching.

10

The Heretical Bloggings of Ham

"An all-out attack on evolutionary thinking is possibly the only real hope our nations have of rescuing themselves from an inevitable social and moral catastrophe."

—Ken Ham

"These heretics, since they are blind to the truth, and deviate from the [right] way, will walk in various roads; and therefore the footsteps of their doctrine are scattered here and there without agreement or connection."

—St. Irenaeus of Lyons

ONE OF KEN HAM's favorite things to do on his blog is to disparage and condemn Christians who don't share his view on Genesis 1–11. Even in the midst of that, he still finds time to condemn NASA, John Glenn, the Huffington Post, the Smithsonian Institute, and the president as well. If anyone holds to a position he feels goes against "biblical authority" and his personal scientific interpretation of Genesis 1–11, Ken Ham will take to his blog and warn his followers about how "the voice of the serpent" is out to deceive them. Now, it is one thing to read arguments against Ken Ham. It's quite another to read Ken Ham in his own words. It is, by far, the best thing to do in order to be convinced that what he is promoting is anything but the historic Christian faith.

IS EVOLUTION A SALVATION ISSUE?

On January 1, 2014, Ken Ham wrote a blog post titled, "Millions of Years—Are Souls at Stake? Biblical Authority," in which he engages in an impressive display of double-speak regarding whether or not belief in the historicity of Genesis 1–11 is a salvation issue. Early on in the post he said, "nowhere does the Bible even imply salvation in Christ is conditioned upon one's belief concerning the days of creation or the age of the earth or universe." But then, by the end of that very paragraph, after re-asserting that "Salvation is conditional upon faith in Christ—not belief about the six days of creation or the earth's age," Ken Ham then immediately said, "So these are not salvation issues per se. But it is a salvation issue in an indirect sense."[1]

This is truly astounding. In one breath, he says the age of the earth isn't a "salvation issue," but in another breath he says it really is, *just indirectly*. He reiterated this again at the end of his post, where he once again said, "to believe in millions of years is a gospel issue. This belief ultimately impugns the character of the Creator and Savior and undermines the foundation of the soul-saving gospel."

Are you confused? Let me try to explain: (a) the *gospel* is the *salvation* message; (b) believing in millions of years isn't a *salvation* issue, but it is a *gospel* issue, because (c) believing in millions of years undermines the "*soul-saving gospel*," but (d) it isn't a salvation issue. Still confused? Just wait. There's more:

> "Many Christians believe in millions of years and are truly born again. Their belief in millions of years doesn't affect their salvation. But what does it do? It affects how other people, such as their children or others they teach, view Scripture. Christians who compromise on the idea of millions of years can encourage others toward unbelief."[2]

> "It is a salvation issue indirectly. Christians who compromise on millions of years can encourage others toward unbelief concerning God's Word and the gospel."[3]

That clarifies everything! Believing in millions of years doesn't affect *your* salvation, but it will affect the salvation *of others*. So, *within the same*

---

1. Ham, "Millions of Years," paras. 2–5.
2. Ham, "Millions of Years," para. 22.
3. Ham, "Millions of Years," para. 25.

post Ham has gone from saying "millions of years" (a) *isn't* a salvation issue, to (b) *it is* a salvation issue, to (c) yes *it really is* a salvation issue, to (d) you can be a Christian who believes in millions of years *and still be saved*, to (e) but if you teach it to others, *it will affect their salvation*.

Such is the kind of double-speak that Ken Ham routinely uses to frighten his followers.

CONTRALOGOS

One of Ken Ham's favorite whipping boys is BioLogos, the theistic evolution organization started by Francis Collins. On January 18, 2014, Ken Ham attacked BioLogos in an article titled, "Should BioLogos be Called, 'ContraLogos' Instead?" In typical Ham fashion, right after saying that BioLogos' goal is to get as much of the Church to compromise on God's Word, Ham turned around to engage in breath-taking double-speak:

> "Now, I am not claiming that such compromising people can't be Christians. Salvation is conditioned upon faith in Christ, not what a person believes about millions of years and evolution. Such compromise, however, undermines the authority of the Word and is dangerous to the health of the church. In reality, an attack on the Word of God is an attack on Jesus Christ, who is the Word. Those academics involved with BioLogos will certainly stand before God one day to give an account of how they handled the Word. And those people who used their influence to teach others many false ideas are warned in Scripture: 'My brethren, let not many of you become teachers, knowing that we shall receive a stricter judgment'" (James 3:1).[4]

In one paragraph alone, Ham has accused BioLogos of trying to get the Church to compromise God's Word, while at the same time saying that doesn't mean they're not Christians. Still, according to Ham, BioLogos is undermining and attacking the authority of the Word, and to attack the Word is to attack Christ himself. And since they are attacking Christ, they will have to stand before God and be judged because of their false ideas.

How can one who attacks Christ be a Christian? That is, quite literally, a nonsensical and contradictory statement. So why does Ham say this? Because in a very passive-aggressive way, he wants to condemn

---

4. Ham, "ContraLogos Instead?" paras. 4–5.

BioLogos without coming across as condemning them. But he can't hide the obvious: the judgmentalism is palpable.

Ham then addressed the claim made by Dr. Haarsma of BioLogos that he is presenting Christians with a false choice: it must be either evolution *or* God's Word, science *or* religion. Dr. Haarsma said, "We at BioLogos maintain that you don't have to choose. You don't have to give up Christian faith in order to accept the best, most compelling science." She also said that even though BioLogos disagrees with Ken Ham on the issues of evolution, fossils, and genetics, that they were still "brothers and sisters in Christ with Ken Ham. We believe . . . that the Bible is the authoritative word of God."[5]

Her statements were even-handed, thoughtful, and reconciliatory towards Ken Ham. But Ham didn't exactly see them that way:

> "But what a contradiction. It's impossible to maintain that the whole Bible is the authoritative Word of God and at the same time say that the first eleven chapters of Genesis are incorrect because man's fallible ideas about origins must override what Genesis clearly teaches. In fact, for secularists, evolution is really man's fallible ideas to explain the universe without God. Molecules-to-man evolution and millions of years are really the pagan religion of our day. Christians who compromise with such pagan ideas are no different than the Israelites who compromised God's Word with the pagan religions of their day (like the Canaanites)."[6]

At no time did BioLogos say that Genesis 1–11 is "incorrect." They say that it is not *historical narrative*. But for Ken Ham, being beholden to Enlightenment thinking as he is, to say that something is not historical fact amounts to saying that it is not true. Let's also be clear, evolution is not the "pagan religion of our day." To continue to accuse it of being so is inflammatory paranoia. Finally, let's note that whereas BioLogos tried to strike a reconciliatory tone, and called Ken Ham a Christian brother, Ham responded by equating them with pagan Israelites...but of course, he's not saying they're not Christians.

After once again claiming evolution is atheistic by nature, Ham then claimed "the scientific evidence confirms the Bible's account." You can read all his posts and look through the AiG website, and you will not find any scientific evidence for YEC—it doesn't exist. So how, you may ask,

5. Ham, "ContraLogos Instead?" para. 9.
6. Ham, "ContraLogos Instead?" para. 10.

can he claim such a thing? It's simple: by virtue of his fictional category of science—*historical science*, the kind that cannot be tested or observed. And where do we find historical science? Genesis 1–11! When Ken Ham says that the scientific evidence confirms Genesis 1–11, what he's really saying is, "Genesis 1–11 is historical science, and it's that historical science that confirms Genesis 1–11!"

NORMAN GEISLER, YOU SELL-OUT!

Another well-known conservative Evangelical scholar that drew the ire of Ken Ham was Norman Geisler. In a February 14, 2014 blog post titled, "The Ultimate Motivation of this Prominent Theologian?" Ken Ham took issue with Geisler's comments regarding YEC. After saying how much he respected Dr. Geisler, Ham then proceeded to attack the man over the "unforgivable sin" for young earth creationists. Geisler had written an article titled, "Does Believing in Inerrancy Require One to Believe in Young Earth Creationism?" and had answered "not necessarily." He stated, as B. B. Warfield did a century ago, one could still hold to inerrancy without insisting the universe was made in six literal 24-hour days a mere 6,000 years ago.

Well, Ham took that article to be a personal slight against him and AiG, and therefore proceeded to accuse Geisler of being "influenced by an authority outside the Bible: the majority view among scientists of very old ages, so that he can allow for or believe in billions of years."[7] Yes, even Norman Geisler has now been deceived by the devil and his secular minions.

After once again making the false claim equating evolution with philosophical naturalism and atheism, Ham then said that the priority at AiG was to take the Word of God "naturally." This means that Genesis 1–11 is straightforward literal history. Ham even claimed that "almost the whole church…for 1,800 years and much of the church…today" has read Genesis 1–11 as straightforward history.

As we have already seen, that claim is demonstrably false. YEC is an interpretation of Genesis 1–11 that has never been universally held throughout Church history. Neither the Orthodox Church, nor the Catholic Church hold to the view that the earth is only 6,000 years old. Even among Protestant pastors, only 46% agree that the earth is only 6,000

---

7. Ham, "The Ultimate Motivation?" para. 11.

years old. How Ham can claim that "almost the whole church" throughout history has shared his view is mystifying.

Deep down, Ken Ham must know what he claimed wasn't true, for right after he made that claim, he turned around and said, "It is true that many of the church fathers and the early creeds did not deal with the age of the earth/universe. But that is simply because almost all of them were young-earth creationists, such as Augustine."[8]

Think about what Ken Ham said right there. The early Church Fathers and the creeds didn't address the age of the earth, *because they were young earth creationists*? If they didn't deal with it, how does Ken Ham know they were young earth creationists? What further complicates things is his assertion that the young earth creationist movement started with Henry Morris' book *The Genesis Flood* in 1961. How anyone can claim that men like Augustine were part of a movement that began in 1961 is beyond me.

In any case, Ham couldn't let himself condemn only Geisler, and so he put famous nineteenth century Christian theologians like Spurgeon, Hodge, Scofield, Warfield, and even the original Fundamentalists who wrote *The Fundamentals* in 1910, in his crosshairs and accused them of "following suit" with the "compromisers" who first suggested "millions of years."[9] That's right. Ken Ham accused the original Fundamentalists of not being fundamentalist enough. The men who came up with the modern doctrine of inerrancy did not insist that that meant the theory of evolution contradicted Genesis 1–11, so Ken Ham criticized them as compromisers.

Ken Ham then concluded his post with yet another instance of double-speak: "I assert that many great men of God in today's world are contributing to a generational loss of biblical authority because of their insistence on accommodating man's belief in billions of years with the infallible Word of God." How can "great men of God" be involved in subverting the authority of the Bible, yet still be considered to be "great men of God"? Well, in the world of Ham, apparently it is possible.

8. Ham, "The Ultimate Motivation?" para. 20.
9. Ham, "The Ultimate Motivation?" para. 21.

MILLARD ERICKSON: REPENT!

Norman Geisler was not the only conservative Evangelical theologian to be judged by Ken Ham. On May 21, 2014, Ken Ham wrote, "Textbook Misleading Many Seminary and Bible College Students," in which he shared a blog post by Terry Mortenson that lambasted Millard Erickson, a well-known conservative Evangelical systematic theologian, not because he particularly embraced theistic evolution, but rather because he didn't endorse six-day creationism *enough* in the third edition to his systematic theology book.

After lauding Erickson as "one of the greatest evangelical theologians of our generation," the post condemns Erickson for not giving enough ink to YEC in the third edition of his *Christian Theology*.[10] Apparently, Erickson's chapter on creation wasn't any different than what it was in Erickson's second edition that came out in 1998. Specifically, Ham was upset over Erickson's treatment of the global Flood theory. In Erickson's book, he referred to the 1923 book by Seventh Day Adventist George McCready Price, but failed to mention John Whitcomb and Henry Morris' 1961 book, *The Genesis Flood*. Ham was upset that Erickson didn't mention the book "that launched the modern creationist movement."[11]

This admission that YEC is a movement that began with Henry Morris' book in 1961 is significant, in that it flatly contradicts Ham's claim that Christians have always been young earth creationists throughout Church history up until Darwin and his "godless evolution" came on the scene in 1859. If YEC started in 1961, then it couldn't have been the position of the Church throughout history. You can't have it both ways.

Well, Ham (and Mortenson) took issue when Erickson said, "The age of the universe is a topic that needs continued study and thought" but then didn't devote more of his chapter to YEC literature. This smacked of suspicion: "It is hard not to conclude that he has deliberately avoided that literature. Why has he? I suggest it is because he has uncritically accepted what the majority of scientists say about millions of years."[12]

Perhaps Erickson really had critically thought about the issue and had decided that YEC deserved nothing more than a brief mention in his book. That might sound harsh, but it probably is true. Erickson's job is to critically analyze the various aspects of systematic theology. Therefore,

10. Ham, "Textbook Misleading," para. 2.
11. Ham, "Textbook Misleading," para. 4.
12. Ham, "Textbook Misleading," para. 5.

for Ham to accuse this Erickson of *uncritically accepting* a certain theological view regarding Genesis is rather insulting to the man.

Ham (and Mortenson) wasn't done insulting Erickson and proceeded to accuse the man whom he had earlier called, "one of the greatest Evangelical theologians of our generation," of producing a book that is "misleading many evangelical seminary and Bible college students not only in America but through translation in other countries as well."[13] Ham can't have it both ways. If Erickson's book is misleading Christians, then he can't be a great Evangelical theologian, can he? As we have already seen, though, this kind of manipulative double-speak is just par for the course for the folks at AiG.

Ham ended his post with some not so surprising judgmentalism: "Dr. Erickson needs to do his homework in creationist literature, *repent of his erroneous teachings* on creation and the age of the earth and his ignoring of creationist writings, and then he needs to do a fourth edition to his theology text *to affirm faith in the literal truth of Genesis*. Join me in praying that he will do so."[14] Yes, AiG has proclaimed it.

BIOLOGOS: STRANGERS WITH CANDY!

Another tactic of Ken Ham is to whip parents up into fear that "compromising organizations" like BioLogos are out to get their children. On July 2, 2014, in a post titled, "BioLogos Targets Children and Teens with Theistic Evolution," Ham once again sounded the alarm that BioLogos had developed a curriculum for students from grade school all the way up to high school. And what better way to make parents afraid than to demonize, and I mean *literally demonize*, BioLogos:

> "The Bible makes it clear that God's people are to train up their children in truth, so they won't be led astray by the evil teachings of this world. But the devil also knows this teaching, so he works hard to indoctrinate children at a young age in false teaching. Sadly, I believe organizations like BioLogos, even if staffed by Christians, are helping the devil in leading this and coming generations away from the truth of God's Word."[15]

---

13. Ham, "Textbook Misleading," para. 6.
14. Ham, "Textbook Misleading," para. 7.
15. Ham, "BioLogos Targets Children," para. 1.

Once again, Ham engages in a breath-taking example of doublespeak. After accusing BioLogos of leading children astray with "the evil teachings of this world," he then says that even though BioLogos might be staffed by Christians, it is actually helping the devil in leading people away from the truth of God's Word. How can one be a Christian if one is actively helping the devil? Methinks the man speaks with a forked tongue.

It should be abundantly clear that Ham would rather smear and judge fellow Christians than try to prove his young earth claims are true. The reason why, of course, is because he can't prove his claims are true. That is why he resorts to (a) *redefining* biology, geology, and astronomy right out of the realm of science, (b) *making up* a category of "historical science," and defining it as "untestable belief about the past" so he can claim that Genesis 1–11 is "historical science," and (c) *judging* any Christian who disagrees with him as a "compromiser of God's Word" who *helps the devil!*

What horrifies Ham is that the curriculum BioLogos has developed to teach children about how God could have used evolution to create the variety of life on the earth is "colorful and filled with rhymes; they could be effective tools in leading children astray." This quite literally is the height of hypocrisy. All you have to do is glance at the AiG website and browse through their curriculum for children. That's exactly what Ken Ham has built his entire organization on.

He doesn't see it that way, though. What *he is doing* is God's work; what *BioLogos is doing* "is teaching children that God's Word cannot be trusted! But with BioLogos, the indoctrination doesn't stop at children—they also want to influence those who teach children."[16]

"Indoctrination" is the word Ham uses to slander and libel anyone who tries to teach something that contradicts what he claims. But what exactly is "indoctrination"? Merriam-Webster defines it as "to teach someone to fully accept the ideas, opinions, and beliefs of a particular group and to not consider other ideas, opinions, and beliefs." So, are groups like BioLogos, or any of the recent Christian academics who have written on this subject, "indoctrinating" anyone? I've read quite a lot of literature from BioLogos, as a well as a number of books from Christian scholars, and I can tell you they certainly do not indoctrinate. They attempt to lay out the various views in the creation/evolution debate, and

---

16. Ham, "BioLogos Targets Children," para. 5.

then (of course) argue for their view—but they make it a point to lay all opposing views out there.

By contrast, AiG deliberately puts out misinformation in regard to the creation/evolution debate. Ham's very post is an example of how he is trying to keep people from even looking at the BioLogos material. I was specifically told by my former headmaster that he did not want me showing even a theistic evolution video in class, for fear that some students might be convinced by it. That is why it is so laughable when Ham accuses groups like BioLogos of indoctrination. He is the one doing the indoctrinating. Consider what he says here:

> "They want to inoculate parents and students against thinking critically about evolutionary claims, so they claim that if you believe anything else, you've supposedly rejected 'science.' Really, it's just a rejection of the completely unproven idea of evolution and the God-rejecting naturalistic worldview that spawned it. Christians who accept evolutionary ideas about the age of the earth and the origin of life…are in effect calling God a liar and rejecting His Word. They are in essence helping the secularists to inoculate children against the Bible as the infallible Word of God."[17]

The only one preventing critical thinking is Ken Ham. He frightens people by claiming if you believe anything other than what he says about Genesis 1-11, you are undermining the Bible, attacking Christ, and working for the devil. Yet how can he say he promotes critical thinking when he claims the theory of evolution is an "unproven idea" that has spawned from the "God-rejecting naturalistic worldview"? How can he claim he wants honest debate when he claims that *Christians* who believe in theistic evolution are "calling God a liar and rejecting His Word"?

In any case, after attacking BioLogos for developing curriculum for kids, Ham ironically launches into an appeal *for people to buy the curriculum he has developed for kids:* "We have to teach our children from a young age (even pre-school) that they can trust the Word of God and answer skeptical questions, so they'll be equipped to handle claims that challenge biblical authority."[18] The irony is blindingly blatant.

---

17. Ham, "BioLogos Targets Children," para. 8.
18. Ham, "BioLogos Targets Children," para. 10.

ALIENS! SAY GOODBYE TO E.T.!

One of the most recent crusades of AiG has been to fight against the idea of life on other planets. Apparently, Ken Ham feels this is an issue that is a threat to the Gospel. In a July 20, 2014 post titled, "We'll Find a New Earth in 20 Years," Ham responded to a NASA scientist who said he expected that we would find a new earth-like planet in the next 20 years. I don't know about you, but I know I have often wondered about the possibility of life on other planets—who hasn't watched *E.T.* and wondered about finding life on other planets?

Ham finds this thought dangerous and sinister. Needless to say, Ham was not happy about this comment by the NASA scientist. He bemoaned the fact that "countless hundreds of millions of [tax] dollars" had been spent over the years searching for extraterrestrial life, because the search for life on other planets is just a secularist conspiracy to disprove God:

> "Of course, secularists are desperate to find life in outer space, as they believe that would provide evidence that life can evolve in different locations and given the supposed right conditions! The search for extraterrestrial life is really driven by man's rebellion against God in a desperate attempt to supposedly prove evolution!"[19]

Think about what Ken Ham actually has said. He actually believes that space exploration is rebellion against God. He actually believes that searching the universe for signs of life is just a secularist conspiracy trying to prove evolution. In any case, Ham felt compelled to give a supposedly biblical perspective on the possibility of extraterrestrial life:

> "Now the Bible doesn't say whether there is or is not animal or plant life in outer space. I certainly suspect not. The Earth was created for human life. And the sun and moon were created for signs and our seasons—and to declare the glory of God.[20]

> "And I do believe there can't be other intelligent beings in outer space because of the meaning of the gospel. You see, the Bible makes it clear that Adam's sin affected the whole universe. This means that any aliens would also be affected by Adam's sin, but because they are not Adam's descendants, they can't have salvation. One day, the whole universe will be judged by fire, and

---

19. Ham, "We'll Find a New Earth," para. 2.
20. Ham, "We'll Find a New Earth," para. 6.

> there will be a new heavens and earth. God's Son stepped into history to be Jesus Christ, the 'Godman,' to be our relative, and to be the perfect sacrifice for sin—the Savior of mankind.[21]
>
> "Jesus did not become the 'GodKlingon' or the 'GodMartian'! Only descendants of Adam can be saved. God's Son remains the 'Godman' as our Savior. In fact, the Bible makes it clear that we see the Father through the Son (and we see the Son through His Word). To suggest that aliens could respond to the gospel is just totally wrong. An understanding of the gospel makes it clear that salvation through Christ is only for the Adamic race—human beings who are all descendants of Adam."[22]

So, Ken Ham doesn't think there is life on other planets *because the Bible doesn't say so*. That really is a peculiar reason for rejecting the possibility that there is life on other planets, don't you think? After all, there are a lot of things the Bible doesn't tell us about: chromosomes, genes, sperm, eggs, the whole process of variation within a species...the existence of America. Are we to reject the idea that those things exist because the Bible doesn't specifically tell us about them? Of course not. So why is Ham so adamant against the possibility of life on other planets?

The answer is obvious. He himself gives the reason: if life came about through natural processes on other planets, then that would mean that's how it could have come about here on earth...and that would be "evolution," and "evolution" equals "anti-God religion" for Ken Ham. Surely, though, that is an odd line of reasoning. Merely explaining the natural process by which life comes about and varies within creation does not, by any means, mean you're denying God...unless, of course, you're Ken Ham.

This reveals Ham's fundamental problem. He cannot tell the difference between *explaining a natural process*, and *making a philosophical claim* that nature is all that exists. Is explaining the development of a clump of cells the moment after conception into a zygote, then an embryo, then a fetus, then a baby a denial of a Creator God? Everyone knows that the process of development from zygote to a baby is the natural process by which God brings about life. Apparently, Ken Ham can't conceive the same thing applies to all of nature.

---

21. Ham, "We'll Find a New Earth," para. 7.
22. Ham, "We'll Find a New Earth," para. 8.

In addition, in the above quote, Ham claims the Gospel indicates that there can't be alien life, because Adam's sin affected the entire universe, therefore aliens would be affected, and thus couldn't receive salvation. But where in Genesis 3 does it say that Adam's sin affected the entire universe? It doesn't. To claim that Genesis 3 is making a definitive statement that human sin somehow affects (or is even talking about) any potential life that might or might not be in the Andromeda galaxy is just silly. Ham is clearly reading into the Bible things that aren't there, and then using those things that aren't there to support his claim that there can't be life on other planets because the Bible doesn't say they're there.

Finally, his comments regarding how only human beings can be saved because Jesus was not the "GodKlingon" or "GodMartian," and how "to suggest that aliens could respond to the Gospel is just totally wrong," are just absurd. I've *never* heard anyone ever suggest that. Given the fact the Bible doesn't even touch upon the issue of life on other planets, the only thing that is "just totally wrong" is Ken Ham claiming biblical authority and proclaiming there can't be, because the Bible doesn't mention it.

ALVIN PLANTINGA: THAT PHILOSOPHICAL NATURALIST

In a September 29, 2014 post titled, "Christian Philosopher Says Science Doesn't Oppose Faith," Ken Ham went out of his way to condemn Christian philosopher Alvin Plantinga, who works at Calvin College. Just like in all of his other posts, Ham does not hide his hatred of any Christian college like Calvin, or any individual who is open to the idea of theistic evolution: "Calvin College in Grand Rapids, Michigan, is one of the most ardently compromising Christian Colleges in the US that continues to lead so many young people astray in regard to the authority of Scripture beginning in Genesis."[23]

Of course, the only reason why he calls Calvin College "one of the most ardently compromising Christian Colleges in the US" is that it does not agree with *him* on the topic of how to interpret Genesis 1–11, and thus how to understand the theory of evolution. Nothing else matters for Ken Ham. It is his line in the sand, and the litmus test by which he feels

---

23. Ham, "Christian Philosopher Says Science Doesn't Oppose Faith," para. 1.

he has the right—no, the duty—to judge fellow Christians, particularly Christian academics:

> "Evolution is absolutely, completely, and utterly opposed to Scripture. Besides, as is usual for these academics, they refuse to acknowledge the difference between historical science (beliefs about the past or origins) and observational science (that builds our technology)."[24]

The above quote crystalizes Ham's basic argument on which he has built his entire YEC empire: "these academics" (or "those scientists," or "those NASA astronauts") simply refuse to acknowledge the difference between historical science and observational science. Yet we have already seen that Ken Ham's distinction between "observational" and "historical" science is a shell game he has to play in order to legitimize his unbiblical and unscientific claims regarding the universe being only 6,000 years old. It is his attempt to inject his modern interpretation of Genesis into the scientific arena, without actually doing anything scientific.

That is why, when scientists and biblical scholars point out that his claims are neither scientific nor biblical, Ham resorts to condemning them all compromised Christians who are helping the devil and calling God a liar. All the fictitious categories of science and name-calling in the world, though, cannot cover up the fact that the claims of YEC are, in fact, not scientific, not biblical, and have no standing in the history of the Church.

Another astounding part of Ham's post on Plantinga is his demonstrable inability to understand basic argumentation. Plantinga had made the observation that atheists like Richard Dawkins wrongly try to use evolution to prove their atheism. Since evolution is limited to the natural world, it cannot say anything about whether or not God even exists. As Plantinga wrote, "It's a metaphysical add-on they are importing into the scientific notion of evolution."

Plantinga's point is pretty clear: when atheists attempt to argue that evolution "disproves" God, they are not doing science. They are smuggling in their presupposed atheistic worldview and trying to legitimize it with science. Ham, though, was unable to grasp this. He wrote, "Plantinga seems to recognize that naturalism is the philosophical and religious underpinning of evolution and that it is atheistic and diametrically opposed

---

24. Ham, "Christian Philosopher Says Science Doesn't Oppose Faith," para. 2.

to Christianity."[25] I'm sorry, that's precisely what Plantinga *was not* saying: naturalism *is not* the "philosophical and religious underpinning of evolution." He was saying the *exact opposite* thing Ken Ham thought he was saying.

Evolution is a scientific theory regarding the natural world. Naturalism, by contrast, is the philosophical assumption that the natural world is all that exists, and that there is no God. That was the distinction Plantinga was making. Yet that very distinction was lost on Ken Ham, who simply doubled-down on his claim that the scientific theory of evolution was the same thing as the philosophical worldview of naturalism:

> "What [Plantinga] fails to realize is that evolution is not some kind of neutral science that stands or falls on its own. It is an entire worldview that effects how you see and interpret the evidence in cosmology, geology, and biology. The religious implications of evolution are inescapable because to accept evolution means to reject or reinterpret the clear teaching of Genesis in all three of these areas. This puts man as the ultimate authority instead of God, which is exactly what naturalism seeks to do— explain life without God so that we can be our own authority."[26]

That is not true, whether or not you accept evolution. Evolution is a *scientific theory*, not a *philosophical worldview*. It is not a religion. It is limited to observing the workings of the natural world. It is not the same thing as *philosophical naturalism*. Yet Ken Ham seems unable to make such a distinction. Throughout his post, he hammers home this incoherent claim that evolution is an anti-God religion that compromises the Bible:

> "Plantinga also doesn't seem to recognize that evolution and God's Word are utterly contradictory to one another. In order to fit evolution into God's Word, you have to compromise Scripture."[27]

> "While the evolutionary model of history is contradictory to Scripture, this does not mean that science and faith are pitted against one another. Observational science—the kind of science that is in the present and is observable, repeatable, and testable—will always confirm the Bible. You see, molecules-to-man

---

25. Ham, "Christian Philosopher Says Science Doesn't Oppose Faith," para. 3.
26. Ham, "Christian Philosopher Says Science Doesn't Oppose Faith," para. 3.
27. Ham, "Christian Philosopher Says Science Doesn't Oppose Faith," para. 6.

evolution is historical science—the kind of science that interprets the past based on your starting point and is not observable, repeatable, or testable. True science and its conclusions are always in perfect harmony with God's Word."[28]

Science and faith *aren't* pitted against one another; but science *is* pitted against Ham's claims because Ham's claims have absolutely no basis in science. That is why he has to resort to his shell game of "observational and historical science." Let's be clear: not only does Ham reject most of modern science, he also does not hold to a Christian worldview. In reality, he holds to the Enlightenment worldview that insists that only scientific and historical facts constitute truth. That is why Ham tries to legitimize his assumptions with scientific-sounding language. That is why he has made it his life's mission to prove that Genesis 1–11 is scientific. Ken Ham is a slave to his Enlightenment assumptions.

THE POPE...KEN HAM IS GOING AFTER THE POPE?

On October 29, 2014, Ken Ham set his cross-hairs a little higher by calling the Pope to account in a post titled, "Is the Pope Right that 'God is not Afraid of New Things'?" Pope Francis, as many popes before him, made it clear: the Catholic Church does not reject the theory of evolution, and evolution is the means by which God has created and continues to create the world. Simply put, the Catholic Church endorses theistic evolution. Not surprisingly, Ham put it a little differently: "Following in the tradition of other recent popes, Pope Francis has compromised biblical authority in favor of man's ideas in the area of origins."[29]

Pope Francis had said God was not a magician who simply waved a magic wand and "poofed" everything into existence. He said, "Evolution in nature is not inconsistent with the notion of creation, because evolution requires the creation of beings that evolve." Even though Ham said he agreed that God is not a magician, he clearly didn't get the Pope's point. The Pope's comments were directed against organization like AiG, who, by denying modern biology, geology, and astronomy, claim God "poofed" everything into existence within the course of six days, and thus say *God is a magician.*

28. Ham, "Christian Philosopher Says Science Doesn't Oppose Faith," para. 9.
29. Ham, "Is the Pope Right?" para. 2.

This brings up a valid criticism of AiG. Nowhere on their website or in their literature do they ever explain how creation came into being. Yes, God did it—that's the *Who*; but what about the *how*? How did God do it? AiG never addresses that. They put forth the "Who," claim it's the "How," and then condemn anyone who actually tries to explain the "How" scientifically. If I was able to engage Ham on this issue, I imagine the conversation would go something like this:

"God created the universe in six days, 6,000 years ago."

"Okay, but how did He do it?"

"It's right there in Genesis—He spoke and it happened."

"Okay, but how did it happen?"

"God did it."

"Okay, but how?"

"You know, He spoke it into existence…POOF!"

Voila! There you have it! The appearance of Ham's magician god! Ham ended his post by accusing both BioLogos and the Pope of changing the Bible:

> "…if God and His Word are open to change, then God's Word is not an authority on anything—man becomes the authority because he gets to decide when and how God's Word applies. This is simply a recycling of the same old lie from the Garden of Eden, 'Has God really said . . . ?' Sadly, religious leaders all around the world are falling for this lie and choosing to reinterpret God's Word based on man's fallible ideas. By and large, God is not the authority anymore—sinful man is. But it is God's Word—not man's word—that is truth."[30]

This quote captures another thing about Ken Ham and his followers. They love to accuse anyone who disagrees with them of speaking with the voice of the serpent. Apparently, to question Ken Ham is to question God…and to be in league with Satan.

BILL NYE, THE ANTI-GOD RELIGION GUY

No analysis of Ken Ham would be complete without looking at what he has written about Bill Nye since their debate in February of 2014. In a December 19, 2014 post titled, "Who's Really Raising Kids Who Can't Think?" Ken Ham takes issue with Nye's comments that young earth

---

30. Ham, "Is the Pope Right?" para. 9.

creationism makes children scared and uncomfortable with modern science. In response, Ham accuses Nye and "other secularists" of indoctrinating "generations of children in meaningless, purposeless evolutionary naturalism—atheism!"[31] In this post, Ham touches upon virtually every one of his standard talking points.

We have already noted Ham wrongly equates the scientific theory of evolution with the philosophical worldview of atheism. Evolutionary theory does not say, "Everything is meaningless and purposeless." It says, "We see such and such happening in the natural world, and this is the way in which the variety of species may have come about."

In any case, Ham lamented that teachers aren't even allowed to teach the problems with evolution, and that the government had made it illegal to teach young earth creationism in public schools. "This approach by secular academics," Ham claimed, "is not encouraging kids to think. This is indoctrination. And it's really indoctrination in an atheistic religion. In America, the government is endorsing a state religion—the religion of naturalism or atheism!"[32] I'm sorry, but no. Evolution is neither an "atheistic religion," nor the "state religion" of America. Ken Ham is simply upset because the government does not allow schools to teach YEC as science, because Ken Ham's definition of "historical science" is a made up definition.

Ham then proceeded to outline the "very glaring problems" with evolution. First, he claimed that evolution violates the "Law of Biogenesis," and cannot say how life began in the first place. The problem with that "problem," of course, is that evolution doesn't address the origin of life at all. So the "problem" Ham accuses evolution of having, evolution doesn't have, because evolution doesn't attempt to even address that issue.

Second, Ham claimed that "there is absolutely no known process that can add new information into the DNA to make these types of changes."[33] This is misleading as well, for modern studies in genetics indicate that it is not that new information is added, but rather that there are "switches" within the genome that essentially turn on and off, and thus act as keys that open genetic doors to genetic information that is already there that allows organisms to adapt to their environment.[34]

---

31. Ham, "Who's Really Raising Kids Who Can't Think?" para. 3.
32. Ham, "Who's Really Raising Kids Who Can't Think?" para. 5.
33. Ham, "Who's Really Raising Kids Who Can't Think?" para. 9.
34. "What Darwin Never Knew." *Nova*. December 2009.

Let me prove this further with an example we can all get interested in: sex...and babies. Any time a man and woman have sex and conceive a child, that child is a genetic product of that man and woman—but lo and behold, that child is genetically different from both parents. Yes, there are a host of genetic similarities, but there are genetic variations and mutations that work in different combinations that produce an entirely different person.

So, let's say a certain man was 5'2" and his wife was 6'8." The gene that determined height in their son could be from the man and not mutate at all, and therefore their son will be short. Or it could come from the wife, and therefore their son could become tall. Now, let's say he becomes tall. If in his future lineage, his descendants routinely marry other tall people, chances are they will produce tall offspring, quite unlike that one ancestor in their past who was the size of an Oompa-Loompa. The point is, in the very creation of life, a baby, there is genetic variation and mutation that leads to a wide variety of new genetic information, and changes in future organisms.

Now, someone might say, "That's one thing; the idea that such changes can happen to such an extent that an ape-like ancestor could develop into a modern human being is quite another thing." I agree. That is a valid point. I wonder about that too. But Ken Ham doesn't even let you ask that question because he denies the very fact that new genetic information can be produced in the first place. Simply put, he does not let you even adequately analyze the claims of evolution because he purposely misrepresents them

Ham's third "problem" is that no one has ever observed evolution happening. That statement too is deceiving. Evolution can be observed—we see it in the fossil record, we see it in DNA studies. Ham will no doubt say, "You didn't see a finch turn into a cougar! You just saw a finch produce another finch with a bigger beak! It's still a finch!" Well sure, but evolutionary theory says that over the course of time, those minor adaptations eventually lead to larger changes, and we see evidence of these very things in the fossil record and in the genetic code. So we are, in fact, able to observe it. Just because you can't observe an alligator giving birth to a duck doesn't mean evolution isn't true; it just means you don't understand what evolution claims.

The real shocker in the article is when Ham argued evolution is *actually holding back research and medicine*. I'm sorry, the exact opposite is true. The study of DNA, genetic diseases, vaccines, and a host of other medical advances have come about precisely because of evolutionary theory. Yet still, Ham says evolution has actually hindered research and medicine.

How, you ask? Ham pointed to what was originally thought to be "junk DNA." Early on in genetic studies, scientists had no idea what 98% of the genome was there for, so they labeled it "junk." Ham pointed out that further study has shown that it isn't junk at all. He said, "around 80% of the 'junk' DNA has a useful function and many researchers predict that as more research is done, this number will rise to 100%. A belief in evolution actually held research back!"[35]

Let's look at Ham's comments. Yes, he's right—research has shown that what was previously labeled "junk DNA" actually has a useful function. But how has belief in evolution held that research back? Research has shown it has a function; it has furthered knowledge. Not only is Ham's claim that evolution has held research back nonsensical, but the man who headed the research on the human genome, Francis Collins, is an Evangelical Christian who believes in theistic evolution! So again, Ham's fourth attempt of discrediting evolution is found to be false.

Ham ended by claiming the scientific method doesn't apply to historical science: "The scientific method involves testing a hypothesis, repeating that testing, and observing the results. Historical science deals with the past and therefore it cannot be tested, repeated, or observed in the same way—you can't use the scientific method directly on the past."[36]

That is the essence of Ham's shell game. That's how he can claim the earth is only 6,000 years old. He says, "My 'scientific claims' are 'historical scientific claims' that are not based on the scientific method!" Given the fact that Ham clearly spells this out in his writings, it is absolutely true to say that YEC rejects modern science, and instead relies on a fictitious category of science that doesn't use the scientific method.

NOAH HAD HELP…AND APPARENTLY ADVANCED COMPUTERS

Back in July of 2016, Ken Ham's "Ark Encounter," a life-sized replica of Noah's Ark, opened in Kentucky. Ham claims the project will "prove God's Word is true," although I'm not sure how building a giant boat with

---

35. Ham, "Who's Really Raising Kids Who Can't Think?" para. 17.
36. Ham, "Who's Really Raising Kids Who Can't Think?" para. 19.

modern technological equipment proves that Noah could have built the Ark with primitive tools. If you really wanted to prove it could be done, get some basic hammers, nails, and saws, take your wife and six kids, and try to build that thing without modern technological equipment.

Ken Ham, though, anticipated this objection. On a June 5, 2015 post titled, "Answering Claims About the Ark Project," Ham claimed the Bible doesn't say Noah couldn't have hired workers (who, Ham says, probably mocked Noah while they were building it). Given the fact Ham routinely condemns anyone who believes the universe is a lot older than 6,000 years as smuggling man's speculations into the Bible, it's ironic that he is doing the exact same thing. The only difference is that when astronomers speculate the universe is 14 billion years old, that claim is based on the measurable speed of light that is consistent throughout the universe. Ham's claim is based on nothing other than his own imagination.

Ham then made a truly remarkable claim. He said that people today wrongly assume that people back then only had "primitive" items like stone tools, and that there was actual evidence that primitive people had the ability to create sophisticated technology. In addition to that, people lived for hundreds of years, so if there was a pre-flood genius like Thomas Edison or Albert Einstein, they would have had hundreds of years to develop astounding technology:

> "By the time of the Flood, who knows what technology people may have invented? The fantastic technology we enjoy today is the result of an accumulation of knowledge gained over the past few hundred years. Think how far technology has advanced in just 200 years!"[37]

Think for a moment what Ken Ham has claimed: *people living 4,000 years ago had sophisticated technological machinery that matched or exceeded the modern technology we have today!* You read that right. In order to justify his rationale that building a life-sized 'Ark' in Kentucky somehow proves God's Word is true, Ken Ham has claimed that Noah had access to smart phones, computers, cranes, forklifts...and maybe even a flux-capacitor.

A logical question would therefore be, "If that was the case, then why is there absolutely no evidence whatsoever, anywhere in the world, that ancient people were more advanced technologically than we are today?" Well, Ham has an answer to that as well: "*...for those scoffers who*

---

37. Ham, "Answering Claims About the Ark Project," para. 15.

say that if Noah had such technology we would find evidence of it, they need to understand the sheer destructive processes of the global Flood. It essentially obliterated the pre-Flood world."[38]

Such is the shell-game that is AiG: deny modern science, claim Genesis 1–11 is the kind of "historical science" that can't be tested or proven, call every Christian who disagrees with you a "compromiser," convince people that evolution is an "anti-God religion," ignore the historical testimony of the Church, make up outlandish explanations with no basis in reality to support your claims, and then claim that Noah's flood wiped out any evidence of your claims.

THE HERESY OF YOUNG EARTH CREATIONISM

One of the most common accusations the Old Testament prophets made against the leaders of Israel was that they had led the people astray. Jeroboam claimed to worship YHWH, but then set up two golden calf altars in Dan and Bethel. By patterning Israel's worship after the practices of the surrounding pagan people, he led Israel away from the true worship of the God of Israel, and into a legacy of perversion and idol worship.

A few hundred years later, Jeremiah essentially accused the Temple priesthood of something similar (Jeremiah 7). The Jews of Jeremiah's day would cry, "The Temple of the Lord! The Temple of the Lord!" all the while continuing in the immoral practices of the pagan nations around them. They treated the Temple as just another idol to manipulate to gain YHWH's favor. Jeremiah condemned them for doing this. He warned them that if they refused to abandon their pagan ways that they would suffer the judgment of YHWH in the form of an invasion from Babylon. For speaking the Word of God, he was mercilessly persecuted.

Still later, both Jesus and early Christians like Stephen condemned the Temple priesthood of the exact same thing: taking the place where the LORD God had chosen to let His presence dwell, turning it into an idol "made by human hands," and greatly profiting from it. The Temple priesthood conspired to not only have Jesus crucified, but to also have Stephen stoned to death a short time later.

They had to destroy anyone who exposed their idolatry for what it was. Neither Jeremiah, Jesus nor Stephen spoke against the Temple, per se. They spoke against how the Jewish religious leaders had turned the

---

38. Ham, "Answering Claims About the Ark Project," para. 16.

Temple into an idol that they could manipulate for their own purposes, namely to line their own pockets and, to stir up even more hatred and division among their own people and with the Babylonians and Romans.

Well, history has a way of repeating itself, for the same kind of thing is happening within Evangelicalism. The ultimate result of Protestantism's rejection of Christian Tradition, and of any kind of authority other than one's private, individualized interpretation of the Bible, has led to *biblical literalism*, or more properly speaking, *Bible idolatry*. Young earth creationism is the clearest expression of it.

By rejecting all historical Church teaching and putting the Bible on a pedestal, biblical literalists have lost any kind of understanding of the Church as the Body of Christ and God's instrument of revelation in the world. In its place, they have reduced the Bible to a decontextualized book to be blindly obeyed and worshipped.

Remember, Jeroboam *claimed* to worship YHWH, but he *rejected* the Temple where YHWH had chosen to dwell. Instead, he set up golden calf idols. In the same way, biblical literalism has rejected the very concept of the Church as the Temple of Holy Spirit and has instead set up a decontextualized Bible as an idol that men like Ken Ham can manipulate. The creation/evolution debate, therefore, is simply a symptom of a deeper problem within Evangelicalism: the tendency to turn the Bible into an idol and neglect the importance of the historical and worldwide Church.

If one has no concept of what the Church is, and if one elevates, or more properly speaking, *devalues* the Bible to the status of an idol, one's understanding of God, Christ, salvation, the Bible, the Church, and reality itself is going to be a muddled mess of uncritical, private interpretations, political assumptions, and cultural biases. And in the midst of all that, well-meaning individuals who are truly seeking the truth will get hurt.

By the time of Jesus, the Temple in Jerusalem, the place where God's Name used to dwell, and that was intended to be a light to the nations, had been turned into a national symbol for Jews *against* the nations. The priesthood had taken God's House and had manipulated it into a money-making machine for themselves. By stoking fear and hostility toward the Gentiles, the priesthood goaded the Jewish people to further devotion to the Temple, and hence more lucrative business for themselves.

The Temple priesthood had turned the Temple of YHWH into an idol, and since that tree was no longer bearing any fruit, Jesus prophetically declared it would be destroyed. In its place, Christ said *his body would be the new Temple.* That body, *that Temple,* is the Church. Stephen, the first Christian martyr, echoed Jesus' condemnation of the Temple when he said the Temple was "made by human hands," the prophetic designation for idolatry. For calling out the Temple priesthood for their "temple idolatry," Stephen was stoned to death, and within a generation, both the Temple and the entire city of Jerusalem, was destroyed, just as Jesus had prophesied.

Evangelicalism is faced with a similar challenge. Having lost a proper understanding of the Church, it has let biblical literalists to turn the Bible, particularly passages like Genesis 1–11, into a theological idol. I am afraid that the results will be devastating. Many might not see it coming, but that's the nature of idolatry: you become what you worship, and if you worship a blind and deaf idol, you will become spiritually blind and deaf.

The large number of children from Evangelical homes who are leaving their churches by the time they graduate college should be telling. Contrary to what Ken Ham says, though, the remedy to that trend *is not* to put build bigger temples of biblical literalism. It *is not* to put the Bible on a bigger pedestal and force children to bow down to it even more, with their faces buried further in the sand. The remedy is to reject biblical literalism and return to the traditional understanding of the Bible that has guided the Church for 2,000 years.

Having taught Bible in Evangelical high schools for sixteen years, my concern is for my former students, for young people who have been subjected to YEC indoctrination yet who just feel something isn't right but are afraid to say anything. Or, if they have questioned it, have been met with shaming and intimidation. My concern is for everyone who has grown up in the Evangelical world and who is struggling with their faith because they have been told that if they doubt the universe is 6,000 years old, then they are questioning the Bible and calling God a liar.

I want to say that it is okay to raise questions when something doesn't seem right. Don't let yourself be intimidated and condemned by heretics like Ken Ham. Walk away from the idolatrous temple he has built. He does not represent the historical Christian faith.

This book is not an attack on Evangelicalism. I grew up within Evangelicalism, most of the Christians I know are Evangelicals, and most Evangelicals I have known in my life are sincere, godly, wonderful people, faithful in their following of Christ. Despite the problems within Evangelicalism, by and large it still reflects a vibrant expression of the

Christian faith. That is why I've written this book: not to attack the Evangelicalism, but to warn it: YEC is neither scientific, biblical, or has any standing in the history of the Church. It is the most glaring heresy of our time. To reject YEC is not a rejection of Christianity, and it is not a rejection of the Bible as the inspired Word of God. It is rightly rejecting a very dangerous heresy.

THE POLITICS OF PHARISAISM

The more insidious problem with the biblical literalism of YECism is that it is nothing less than pharisaical. The Pharisees of Jesus' day loved to distinguish themselves from any others in specific ways. It wasn't enough for Jews to be a "peculiar people" in the eyes of the surrounding pagan world. It wasn't enough that they observed the Sabbath, worshipped one God, love their neighbor, or strived to obey the Torah. The Pharisees went "over and above" what was prescribed by God in the Torah and established extra requirements in their own "oral tradition" that they then elevated to the same level of authority as the Torah.

Why? Because the Pharisees were all about *boundary markers* that helped distinguish themselves from not only the pagans, but also Jewish "sinners." Next time you read where the Pharisees get angry with Jesus for eating with "tax-collectors and sinners," realize that the "sinners" they are referring to are their fellow Jews who didn't obey their oral tradition. In the eyes of the Pharisees, such people might still be *Jews*, but they certainly weren't as "holy" as the Pharisees were...therefore, why would the Messiah eat with *them*?

Well, a quick glance through the gospels should give you a pretty clear indication as to how Jesus felt about Pharisees. Perhaps the starkest image Jesus uses to describe them is "white-washed tombs": nice, white, and clean on the outside, but full of death and bones on the inside. Wash your hands all you want, count all your steps on the Sabbath, be as outwardly pure and moral as you can be—if you condemn others, place extra burdens on the faithful, and destroy people's lives with your oral tradition, you're still nothing but a white-washed tomb.

In a similar vein, Evangelicalism also has within its ranks its own Pharisees, with their own boundary markers to distinguish them from secular humanists, atheists, and other "compromised Christians" who, because they don't believe the universe is 6,000 years old, are seen as undermining the authority of the Bible, listening to the voice of the serpent, and being deceived by the devil. Any deviation from their boundary markers will put you in line for a whole world of shaming, guilt, and 'O so polite' persecution.

I grew up in a rather conservative Evangelical home. I've read the Bible stories a hundred times over since I was a kid. I knew who the Pharisees were—they were the "bad religious guys" that Jesus condemned. But up until rather recently, that detail about the Pharisees just never really sank in: they were *the bad religious guys*. And the reason they were so bad wasn't because everyone thought they were bad. In fact, quite the contrary: most Jews considered the Pharisees to be the *really serious and spiritual Jews*.

The Pharisees were the kind of guys who made the Jewish "sinners" feel guilty all the time because the Pharisees never missed an opportunity to show the world just how righteous and holy they were. They were going to stand firm on *the authority of the Torah*, and they weren't going to compromise one bit on it. Letting any single, solitary portion of the Torah slide was just pushing Jewish society down the slippery slope of compromise, paganism, Roman gladiator games, and gay orgies.

So, when a certain Galilean peasant from Nazareth showed up claiming to be both prophet and Messiah but seemed ambivalent to some of the Pharisees' idolized boundary markers of their oral tradition, well, then, sometimes it's necessary that one man die on behalf of the nation.

Oh, they put on a good face. They would be smiling the whole time while they "lovingly" judged you for a whole list of rules you were breaking that, although not explicitly stated in the Torah, were nevertheless part of their "oral tradition" that touched upon a wide range of issues that the *truly righteous Jews would undoubtedly take*. "Oh, we're not saying you're not a Jew," the Pharisees would say to Jesus, "but you *did* pick those grains off on the Sabbath! Repent of your compromising the authority of the Torah!"

"You're a Jewish brother," the Pharisees would say, "but Jesus, she's a prostitute, he's a leper, and *that guy* is a Roman soldier who buggered his servant. If you don't immediately condemn them, how are they going to know they're sinners? You can't be the Messiah, you're not like us!"

I've met modern-day Pharisees. I've been fired by modern-day Pharisees. They abuse their authority and condemn anyone they deem a threat to the sanctity of their particular "oral tradition." Such is not the kind of authority Jesus urged his followers to exercise. When his disciples had gotten into an argument over who was to be the greatest, Jesus told them:

> "The kings of the Gentiles lord it over them; and those in authority over them are called benefactors. But not so with you; rather the greatest among you must become like the youngest, and the leader like one who serves. For who is greater, the one who is at the table or the one who serves? Is it not the one at the table? But I am among you as one who serves." (Luke 22:25–27, NRSV)

Jesus wanted his Church to exercise its authority as a servant community, not as authoritative tyrants. Granted, in any business, church, or school, there is going to be people in charge, and sometimes those people must make decisions that are unpopular. But the way you go about making those decisions is often more important than the decision itself. The way I was treated was, to say the least, not honoring of Christ. It was abuse of the authority of the leaders of the school, masking itself as a defense of "the authority of Scripture." That is the nature of Pharisaism. That is the nature of idolatry. That is the nature of heresy. Under the mask of biblical authority, these three things combine into some very peculiar politics.

THE IDOLATRY OF PHARISAICAL POLITICS

Unfortunately, YECism can no longer be considered just a quirky fringe group. Its heretical theology and pharisaical mentality has worked its way into the mainstream of Evangelicalism, and the results are proving to be devastating. As bad as it is, the main problem has never been young earth creationism's rejection of, or Evangelicalism's general distrust of, modern science. The main problem can be seen in the current obsession to winning the supposed "culture war," and the "politicization" of American Christianity. Let me explain how this has happened.

The thing to remember about biblical literalists like Ken Ham is that, despite their claims that they are simply reading "the plain meaning" of Genesis 1–11, in reality they are doing no such thing. By putting the Bible (or more properly, Genesis 1–11) on a pedestal, they have treated it as an idol, and have rejected the very biblical exegesis and Church Tradition that enable one to properly interpret it. In their place, they have instead chosen to interpret Genesis 1–11 in the context of modern science, in the context of an Enlightenment view of reality, and yes, in the context of modern politics. Pharisaical moralism always has a political component.

What makes YEC so dangerous is that it has linked the interpretation of Genesis 1–11 and the issue of evolution to the politics of the supposed "culture war." Right-wing Evangelical gatekeepers like Ken Ham and Al Mohler are convinced that the battle between the historicity of Genesis 1–11 and the theory of evolution is ground zero in that culture war.

Their thinking goes like this: if you say Genesis 1–11 isn't historical, then you are saying the Bible is full of errors; saying the Bible is full of errors is to undermine the authority of the Bible, and that means you just pick and choose which parts of the Bible you want to obey, and probably question Jesus' miracles and his resurrection as well. Therefore, that must mean you are in rebellion against God's Law, have an "anything goes" attitude toward morality, and compromise on issues like abortion, racism, gay marriage, pornography, and a host of other evils of secular society.

They think if you deny the historicity of Genesis 1–11, that opens the door for evolution, which opens the door to immorality, atheism, liberalism, and the Democratic party. This mindset has fostered a paranoia throughout many segments of Evangelicalism that thinks if we "compromise" on Genesis, then we'll lose the culture war. Our society will descend into moral anarchy and conservative Christians will be rounded up and put in camps. So you need to repent, stand on God's Word, proclaim the Flood really happened, and save our culture!

This paranoia has caused Ken Ham to condemn countless Christian pastors, theologians, and scholars because they don't agree with his interpretation of Genesis 1–11. This paranoia has been the reason why so many ultra-Fundamentalist gatekeepers have put pressure on Evangelical colleges and universities to crack down on and dismiss countless academics who have devoted their lives to teaching in the fields of Biblical Studies or Science, yet who don't hold to the tenants of young earth creationism. Drastic measures must be taken, for there's a culture war going on, and Genesis 1–11 is our political litmus test to determine which side you are on!

Yet the question of the proper interpretation of Genesis 1–11 should not be a political or cultural issue—*it is an exegetical issue*. For that matter, the question of evolution isn't a political or cultural issue either—*it is a scientific issue*. When you turn Genesis 1–11 into a political and cultural issue, you are allowing God's Word to be manipulated to serve the political agendas of this world. You are not fighting the rulers, authorities and cosmic powers of this present darkness (Ephesians 6:12); you are allowing yourself to be their pawn.

I agree with Ken Ham that we are becoming a more secular society. I agree that there are serious moral problems in our culture. The way to address those problems simply isn't insisting that Adam and Eve had a pet dinosaur, and it certainly doesn't lie in pharisaical attempts to obey God's Law even more so that He'll let us "rule the culture" for Jesus.

Remember, that was the exact mindset of the Pharisees: they thought if they were really good at keeping the Torah, then God would return, bless them, and give them political power to rule so they could fix the godless culture around them. They were trying to be morally good in order to gain political power. Jesus saw them for what they were: white-washed tombs, and a brood of vipers—very moral, no doubt, but ultimately very godless, very political, and violently opposed to the Word made flesh.

WHICH SIDE OF POLITICAL AISLE ARE YOU ON? SHOULD YOU BE?

The proof we are becoming a more godless society is not that we are becoming more liberal or more conservative. It's that we are becoming more politically idolatrous. This is happening throughout American Christianity, with both conservatives and progressives. The baffling thing is how both camps have somehow linked the creation/evolution debate to the host of cultural issues facing our society today.

"Conservative Christians" tend to believe Genesis 1–11 is historical and evolution is false. This view is then tied to being pro-life, anti-gay marriage/LGBTQ+, tough border security, pro-gun/second amendment, and denying climate change. It apparently also means blindly supporting the Republican candidate and hailing him/her as the savior of the country.

"Progressive Christians" don't believe Genesis 1–11 is historical and accept evolution as true. This view is then tied to being pro-choice, pro-gay marriage/LGBTQ+, claiming a wall is racist, pro-gun restrictions, and climate change is real. It apparently also means supporting the Democratic candidate and hailing him/her as the savior of the country.

Why is that? Without making any judgments on those cultural issues or candidates, what logical connection is there between believing the historicity of Genesis 1–11 and supporting the second amendment? Why does accepting evolution seem to always mean one is pro-gay marriage? And, depending on your political bent, why are some of you are thinking right now, "Joel, hold on…are you saying you're pro-choice? How can you be a Christian, if…." or "Joel, you're not an intolerant bigot toward the LGBTQ+ community, are you? How can you be a Christian, if…."

Let me suggest that impulse within all of us is the root problem in virtually all the hot-button cultural issues of our day. And somehow, the scientific theory of evolution and the exegetical question regarding Genesis 1–11 has been lumped in together with all of this.

Yes, far too many conservative Christians are beholden to an agenda that is more aligned with the GOP party platform than the Kingdom of God. At the same time, far too many progressive Christians are beholden to an agenda that is more aligned with the Democratic party platform than the Kingdom of God. Obviously not all conservative and progressive Christians are like this, but some certainly are. That is why I've come to disdain any label like "conservative" or "progressive" that comes before the word "Christian." When you label yourself (or others) in that way, there is a danger of aligning yourself more with a certain political party than with Christ, and inevitably that means war…*a culture war.*

I'm not saying Christians shouldn't be involved in politics. By all means, support the political party or candidate you think is best be able to run the government. What I am saying is that Christians in America, both conservatives and progressives, sometimes get dangerously close to equating the Gospel of the Kingdom of God with a particular party platform. When that happens, each side comes to view each other as the enemy, rather than fellow Christians in the Kingdom of God. Simply put, far too many Christians have taken hold of the political platforms of the Left and Right, slapped "Jesus" on them, and then have proceeded to beat the holy hell out of the other side. And thus, we end up with this: "compromising, pro-evolution, gay-loving, liberal secularists" vs. "intolerant, anti-intellectual, bigoted, fascists."

That is the indication of the growing godlessness and secularization in our society: people *thinking* they're serving Christ but are looking to just another Caesar to be their savior and devouring each other in the process. It is political idolatry, pure and simple. We must remember that the politics and values of the Kingdom of God are not always the same as either the GOP or the Democratic party. We must remember that the pressing cultural issues of our day, be they abortion, gay marriage, gun control, immigration, Muslim-Christian relations, and yes, evolution, do not have simplistic, black and white, clear-cut answers.

It is idol worshippers who give the kind of simple answers that fit on a bumper sticker, are splashed on a 30-second political ad, or come in the form of *Answers in Genesis* cartoons. Human beings made in God's image, though, are not simple, and the issues and challenges that face our culture aren't simple—they are complex and nuanced. It takes real human beings practicing patience, faith, hope and love to discuss those complexities in order to arrive at a clearer understanding of the truth. If the extent of your discussion on controversial cultural issues are bumper sticker slogans and sound bites, and if you use them to tear apart "the other side," then you might want to ask yourself where your true worship and loyalties lie.

In the case of Ken Ham and *Answers in Genesis*, the answer to that question is obvious. Make no mistake: young earth creationism is a heresy, rooted in Bible idolatry and finding its expression in pharisaical moralism, the works of the flesh, and political idolatry. The more it takes root in the soil of Evangelical Christianity, the more it will demand the complete rejection of everything and everyone who does not bow to its claims. The result will be not only a complete rejection of science, biblical literacy and Christian history, but a capitulation of the Gospel itself for the divisiveness of the politics of this age.

The more any group cuts itself off from anything and anyone who might be deemed "dangerous" to their peculiar beliefs, the more that group will devolve into an outright cult. I don't want Dr. Bruce Waltke to be right in this case, but I fear that history will prove that he is. Whether or not Evangelicalism devolves into a cult will depend on how Evangelicals ultimately respond to the young earth creationism and the Heresy of Ham.

11

Taking a Cue from Irenaeus of Lyons

"God having predestined that the first man should be of an animal nature, with this view, that he might be saved by the spiritual One."

[God] "knew the infirmity of human beings, and the consequences which would flow from it; but through [His] love and [His] power, He shall overcome the substance of created nature. For it was necessary, at first, that nature should be exhibited; then, after that, that what was mortal should be conquered and swallowed up by immortality, and the corruptible by incorruptibility, and that man should be made after the image and likeness of God, having received the knowledge of good and evil."

—St. Irenaeus of Lyons

THE REASON I HAVE covered so much territory is that I believe the only way to truly come to grips with the current creation/evolution debate, and specifically the claims of YEC, is to see that there is much more at stake than just the question of the age of the earth or the historicity of Adam and Eve. When seen within the larger context of Church history and biblical studies, it becomes clear that YEC is not only scientifically baseless, but it is rooted in a twisted interpretation of Genesis 1–11 that has no authoritative standing within the first 19 centuries of Church history. It is a heresy that breeds paranoia and fanaticism that in turn has done a tremendous amount of damage. Simply believing the earth is only thousands of years old is not heretical. Making that belief the foundation of the Gospel and claiming that failure to acknowledge that is the root cause of all of society's ills—that is both heretical and dangerous.

I don't want to end on a sour note, though. After all, the Gospel is life-affirming, and I believe, just as Paul did back in the first century and just as Justin Martyr and Irenaeus of Lyons did back in the second century, that part of the challenge to Christians is to show there are seeds of truth in all philosophies and discoveries that can bear witness to the Gospel. For too long evolution has been considered by Christians to be *at best* an odd and inconvenient thing that makes Christians really uncomfortable, and *at worst* an absolute Satanic attack on the Christian faith.

Well, we need to change all that. I believe a better understanding of Church Tradition, the Bible in general, and the Gospel in particular, actually makes it possible for us to see how something like the biological theory of evolution can provide some insights that help us understand salvation and sanctification better. In order to do that, we need to recalibrate our understanding of the early chapters of Genesis to be in harmony with what the early Church taught. If we do that, we may be able to see the theory of evolution, not as a threat to the Christian faith, but actually as another way to help explain it even better.

TRANSLATING THE GOSPEL FOR TODAY'S WORLD

The challenge that faces both Christians today and Christians in every society, culture, and era throughout the past 2,000 years is essentially the same challenge that faced the apostle Paul in the first century: how do you take the Gospel that Jesus Christ himself imparted to his disciples when he charged them to "go out and make disciples of all nations" and "translate" it to make sense in the wide variety of societies and cultures throughout the world?

Paul's challenge was to translate for the Gentile world what was originally a distinct Jewish Messianic movement centered on the resurrection of Jesus. That meant having to deal with a whole new set of circumstances, presuppositions and worldviews, and then finding a way to speak the Gospel into that different culture so that the resurrection power of Christ and the empowering of the Holy Spirit could transform hearts and minds.

Over time, different challenges faced the Church, both geographically, as the Gospel spread across the globe to even more cultures, and timewise, as the inevitable passing of time brought new situations and challenges to face. Just as Moses took the genre of ANE myth and essentially "monotheism-ized" it to tell the revealed truth about God, mankind, and creation, so too did the early Church Fathers and later medieval scholars take the philosophical categories of the Greek philosophy of Plato and Aristotle and essentially "Christianize" it so that the Gospel and Christian worldview could further address the challenges of their respective times.

Translating the Gospel for a world in which cultures and societies are in a constant state of flux is a tricky business, whether you are Paul, Origen, Augustine, or Thomas Aquinas. But at least those men had access to and knowledge of the Living Tradition of the Church that preserved the Gospel that Christ handed down to his original apostles. Modern Evangelical Christians, though, are faced with an additional challenge: they may have the Bible, but it has been divorced from the Living Tradition of the Church.

Many Evangelical Christians today are desperately trying to "get back to the early Church," thinking for some reason that back then things were just perfect. "If only we could get back the to the early Church, then we would be the kind of Church Christ wants!" As well-intentioned as that kind of thinking may be, the fact is, it is entirely misguided. Our challenge as Christians today isn't to "get back to the early Church." Rather, it is to take the creedal fundamentals of the Christian faith—the Capital-T Tradition that defines the Church and that articulates what Christians have always believed—and translate that Living Tradition to our world *today*, and thus let the transforming power of the Holy Spirit work through the Church, which is the Body of Christ, continue to redeem, not just individual people, but communities, societies, and ultimately the world.

Unfortunately, in attempting to "get back to the early Church," Protestants have largely thrown out Church Tradition and have tried to rely on the Bible alone. Thus, have ended up interpreting the Bible, not in light of the Church Tradition, but rather in light of a secular Enlightenment worldview. Instead of redeeming the times by translating the Living Tradition to the current culture, we have lost the Living Tradition and have translated the current culture's worldview into the Bible.

The challenge for us is to re-learn the foundational building blocks of the Christian faith so we can then "translate" the Gospel to our day and age and creatively build up the Church as it rests on Christ the cornerstone.

RECLAIMING THEOLOGY AS THE QUEEN OF THE SCIENCES

With that, in the spirit of the Medieval scholars who taught that theology was the "queen of the sciences," I want to take the time to creatively reflect on how the theory of evolution can help us gain a better appreciation and understanding of Christian theology. Simply put, how can the biological theory of evolution serve Queen Theology and help us understand God and His creation better? What implications does it have for the Christian faith?

I want to emphasize an important point before I begin: you don't have to care all that much about the creation/evolution debate to be a sincere, fully mature Christ follower. When it comes to growing up into the fullness of Christ, understanding evolution simply is not important. There have been tremendous men and women of faith who were artists, scholars, theologians, peasants, monks, nuns, laymen, etc. who never even heard of the theory of evolution, and yet whose love and commitment to Christ was so strong that they proved themselves to be worthy citizens of the Kingdom of God. When it comes to the Christian faith, the theory of evolution is irrelevant.

Still, given this day and age, with evolution being such a divisive topic, it would be smart for Christians to get at least a basic knowledge of the controversy if they want to avoid being easily swayed by half-baked arguments of either Ken Ham or Richard Dawkins. But if you are like me and think that no matter how God created the world, the Bible still reveals to us what kind of God He is, who human beings are, and what God's purposes for His creation is, then you might be able to discover how some of the biological truths connected to evolutionary theory can be creatively related to theological truths regarding salvation and the Christian life.

FRUIT FLIES, THE TRINITY, CREATION, AND RELATIONSHIP

For me, most significant theological insight I got during my research for this book came when I watched a video from Nova titled *What Darwin Never Knew*.[1] The two-hour special is a fascinating look at advances in

---

1. "What Darwin Never Knew," *Nova*, 2009.

evolutionary theory since the time of Darwin, but there is one segment in particular that blew me away...it was all about fruit flies and DNA "switches."

Basically, there are two types of fruit flies: one with dark spots on its wings, the other without dark spots. Scientists wanted to find out why some fruit flies have these spots, while others don't. Well, they looked at the genetic code of both types of flies and found to their astonishment that both flies have that "paint-brush gene" that coded for the dark spots. The natural question became, "If both flies have the same "paint-brush gene," then why does one fly have dark spots and the other doesn't?

The answer was found in the supposed "junk DNA" of the genome nobody really understood—the "dark matter" of the genome. In fact, 98% of the double helix of the DNA structure doesn't code for proteins. What this means, basically, is that the monumental step forward with the Human Genome Project that successfully coded the proteins of the genome, still left 98% of the double-helix uncharted. That fact alone should blow us away and leave us in sheer awe of the complexity, creativity, and mystery of life.

In any case, scientists found a difference in the "dark matter" around the "paint-brush gene" between the two flies: the spotted fly had a stretch of DNA that was different from the unspotted fly. So scientists took that stretch of DNA, combined with the gene in a jellyfish that makes it glow, and then injected it into the unspotted fly. Guess what happened? The unspotted fly developed glowing spots on its wings! What scientists had found was essentially a "switch" in the DNA structure. It basically turns on and off the genes that make stuff. If the switch is turned on, then the "paint-brush gene" paints dark spots on the wings of fruit flies; if the switch is turned off, then that "paint-brush gene" is essentially out of work.[2]

What this all boils down to is that evolutionary theory has been able to show how, at the genetic level, biological organisms interact and adapt to their environment in the natural world. The genetic information and ability is already there in the fruit fly, or bird, or bacteria, or human being, to do a whole bunch of "stuff." Whatever "stuff" any given organism does,

---

2. In personal correspondence, Gregg Davidson has told me these "DNA switches" shouldn't be confused with "epigenetic tags." He said, "polymorphic organisms (like many salamanders) have DNA that is variously triggered depending on the environment to produce different body types... [but] epigenetic tags do respond to environment and can influence what DNA is expressed or not."

though, is dependent upon its interaction with its surrounding environment. What this shows, therefore, is something we should have known anyway: creation is not a static thing, but rather an on-going creative process of life. Creation is happening every second of every day. This is the sort of thing many of the early Church Fathers said almost 2,000 years ago.

What does this say about God? I think it forces us to abandon two extremes regarding God and creation. On one hand, we must abandon the idea that God is like a watchmaker who created the "universe-clock" way back when, and then let it run all on its own. On the other hand, though, we also must abandon the idea that the natural processes we see in the natural world are all there is. I think a proper understanding of evolutionary theory blows both the mechanistic understanding of the universe and the naturalistic view of the world out of the water. The universe, and the world in particular, neither is simply a machine built by an "intelligent designer," nor the product of blind processes. It is fundamentally *relational*.

A machine (like a battery-powered clock, for example) will run in the same way whether it is set in the Himalayas, the Amazon jungle, or the Sahara Desert—the only thing that can "happen" to it is that either its batteries run out, or that something in that given environment destroys it. Simply put, you, me, and creation itself, is not a machine governed by blind natural laws and processes. A machine cannot adapt and evolve—it is not relational. By contrast, living organisms, indeed creation itself, is fundamentally relational—it interacts, adapts, evolves, and creates ever-new life forms in relationship to other forms of life within creation.

From the Christian perspective, this concept of life being fundamentally relational should not surprise us at all. First, this helps us understand the Trinity a bit better. The doctrine of the Trinity reveals to us that God Himself, as the source of all life, is a relational being within Himself. He is not a static "thing," but rather a living, relational, life-giving being. He is, as C.S. Lewis said, sort of a *perichoretic* dance (*perichoresis* is a Greek word that is used to describe the Trinitarian relationship within God), and His purpose for His creatures is for us to enter into that dance.

And so, this biological reality of evolution within the natural world points toward the deeper reality of the life of God Himself: the spiritual dance of the Trinity is being performed on the stage of this natural world. God is dancing, He has created us to enter into the dance by means of relating to everything within creation: a close friendship, a hike in a forest, giving birth, painting a landscape—all of these things require relationship, and the very concept of relationship demands personhood. All these things in the natural world impact who we are on a Spiritual level, for there is interaction, adaptation, and ultimately *transformation* from being mere creatures to being Sons of God who will rule all of creation with our Lord and Brother Christ.

Second, this should also help us understand creation as it relates to God a bit better. Instead of understanding the laws of nature as mechanistic or blind processes, I think evolution, by showing the very relational character of creation itself, reveals that what we call the laws of nature are, in fact, *living, relational laws*, reflecting the very metaphysical nature of the living, relational God, and bringing forth the kind of creative life in the natural world that is ever-present within the Trinitarian life of God. In that sense, just as human beings are made in the image of God, and thus are to reflect the nature of God, the very creation itself also reflects in its temporal, natural life the very eternal life of God. Therefore, to partially quote one of my favorite songwriters, Bob Bennett, the task of human beings as the royal, priestly custodians of God's creation is to enter in, take part in this miracle of creation, and offer it back up to the Lord of Life:[3]

> *A light shining in this heart of darkness; A new beginning and a miracle*
> *Day by day the integration of the concrete and the spiritual*

We see it around us every day. The very theory of evolution itself opens a door to understanding the miracle of creation even more. And in that sense, by further unlocking the mysteries of the natural world, evolutionary theory opens yet another door to deeper Spiritual realities. It is our task, as image-bearing priests of God, to offering everything in creation up to God, and thus integrate "the concrete and the Spiritual."

FRUIT FLIES, TRANSFORMATION, AND ETERNITY

Since I'm on the topic of fruit flies, let me share another theological lesson I was able to apply from my learning more about evolutionary theory. Due to the short life span of fruit flies, scientists can observe generations upon generations of them in a short period of time. A fruit fly's entire life is about 30 days. Let's put that into perspective: from a fruit

---

3. Bennett, "Matters of the Heart," 1982.

fly's perspective, a human being who lives for 85 years would have lived 1,034 lifetimes. For human beings to get an idea of what's that like, try to imagine being alive for 87,890 years. And then try to imagine that being's lifetime of 87,890 years being only one generation in a long history of that species' existence. Time becomes so vast that, from the perspective of the limited blip of a lifetime of a human being, you might as well just say it is eternal.

Trying to understand "eternity" really is impossible from our perspective. Even to say, "God has *always* existed," or "God exists *for all time*" is to, in fact, confine God to the limitations of time. You simply cannot express the concept of eternity in human language, for human language is ultimately a product of this limited realm we call "time." When we consider the difference of perspective of a fruit fly in comparison to a human being, though, I think we can at least get a better understanding of it. One day in the life of a fruit fly is the equivalent of almost three years in the life of a human being. Over the three years of 2011-2014, I lived through some major life-changing experiences in my family: pregnancy, cancer, chemotherapy, major surgery, recovery, birth, raising a toddler, and a long, drawn-out, and bizarre divorce that lasted for 19 months.

From my perspective, at the time, those three years seemed like a hellish eternity. I thought those trials would never end. When they did, Mr. Spencer was so kind to boot me from my job as Worldview teacher, which started another cycle of conflicts. Still, even though they have had a life-changing impact on me, those three years will have amounted to a relatively short period of time in the course of my entire life. The thing I realized in the midst of those trials was that the kinds of changes those conflicts had on me were entirely dependent upon the way in which I chose to react to those conflicts. Or to put it in "evolutionary terminology," my Spiritual life has "evolved" (I think for the better) because I chose to respond to the inevitable conflicts in life in certain ways, whereas if I would have chosen to respond in different ways, my Spiritual life would have regressed, or ultimately might have taken a darker turn.

Genetic studies have shown there is something already in many living organisms capable of adaptation, evolution, and transformation, that, when a certain switch is flipped, makes it capable of adapting to its environment for its relatively brief life. By analogy, God has built into human beings the ability to choose how to react to the inevitable conflicts of life. Our ability to choose, to "flip certain switches" woven mysteriously within the very fabric of our being, will determine if we in our "natural state" (what C. S. Lewis calls *Bios*) will transform (and "evolve," if you will) into the higher form of Spiritual life (what C. S. Lewis calls *Zoe*), into not just more highly developed creatures, but into transformed beings who mature fully in Christ to be revealed as "sons of God," just as Romans 8:19 states, "For the creation waits with eager longing for the revealing of the sons of God" (ESV).

We in our natural, time-limited states, tend to only see the immediate pain and conflict in our lives. We can't really get the big picture of God's eternal perspective. But the evolutionary changes we see in fruit flies, within their brief, natural lives, can help us put our own conflicts into perspective. We are made for eternity. Although we cannot fully comprehend such a thing, we can see that the tribulations we inevitably experience in this life shape, mold, and transform us in ways that have eternal consequences.

As long as we respond to those trials and tribulations with faith, hope and love, we can be assured that such "fiery ordeals," however presently painful, will turn out to be fires that purify us into eternal righteousness. But if we respond to those "fiery ordeals" with hatred, contempt and bitterness, those very same fires that could purify us will end up enveloping us in our own personal hell.

Strange as it may sound, evolution can help us view such trials from an eternal perspective. Now, it is true that the "DNA switches" and short lifespans of fruit-flies are not *directly* related to the larger theory of evolution. And yes, evolution works over multiple generations, affecting populations, not specific, individual organisms. But like I said earlier about fruit-flies, I have found that if you are a Christian and take the time to study a little bit about evolution, you're going to find things that can actually help you understand salvation and the Christian life better. If theology truly is the "queen of the sciences," this should not be surprising.

IRENAEUS, AND RETHINKING ADAM, EVE AND "THE FALL"

Ultimately, evolution impacts the way we look at human beings and "the Fall" in Genesis 2—3. Young earth creationists like Ken Ham claim evolutionary theory is an attack on the trustworthiness of the Bible. If there was no special creation by God of a first couple, perfect genome intact, directly from the dust 6,000 years ago, then the Bible is untrustworthy, and the gospel is undermined...thus says Ken Ham. But let's take Ken Ham out of the picture for just a moment and keep things really simple.

Chances are you've been taught since Sunday school that God created a perfect world, where nothing ever died. Then, when Adam and Eve ate from the Tree of Knowledge of Good and Evil that they "fell" from their perfect state and opened the door for sin and death to run rampant throughout the rest of human history. The reason why *we* sin is because *they* sinned first, and since we've descended from them, we've somehow inherited that sin nature. Quite obviously, the theory of evolution and the idea that there was no historical Adam and Eve throws a big monkey wrench into that whole scenario, doesn't it? In that respect, it is perfectly understandable why evolution and the idea that there was no historical Adam and Eve has traditionally been viewed by Evangelicals with suspicion and fear.

Yet what most Evangelicals don't know is that *that view* of an originally perfect and historical Adam and Eve who "fell" from that perfect state and screwed things up for the rest of humanity largely came from Saint Augustine in the fourth century. It was his interpretation of those early chapters in Genesis in his own commentary of Genesis that ended up shaping the way most Catholics and Protestants have come to view Adam and Eve.[4] What most Evangelicals don't know is that there was an earlier second century Church Father, Irenaeus of Lyons (AD 130-202), whose interpretation of Genesis 2—3 was quite different than that of Augustine's.

Ironically, far from getting us away from the original understanding of Genesis 2—3, evolutionary theory can very well help us get back to the way early Christians like Irenaeus of Lyons read and interpreted these chapters. In chapter 6, when I commented on Genesis 2—3, I mentioned that a plain reading of the text actually indicates that Adam and Eve *were not created perfect*. The fact that they were so naïve that they got tricked by the serpent seems to suggest that they were, in fact, not perfect: a perfect person wouldn't have gotten tricked, right? Therefore, if they were not perfect, can we really say that eating of the Tree of Knowledge of Good and Evil constituted a "fall" *from perfection*? I'm not sure we can.

Don't misunderstand me. Genesis 3 obviously teaches we are imperfect, sinful creatures. Still, I'm just not sure that it is teaching that

---

4. John R. Schneider provides an excellent overview of the problems with Augustine's interpretation of Adam in his article, "The Fall of 'Augustinian Adam': Original Fragility and Supralapsarian Purpose." *Zygon: Journal of Religion and Science.* December 2012, Volume 47, Number 4.

humanity at one point in the past was literally perfect. In fact, such a view is that of the early Church. We know this because we have the writings of the early Church Father Irenaeus of Lyons. He was a disciple of Polycarp, who was a disciple of John himself. When it comes to early Church testimony outside of New Testament times, you can't do much better than Irenaeus of Lyons.

His most famous work is called, *Against Heresies*, in which he not only wrote about the various heresies that threatened the second century, but also explained precisely the Church Tradition that had been handed down to the apostles by Jesus himself. Now, in order to understand precisely what Irenaeus had to say about Adam and Eve, you have to first understand what the heretics of his day were saying about Adam and Eve. Interestingly, some of it is going to sound awfully like the claims made by Ken Ham and young earth creationists. And I have to warn you of one more thing: a little bit of Greek Philosophy is going to be involved in the discussion.

The Heretical View of Adam and Eve

The heretics in Irenaeus' day taught that God had created Adam as essentially a celestial-like being—a veritable superman, if you will, who possessed an amazing intellect, and who was perfect in every way. Therefore, when Adam and Eve were tempted by the serpent, the heretics said they, along with a previously perfect creation, had fallen from that state of perfection. Therefore, when it came to Christ, the heretics taught that he came to restore us to that original state of perfection. Thus, their version of Adam and Eve was very Gnostic in its outlook. It pictured Adam and Eve as purely spiritual, non-material beings who "fell" into the dirty world of materiality and physicality. They viewed this present material creation as a result of that "fall." They taught that Christ was going to restore us to that original "pre-material/spiritual state" of Adam and Eve's initial perfection.

Now, many of you might be thinking, "Well, I think Adam and Eve were real, physical people, but they were perfect, weren't they? Isn't that the point? They fell from God's perfection? How could God create something that wasn't perfect? The reason why nature has earthquakes and tornados and hurricanes is because of their sin, right? Christ came to restore us to the original state of perfection that Adam and Eve had, right?"

Well, if you think that, that means your view of Adam and Eve and the "fall" isn't the view of the early Church. In fact, it was this heretical understanding of Adam and Eve as perfect beings with towering intellects and supreme powers that Irenaeus made a point to mock.

Irenaeus' Response to the Heretical View of Adam

The first way Irenaeus mocked this heretical view of Adam was to emphasize that Adam was created out of *dirt and mud*: he wasn't some sort of glorious, towering, angelic-like superman; he was a material being, formed from the base earth, as much a part of the natural order as everything else, and that was what God intended, and that was "good." Irenaeus was not going to let the heretics claim to be so "spiritual" that they rejected God's good creation, and human beings' relationship to it.

The second way in which Irenaeus confronted the heretical teaching of Adam was by making it clear that none of the early Church Fathers had, in fact, taught that Adam was a perfect being. In fact, given Irenaeus' close proximity in time to Christ himself, it is safe to say that neither Christ nor his Apostles taught that Adam was some sort of perfect being either.

Quite the contrary, Irenaeus said that Church Tradition had always taught that Adam and Eve were essentially children who had yet to develop into full maturity. He said, "Adam and Eve were naked and were not ashamed, for their thoughts were innocent and childlike."[5] Therefore, their sin was not so much a "fall from perfection," as it was the result of childish immaturity. If that shocks you, consider something else. Irenaeus viewed Adam and Eve as symbolic of all humanity. The very name "Adam" means "humanity." For Irenaeus, the story of Adam was never just the story of an individual, it was the story of each one of us.

Therefore, Irenaeus interpreted Genesis 1:26, which says, "Let us make Man (Adam) in our image, after our likeness," as describing the nature and purpose of humanity. He taught that we are created in God's *image*, but our purpose and task as human beings is to grow into the full *likeness* of God by means of relationship with Him.

The Orthodox Church has always made a distinction between "in God's image" and "after God's likeness." Simply put, God's image is something we are born with—it is part of our nature; God's likeness is

---

5. Irenaeus of Lyons, *Proof of the Apostolic Preaching*, 14.

something we grow into, if we so choose. Think of it this way. My son is "in my image"—meaning, he looks like me. Even in the womb, the ultrasound showed he had my profile. But as of yet, he is not "in my likeness." He has yet to grow up. If I raise him right, and if he makes good decisions, in time he will not only just look like me, he will also grow up to be very much like me. It's not a perfect analogy, but I think it is one that will do very well.

A Brief Lesson on Greek Philosophy in the Early Church

The reason why early Church Fathers like Irenaeus saw Adam and Eve as children was because of their very understanding of reality. This requires a quick course on Greek philosophy. Borrowing from Greek philosophy, they understood God as being an uncreated, eternal being, and therefore perfect, "pure actuality" as Aristotle would say. There is nothing about God that is in a state of "becoming," because God already perfectly "is." When He reveals himself to Moses at the burning bush, God does not say, "I am a being with potential to become something more." He simply says, "I AM."

When God creates, though, He creates within time, and so the creatures he creates are in a constant state of "becoming." I am a 54-year-old man, but I am not the totality of Joel Anderson because I still have, more than likely, a large portion of my life to live. If you've ever seen the bumper-sticker that says, "Be patient with me, God's not finished with me yet!" you're getting a glimpse of this very concept. As long as we are creatures within time, we are works in progress, creatures in a state of "becoming," full of potential to become something more than we currently are. That means we aren't perfect.

This means everything must come in due time. When I was 12, I wasn't mature enough to handle the responsibilities I have at 54. Growing up takes time—there is no other way. This fact of reality is what Irenaeus is getting at when he describes why Adam and Eve were child-like:

> "But things which are made by God, in as much as they have received a beginning of their existence at a later time, must fall short of [He] who made them. Things which have come into existence recently cannot said to be unoriginated. To the extent… they are not unoriginated they fall short of being perfect. In as much as they have come into being more recently, they are infants, and, in as much as they are infants, they are unaccustomed

to and unpracticed in perfect discipline. A mother can offer adult food to an infant, but the infant cannot yet digest food suitable for someone older. Similarly, God, for his part, could have granted perfection to humankind from the beginning, but humankind, being in its infancy, would not have been able to sustain it."[6]

This is what we see in Genesis 3 with the Tree of the Knowledge of Good and Evil. The fruit on it was "adult food," and Adam and Eve were still on Gerber's baby food. To use another analogy, the fruit on the tree was like wine and Adam and Eve were still under-aged. In their immaturity and curiosity, they snuck a bottle of wine back to their room, drank the whole thing, and ended up throwing up, and waking the next day with a massive hangover. Thus, not only did they suffer in their bodies, their relationship with "Dad" was also affected, for they proved themselves to be disobedient. They were not fully grown up, and it showed.

Given that, when Genesis 1:26 says that God created Adam "in His image" and "to be according to His likeness," the early Church Fathers taught that was saying that even though we are mere creatures, not only do we bear the stamp of God's image, but God's intention all along was for us to become like Him. That state of "becoming" necessitates time and history, so that God's imperfect, incomplete creatures can progress and grow into His likeness. Simply put, being creatures, our "potentiality" is that we can (if we enter into an obedient and trusting relationship with God) become like God. That was, and still is, God's purpose for humanity all along. That's why the early Church Fathers didn't view Adam and Eve as being created perfect. Only God is perfect, and God's purpose for mankind, and the reason for creation itself, is for His creatures to enter into relationship with Him, and by doing so, become ever-more like Him.

Christ is the Alpha and Omega, not "Plan B"

This leads us to something else to understand. Irenaeus points out the reason why Adam and Eve disobeyed and sinned was because, even though they were made in God's image, they didn't yet fully understand what that meant because Christ, the one who is "the image of the invisible God" (Colossians 1:15), had not yet been made known or visible. They were led astray so easily because they were child-like. They did not yet

---

6. Irenaeus of Lyons, *Against Heresies*, IV.38.1.

have full knowledge of good and evil, because they had not yet acquired the wisdom that comes through living.

In that sense, one can say that "the fall" was inevitable, in the same way it is inevitable that every person, being childish and immature as we are, is bound to make bad choices and be led astray by countless temptations throughout life. You might be alarmed by such an understanding of this idea that "the fall" was inevitable and say, "You're saying God is responsible for this sinful world, for He created Adam and Eve imperfect, knowing they would sin." Well, He *did know* they (and we) would sin, and it's obvious, they (and we) *aren't perfect*. But the good news is that's not where the story ends.

Irenaeus' teaching on Adam and Eve makes a lot of sense when seen in the light of Christ. He saw Christ as truly the Alpha and Omega of the entire creation: God's fundamental purpose for creation was to bring all creation to fullness in Christ. That was the goal all along. The way by which God intended for humanity to become like Him had always been through Christ. It wasn't like God created the world, then was surprised that His "perfect" human beings screwed up His perfect masterpiece, and so decided to resort to "Plan B" and sent Christ to clean up the mess.

This is a very important point: there is no "Plan B" with God. This creation, this history, this life we experience—this is the plan. It always has been the plan. Christ is to be the savior of the world. And, as Anthony Zimmerman points out, the word "savior" doesn't just narrowly mean "someone who pays the ransom for sinners." It carried with it the notion of a "sanctifier:" someone who offers something up to God to make it holy and set apart for God's purposes.[7] Christ's purpose all along as Savior-Sanctifier was to take "natural man" and bring him into the supernatural.

Now the thing to realize is that all of that original childlikeness and immaturity is inherently *natural*, it's part of what it means to be a created being. To be created inherently means that we are *not* like God. He is uncreated perfection, whereas we are created as imperfect creatures, but with a purpose: to relate to God in obedience and trust so that we can forever grow into further likeness of God—and the one who makes that possible is Christ, our Savior and Sanctifier.

We will never be perfect in the same way God is perfect, but He has created us in His image with the capacity to enter into a relationship with Him so we may forever become more like Him. As Irenaeus said, that has

---

7. Zimmerman, "Irenaeus on Original Sin."

always been God's plan for humanity and His creation: to create natural, imperfect creatures who have the capacity to be saved and sanctified by Christ, and to grow into the likeness of God:

> "God having predestined that the first man should be of an animal nature, with this view, that he might be saved by the spiritual One. For inasmuch as He had a pre-existence as a saving Being, it was necessary that what might be saved should also be called into existence, in order that the Being who saves should not exist in vain."[8]

To put it another way, the whole purpose of humanity and creation itself was to give something to Christ to save and sanctify. This means that the entirety of human history is salvation history. As Denis Minns said, "This path may twist and wander through many detours, but there is no radical bifurcation.... The human race was predestined in Adam, but it was predestined to come to be in the image and likeness of God."[9]

The Tragedy of Genesis 3 and the "Fall"

If we understand what Irenaeus is saying about Christ and His relationship to humanity, we'll understand the story of Adam and Eve is not a story of two people way back when. It is the description of the reality of human experience. The Adam and Eve story is my story, is your story, is our story. The tragedy of Genesis 2—3 wasn't that God created two perfect people who sinned, fell from perfection, thus making God resort to some sort of "Plan B of Christ." The tragedy was that the childish and immature Adam and Eve tried to grow up too fast, and they didn't trust God to grow them up in His good time. They were indeed created in God's image, but the point of human existence was to grow up into full maturity, into God's likeness. Being immature as they were, they didn't want to wait—and so they disobeyed. In that sense, Genesis 3 isn't about the first couple's "fall from perfection," as it is about human immaturity, disobedience, and the inevitable mess we make of things.

We all know this to be true in our own lives. Think about it. We are born immature, naïve, innocent and childish—of course . . . we're children! When our parents try to teach us patience and wisdom, and try to guide us into maturity, what do we do? We don't want to wait. We

---

8. Irenaeus of Lyons, *Against Heresies*, V.22.3.
9. Minns, *Irenaeus*, 58–59.

want the "freedom" of adulthood right now. When our parents say, "Now you're in high school, curfew is 10:00 pm on school nights," we want to prove to our parents that we're adults…so we disobey and stay out until 11:30 pm. And what does that act of disobedience really show? That we're mature? Absolutely not. It shows just the opposite—our disobedience shows that we are still woefully self-centered, immature, and foolish.

Consequently, punishment ensues, and distrust is sown. Our little disobedient act gave us a real knowledge of "good and evil." Our eyes certainly were opened, and we saw how foolish and sinful we really are and how much hard work it will take to grow up and regain the trust of our parents, and how much work it will take to truly grow up and become mature adults. As is true with us, so that truth is reflected in Genesis 3.

After all, how else does one gain wisdom, knowledge, and maturity, if one doesn't step out and miserably fail first? Wisdom, knowledge, and maturity only come about after a series of steps and inevitable failures. Consider what Irenaeus says here about Adam, and thus humanity:

> "He learns from experience that disobeying God, which robs him of life, is evil, and so he never attempts it. But how would he have discerned the good without knowing its opposite? For firsthand experience is more certain and reliable than conjecture. The mind acquires the knowledge of the good through the experience of both and becomes more firmly committed to preserving it by obeying God. First, by penance, he rejects disobedience, because it is bitter and evil. Then he realizes what it really is, the opposite of goodness and sweetness, and so he is never tempted to taste disobedience to God. But if you repudiate this knowledge of both…unwittingly you destroy your humanity."[10]

This is the way God has planned it all along. Even though God creates us in His image, He knows we will disobey and invite suffering into our lives. Still, the plan all along was that through our sin, and the suffering and pain that comes with it, God, through Christ, meant it all for our ultimate perfection, to where we grow up in Christ, and become ever more transformed into the likeness of God. As John Schneider wrote, "Irenaeus thought that the Fall must have been a part of a foreordained plan, and that the plan was for a better world than any other. It would be a world brought to maturity and flourishing in and through the

---

10. Irenaeus of Lyons, *Against Heresies* IV.39.1.

Incarnation and Atonement, the Person and Work of Christ."[11] Consider what Irenaeus says here:

> "How could man ever have known that he was weak and mortal by nature, whereas God was immortal and mighty, if he had not had experience of both? To discover his weakness through suffering is not in any sense evil; on the contrary, it is good not to have an erroneous view of one's own nature. The experience of both [good and evil] has produced in man the true knowledge of God and of man and increased his love for God."[12]

Contrary to what some might think, this does not make God responsible for evil. Irenaeus is not saying God is the author of evil. As Schneider writes, "It was in the *nature* and *character* of God...to bring about a world that would emerge through divine victory over imperfections and evils. In these metaphysics, God *authorizes* the existence of evils for that purpose, but is not the 'author of evils' in the sense of being *culpable* for anything wrong. In its totality, beginning to end, the creation is 'very good,' and so is God."[13]

Reading and understanding Genesis 2—3 through that lens makes a whole lot more sense than the way we have always been taught to read it, as if it were literal history about the first two people in the world. If one listens to what Irenaeus says, and realizes the symbolism in the story, one realizes that the story is spelling out a fundamental truth regarding humanity as a whole, and each one of us as individual human beings.

Think about times when you tried to be wise before your time, when you were deceived, when you reached out for some "forbidden fruit," when you felt shame and guilt for doing something you knew was wrong, and when you experienced broken relationships because of something stupid you did. Then go and read Genesis 2—3. You'll find that Genesis 2—3 speaks directly to you. Despite the pain and suffering that has come about through your bad decision, God has promised to work through you, the woman's offspring, to eventually crush the head of the serpent.

---

11. Schneider, "The Fall of 'Augustinian Adam,'" 23.
12. Irenaeus of Lyons, *Against Heresies* V.3.1.
13. Schneider, "The Fall of 'Augustinian Adam,'" 23.

Challenge, Failure, and Reassurance

Perhaps this can get us to at least a slightly better understanding to the age-old question, "Why does God allow suffering and death?" I can't even begin go through all the passages in the New Testament that talk about the inevitability, and dare I say, the necessity of suffering and death when it comes to salvation. On virtually every page of the New Testament you will find something about how trials, tribulations, suffering and death itself produce endurance, maturity, righteousness, and growing up into the fullness of Christ. It seems quite clear in the New Testament that you cannot become fully mature in Christ without going through suffering, because suffering is the "sparring partner" that challenges us to become fully mature in Christ.

Perhaps an analogy will help: the show *The Biggest Loser*. At the beginning of the show, you see various people overweight and out of shape. They are given the challenge to get healthy and work out. The first few workouts are not only extremely painful for them, they are painful for us to watch! Those contestants are in hellish pain—their muscles haven't worked that much in years; their heart is pumping as if it will burst. They feel like they're going to die. But little by little, the weight comes off, the muscles get toned and get stronger, and by the end of the show, the ones who really worked hard are not only 10 times healthier than they ever thought they could be, but they have experienced an additional transformation other than their bodies alone. Their self-esteem, their confidence, and their spirit has returned—they are *new people*. The workouts that once seemed like hell to them are now a source of invigorating life. They love to work out now. Yes, their muscles still hurt after a workout, but it's a different kind of hurt . . . it's a "good hurt," as opposed to the "hellish hurt" they first felt.

Now obviously, the Bible does not say sin is a good thing, but it does acknowledge that challenge and struggle are inevitable within God's purposes for humanity to become like Him. What Genesis 3 shows is that a relationship with God involves a *challenge*: the challenge to obey Him, and to trust that He will grow us up into His likeness in His good time. Genesis 3 also shows us something else: Adam, Eve, you, me, and every human being *fails at that challenge*. We don't trust. We don't obey. That's why we find ourselves estranged from God. Such failure not only fractures our relationship with God, it also fractures our relationship with other human beings: spouses, children, parents, friends, everyone.

Yet still, Genesis 3 shows us one other thing, something that doesn't get fully revealed until Christ, but it is still there in Genesis 3: there will be a "war" throughout history between the serpent's offspring and the woman's offspring, and eventually the woman's offspring will crush the head of the serpent. Despite Adam and Eve's disobedience, despite our own sin and disobedience, God, in His providence, works through the struggle of history to still bring about His purpose: taking creatures made in His image, and growing them up into His likeness.

In that respect the history of God's creation itself is salvation history. Each one of our stories, and indeed the story of all creation, isn't one of trying to recapture some lost perfection, but rather of choosing to take part in the transformation of God's creation He has intended all along: from being men of the dust to being transformed into men of Heaven; from the old creation being transformed to the New Creation, from being spiritual infants "in Adam" to being spiritually mature Sons of God "in Christ."

THE IRRELEVANCY OF A HISTORICAL ADAM

With all that being said, it may very well be true that Irenaeus (and most Christians throughout Church history) *assumed* Adam and Eve were historical people. The fact is, though, at least with Irenaeus, one simply cannot make that argument from the text at all. Irenaeus' argument regarding Genesis 2—3 was focused on human identity in relationship to creation and to God, His purposes involving His creation, and the goal of salvation in Christ. Irenaeus simply was not making a historical argument. Even if he did view Adam and Eve as two historical people, it is abundantly clear from his writings that such a point was incidental in light of his teaching regarding how Adam symbolizes all humanity.

If Irenaeus was transported to today, and it was explained to him how the findings of both the Human Genome Project and other advances in evolutionary studies have cast doubt on the notion that all humanity has descended from two people a mere 6,000 years ago, I have to think it would not have phased him, because he already clearly understood back in the second century that Genesis 2—3 was speaking to the human condition of which we all are a part.

Obsessing over the historicity of Adam and Eve is, I believe, actually an attempt to keep Genesis 2—3 at arm's length, and to keep it from directly challenging and speaking to our lives in the here and now. To do so is to treat it as nothing more than a fact to be proven and defended. Instead, we should see it as God's revelation that speaks directly to each of us, for we are human beings, we are Adam. In that respect, Genesis 2—3 becomes intimately relational. It tells us who we are, why we do what we do, and it challenges us to respond to God in obedience and trust. If I can put it this way: whether or not Adam and Eve were historical people, that doesn't change the fact that Genesis 2—3 is about your condition as a human being.

As things stand, as Christians we know we can respond to God in obedience and trust because we know the goal: Christ, who is the image of the invisible God who has been revealed. Read through your New Testament through this lens, and you'll see this view everywhere. It is inescapable. It permeates the Gospels, Paul's letters, and the entire New Testament. Irenaeus bears witness to it in his writings, and it is something we know deep in our bones, because it is that transformative salvation that we live out and in which we grow every day of our lives. Just consider these two passages from Paul:

"He will transform the body of our humiliation that it may be conformed to the body of his glory, by the power that also enables him to make all things subject to himself" (Philippians 3:21, NRSV).

"I consider that the sufferings of this present time are not worth comparing with the glory about to be revealed to us. For the creation waits with eager longing for the revealing of the children of God; for the creation was subjected to futility, not of its own will but by the will of the one who subjected it, in hope that the creation itself will be set free from its bondage to decay and will obtain the freedom of the glory of the children of God" (Romans 8:18–21, NRSV).

IRENAEUS AND EVOLUTION

In a roundabout way, I think Irenaeus' teaching on Genesis 2—3 can have an impact on the current creation/evolution debate. I say "roundabout" because obviously he did not directly comment on the debate. But because of Irenaeus' teaching on Genesis 2—3, I believe we can see salvation itself, by virtue of the indwelling presence of the Spirit, is a process of Spiritual transformation and evolution. The biological theory of evolution, therefore, can serve as yet another example in creation that reflects God's purposes, and thus can give further glory to Him.

Of course, there is a difference between salvation and evolution. On the biological level, evolutionary changes happen all on their own, depending on the environment in which an organism finds itself. The organism really has no say in the matter. On top of that, evolution works over an extremely long period of time, over generations and affecting population groups. With human beings, though, in addition to the mere biological life that we share with the rest of creation, we also possess a spiritual life. And when it comes to the spiritual life, it is not just a matter of automatic genetic switches. It is entirely dependent on the choices we make. When faced with the inevitable sufferings in life, we have the choice to adapt, evolve, and be spiritually transformed by them. Whether or not we are transformed into more heavenly creatures is entirely dependent on our choices. Just as an organism that fails to adapt to its environment soon goes extinct, we, if we fail to trust and obey God through those times of trials, will eventually lose our lives as well.

Simply put, evolution helps us understand that our Christian salvation is not an "I got saved and now I have my get out of hell card all sown up!" It is not a one-time transaction. Christian salvation is a transformative journey of Spiritual evolution, where God, through Christ and the indwelling presence of the Holy Spirit, slowly re-creates us into the fullness of Christ, into beings who grow into the likeness of God.

The biological evolution we see in the natural world acts as a pointer to the reality of our Spiritual evolution by the transformative power of the Holy Spirit. It helps us get a better grasp of eternity and how God's plan and purposes stretch far beyond what our limited perspective can clearly see—and that necessitates faith. It also helps us get a better grasp of suffering and tribulations in this world—they too are part of God's purposes. They either will be the means by which we achieve maturity in Christ, or the instruments of our ultimate destruction—and it all depends on how we react to them. Do we accept them as Christ accepted the cross, or do we let them embitter us and push God away, and thus reject the very source of life that can redeem us? Finally, we have to remember that our individual "Spiritual evolution" is not an end in and of itself. Ultimately, we are part of something bigger than ourselves—through Christ, God has promised to renew *all creation.*

RECLAIMING THEOLOGY AS THE QUEEN OF THE SCIENCES

If we can reclaim the early Church's understanding of salvation as an infinite process of becoming more and more like God in Christ—always being God's creatures, but ever being taken up into the transformative life of the Trinity—I think we would be much better off in our understanding of God, Christ, salvation, ourselves, and creation around us. If we understood that, we would be able to look at something like the theory of evolution, and instead of being frightened by it, be able to reflect and contemplate how that natural biological process mirrors the very salvation history we find in Christ.

It was in the Middle Ages when Christian theologians and scholars saw theology as the "Queen of the Sciences." What we call science they called "natural philosophy." But they did not see an insurmountable divide between science and faith. Rather, they saw everything in nature, even what we call the "natural sciences" as being the "handmaiden to Queen Theology." Everything that they discovered about the natural world, they would use to help further explain the Christian faith and theology.

Yet during the Enlightenment, secular thinkers took a philosophical axe and completely cut the cord that bound theology and the natural sciences. Everything changed in the Western worldview after that. Before, what was discovered about the natural world was used in the service of theology; helping to further explain the wonderful world God had created.

Now, though, in parts of the Evangelical world, we have men like Ken Ham rejecting the natural sciences altogether. Instead of allowing the discoveries in the natural sciences to serve as handmaidens to Queen Theology and serve as examples in the natural world that reflect theological teachings, he not only tells people that the natural sciences are the enemy to Christian faith, but he also ignores what the true fundamentals of the Christian faith are. In their place, he has taken Genesis 1–11 and has constructed his own idol of "historical science," and teaches people that a belief in a young earth and a historical Adam is a fundamental tenant of the Christian faith. It isn't. It never has been. We have the writings of the early Church—that's never been claimed.

A LIVING PAINTING

I do not know whether every single detail in the biological theory of evolution is true, but from what I've researched, it certainly has unlocked a lot of mysteries about the natural world. I know one thing, though: in the course of my research for this book, what I've learned about the theory of evolution has made me interested in science for the first time in my life. It is pretty fascinating—there's no other way to say it.

In addition, it has actually further strengthened my faith in God. I now look at the standard caricature of God as "the great watchmaker" and I realize that concept of God is way too small. In my opinion, the complex artistry and creativity that evolutionary theory reveals about the ongoing creation of natural world puts all other depictions of God and creation to shame, whether it be Old Earth Creationism, Young Earth Creationism, Intelligent Design, or Ultra-Darwinism.

Such theories seem to me to be attempts to paint a picture of God and creation using a "color-by-numbers" book, or (in the case of Ultra-Darwinists) an attempt to paint a picture of a godless creation by throwing random paint cans off a five-story building, letting them smash onto the pavement and explode the paint everywhere, and then say, "Look! Complete random chance! No one is responsible for it!"

Evolution, properly viewed through the lens of theology, shows all that to be mere child's play. Instead, it gives us a picture of *a living painting*—one that seems to paint itself because God has breathed life into it and given it the ability to create beauty along with Him. Yes, He is ultimately doing the creating, but He has filled creation with so much life, that it seems to paint itself. It improvises, adapts, and creates different colors and hues as it continues to live and grow.

His crowning achievement is human beings, biologically a part of the living painting, but also having access to the Spirit of God. As they grow in their relationship with Him, they come to reflect His image more each day, and they are able to fulfill His purposes for them to be priestly king-custodians of this living painting of creation, and His co-creators and artist-apprentices. The knowledge derived from evolutionary studies have made it possible to create vaccines, medicines, healthier foods…the list can go on. All of these things point to something we can rejoice in—fulfilling our calling as God's image bearers who are to not only exercise dominion over His creation, but to care for His creation.

So let me urge you not to get bogged down and distracted by oversimplistic arguments how the earth can only be 6,000 years old, or overblown proclamations how "evolution disproves God." If you understand what Genesis 1–11 is really doing, then you don't have to be afraid of evolutionary theory, and you'll be smart enough not to get duped by men like either Ken Ham or Richard Dawkins. There is so much truth and wonder found within evolutionary theory, and Christians should be able to embrace it and give glory to God for what evolutionary theory has discovered.

Just keep it subservient to theology, and let it bear much fruit.

12

Hamming It Up

"I do not like green eggs and ham/I do not like them, Sam-I-Am"

—Dr. Seuss

IT HAS BEEN TEN years since Mr. Spencer first informed me at Panera Bread that he no longer had confidence in me as a Worldview teacher and would not be renewing my contract at the end of the following school year. Two years later, in the summer of 2016, I came out with *The Heresy of Ham*. I wrote for the very personal reason that I was just trying to make sense of what had happened. That ordeal made no sense to me.

What I concluded about YECism can be seen in the first eleven chapters of this book. YECism is not scientific or biblical, has never been a fundamental tenet of the Christian faith, and has caused a great deal of hurt to countless Christians, and doing so, has actually contributed to the loss of faith of many. Ultimately, the primary concern of YECism is "fighting the culture war." That is why YECists like Ken Ham tend to be so divisive—they are *fighting a war*. They think if they can convince people that Genesis 1–11 is historically and scientifically accurate, then people will submit to biblical authority and America can get back to its Christian foundations and be a Christian nation again.

There are so many things wrong with that mentality that I can't begin to list them all. It would take up an entire book in and of itself and would ultimately veer off into topics, "culture war" topics, that go beyond the scope of this book. Now, there really are challenging and controversial cultural issues facing our society today. I would never suggest that Christians should not speak out about issues they feel are important. I certainly have some very strong opinions about many of them. How you choose to go about engaging in those issues is up to you. All I will suggest, though, is don't go about it in the way YECists like Ken Ham do. I've gotten an up close and personal view of that "battle plan." It is as absurd as it is comical, not to mention extremely hurtful.

With that, let me tell you a few more personal stories. Let's go back to where I began this book—to that fateful day in June of 2014, when Mr. Spencer first shared "his concerns" about the fact that I was not a YECist—and let me tell you about how I found myself sojourning among the tents of Ham…

"WOE IS ME, THAT I SOJOURN AMONG THE TENTS OF HAM"

I walked out of Panera Bread that day, shell-shocked. Mr. Spencer, the headmaster at my school, had spent an hour expressing his "deep concerns" about my staying on at the school after the next year because… why? I didn't agree with the YECist claims of Ken Ham, and because I was Orthodox? Really? That didn't make any sense. As I walked to my car, I half-expected Ashton Kutcher to pop out from behind my bumper with a camera crew and tell me this was going to be on the next episode of *Punked*.

Well, Ashton was nowhere to be found. All I found was a host of thoughts racing through my mind: *There had to be a misunderstanding* (there wasn't); *Mr. Spencer couldn't really be that clueless, could he?* (he was); *If he wants me to write my understanding of Orthodox Christianity to alleviate his concerns, it looks like I have some writing to do if I want to save my job.* Deep down, I suspected it would be a futile exercise, but although I couldn't articulate at the time, there was a sense of fascination of it all. I told myself, "I am under contract for the next year, so if I my career is going to perish in a Hamean flood, I might as well catch a wave and enjoy the ride." At that point, I had nothing to lose.

I went home, and over the course of the next week, I wrote my "explanation of Orthodoxy" for Mr. Spencer, even though it was obvious that his real concern was that I didn't believe Ken Ham's YECist claims. In any case, I went out of my way to be as conciliatory as I possibly could and to alleviate any concerns he might have about both Orthodoxy and my view of the creation/evolution debate. I emphasized that what I appreciated the most about Orthodoxy was its commitment to preserve the core teachings of Christianity, what Orthodoxy calls "Church Tradition," that have existed ever since the early Church that virtually every Christian shares, regardless of one's denomination. I pointed out that virtually every statement of faith in most Evangelical churches and organizations comes from the Nicene Creed and the Orthodox Church. In fact, what attracted me to Orthodoxy was how it focused on those "creedal fundamentals" of the Christian faith *that all Christians share*. Seriously, how could Mr. Spencer have a problem with that?

I also told him that one of the most influential books in my life had been *Mere Christianity* by C. S. Lewis. In my opinion, what he articulated as "mere Christianity" pretty much summed up the Church Tradition of Orthodoxy quite well. Again, I thought, "What Evangelical Christian is going to have a problem with C. S. Lewis?" I also went out of my way to emphasize that I obviously didn't think everyone had to become Orthodox to be a true Christian. I just felt a better understanding of the Church Tradition Orthodoxy had preserved could only strengthen one's faith.

As for the creation/evolution debate, I said that even though I critiqued the Nye/Ham debate on my blog, I never had taught my view in my classes. For that matter, my own view wasn't even fully developed yet. Sure, I wasn't convinced with Ken Ham's YECism, but I still wasn't convinced of all the claims within evolutionary theory either. Yes, I thought evolution happens to an extent, but to what extent, I didn't know. In any case, the only time I ever touched on the creation/evolution debate was in Senior Worldview. Even then, all I did was lay out the different views people had in the debate, have the students discuss the strengths and weakness of each view, and then tell them that if it was something they really care about, that they'll need to investigate it further. That is what I felt Christian education *should* do regarding this topic.

When I finished writing out my explanation, I thought it was pretty good. I couldn't see how any rational, thoughtful Christian of any denomination would have any real problem with what I had written. For that reason, when I emailed my explanation to Mr. Spencer, I still had a faint glimmer of hope that this whole thing could be resolved.

It didn't take long for that glimmer of hope to be extinguished. Amazingly, my simple and straightforward explanation "evolved" that summer into a wide-ranging, extremely uncomfortable, and utterly baffling exchange that branched out considerably from what I explained in my initial email. If I were to include the entire contents of the emails that went between Mr. Spencer and me that summer, it would take up well over fifty pages, and I wouldn't want to subject anyone to that mess. I will summarize it, though. In the end, the summer-long email exchange centered around five topics: (1) Orthodoxy, (2) C. S. Lewis, (3) the creation/evolution debate, (4) Adam and Eve, and surprisingly (5) homosexuality.

Orthodoxy

When it came to Orthodoxy, Mr. Spencer was deeply concerned when I said I liked Orthodoxy because it emphasized the core tenets of the Christian faith all Christians share. He then accused me of trying to push Orthodoxy into the school. He called it a "foreign worldview" that didn't reflect the worldview of the school community and said I was subverting the authority of Scripture by adhering to the "traditions of men" and putting "man's interpretation over the Bible." He said the sole source of God's truth was Scripture, not the Orthodox Church. Therefore, what I was doing was telling students they could find out their own truth, *and that opened the door to liberalism.*

No matter how much I tried to get him to see that I was emphasizing the things that all Christian denominations shared, he insisted I was being divisive. You read that right: *the more I emphasized the core teachings that all Christians share, the more he accused me of causing division.* On top of that, the supreme irony of this was that a good 99% of the school community had no idea I was even Orthodox. I never brought it up. In addition, it can be argued that Orthodoxy is the most theologically conservative branch of Christianity, so for Mr. Spencer to accuse me of "opening the door the liberalism" was just baffling. Nevertheless, it showed me where his real concerns were. In his mind, the creation/evolution debate was really about *fighting the culture war*. Since I didn't believe Ken Ham's YECism, *that meant I must be a liberal.*

C. S. Lewis

Another contentious topic in those emails centered on none other than C. S. Lewis of all people. Mr. Spencer zeroed in on one of my blog posts where I had talked about how, in *Mere Christianity*, Lewis had said that there was no such thing as a 100% Christian or 100% non-Christian. To clarify, Lewis was emphasizing that everyone is either becoming more or less like Christ throughout their lives, because the Christian life was essentially a process and a journey. Therefore, salvation isn't just a "get out of hell free" card but is ultimately the restoration of a relationship with God through Christ that continues to grow and deepen throughout one's life. The goal of salvation, therefore, is to grow into the fullness of Christ, and that is why the Apostle Paul tells Christians we are to "work out our salvation with fear and trembling." That has made absolute sense to me ever since I first read *Mere Christianity* while I was a student at my Christian high school in Illinois.

For some reason, though, Mr. Spencer was deeply troubled by what Lewis said. No, he said, salvation wasn't a *journey* or a *process*—that sounds too much like evolution! Salvation was an instantaneous new creation. Christians did not have to "work to earn their salvation."

When I read what he wrote, I was baffled. Lewis wasn't saying Christians had to "work to earn their salvation." He was simply making the obvious point that the moment you are saved, you're still not fully Christ-like yet. Therefore, your Christian life is one in which (hopefully) you are becoming fully Christ-like. That is the goal of salvation, *to be like Christ*. Throughout your whole life, by following Christ and being faithful to him, by allowing the Holy Spirit to work within you, you are becoming more Christ-like every day. That's what Paul means by *working out your salvation with fear and trembling*.

Unfortunately, this went over the head of Mr. Spencer. He found it suspicious and told me that because I was claiming salvation was an ongoing process whose goal was to become fully Christ-like, I was "advocating the serpent's position of Genesis 3:5" and saying that we can "become like God." Since he was confused with what I was saying, he was concerned that my students could be susceptible to such views. It was dangerous.

How could I respond to that logic? "Working out your salvation with fear and trembling" and "becoming Christ-like" is the serpent's position of Genesis 3:15? In one fell swoop, he unwittingly rejected the goal of salvation and accused me of pushing "the serpent's position" for stating what the goal of salvation was! His reply was so absurd, I couldn't even be mad. Yes, this man was taking a blowtorch to my teaching career in Evangelical schools, but my gosh, I couldn't help but be fascinated by it all. By accusing me of "advocating the serpent's position," he was accusing *the apostle Paul* of "advocating the serpent's position, because I was quoting Paul!

The Creation/Evolution Debate

Then there was the topic of the creation/evolution debate, Mr. Spencer's real concern. Obviously, he was deeply troubled I didn't accept Ken Ham's claim that the earth was only 6,000 years old and had said we should all accept the fact that evolution "happens to some extent." Of course, he didn't say he was upset that I didn't accept *Ken Ham's view*. No, Mr. Spencer accused me of *not having enough faith in God's word*. Evolution was in conflict with Genesis, he said, and it didn't "happen to an extent." He then defined evolution as "particles to people over time, without the need for an intelligent Designer," and said "that worldview" was in direct contradiction to God's word. A Christian had to choose: *evolution or God's word*.

He then told me I was no longer allowed to show the documentary *Did Darwin Kill God?* during my Darwin Unit in Senior Worldview. To be clear, what I tried to do in that unit was to show some kind of video that represented the varying positions in the creation/evolution debate, so that the students would have a better understanding of what each view said and so that they would be in a better position to critically analyze each view. I showed an Answers in Genesis video, an intelligent design video, a video of Richard Dawkins, as well as *Did Darwin Kill God?* which held to the theistic evolution view. Mr. Spencer said he had no problem with showing students opposing views, as long as I *told them ahead of time that they were in error*. And since I wasn't doing that, he said I was guilty of "promoting intelligent design and theistic evolution," and was thus "in conflict with our school community according to our new statement of faith." (I'll explain what that "new" statement of faith was shortly).

I decided not to point out to him that intelligent design and theistic evolution were two distinct positions. I'm sure if I did, he would just say something to the effect that I was trying to confuse him, just like the serpent tried to confuse Eve. Instead, I told him that if he didn't want me showing the video in Senior Worldview, that was fine, but I felt that purposely eliminating one of the major views in the creation/evolution debate was antithetical to the purpose of education. He replied by telling me, "True Christian education is to make sure students have the answers they need."

As for what he said about evolution itself, I told him that even Ken Ham, even though he wouldn't use the word "evolution," believes that evolution happens to an extent. He just claims all the variation of species happened within a few thousand years. That was my point—ultimately, everyone agrees with the basic premise of evolution, that organisms adapt and change over time. I also said that Genesis 1 simply isn't trying to give modern scientific information. Since we held the Bible to be the inspired word of God, we needed to realize that Genesis 1 was originally addressed to a pre-scientific Israelite people who were living in an ancient pagan world and were fleeing Egypt. They weren't asking modern scientific questions, so we shouldn't impose modern science back onto Genesis 1.

As for his definition of evolution, I tried to explain to him that it wasn't an accurate definition. I said evolution is a *scientific theory* that is limited to studying things in the natural world and that it is utterly incapable of even addressing the possibility of something that is beyond the natural world. It simply isn't the same thing as the *philosophical worldview* of atheism. If he wanted a better definition of evolution, I said he should consider the one put forth by Ernst Mayer: "Evolution is the change in the properties of populations of organisms over time." That was it, nothing more.

Not surprisingly, Mr. Spencer accused me of being deceptive (like the serpent), undermining the authority of Scripture, not having faith in God's word, and putting "man's word" above "God's word."

Adam and Eve

Then there was Adam and Eve. Mr. Spencer said if Adam and Eve weren't historical, then the origin of sin and marriage are called into question, and Christ is a liar because he refers to Genesis 2. Mr. Spencer also said he found it disturbing I had pointed out that early Church Fathers like Irenaeus taught that Adam and Eve weren't created perfect but were rather created immature and child-like, and that therefore the real story of Genesis 2—3 was that we human beings sin, and thus need to trust and obey God so we can grow into the full image-bearer that He intended us to be. Mr. Spencer insisted that was not the position of the school or the Evangelical church.

I told him this was a basic tenet of the faith that was taught throughout Church history, in virtually all branches of Christianity, and by most well-respected Evangelical theologians and scholars in our world today in Bible and Theology departments in Evangelical colleges across the country. I should know, I got my two master's degrees from *Evangelical graduate schools*. That's where I learned it. Once again, he accused me of being deceptive.

Homosexuality

The final topic in those emails had to do with, of all things, homosexuality. Ever since Mr. Spencer found out I did not accept YECism, he had scoured my blog to find evidence that I was some kind of "liberal" in the culture war. A few years earlier, before the gay marriage issue had been decided, I had written a post in which I tried to just lay out what the Bible actually said about the topic and what the Church had always taught about it. The only reason I am including this discussion here is because (as I will show) it reveals the deeper motivation of modern YECism, namely fighting the culture war. Regardless of what your personal view regarding gay marriage and homosexuality might be, I'm going to say up front that I doubt you will find the view I expressed to be "liberal" in any way.

In a nutshell, I made the following points: (1) the Church has never sanctioned gay marriage, but if the State wanted to legalize gay marriage, that's its prerogative—it wasn't something I was going to obsess over; (2) the Bible condemns same-sex sexual activity; but (3) the Bible doesn't address the modern concept of *sexual orientation* and doesn't condemn someone for being attracted to someone else. Simply put, *attraction* and *engaging in actual sex acts* are not the same thing. God doesn't condemn someone for feeling a certain way, just as He doesn't condemn me for being more attracted to brunettes. The Bible addresses specific behaviors, not feelings.

Mr. Spencer found what I had written deeply disturbing. He said attraction was the same thing as lusting, and since Jesus condemned lusting in Matthew 5:28, my view put me in conflict with him as a father and with the school community. No matter how much I tried to make him see the difference between *actual sexual behavior* and simply *finding yourself attracted to someone*, or how attraction isn't the same thing as lusting, he insisted that what I was saying was dangerous and was essentially giving students struggling with same-sex attraction to go out and engage in homosexual acts.

Well, there's no arguing with that logic, I suppose.

～

Later that summer, Mr. Spencer said he wanted to meet for coffee at a local coffee shop to discuss the upcoming year. At that meeting, Mr. Spencer showed me the updated "statement of faith" he and a few Board members had made for the school. He said he wanted to get my reaction to it.

The first two pages were the standard "statement of faith" that most Christian schools and churches have (the core tenets of the Christian faith that actually came from the early Church councils!). The two new pages, though, consisted of a heavy dose of young earth creationism and end-times dispensationalism. From that point on, any teacher applying for a job at the school had to sign off on the school's stated belief that God created the universe in seven 24-hour days a mere 6,000 years ago, as well as the "end times" views of Hal Lindsey and Tim LaHaye. If they had any qualms about those two stances, they had to provide a written explanation of their position on the teacher application.

It was clear to me that Mr. Spencer was changing the school's statement of faith so he could justify not renewing my contract at the end of the school year. Besides, I bet he was hoping I would be so offended that I would quit right there and then. He didn't know me that well. Instead of quitting, I told him how perplexed I was over what he was doing. I had been at the school for seven years and there had been no problems or objections to anything I had taught. I even reminded him that when he first interviewed for the job of headmaster, he had met with me and two other teachers at the school and had told me at the time how he had heard I was "the heart and soul" of the school and had heard nothing but good things about my Worldview classes.

"When did you start having problems with my teaching?" I asked.

His answer did not surprise me. "I'd have to say it was last fall when you told me of your conversation with Pastor Clark. Then when I read what you wrote to him when you answered his questions, that caused me deep concerns and made me question your ability to teach Worldview anymore." *Why, of course!* Of course, Pastor Clark was somehow in the mix. Of course, Pastor Clark showed Mr. Spencer what I had written to him. I was in the middle of a theological handicap match, two on one. Why wasn't I surprised? And all this was happening because I didn't agree with Ken Ham's claim that the earth was only 6,000 years old.

A few days later, Mr. Spencer sent an email to the faculty to announce he was sending a few teachers to an AiG conference for a few days at the beginning of the school year and arranging for Bodie Hodge to speak in one of our chapels. In addition, he announced he had chosen Ken Ham's book, *Already Gone*, as the focus of our morning devotional meetings in the fall. My final year at the school was going to be interesting!

A few weeks later, Mr. Spencer sent me another email in which he reiterated that he had no confidence in me whatsoever. And, once again, almost like a tick, he accused me of being deceptive. There was no doubt in my mind he was trying to get under my skin and make me just quit. That wasn't happening. I never have been one who wilted under intimidation. I determined I was just going to keep my mouth shut that year and not cause any problems. That being said, I knew I had to write a reply. In my email, I again reiterated my belief that the age of the earth was not a fundamental tenet of the faith and that YECism was wrong to make it a primary issue of the faith. The fact that he did not want me at the school anymore because of that issue told me that he saw it as a primary issue too, and I found that extremely unfortunate. I then ended with the following:

> "Obviously, your main concern with me is over the creation/evolution debate. That's why you are requiring the faculty to read *Already Gone*. The fact you are also sending some teachers to the AiG conference and are having Bodie Hodge come and speak in chapel tells me you want to push YECism at the school this year. That is your prerogative. If you want to indeed push YECism more in Worldview and the Science classes, then you are right—I'm not going to be a good fit.
>
> "Still, I would advise against it. It's fine to present YECism as one of views Christians have and encourage students to think through all the views. But to push YECism as the only Christian option to 'godless evolution' is a huge mistake. There are a host of things wrong with YECism, the least of which is the claim the earth is only 6,000 years old. It contradicts biblical scholarship

and exegesis, it has no precedent in Church history, has never been a fundamental tenant of the Christian faith, and is not accepted anywhere in the scientific world.

"I fear that pursuing such a course of action will not only fail to prepare students for successful engagement in the academic world many of them will encounter after high school graduation but will also fail to reverse the trend of defection by Evangelical youth from their spiritual heritage. In fact, it will probably accelerate it. If you tell a student that if he doesn't believe in a literal six-day creation 6,000 years ago, then he can't believe in the Gospel and resurrection of Jesus Christ, when that student just takes an entry level biology class and learns just the basic facts about biology, do you know what he's going to do? *He's going to completely throw away his faith because you will have told him that he has to.* You will have attached to the Gospel of Christ a debatable scientific claim and an interpretation of Genesis 1–11 that has never been universally held in Church history, and you will have made adherence to that debatable scientific claim a prerequisite for the Gospel of Christ. That is indescribably sad."

I didn't want to be confrontational, but I felt it was important to be direct and to the point. Besides, what could he do? Fire me?

Mr. Spencer clearly didn't appreciate it. On the first day of teacher meetings, before the school year began, I walked into my classroom to find that all the new desks that were given to me the previous year had been taken out and replaced with old, rickety desks. Mr. Spencer had given the nicer desks to another teacher.

I then sat down at my desk, turned on my computer, and found that Mr. Spencer had sent me yet another email. What a great way to start the new school year! Once again, he reiterated that he had no confidence in me and was not going to renew my contract at the end of the year. He also threatened me and said that, although I hadn't tried to stir up any trouble among the faculty, he was not going to tolerate any divisive behavior. He said that my worldview was contrary to the worldview of the school community, that I didn't believe that Scripture could stand up to the scrutiny of science, and that I was casting doubt on the accuracy of Scripture in Genesis 1–11. By doing so, I was casting doubt on what Scripture says about sin and salvation. He ended his email by telling me that either I was ill-informed about evolution, or I was being intentionally misleading about it, and thus was "a wolf in sheep's clothing."

I sat back in my chair and took a deep breath. I felt numb. He had actually called me a "wolf in sheep's clothing." He said I was intentionally trying to mislead people. The entire email screamed, "You are bad. You are dangerous. One hint of trouble from you, and you're gone." I'll be honest, that stung. Still, I've never been one to back down when I felt bullied. I quickly wrote a very short reply in which I said that Genesis 1–11 simply wasn't doing science, therefore anything modern science discovers can't threaten the authority of Scripture. For that matter, I wasn't casting doubt on the authority of Scripture. I was questioning Ken Ham's interpretation of it—the two were not the same. I ended by saying, "I am sorry that you see this issue as a primary issue in the Christian faith. I'm sorry to find that you see me as a wolf in sheep's clothing. And I'm sorry that you see fit to end my employment here over an issue that I hardly even address over the course of the entire four-year Worldview curriculum."

That morning, the reality of those two months hit me like a ton of bricks. I wasn't so much hurt as I was just sad. I had devoted my career to Christian education and had poured seven years of my life into developing what I felt was a quality Biblical Worldview curriculum. It was something I thought was my life's calling. Seeing it all just cast aside over the fact I didn't agree with Ken Ham was just comically devastating. Because *of that*, Mr. Spencer viewed me with suspicion. He seemed to either not understand, or purposely twist, everything I tried to say. In his mind, since I didn't accept YECism, I had to be on the opposing side of the culture war. Therefore, he was not going to even try to really listen to what I said—he had already predetermined that I was simply trying to deceive him. Despite anything I might say to him, he already knew what I *really thought*, and any attempt by me to convince him otherwise was interpreted as, *"Hiss! Hiss! Do God really say . . . ?"*

This is the core problem with YECism. It's not that Ken Ham believes the earth is only 6,000 years old. It's not that he thinks Genesis 1–11 is conveying journalistic history and is God's historical science textbook. The core problem, and Ken Ham has said it himself, is that YECists insist that *a literal/historical reading of Genesis 1–11 is the foundation to the Christian faith*. I'm sorry, it's not. It is foundational to YECism, and YECism's goal is to win the culture war. And since it is all about fighting a war for YECists, *it is all about fighting a war*, and one's stance in the creation/evolution debate serves as the litmus test to determine whether or not you are a true Christian, a secular liberal, or in my case, a compromiser who is undermining biblical authority. From a YECist perspective,

Pastor Clark was right: *YECism is something worth dividing the Church over.* That's the problem. The age of the earth is a secondary issue at best and making it the singular foundational issue *divides the Church.* That's what heresy does. Read the early Church Fathers, they pound that home over and over again.

MORNINGS WITH KEN HAM (WHEN I WAS "ALREADY GONE" ANYWAY)

Despite all that, even though I am now Orthodox, I haven't given up all hope for Evangelicalism. Yes, there are problems within Evangelicalism these days, and dealing with YECism is certainly one of them. But I am convinced that the ones who are pushing YECism are a relatively small minority. They just have the soapbox and a bullhorn. In fact, my experience that year convinced me more than ever that the majority of Evangelical Christians, despite what they may say if asked about the creation/evolution debate, really are not too concerned about it. It doesn't play any significant role in their Christian faith, nor should it. I am not going to relate all that transpired in the course of that final school year, but there are a two particular events that I think crystalize not only another major problem with YECism in terms of the "culture war," but also have convinced me that, despite the current vitriol in the creation/evolution debate, most Evangelical Christians know deep down that this whole debate is not fundamental to the Christian faith.

The first event concerned the morning devotions in which Mr. Spencer had the faculty discuss Ken Ham's book, *Already Gone*. If you have read the book, you'll know that the first few chapters simply lay out a standard Evangelical view of the current culture: there are cultural problems in our society, young people are leaving the church, and churches need once again to provide a solid Christian witness to our world. Naturally, that kind of general message of how Christians need to stand on God's word and be lights in the world was met with approval among the faculty.

When we got to chapter four in the book, many teachers started to feel uneasy. In chapter four, Ken Ham really starts to obsess over Darwin, Genesis 1–11, and evolution…*a lot.* Consequently, the day we were to discuss chapter four, there was a lot of silence in the room. No one really knew what to say. A few of my friends leaned over and quietly said to me,

"Did you get why he brought up geology?" I just shrugged my shoulders. I saw another teacher mouth "dinosaurs?" to another friend. I just kept quiet. Inside, though, I was thoroughly enjoying it.

By chapter five, after another largely quiet discussion, with about five minutes left in the meeting, one of the science teachers finally spoke up and voiced her concerns about the book. She said that what Ham was saying about the earth being only 6,000 years old just wasn't true. After that, the librarian chimed in and asked whether or not Ken Ham knew there was more in the Bible than just Genesis 1? The floodgates then opened, and Mr. Spencer experienced a veritable deluge of complaints from the faculty. He was legitimately shocked to find that almost everyone thought Ken Ham was obsessing over evolution and Genesis 1-11 way too much. It seemed that many in the school community didn't share his YECist worldview after all! The morning bell rang, and we all left to go to our classrooms. As we walked out of the library that morning, I was beaming.

The next morning, Mr. Spencer called a special faculty meeting to clear the air regarding the previous morning's discussion. He said the main issue the book was getting at was *biblical authority*, and to accept "millions and billions of years" would be to undermine the *authority of the Bible*. He concluded with, "We all love science. I want our science classes to be full of rigor and to really challenge our students. But we must filter everything, *including science*, through the Word of God. We have always been a YECist school, and we must stay uncompromised on the *authority of Scripture*." His comments were met with dead silence. A few science teachers were scowling. I tried to conceal a smile. After an awkward pause, Mr. Spencer stammered out, "…and that's my story, and I'm sticking to it! You're dismissed."

That meeting left a bad taste in many teachers' mouths and served as a precursor to how the year would go. When it became painfully obvious to everyone that Mr. Spencer had decided to push YECism at every level of the school, a good number of teachers simply decided not to fight it and resolved to look for another job the next year. They wanted no part of it.

Up to that point, the faculty was like a close-knit family. Throughout that year, though, the entire atmosphere among the faculty changed. It just became depressing for everyone to work there because hardly anyone approved of what Mr. Spencer was doing. So, when Grandparents Day in the elementary school rolled around and Mr. Spencer arranged for the grade school children to sing "I Don't Believe in Evolution" by Buddy Davis of AiG, there were a lot of sideways glances and eye-rolling among the faculty. And when Mr. Spencer took a few high school chapels to push YECism, there were a number of quiet sighs coming from the teachers.

As sad as that year was for the entire faculty, in an odd way, it felt good to know that most of the faculty did not, in fact, share Mr. Spencer's YECist outlook. I'm sure most of them would have said they didn't believe evolution and that they believed Adam and Eve were historical people, but it was abundantly clear that for most of the faculty, none of that was a crucial, fundamental part of their Christian faith. They believed that ultimately, God created the world, and that was what was important, not how exactly He might have done it. They read the story of Adam and Eve, probably assuming it was historical, but knowing full well that ultimately the point was that human beings were sinful and in need of salvation, and that was enough. That gave me hope and helped me get through the year.

"DOWN IN CAROLINA WAY, LIVED A MAN NAMED BIG BJ" [1]

The other event that crystalized another problem with YECism happened near the end of the school year, in April, when Mr. Spencer arranged for a teacher-in-service titled *Integrating a Biblical Worldview in the Classroom*. It amounted to a three-hour long announcement that, starting the following year, the elementary school was going to be using Biblical Worldview books published by Bob Jones University Press.

In one example of how the books "promoted critical thinking," the BJU press spokeswoman showed us a section in the book that dealt with, what else? *The creation and evolution debate*! Of course, what they considered critical thinking amounted to saying, "In the Bible, the genealogies total 6,000 years!" That was it. Even though it was curriculum for the junior high, the high school teachers were clearly horrified.

What made Mr. Spencer's move so surreal was that Bob Jones University doesn't really have a stellar track record when it comes to things like racism. In addition, at that time, it had just recently been discovered that the university had routinely counseled young women who had been the victims of sexual assault and rape to repent of their part of the sexual encounter, to repent of their not being able to forget about it, and to not

---

1. The first line in the song, "We Don't Need No Color Code" by Steve Taylor.

report the assault to the police. Putting YECism to the side just for a second, one has to question the judgment of anyone who doesn't see the potential problem in promoting curriculum from a university currently known for not only having a blatant racist past, but also being guilty of shaming rape victims. Mr. Spencer, apparently, didn't see it that way.

Needless to say, a lot of women weren't too happy. My closest friend at the school, Kennedy Harris, whose classroom was across the hall from mine for eight years, was especially not happy. She was an African American woman whose daughter was in the elementary school. She took it upon herself to write a letter to Mr. Spencer expressing her displeasure at the decision. And since she was the one person I confided in that year, she shared her letter to Mr. Spencer with me. After voicing her displeasure with what Mr. Spencer was doing, she ended her letter by saying:

> "I am not a fan of BJU. Their racist and misogynistic tendencies in the recent past are offensive to me and to some other faculty members, as well. I understand that many schools in the past had similar issues, but if it is happening in the twenty-first century, I cannot be a part of it. If my children are going to be studying from that curriculum, I don't want them, or me for that matter, to be looked at as 'Uncle Toms.' If you were not aware of their reputation, I'm sure you can google it."

Mr. Spencer's response was the epitome of tone-deafness. He actually went about defending BJU to an African American woman. He told her that he knew about BJU's past reputation, but he really felt they had some extremely effective tools for Christian education. He then told her that he had just been at a conference at BJU that past January, and he really felt there was a positive atmosphere in regard to race relations. After all, *African Americans were visible on campus*, and not only just as students. *There were even a few African American faculty members.* He had come away from that conference with a lot of respect for the quality of their curriculum and their commitment to promoting a biblical worldview.

The response didn't sit well with Kennedy. When she showed me his email, I wasn't surprised at all. Now, neither Kennedy nor I thought Mr. Spencer was a racist or a misogynist. He was just incredibly tone-deaf. So, Kennedy wrote a response, expressing her extreme displeasure:

> "I really don't know how to respond. I'm even more offended that you openly admit that you are well aware of BJU's past

unbiblical and racist stances, and yet are so quick to embrace their curriculum when those wounds are still so fresh. That hurts more than you can possibly understand. BJU did not begin admitting African Americans until the late 1970s and even then, there were restrictions. The ban on interracial dating wasn't even dropped until 2000. And it is not easy to forget that BJU has gone on record stating that African Americans should be glad that they were put into slavery because otherwise they would still be in the jungle. I know that statement was of the past, but it still hurts. The wound is still too fresh.

"You mentioned you saw some African Americans on the BJU campus. So what? That's like saying it's okay to fly the Confederate flag at the courthouse because some African Americans fought on the Confederate side in the Civil War. I have worked hard to be judged by the content of my character and not the color of my skin, so I have a really hard time swallowing the fact that you are such a BJU supporter. I don't anticipate us agreeing on the issue of the BJU curriculum, but I wish you would strongly reconsider your decision."

He didn't. The BJU textbooks were implemented the very next year. One thing had become abundantly clear. In the culture war, promoting YECist ideology covers a multitude of sins, even racism and misogyny.

That incident revealed to me another problem with YECism. For all its focus on fighting the culture war, it is astonishing to see how quickly certain cultural sins are papered over *if the school, organization, or person is promoting YECism*. I'm not suggesting YECists really endorse racism or misogyny. I'm not going to do what YECist leaders like Ken Ham routinely do and accuse people of certain "cultural sins" based solely on whether or not they embrace YECism. Like I said, I don't think Mr. Spencer was racist or misogynistic. In most respects in everyday life, he was a decent and friendly person. But his YECist ideology clearly skewed his perspective on certain things. Not only did he see "liberalism" in me when there was none, but he failed to see how embracing curriculum from a place that recently was guilty of very real racism and misogyny might cause some very fresh wounds to be re-opened.

Simply put, *the worldview of YECist ideology screws up people's spiritual vision*. By making YECism a litmus test for Christianity, YECists not only make fellow Christians enemies, but they become blind and deaf to the very real cultural sins of their perceived allies, rationalizing that since they are promoting YECism, those cultural sins aren't *really bad*, at least not anymore.

That really lies at the heart of what I've called the "heresy of Ham." When you take secondary issues, elevate them to the cornerstone of your faith, and make them the basis for your whole worldview, you're not going to see anything clearly. And since you think you're in a culture war, the casualties in your not-so-friendly fire are going to be high.

THE END OF THE ROAD

A week before finals, Mr. Spencer made the official announcement in a school newsletter that I was leaving and that a local youth pastor was being hired full-time to take my place. In the newsletter, he had given the impression that I was simply choosing to move on and had assisted him in the transition process. There is no other way to say it, he misled the school community. In fact, a couple pastors whom he told me agreed with his decision not to renew my contract later told me he had told them I was just choosing to leave. They had no knowledge of what really had happened.

Then, on the second to last day of school, Mr. Spencer sent an email to the entire faculty about an event that was going to happen during the next school year. Pastor Clark was going to host an *Answers in Genesis* conference at his church the following February and Mr. Spencer was going to have the entire school, both students and faculty alike, attend this "exciting conference." As I read the email, I just sat at my desk and gave an exasperated smile. There couldn't be a more fitting conclusion to the year. *Of course,* Pastor Clark was going to have an AiG conference at his church. *Of course,* Ken Ham was to be the main speaker. *Of course,* Mr. Spencer was going to have the entire school attend. *Of course!*

Once the school year was over, I cleaned out my classroom and left. Over the course of those eight years, I had turned my classroom into artwork by painting numerous murals on my classroom walls: Deuteronomy 6:4–5 in Hebrew on one wall, John 1:14 in Greek on another wall, a quote from Thomas A 'Kempis on the wall behind my desk, as well as a painting of Jesus, the Temple in Jerusalem, the Book of Kells, and the three Cappadocian Fathers. I looked at those walls one last time, knowing that Mr. Spencer was probably going to paint over everything over the summer.

Sure enough, they were painted over in a flood of beige the following week. No trace of me was to be left behind.

Once the school year was over, I started researching Ken Ham and AiG in earnest and writing about YECism on my blog. About three months later, at the end of the summer and the beginning of the new school year, I finally broke my silence on what had happened and wrote a blog post titled, "Why I am Not Teaching This Year…and the Heresy of Ken Ham." I didn't name any names, but I'm sure people at the school knew who I was talking about. I didn't write the post to "get them." I wrote it because I really did love teaching at that school and I didn't want to see an overzealous YECist headmaster destroy a good school. I ended that post with the following:

> "I fear for my former students who are walking away from Christianity because they are told that what Ken Ham is claiming is Christianity—*no it's not*. It is a heresy. You are right to reject Ham's "gospel," because as Paul says, it is no gospel at all. But don't reject Christ because you've been told that Christians have to believe that Noah hired mocking workers who had access to cranes, bulldozers, or any number of advanced technological machinery to build the ark. Use your God-given intelligence and reject such nonsense."

I still feel that way. In fact, over these past eight years since the original publication of *The Heresy of Ham*, it has been heart-breaking to encounter a number of former Christians who have walked away from Christianity, and, when asked as to what started their walking away from the faith, have said that it was when they realized that the YECism they were taught as kids was, in fact, nonsense. They felt lied to, and immediately started to suspect that the entire Christian faith was just a bunch of lies as well.

In any case, over in the course of the next year, as I was writing *Heresy of Ham*, not only did I get to meet Ken Ham himself at the AiG conference in my town, but I also was able to visit his Creation Museum and Ark Encounter, a mere four days after it opened. After a tough and stressful year, those "ark encounters" provided me with some disturbing, yet darkly comic relief. Want to hear about it? I have a couple more stories to tell.

13

Ark Encounters

My Close Encounters with the (un)Biblical Kind

"Do it! Do it! Do it! Do the Hustle!"
—Van McCoy

BETTER WATCH OUT, KEN HAM IS COMING TO TOWN

The following February was the long-awaited AiG conference at Pastor Clark's church that Mr. Spencer arranged to have the entire school attend. It was free admission and open to the public, so I just had to go. I had the date circled on my calendar for quite some time. After a good six months of researching AiG and YECism, I knew I had to pop in for at least one session to hear the man himself.

When I walked in the church, I was a bit nervous. Yes, it was nice to see a number of my former co-workers and students, but I was still pretty uncomfortable. I decided to sit in the back in order to not draw attention to myself. That didn't stop Pastor Clark and a few other pastors from coming up and sitting behind me for a while. What did they think I was going to do? Shout out "Nye is the Science Guy!" and dowse myself in flames in protest?

As far as Ham's presentation went, I wish I could say I wasn't disappointed, but I would be lying if I did. The fact is, it is a truth universally acknowledged (at least by those who have spent any time reading up on Ken Ham and AiG) that when it comes to YECist arguments, there is nothing new under the sun. It is always the same rehashed clichés and talking points that are ripped through in such a frenetic pace that those in the audience never have time to process or think about them. If Duane Gish popularized what became known as the "Gish Gallop," Ken Ham's version might well be coined the "Ham Hustle." In any case, if the ability to time travel really is possible, I am certain what inspired the writer of Ecclesiastes to write, "There is nothing new under the sun" was, in fact, an AiG conference.

When Ken Ham took the stage, the first thing he did was to make clear what the motivation and purpose of AiG was: *to equip young people to give a defense of the Christian faith.* With that, the "Ham Hustle" was off and running.

First, he mentioned the "Seven C's of History" was one of AiG's primary witnessing tools: *Creation* (Genesis 1—2), *Corruption* (Genesis 3), *Catastrophe* (Genesis 6—8), *Confusion* (Genesis 11), *Christ* (Gospels), *Cross* (Gospels again), *Consummation* (Revelation). I couldn't help but notice that he seemed to miss a small portion of the Biblical story, namely the entire Old Testament Story after Genesis 11. I mean, geesh, just use *Covenant!* That's kind of a big deal in both the Old and New Testament stories, don't you think?

Don't think about that . . . keep moving . . .

From there, Ham launched into his explanation of there being two different kinds of science: observational and historical science. But it really wasn't an "explanation," per se. It was simply what AiG always says: "observational science" builds our technology; "historical science" is untestable belief about the past. (Wait, did Ham just define "historical science" as "untestable belief about the past"?)

Let's keep moving!

Next, Ham said there was rock solid scientific evidence for an infinite God. Romans 1:20 says, "*Ever since the creation of the world his eternal power and divine nature, invisible though they are, have been understood and seen through the things he has made. So they are without excuse.*" Take that, atheists! The laws of nature and the "laws of logic" prove there is a God! (Romans 1:20 is "scientific evidence"? What is a "law of logic"?)

Go . . . go . . . go! We've got a lot to cover!

Ham then took direct aim at evolution by falsely equating it with atheism. He asked the students, "If there was no God, and just 'evolutionary processes,' where did morality come from? If we are just 'evolved animals,' how can anyone determine right and wrong?" I thought, "Sure, *if* there is no God, and *if* human beings are nothing more than evolved animals, then yes—the concept of morality is problematic. But evolution does not say there is no God. It's just a description of the natural process that leads to the varieties of life we have in the world."

Keep it moving! Next up...

Ham then turned his attention to DNA as "evidence" for God. DNA is the code that provides information for things necessary to live, grow, and develop, but that information is immaterial. So, where does the information come from? God, of course! He then exclaimed, "It's a fairy tale! Evolution is just a fairy tale! They don't know! Evolution can't explain the origin of life! Atheism is just blind faith!"

To bolster his point, Ham showed a clip from the Intelligent Design movie, *Expelled*, where Ben Stein asked Richard Dawkins where life on earth could have come from. Dawkins said it could have been "seeded" by some alien life form. Now, let's all agree that Dawkins' answer is rather "out there" (both literally and figuratively). What I couldn't get over was that Ham showed a clip from *an Intelligent Design movie* and even said it was a good movie! Ham routinely savages *anyone* who is a proponent of Intelligent Design.

There's no time to think about that inconsistency! Go! Go! Go! It's culture war time!

After that, Ham then went "full culture war." He asked, "So, why did atheists come up with the fairy tale of evolution?" Can you guess Ham's answer? If you guessed, "It's because they are in rebellion against God," you'd be right! Ham told the students, "God *owns you,* and He *made the rules.*" Therefore, the reason why atheists invented evolution was because they didn't want to obey God's rules in the Bible...and that's why we have abortion and gay marriage.

Regardless of your views on those issues, you have to admit Ham's claim makes no freaking sense. Maybe I missed it, but I don't believe Charles Darwin was touring the Galapagos islands and suddenly thought, "Damn those rules in the Bible! I think I'm going to invent evolution so I can abort babies and have sex with those fine, strapping sailors!"

Ham then ended his first 20-minute talk (yes, he covered *all this within 20 minutes*) in an absolute flourish. He told the students three basic things to remember: (A) "Atheism is evolution, and evolution is a religion that says there is no God;" (B) "Science confirms the Bible;" and (C)"Genesis 1:1 is the most scientific statement one can make."

The Last Jedi had not come out yet, but I swear that in my head, Luke Skywalker was saying (not to Kylo Ren, but to Ken Ham), "Amazing, every word that you just said was wrong."

After a short break, Ham resumed by talking about how Noah was able to fit all the animals on the Ark. With absolutely no evidence (scientific or biblical) whatsoever, Ham confidently declared there were only 2,000-3,000 "animal kinds" on the Ark, and that Noah was able to fit them in with room to spare because "most average land animals are smaller than a rat."

"Really?" I thought, "Most land animals are smaller than a rat?" I'm no expert scientist, but that claim sounded highly suspect. Was Ken Ham really claiming that the original cow-kind, dog-kind, elephant-kind, and Tyrannosaurus Rex-kind were all...smaller than rats?

As it turns out, he wasn't claiming that...exactly. According to Ham, all the animals that Noah brought on the Ark were probably *baby animals...and they were no bigger than rats.* Since the Bible doesn't say exactly how Noah was able to bring all those animals on the Ark, *that's probably how it happened.* Problem solved! He then quickly moved on to showing a video that made more false claims about evolution.

I couldn't help but think that perhaps he was selling himself short with this explanation. After all, as AiG has argued, Noah had access to advanced technology that would put our modern technology to shame. It would require really advanced knowledge about that advanced technology, right? Therefore, is it really out of the realm of possibility that Noah was one of the greatest scientists of the ante-diluvian world? The Bible doesn't say he wasn't, so logically *he probably was.* And since that *probably is the case,* maybe he didn't have to bring in baby dog kinds, cat kinds, elephant kinds, and T-Rex kinds onto the Ark. Maybe, since he *probably* was the greatest scientist of the time, he *probably* was also an advanced geneticist and *probably* was able to simply bring on board two eggs of each animal kind and store them in cryogenic chambers.

Who is to say this wasn't possible? After all, Genesis 4:22 says, "Zillah bore Tubal-cain, who made all kinds of bronze and iron tools." Right there, as AiG has claimed, the Bible is talking about advanced technology, so perhaps cryogenic chambers and in vitro fertilization isn't so far-fetched? I mean, if the criteria for AiG was, "The Bible doesn't exactly tell us how, then *probably it happened this way*," why not just take full advantage of that "probable" pre-flood advanced technology? Maybe I was just being silly. In any case, contemplation of the wonders of all that pre-flood technology had to wait. Ham was already on the next leg of the Ham Hustle.

Ham went on to the subject of Darwin's finches and told the students that the changes in their beaks were the "best evidence" atheists give for evolution. "But finches are still finches are still finches!" Ham exclaimed. Wow! Using "atheist" as a synonym for "someone who accepts evolution" is rather bold, isn't it? And even I, someone who doesn't have expertise in the biological sciences, knew enough to know that Darwin's finches are not the "best evidence" for evolution. There is quite a bit more.

There was no time for further contemplation on that point because Ham quickly moved on to the relationship between biology and…*morality*? That's right! He told the students that evolutionists try to claim human beings are genetically related to everything in the natural world, but that was false. The only reason they say that was so that they can say abortion is okay.

WHAT? I was confused. How did he make that jump? It didn't make sense. Human beings *really are biologically and genetically related to other organisms*. For example, we share 22 identical chromosomes with chimpanzees, and our 23rd chromosome (chromosome #2) is the result of the other two chimpanzee chromosomes being fused together. That's the only difference. Does that mean it is now morally acceptable for human beings to start throwing feces at each other? Of course not. For some reason, though, Ham equated biological similarities with morality, and then (you guessed it) linked it to another front in the culture war. I do not agree with abortion, but Ham's argument and claim was pure nonsense.

After that, Ham kicked it into high gear as he came into the home stretch of the Ham Hustle, picking up and putting down random topics and claims as fast as Usain Bolt's feet in the 100-meter dash:

- Andrew Snelling is a geologist who gives evidence for a global Flood. Billions of dead things are buried in rock layers all over the earth! Who are you going to believe? Man's word or the Bible?

- Psalm 104 gives a detailed description of how God drained off the earth after Noah's flood! (It doesn't say that—*it's a freaking Creation Psalm, for goodness' sake!*).

- Genesis 1 is about a literal six-day creation only 6,000 years ago. Christians who accept evolution are trying to fit millions of years into Genesis 1, but it can't be done!
- You don't need the sun to have a 24-hour day. Light for the first three days came from somewhere else. (Your evidence is?).
- Genesis 3 tells us about the origin of clothing, but feminist groups are rebelling against God because they want to walk around nude!
- Don't trust those atheistic dating methods scientists use! The Bible is the only reliable dating method! They said this diamond was two-million-years-old, but when it was re-tested, it turned out to be 58,000 years old. Now, we don't believe it was 58,000 years old, but... (WAIT A SECOND! You can't use a scientific dating method to show that a diamond was 58,000 years old and not two-million years old, and then turn around and dismiss the dating method you used to show it was 58,000 years old!)
- Biology, geology, anthropology, and astronomy all confirm the Bible!

That was quite the sprint! I was out of breath just listening to it. After he crossed his finish line, just like an Olympic runner grabs his country's flag after a race and carries it around the track, Ham grabbed his culture war flag and ended with a flourish. He told the kids that he had a message for President Obama: *God created marriage, not him. Evolution was the worship of creation; homosexuality was a sign of God's judgment of America; and human life begins...not at conception, but at fertilization. There are two religions: Man's word (which includes lawlessness, gay marriage, euthanasia, and abortion) vs. God's Word (which includes law, traditional marriage, the meaning of life, and the sanctity of life)—and the reason why these values are collapsing in our culture is because of the theory of evolution.*

Now, I am not a Democrat and have always considered myself as someone who leans conservative, but Ham's culture war crescendo at the end of his presentation made me cringe. Yes, there are serious social issues out there, but linking them to the scientific theory of evolution and then claiming evolution is the cause of the collapse of morality is just flat out bizarre...and offensive to anyone who values their God-given ability to think rationally. And for the record, I'm not sure I know what the difference is between conception and fertilization. I always thought they were the same thing.

As the presentation was coming to a close, I found myself feeling sorry for the man. In fact, I don't think I have ever seen him smile. At the same time, it was sad to see that this is what he was pushing, and this is what was being passed off as critical thinking and a biblical worldview.

Once it was over, a friend of mine, a science teacher at the school, came over to say hi and ask me how I was doing. Ken Ham was up on the stage, shaking hands and talking to a few people who came to meet him. I jokingly said, "Hey, I should go up and get a picture with him," to which my friend said, "Oh you should! Do it! When else are you ever going to have the chance?" She was right. I had to do it. Still, my heart started to race. She held my notebook, I took a deep breath and hustled up to the stage. A minute later, I was shaking hands with Ken Ham. I told him I liked his talk and asked if I could get a picture with him. I got a picture… he never smiled.

CLOSE ENCOUNTERS AT KEN HAM'S ARK

Five months later, on July 10th, 2016, a mere four days after the official opening, my friend Ian and I went aboard Ken Ham's Ark Encounter. Apparently, on opening day there had been a number of protests, but as we arrived that morning, the parking lot was largely empty, and all things were pretty quiet. Ian and I went up to the ticket gate, bought our $60 tickets that got us in to not only the Ark Encounter, but also the Creation Museum that was about 45 minutes away. It was going to be quite a day!

Our group of ticketholders hopped on board the shuttle and we were off to see the Ark! Now, it is true, as you drive up to the Ark, you are bound to say (or at least think of) a certain catch phrase of Donald Trump, "It's huuuge!" It really is. Architecturally, it is quite impressive. At the same time, the entire spectacle of seeing this huge boat in the middle of land-locked Kentucky is rather odd.

After getting off the shuttle and taking some pictures, we made our way into the Ark. As we got in line (which was pretty short at 10:00 am on Monday), we noticed a number of television monitors on which were playing the Ark Encounter's reenactment of a scene from the life of Noah. To be clear, it wasn't any biblical scene. Rather, it was a fictional scene in which Noah encountered three "newspaper reporters" from the nearby city who came out to do a story on his building of his 'Ark.'

The reporters looked like rebellious teenagers, pre-flood goth kids, if you will. Predictably, the more Noah pleaded with them to repent of their sins and come with him on the Ark, the more they sneered and made fun of him. After they left, when Noah expressed his frustration to his wife, she said, "There will always be some people who will just mock us!"

I couldn't help cracking a smile. What an odd way to introduce people to your attraction! Seriously, the first "encounter" one has at the Ark Encounter is the message, "This is going to seem really, really stupid to many of you, but all that means is that you are no better than rebellious pre-flood goth kids." Regardless of whether you think Genesis 1–11 is historical or not, it certainly comes across as an odd marketing strategy, doesn't it?

Deck One

Before we got into the actual Ark Encounter, Ian and were told to stand in front of a green screen, so that we could get our pictures taken. At the end of the Ark Encounter, these pictures were made available for us to purchase. When we got the pictures, I must say, it was all very impressive. There we were, standing right along a host of animals at the entrance to Noah's Ark: a stegosaurus, a pterodactyl, as well as other animals like monkeys, elephants, giraffes, gorillas, and tigers. The irony of it all is that you won't see any monkeys, elephants, giraffes, gorillas, or tigers anywhere in the Ark Encounter. But you will see plenty of dinosaurs, *as well as some animals that never have existed.* You know, just like what we are told in the Bible.

As we walked into deck one, the first section was a room that included a lot of small cages to which were attached the kind of feeders you would find attached to gerbil cages at PetSmart, only they were all made with clay. From these cages came a variety of animal sounds. There were no actual animals in these cages, obviously, but the impression was that these were the very small animals Noah had on the Ark. The fact that these cages took up only one room had me a bit confused, though. After all, didn't Ken Ham say at the AiG conference that most of the animals Noah brought on board were no bigger than the size of rats? What could possibly occupy the rest of the Ark?

In the very next room, we started to find out. There were much bigger wooden cages in which there were models of much bigger animals: a "bear" kind, a "wild boar" kind, a "deer" kind, along with a couple of pterodactyls, and some other animals that I simply had no idea what they were supposed to be. The reason why I didn't know what they were supposed to be was because they were, in fact, animals that never existed. They were what AiG speculated were the "original kinds" from which all our modern species descended. The Ark Encounter would have you believe, for example, that over the span of a few thousand years, polar bears, grizzly bears, black bears, brown bears—and every species associated with bears—descended from those two survivors of the "bear" kind on the Ark.

Sprinkled throughout these largely fictional animals of AiG were lots of written explanations on the walls that summarized all the standard AiG talking points regarding how it is possible that the universe was only 6,000 years old and that there was a literal universal flood only 4,000 years ago. As I perused all the written explanations and displays, I couldn't help but notice how often the following words came up: *may have, probably, could have been.* Indeed, they came up…a lot. The reason should be obvious. When certain claims have no scientific evidence and aren't actually addressed in the Bible, the only real recourse is rampant speculation, combined with a lot of *maybes, probablys,* and *could have beens.*

Deck Two

The second deck could have easily been titled either "Dinos Gone Wild" or "Ken Ham's Fantastic Beasts, and Where to Find Them," for that was where the majority of the dinosaurs and fictitious animal "kinds" were found. Now, I expected AiG was going to have dinosaurs on Noah's Ark, but I was quite surprised to find no one had apparently thought through where they were to be displayed. Amazingly, there were flesh-eating dinosaurs caged right next to animals that resembled succulent chipmunks, giraffes, and ponies...and none of them were the size of rats. Maybe I just didn't appreciate that advanced pre-flood technology, but I couldn't see how a wooden cage would be able to contain a velociraptor who would have been whipped up into a frenzy at the sight of such tasty morsels.

All the animal displays were situated in the center of the second deck. Up and down each side were various displays of Noah and his sons. In one display, we were told, "driven by a desire for adventure and a love for construction, Noah travelled to a small port city where he became an apprentice shipwright. He learned blacksmithing and shipbuilding and eventually married the daughter of his employer." (I was shocked to realize that I had somehow missed all that before; to this day, I still can't find that information anywhere in Genesis 6—9).

In another display, an animatronic Shem, Jephthah and Ham were at work in the blacksmith shop that apparently was on the Ark. (The Bible doesn't say there wasn't one, so that means there *may have been one*). In yet another animatronic display, Noah was in his library (which also *could have been* on the Ark!), explaining to those who passed by how he was recording the evil deeds of the pre-flood world. Amazingly, there was a globe in the corner of his library.

In case there were any people who wondered how Noah could have had a globe on the Ark, there were other displays that argued the ancient civilization of the pre-flood world *probably* knew the earth was spherical and *may have had* advanced technology. Accompanying these arguments were artistic renderings of what that ancient pre-flood civilization *probably* was like. Apparently, they hunted triceratops for their tusks and performed child sacrifice to a golden snake-headed god. Granted, there is no evidence of any of that anywhere, and there is no mention of any of that in the Bible, but in AiG world, *that doesn't necessarily mean that it couldn't have been that way.*

As a side note, since my visit to the Ark Encounter back in 2016, AiG has continued to make updates and additions to the exhibits. One particular addition to the Ark Encounter's depiction of the pre-flood civilization is a diorama that depicts a sort of pre-flood colosseum, in which the wicked people of the pre-flood world are cheering on innocent people being thrown to wild beasts...the wild beasts, of course, being giant, carnivorous dinosaurs. Also seen in the diorama is a rather giant figure (perhaps a Nephilim gladiator?) ready to impale a small, fearful girl with a giant spear. Again, there is no evidence of any of that anywhere, and there is no mention of any of that in the Bible, *but that doesn't necessarily mean that it couldn't have been that way.*

Along with these fictitious stories about the pre-flood world, there were also displays and claims regarding what happened after Noah's flood. According to the Ark Encounter, there was only one ice age. It happened immediately after the flood and lasted for 200 years between the time of Noah's flood and the time of the Tower of Babel. That was when all the dinosaurs (that Noah had saved on the Ark) went extinct. Unless you are the equivalent of a pre-flood rebellious goth kid, it is all very convincing.

Deck Three

On the third deck we found the living quarters of Noah and his family, complete with biographical details of each one's background. I was amazed at just how much we actually know about Noah's family, especially given the fact that the Bible gives us no information whatsoever. Ham (Noah's son, not Ken!) was an expert engineer who designed the waste removal and freshwater systems on the Ark. His wife, Kezia, was a medical expert who fell in love with him when she helped him recover from an animal attack. Shem was a scholar and astronomer. Japheth was the tallest of the sons and was an excellent farmer.

Nearby the living quarters, there was a video representation of Ham's waste removal system. It was an elaborate system of pulleys and buckets, powered by an elephant walking on a treadmill. Now, I had read about this in an earlier AiG article from August 24, 2012, that described how Noah and his sons were able to deal with all the piles of manure that would obviously mount up with all the thousands of animals on the Ark. In this article, AiG mentioned that although Noah could have simply dumped the manure overboard, he probably used it as compost to enrich the plants that had been brought on the Ark.

Then the article proposed something quite ingenious. Noah *could have* developed a "methane digester." All he would have needed was "a simple airtight container to hold the manure, the proper bacteria, and a way of piping the resulting bio-gas to places where it could perform useful work—like a heating, cooking, and lighting inside the ship." The article further said that Noah *could have* used "hollow reeds" from the rubber tree to act as the gas pipes, and that these pipes *could have* also provided "reliable gaslight" to illuminate the interior of the Ark! After all, the inner recesses of the Ark *must have been* pretty dark! The article reminded us that Noah built the Ark 4,450 years ago, "when mankind was still highly intelligent (Noah's ancestor, Adam, possessed a nearly perfect brain as God created him), and Noah could easily have mastered this simple technology."

Needless to say, that was quite a claim. Now, I don't remember anywhere in the Bible where it said that Adam possessed a "nearly perfect brain," but whatever! I wanted to see this ingenious technology at work. Sadly, in the video that demonstrated how this waste removal system would work, I couldn't see any methane digestor or hollow reeds that acted like pipes. But maybe I just didn't recognize them because my brain wasn't nearly as perfect as Adam's. In any case, the video was really imaginative, and actually kind of cool, but I was pretty sure I saw something like that on *The Flintstones*. And I couldn't help but notice that the elephant was not some kind of "pre-flood elephant kind" of animal. It was a modern-looking elephant, certainly much bigger than a rat.

In all fairness, all the displays at the Ark Encounter were very well done and highly imaginative. Of course, they were not in any way, shape, or form *actually biblical*. They were, in fact, highly imaginative fictions. Now, the Ark Encounter obviously knows this, for throughout the entire thing there are small plaques that tell people that there is a certain amount of artistic license being used in the displays. That is all well and good, if it wasn't for the fact that the stated purpose of the Ark Encounter is to try to convince people that Noah's Ark and a worldwide Flood is historically and scientifically provable and true. But there isn't any historical and scientific evidence for it, and to make up for it, we find highly imaginative fictions, a lot of *may haves, probablys,* and *could have beens,* along with very colorful artistic renderings of dinosaurs on the Ark with human beings, pterodactyls being released out of the Ark, the larger dinosaurs perishing in the flood, and evil pre-flood people on a pre-flood safari, hunting triceratops for their husks. Don't mock it—*it may have happened this way. . . . or it may not have.*

Now, I have to make it very clear that I can well understand, and even applaud, the liberal use of artistic license if the whole Ark Encounter was an attempt to creatively display the stories in Genesis 1–11 in order to emphasize the theological and worldview themes and lessons of those chapters. Those chapters are incredibly important stories that lay out the fundamental worldview regarding the nature of God, the goodness of creation, and the inherent dignity yet tragic sinfulness of mankind. Throughout Church history, these stories have been creatively and artistically interpreted in a variety of ways in order to bring the reader to those fundamental truths, and that is a great thing to do.

Ken Ham, though, has decided it is his mission to prove Genesis 1–11 scientifically and historically. But as is obvious to anyone who walks through the Ark Encounter, if you try to do that, you are faced with a host of impossibilities and unresolvable problems. And here comes the ultimate irony: in order for him to "prove" Genesis 1–11 is scientifically and historically true, Ken Ham resorts to artistic license and flat-out fictions. I'm sorry, that is a boat that just doesn't float.

Not only that, but it also draws people's attention away from the purpose and power of the stories in Genesis 1–11. Instead of challenging people to consider things like, "What does it mean we are made in God's image?" "Why is it important that God address evil?" "What does it say about God that He attempts to redeem mankind, despite mankind's propensity to destroy His creation?" Ken Ham chose to focus describing how the pre-flood civilization *could have* killed triceratops for their horns, and how Noah and his sons *could have* invented and used an imaginative waste disposal system while on the Ark. I'm sorry, but who cares?

As Ian and I left the Ark Encounter, I couldn't help but realize that most of the things one sees in the Ark Encounter *aren't in the Bible.* That's what made the whole thing so ludicrous. Yes, it is an incredibly creative project, but in order to try to convince people Genesis 1–11 is history and science, it presents non-biblical fictions and fantastic animals that are nowhere to be found in the Bible . . . or the scientific record. It could have been a tremendously artistic rendering of Genesis 6—9 that helps people, through a creative means, to understand the story of the flood in a much more profound way—the way that the author of Genesis 6—9 intended.

As it stands, though, the Ark Encounter is filled with bad science, unbiblical claims, and fictitious beasts that have never existed in history, all while claiming the Ark Encounter is scientific, biblical, and historical. Ken Ham has turned those early chapters in Genesis into a joke, a really bad joke. All that said, I do want to go back one day and visit it again. Apparently, Ken Ham is planning to build his own Tower of Babel. Some skeptics and compromised Christians might object, but I think it is a really good idea. I think he can really make a name for himself, and I'd love to be there to see what God thinks about it.

THE CREATION MUSEUM: DOWN THE VELOCIRAPTOR HOLE

After getting a bite to eat, Ian and I hopped in my car and drove 45 miles north on I-75 to the Creation Museum. After we parked, we made our way to the front door and were confronted by a large statue of a dinosaur at the entrance. After we got inside, as we glanced around the foyer, it was pretty obvious that Ken Ham was obsessed with dinosaurs. In fact, now that I've been to both the Ark Encounter and the Creation Museum, I'm convinced that Ken Ham's primary objective isn't so much to prove that Genesis 1-11 is scientifically and historically true (although he certainly tries to do so), but rather to convince people that dinosaurs and human beings lived together only a few thousand years ago.

In any case, the foyer was filled with banners and signs that made statements like, "Dragons were dinosaurs!" I thought to myself, "Dragons were dinosaurs? What dragons? Like the one in *Shrek*? What can they be talking about?" To my shock and horror, I soon got my answer as I walked up to the display regarding the Anglo-Saxon epic *Beowulf*. My undergraduate degree was in British Literature, so imagine my surprise to find this display in the Creation Museum. After giving a brief summary of the story of *Beowulf*, the display read, "The epic contains accurate historical information . . ." and went on to claim that the dragon in *Beowulf* "may have been based on real events," and therefore this would be "consistent with the Bible."

My jaw dropped through the floor. I wasn't at the Creation Museum. I was in Bizarro World! To prove Genesis 1–11 was historical, AiG was appealing to an Anglo-Saxon *work of fiction* that dated back to around AD 449 (450 years *after* the birth of Christ!) to show that . . . dinosaurs at one time lived with human beings!?!?! The dragon in *Beowulf* was "consistent with the Bible"?!?!?!? *Beowulf* also has a character named Grendel who had spawned from various demons, goblins, monsters, and giants who traced their lineage back to Cain, and who devoured Danish soldiers at night. And then there is Grendel's mother who lived at the bottom of a fiery, burning lake, whom Beowulf killed with a magical sword made by giants. Are we to think these were actual historical creatures? Really?

And let's not overlook the fact that the Creation Museum was claiming that the dragon in *Beowulf* was actually a dinosaur of some sort that would have been alive and fighting with human beings *in AD 449…450 years after the birth of Christ*, and that would mean fire-breathing dragons were apparently roaming the countryside of the Roman Empire at the time of Christ! And I thought the Creation Museum would be stupid. I couldn't wait to get out of the foyer and into the museum proper to the exhibits. If *Beowulf's* dragon was a historical dinosaur that lived (let's do the math!) *during the same time as Saint Augustine*, I couldn't imagine what else I'd discover at the Creation Museum.

On our way to the exhibits, we passed a giant display of AiG's *Seven C's of God's Eternal Plan*: Creation, Corruption, Catastrophe, Confusion (that takes us up to Genesis 11), then Christ, Cross (that's the gospels), and Consummation (that would be Revelation). I found it highly ironic that not only does AiG insist that Genesis 1–11 is "history" when it clearly is not, but then it turns around and ignores the actual history that is in the Old Testament that talks about God's covenant relationship with ancient Israel. This really was the portal to Bizarro World.

There was another display that highlighted the variety of plant and animal life, along with a sign that read, "There is not enough time—even billions of years—to get such differences by small steps from a common ancestor. The Bible tells us where this amazing variety came from—created by an all-knowing, all-powerful, creative God." The irony of that claim, of course, is that while Ken Ham claims "billions of years" isn't enough time to account for all the differences we see in the natural world today, he does believe that natural selection and genetic mutations are, in fact, the processes that account for the variety of species and life forms in the world, but that it all has come about *within the past 4,000 years, since Noah's flood*. Now, I'm no mathematician, but if "billions of years" isn't enough time, then I'm pretty sure that "4,000 years" would constitute a considerably less amount of time for all that to happen. Such a claim has about as much historical merit as the dragon in *Beowulf* being a dinosaur living at the time of the Vandal's sacking of Carthage.

The First Main Exhibit: Dinosaurs . . . and the Battle for God's Word

After what we encountered in the foyer, it was no surprise to find that the first main exhibit focused on . . . you guessed it . . . *dinosaurs*. There was a life-sized display of an archeological dig, with two archeologists looking at a dinosaur fossil in the rock layer. The explanation in this display said, "Dinosaurs don't come with tags on them telling us how old they are, where they lived, what they ate, or how they died. . . . Because we never have all the evidence, different scientists reach very different conclusions, depending on their starting assumptions." Above the display was a video screen where the two archeologists were talking about the fossil. The first one concluded it was millions of years old. The other one, a creation scientist, said, "You see? He's just interpreting this fossil based on his assumption that the earth is millions of years old. I look at this fossil and conclude that this dinosaur lived 4,000 years ago and was instantaneously buried in the waters of Noah's flood. It's all about starting points!"

I thought, "That pretty much sums up the way AiG believes science is done, doesn't it?" There is no actual studying of the fossil record or geological strands in which fossils are found. Scientists just dig up a fossil, and, depending if they are "secular scientists" or "creation scientists," they look at it and declare their conclusion based on their respective "starting points"! I'm no scientist, but I'm pretty sure that real geologists, astronomers, and biologists don't do that. That's what AiG does, though. That's why it was clear to me that what they're doing isn't real science.

As for what these "starting points" were, next to the display were other charts involving astronomy and the variety of species, including human beings. Each one was clearly labeled with *Man's Word* ("secular science") on one side, and *God's Word* (Genesis 1) on the other. The message couldn't be any clearer: Genesis 1 was presenting accurate scientific information in the fields of astronomy and biology, so if you accept evolution, you are accepting "man's word" (modern science) and rejecting "God's word" (the Bible, which gives us "historical science").

At the entrance to the next room, there were several signs with questions on them: *"Why am I here? Am I Alone? Why do I suffer? Is there any hope? Why do we have to die?"* These are important questions, for sure. I just was at a loss to see how they had anything to do with inspecting dinosaur fossils.

We went to the next room to see the next display. It was all about *biblical authority*. In this room were life-sized representations of various figures in the Old Testament, from Moses, to Jeremiah, Isaiah, and David, followed by an empty tomb, and then the Apostle Paul. The emphasis was clear: if you want to get answers to life's important questions (i.e. the ones right outside the door), you'll find them in the Bible. As a Christian, and as someone who has devoted over twenty-five years of studying and teaching the Bible, I agree with that sentiment. I just didn't see how that had anything to do with dinosaur fossils and distant starlight.

Well, AiG made the connection for me with the very next exhibit titled, *Attacks on the Bible*. These "attacks" come from "secularists" and "evolutionists" who question the scientific and historical accuracy of Genesis 1. To say the earth is millions of years old is to "attack" Genesis 1 and to undermine the authority of the Bible. If you tell people Genesis 1 isn't scientifically reliable, then you are telling them the Bible isn't truthful, and therefore is unreliable to answer life's important questions… and any society that questions the Bible will find itself going to hell in a handbasket.

Who would have thought that any mistake in dating any given fossil could have such dire consequences for the eternal destiny of society? Well, get your handbaskets ready. Ken Ham is about to show you the dystopia that secular scientists have wrought.

The Second Major Exhibit: Hell in a Handbasket

In Canto III of Dante's *Inferno*, when Virgil and Dante enter Hell, inscribed on the gate of Hell are the famous words, *"Abandon all hope, ye who enter here!"* Well, I had abandoned all hope of finding rational thought at the Creation Museum back at the *Beowulf* display, so I almost expected to find a taste of the fiendish underworld at some point on my journey. Sure enough, it was in the next room: *Moral Decay in Society*.

As Ian and I entered, we read the two signs at the entrance: *"Scripture abandoned in the culture leads to relative morality, hopelessness, and meaninglessness"* and *"Scripture compromised in the church leads to scripture abandoned in the home."* We were then bombarded with images of things like a giant wrecking ball crashing into a church, graffiti, riots, drugs, and drinking. There were scenes that depicted a dysfunctional family in various stages of family breakdown. Why is little Jimmy uninterested in the sermon, and is instead eating peanuts while the pastor is preaching? Because the pastor is telling his congregation that Genesis 1–11 is only a "story," and therefore isn't important!

The scene reminded me of those ridiculous "hell houses" some ultra-Fundamentalist churches put on during Halloween. Only this wasn't scary at all. It was ridiculous. Don't get me wrong, I'm not denying there are serious societal problems these days, but who in their right mind really thinks that the "genesis" of all these problems is "compromising pastors" telling their congregations that Genesis 1–11 is "only a story"? Of course, the supreme irony of all this is that this is coming from an organization that built a giant 'Ark' in Kentucky, and then filled it with *fictitious beasts* and *fictitious stories* in an attempt to "prove" Genesis 1–11 is historical!

The Third Major Exhibit: The "Good News" of Genesis 1–11

In any case, what is the best way to confront such compromise in the church? Show how all the historical answers are in Genesis, of course . . . specifically Genesis 1–11. The rest of the Creation Museum was devoted to doing just that—well, sort of. For in its attempt to prove Genesis 1–11 was historical, the Creation Museum took certain "creative liberties" and let's not beat around the bush, included quite a bit of fictitious speculations that are nowhere to be found in Genesis 1–11.

First, there was a giant recreation of the Garden of Eden, complete with Adam and Eve frolicking in what seemed more like a lush jungle than a garden. With them, of course, were . . . *dinosaurs, vegetarian dinosaurs*. A little further on, in the next scene, we saw Adam and Eve being tempted by the serpent, and after that came "Corruption Valley." And what is the first thing we saw in Corruption Valley? *A velociraptor, of course, just like Genesis 3 tells us!* Unlike the fruit-eating dinosaurs in Eden who liked to snuggle up to Adam and Eve, though, this one was now feasting on flesh.

You see, AiG is so committed to biblical authority, even though the Bible says absolutely nothing about vegetarian dinosaurs in Eden who immediately because savage meat-eaters as soon as Adam and Eve ate the forbidden fruit, they know that had to be the case, *because it is all about starting points.* You've got to fit dinosaurs into the Bible somewhere, or else people will think the Bible isn't true and the secularists will win.

In any case, we passed by the velociraptor, took in the Cain and Abel display, saw a few more dinosaurs side by side human beings, and then, in the next room, came to the display of Noah building the Ark. The room looked like the interior of the Ark, complete with an animatronic Noah discussing the building of it, as well as "pagan workers," saying Noah was a religious fanatic, and how they were just building it to get paid.

I couldn't help but smile and think that if this scenario in the Creation Museum had really happened—if Noah hired pagan workers to build the Ark—the last thing they would accuse Noah of being would be a "religious fanatic." Pagans worshipped many gods and had idols that represented them. They would have seen Noah as a veritable atheist. An invisible God, with no idol to represent him? That's no god (at least it wouldn't be to an ancient pagan culture)! All that is irrelevant, though. Not to be a killjoy or anything, but none of that scenario *is actually in the Bible anyway.*

In the next room, Ian and I found some cool models of the Ark, complete with animals making their way in, two by two: elephants, giraffes, lions, bears...and *dinosaurs*! I couldn't help but realize just a few things that might be, could possibly be, considered problematic. First, the elephants, giraffes, lions, and bears were, well, elephants, giraffes, lions, and bears. They weren't the original "kinds" from which eventually came elephants, giraffes, lions, and bears. "How is this possible?" I asked myself. But then I remembered, according to Ken Ham, Noah had access to all that pre-flood advanced technology. Is it really that far-fetched to think he might have had a flux-capacitor and had the ability to time travel? After all, the Noah figure in the model did sort of look like Doc Brown.

Second, all the animals were much bigger than rats. Ken Ham himself said at the AiG conference earlier that year that most of the land animals Noah took on the Ark were no bigger than rats. Something was amiss.

Finally, according to the model, *there were large dinosaurs on the Ark.* For the life of me, I couldn't recall where in Genesis 6 dinosaurs were mentioned.

Oh well . . . just inconvenient details, I suppose.

The Bookstore

With the major exhibits done, Ian and I passed through a few other side exhibits and then made our way to the bookstore. It was filled with merchandise and books, all touting the YECist doctrine of a young earth and dinosaurs being in Eden and even on Noah's Ark. While perusing the bookstore, I noticed one book written by Ken Ham's son-in-law, Bodie Hodge, titled, *World Religions and Cults*. I opened it and found there was a chapter on Eastern Orthodoxy. I'm not sure if Hodge thought it was another religion or a cult, but skimming the chapter it was clear that he felt something was really wrong with it because Eastern Orthodoxy relies on Church Tradition along with the Bible.

Imagine that. Eastern Orthodoxy isn't truly Christian because it values Church Tradition and practice. I wasn't really surprised to find this in the Creation Museum bookstore, though. After all, I had just spent a couple of hours being told that Beowulf was historical, that dragons in folklore and literature were based on dinosaurs, that scientists just make conclusions based on their own biases alone, that dinosaurs were vegetarians in Eden, that dinosaurs started eating meat shortly after that, and that dinosaurs were on Noah's Ark.

. . . did I mention the dinosaurs? Because at the Creation Museum, dinosaurs play a vital role in proving the Bible is true. The message of the Creation Museum is clear: to be a faithful, Bible-believing Christian, one has to believe dinosaurs are in the Bible (. . . even though they aren't).

14

The Historical Adam Debate Today

IN THIS FINAL CHAPTER, I want to offer some comments on what I feel is the current state of the debate within Evangelical circles regarding the issue of the historicity of Adam. Second, I want to expand a bit more on what I feel is the underlying issue that so often instigates the hostility and division that is so often characterized in these two issues of the creation/evolution debate and the question regarding the historicity of Genesis 1–11.

THE HISTORICAL ADAM DEBATE IN TODAY'S EVANGELICAL WORLD

Up until BioLogos, I think it is safe to say that YECist groups like AiG had cornered the market of the Evangelical world without too many people truly realizing what sort of things they actually claimed. BioLogos essentially was the first concentrated effort by Evangelical Christians like Francis Collins to challenge, not only the YECist narrative, but also the general antipathy within Evangelicalism against evolutionary theory as a whole. This obviously has been a good thing because, as hopefully I've shown in this book, there has been a lot of misinformation and hostility coming from YECist groups like AiG for far too long that has really scared and silenced many people.

Not surprisingly, over the past fifteen years or so, there has been many books, articles, social media forums, and podcasts that have sought to make sense of not only the general creation/evolution debate, but more specifically the historical questions surrounding Genesis 1–11, particularly that of Noah's Flood and the historicity of Adam and Eve. I would be remiss if I didn't specifically highlight two books that do a tremendous job on these issues: Gregg Davidson's *Friend of Science, Friend of Faith: Listening to God in His Works and Word*, and Sy Garte's *Science and Faith in Harmony: Contemplations and a Distilled Doxology*. I have added a number of other books that have come out since 2016 to my recommendations at the end of this book.

I'm not going to comment on all these books in this final chapter, but I do want to share a few thoughts about recent attempts to wrestle with the question of the historicity of Genesis 1–11 (specifically Adam and Eve) within the Evangelical world today. It is very gratifying to see this issue more openly discussed. Christians need to ask questions and wrestle with Scripture, particularly hard to understand passages like Genesis 1–11.

The Evangelical world has come a long way over the past fifteen years or so, when scholars like Peter Enns, Bruce K. Waltke, Karl Giberson, and John Schneider all faced severe repercussions from their respective universities in regard to the issues of evolution and the historicity of Adam. The fact there is now be a bit of an open space to talk about these issues shows tremendous progress. Steps are being taken in the right direction. That being said, even though I've read and appreciated a number of the more recent books, I still want to touch upon a few more observations I think need to be taken into more consideration.

First of all, it has always struck me as odd to see that the *starting point* within Evangelical circles when interpreting Genesis 1–11 is to initially come at the question through a scientific lens. The questions that dominate most of these books and articles on the topic are scientific ones: *"Does evolution disprove the historicity of Adam and Eve?"* Or *"If one accepts evolutionary theory, is it still possible to retain the claim of the historicity of Adam and Eve?"* The entire debate inevitably gets framed as a "Science vs. the Bible" debate, and ironically YECists like Ken Ham and militant atheists like Richard Dawkins find themselves strange bedfellows who give the same answer: *Evolution and the Bible are in conflict—you can't have it both ways, it's one or the other.*

I don't think that is the right way to go about things. As I've argued in this book, the starting point in trying to understand Genesis 1–11 should not be to start with an assumption that Genesis 1–11 is historical and then ask the scientific question, *"Does evolution call the historicity of*

Adam and Eve (or Noah's Flood) into question?" Rather, the starting point should simply be, "What is Genesis 1–11? What are we reading? What is the genre of Genesis 1–11?" That is the question that needs to dominate the discussion. How one answers that question will determine how to proceed in the analysis of Genesis 1–11. The fact is if you misinterpret the genre of a text like Genesis 1–11, if you, like Ken Ham, insist it is "historical science" and a literal historical account of origins, all the questions and analysis stemming from that misinterpretation are going to become more convoluted, confusing, and downright silly.

Now, even though more Evangelical books are coming out and rejecting the claims of YECism, many still have a hard time separating the scientific question of material origins with the literary question of the genre of Genesis 1–11. They acknowledge the *literary similarities* between Genesis 1–11 and other ANE myths, but then spend their time trying to make *scientific arguments* that seek to show how scientific discoveries might or might not be able to coincide with the events in Genesis 1–11, as if the entire point of Genesis 1–11 is to be a platform to discuss modern scientific discoveries. It isn't.

Secondly, the biggest historical hang-up continues to center on Adam and Eve. Slowly, it seems more Evangelicals are willing to acknowledge those literary connections between Genesis 1–11 and other ANE myths. More are willing to say that Genesis 1 shouldn't be taken as a literal, blow by blow historical/scientific account of the creation of the world a mere 6,000 years ago. Despite that, most still seem to say, "Yes, *but there still had to have been a historical Adam and Eve*." They then give reasons that sound eerily similar to that of YECism: (A) It's an issue of biblical authority—if you question the historicity of Genesis 1–11, then what's to stop you from questioning the historicity of everything else in the Bible? (B) If there was no original couple, then how can you explain the universality of sin? (C) But there are genealogies in Genesis 1–11. (D) Paul and Jesus refer to Adam, therefore Adam must be a historical person.

I honestly do not understand that. In terms of genre recognition, *if it walks like a duck and quacks like a duck... it's probably a duck*. If all the literary indicators in a text point to a certain genre, maybe we just need to accept the fact that *that is the genre in which it was written*, and then proceed to analyze that text within that framework without constantly trying to force our modern, scientific understanding of the natural world back onto the text. That isn't undermining biblical authority, that isn't calling the veracity or inspiration of the Bible into question—*that's accepting what the Bible is presenting in the given genre in which it is presented*. If we do that, then we are able to see just how important Genesis 1–11 is to the entire biblical story and to understanding the Gospel itself, for it lays out both the very existential situation all of us share and the theological framework to understand God's involvement in history. That's what Genesis 1–11 challenges us to contemplate.

Unfortunately, ever since the Enlightenment, we've been conditioned to filter everything in the Bible through more or less a scientific lens, so when it comes to texts like Genesis 1–11, instead of contemplating what it is teaching, we automatically go about using it as a basis for scientific speculation as to "what really happened." I've noted in this book how much of the YECist speculation comes across as rather convoluted and downright silly—claims of extraordinary pre-flood technology, perfect genomes, dinosaurs on Noah's Ark, an elephant-powered waste removal system, and, of course, Nephilim giants in pre-flood colosseums, throwing innocent pre-flood people to, you guessed it…vicious dinosaurs. None of that has anything to do with the message being taught in Genesis 1-11.

That being said, there have been a number of recent books like William Lane Craig's *In Quest for the Historical Adam* and S. Josh Swamidass' *The Genealogical Adam and Eve* that have argued that perhaps God imprinted His image on a certain historical hominid couple 200,000 years ago (who either evolved with the rest of the eventual human race or who were uniquely created by God de novo at that time) who then interbred with the rest of the hominids who didn't bear God's image.[1] They acknowledge that what we read in Genesis 1–3 isn't some sort of journalistic account of the first historical human couple, but they still argue that there is possibly some actual history behind it.

Indeed, as is always the case with scientific research, our understanding of our past is constantly . . . evolving. In personal conversations, Gregg Davidson has told me, "Genetic studies have indicated all humanity can be traced to a common female, and to a larger population. This is exactly what one would expect if a first couple were selected from a population and set apart, yet mixed anyway." Therefore, he argues that genetic evidence does not, in fact, eliminate the possibility of a first "imago dei."

---

1. See also Gregg Davidson's article, "Genetics, the Nephilim, and the Historicity of Adam," in *Perspectives on Science and Christian Faith* (24–34), 2015.

This kind of scientific research is vastly different than the baseless speculations put forth by Ken Ham, AiG, and other YECist organizations. It is actually rooted in genetic studies and makes clear, definable scientific arguments. To that extent, it is a valid field of scientific research in and of itself. Theoretically, perhaps one day, through genetic studies, scientists will be able to trace the origins of human beings back to an original couple.

That being said, although I understand the interest and fascination with studying the biological origins of the human race and the ultimate origins of the universe itself, I still do not think any such discovery would have much of an impact on what, in this case, Genesis 1–3 is teaching. The inspired meaning and teaching of Genesis 1–3 is not dependent on being able to prove there was a first historical couple. Or to put it another way, even if we were able to literally pinpoint a first human couple, that fact wouldn't change the theological message being taught in Genesis 1–3. Human beings are made in God's image, whether or not there was a historical Adam and Eve, and human beings are sinful and succumb to death, whether or not there was a historical Adam and Eve. The truth of what Genesis 1–3 is teaching is not dependent on the historicity of Adam and Eve.

If genetic evidence points to the possibility of an original couple, investigate it and see where it leads. There is nothing wrong with that. Ultimately, though, I just do not think that impacts the inspired message in Genesis 1–11. Genesis 1–11 is written in the genre of ANE myth. That is the "literary package" in which the chapters are written, so we need to interpret it along those lines. It doesn't have to be "proven" to be historical in order for it to be inspired and true.

The mentality that thinks it has to prove Genesis 1–11 is historical in order for it to be true betrays the fact that, generally speaking, Evangelicals are still really uncomfortable with any notion of uncertainty, especially about anything in the Bible. Everything has to be figured out, or else uncertainty and doubt can creep in, and you can lose your faith. It is this kind of mindset that has often crippled Evangelicals in their search for truth and understanding, not only about the Bible, but about life in general. It is what Daniel Taylor calls "the myth of certainty" in his book by the same name, *The Myth of Certainty*. What I learned from that book over 20 years ago is that it is okay to admit you don't know the answers to everything. Therefore, whenever I get into discussions related to Genesis

1–11 and inevitably get asked the same kinds of questions, I respond in the same way:

"If Adam and Eve weren't historical, where did sin come from?" *I don't know—but I do know the Bible clearly teaches that all human beings are sinful.*

"If human beings just evolved, exactly when did God 'make man in His image'?" *I don't know—but I do know the Bible teaches that all human beings are made in God's image and therefore have inherent dignity and worth.*

"What about Neanderthals, or homo erectus? Does God consider them human? Are they made in God's image?" *I don't know, and quite frankly, don't care. The Bible doesn't address that.*

I'm okay with not knowing the answers to those questions. My Christian faith is not dependent on being able to give conclusive answers to things that the Bible doesn't address. All I can do is do the best I can to understand the Bible (in this case, Genesis 1–11) in its original context, contemplate what it is teaching, and let the truth of that teaching shape my life. I think we'd all be better off if we did the same.

Epilogue

An Ever-Evolving Personal Story

"Don't you know I'm still standing, better than I ever did?
Looking like a true survivor, feeling like a little kid,
And I'm still standing after all this time,
Picking up the pieces of my life without you on my mind"

—Elton John

EVER SINCE DARWIN PUBLISHED *The Origin of Species* in 1859, Christians have wrestled with the whole creation/evolution issue, as they should—it is a difficult and complex issue, to be sure. But let's be clear: the theory of evolution did not challenge *the Bible*—it challenged certain *Enlightenment assumptions about the Bible,* and those assumptions needed to be challenged because *those assumptions were wrong.* Genesis 1–11 is not trying to give a scientific/historical account of the beginning of the physical universe. To claim that it does is to claim something that flies in the face of both biblical exegesis and Church history.

In the beginning of this book, I stated three things: (A) the truthfulness of the Bible does not hinge on the issue of creation/evolution; (B) Christians throughout history have interpreted Genesis 1–11 in a variety of ways, and at no point was anyone's faith called into question because of it; and (C) the "heresy" I am warning about isn't belief in a young earth, historical Adam and Eve, or literal Flood—it is the insistence that those things are the foundation to the Gospel itself. I hope that I've made my case.

Now, I'm under no illusion. Staunch YECists will not be convinced by anything I've said. That's okay. I didn't write this book to convince them. I wrote this book for the scores of good Evangelical Christians who simply don't know what to make of this issue. I wrote it for people like my former colleagues at the Christian school where I used to work, and for my former students, many whom have been told their entire lives that they can't trust the Bible or be Christians if evolution is true.

At best, YECism is a distraction from the Gospel and the traditional Christian faith. At worst, it is a dangerous heresy that antagonizes non-believers and sows division within Christian communities. It is not something that can be ignored. Sadly, I've found that it is almost impossible to engage in discussion with many YECists like Ken Ham without soon being called a compromiser and hypocrite. They don't want to engage in discussion. They're fighting a culture war and demand submission.

That being said, when it comes to the so-called "culture war," that kind of black/white, either/or, us/them mentality seems to be common on both sides. There are vitriolic "culture warriors" on both sides of the political and cultural divide who paint *everyone* on the "other side" with the absolute worst stereotypes and extreme caricatures possible, and then engage in their own scorched earth policy of cultural annihilation. One side screams, "compromiser," "secularist," and "liberal," and the other side screams, "apologist" and "Christian nationalist." Both sides are militant in their insistence that there can be no gray area or room for discussion on their pet issues. After all, it's a *culture war*. If you seem to deviate in any way from either side's prescribed political ideology regarding these issues, bombs away.

I don't have any easy answers as to how to navigate a way through that kind of no man's land. That kind of mentality leaves no room for actual discussion and debate because there is no acknowledgment or humility that says, "Maybe I don't know everything. Maybe I need to take the time to think things through and figure these things out." Instead, it is just, "Here are my ideological stances. They are not to be questioned. If you do, you're the enemy and must be destroyed."

And for some reason, exegetical questions regarding Genesis 1-11 and scientific questions regarding evolution get shoehorned into that culture war. I honestly don't get it. All I'll say is that if you think someone's opinion on those issues is either "liberal" or "conservative," perhaps you've let your political opinions ossify into a divisive ideology that drives the way you react to anyone who doesn't think like you.

I believe Christians need to stay focused on what the goal of Christianity is. It isn't "winning the culture war." It is *becoming like Christ, what Orthodoxy calls theosis.* Instead of letting ourselves be conformed to the political ideologies of the world, we need to be transformed by the renewing of our minds so we can discern the will of God when we face inevitable cultural and political challenges. Our goal should be to be Christ-like in the way we go about addressing difficult issues and challenges, be it seeking clarity in the creation/evolution debate, seeking a better understanding regarding passages like Genesis 1–11, or navigating through so many of the very difficult and confusing cultural issues that face us today. Getting to the truth is important, but the way we go about getting to the truth and conveying the truth is even more important. For the Christian, it isn't about "winning the culture war." It is about shining light on the truth. If we do that in a Christ-like way, our witness is bound to have a healing effect on our culture. We won't be "fighting a culture war." We'll be healing the culture.

Christians need to remember that the truth we are attempting to get to is ultimately Jesus Christ Himself. He is the heart of the matter in all of this, and if our goal is to seek Him, to be conformed to the image of His likeness, and to bear that image to the world, we won't be so easily deceived by serpents who tell us that the way to true wisdom is found in disobedience and divisiveness.

When I was a kid, one Christian music artist I loved was Bob Bennett. I've already quoted from his song *Heart of the Matter* earlier in the book. That song, though, begins with these lines:

> *I'm just a man in a world full of men just like me,*
> *With a heart full of questions and answers*
> *that seem to be somewhat connected*
> *And a headful of preconceived notions that manage to get in the way.*
> *And I find myself longing to return back to the place where I started,*
> *Back when I knew next to nothing . . . back to the heart of the matter.*

I think the humility and longing expressed in those words crystalize what I hope more Christians strive to have as they engage with each other when discussing difficult and challenging issues, whatever they may be.

By all means, state your views on whatever issues come up and articulate the reasons for your views. State as clearly as you can what you think is the truth and be open to listen to those with other views. But if someone attacks you for it, don't fight back in the same way. Don't hate the person. Don't view him as the enemy. The fate of our culture and society does not depend on you defeating the "other side" in the culture war. Just strive to be Christ-like, speak the truth, and if need be, take the beating. That is the kind of witness that will have a healing effect on the culture.

It has been ten years since Mr. Spencer told me my contract would not be renewed, nine years since I walked out of my classroom at that Evangelical Christian school, and eight years since *Heresy of Ham* originally came out. I started working on *Heresy of Ham* that very summer, immediately after I left the school, as a way to make sense of everything that had happened to me. As I began to read books and articles by Ken Ham and the AiG organization, I realized just how influential and dangerously zealous YECism had become within the Evangelical world. At the same time, though, I couldn't help but find the whole thing just absurd. That is why I wrote the book. It wasn't just to make sense of what happened to me. I wanted to warn Evangelicals what YECism actually teaches and how its adherents treat fellow Christians. I knew, and still know, far too many good, sincere, and thoughtful Evangelical Christians to assume "all Evangelicals" really buy into YECism. I hope that simply shining a light on what YECists like Ken Ham really teach and really claim will convince most Evangelical Christians to reject it.

As things turned out, a little over a year after my departure, Mr. Spencer left the school as well. Under his leadership, enrollment had plummeted so much that the Board decided to make a change. Who knows? Maybe my blog post about why I was no longer teaching that year got some people's attention about Mr. Spencer.

Fortunately, after he left, my friend Kennedy Harris was hired to be his replacement and she got the school back onto a sound (and sane) footing. As for me, I was able to get a part-time position in the History department at the local university. All in all, it turned out to be a blessing in disguise. It allowed me to spend more time raising my autistic son, as well as gain valuable teaching experience at the university level. In addition, it gave me time to complete a number of writing projects. I have been able to write my own translation of both the Old and New Testaments, as well as write both *Heresy of Ham* and another book titled *Christianity and the (R)evolution in Worldviews in Western Culture*. I've also just recently published *The Blue-Collar Bible Scholar: Reader's Guide to the New Testament* and hope to have the Old Testament volume out within a year.

As I briefly alluded to earlier, though, my career path has now taken me back to teaching high school English again. I will no longer be teaching Biblical Studies at the high school or university level anymore. That chapter in my life is over, and the page has turned. I'm at peace with it.

Although those were a rough few years, I'm not bitter about any of it. Gaining a better understanding of evolution has helped me appreciate more what the Bible and early Church Fathers like Irenaeus say about salvation and the Christian life. God has created us as these curious biological organisms made in His image, and within the natural world, biological organisms, over long periods of time and within population groups, adapt to their environment and continue to grow and evolve into different life forms. In a similar, albeit obviously not exact, way, salvation involves facing hardships, learning to adapt to the inevitable trials in life, and submitting to the death of your hopes and desires, offering it all up as a sacrifice to God in the knowledge and faith that, through Christ, God will transform us from being mere natural creatures (in Adam) made in His image, into a being Spirit-empowered children (in Christ), according to His likeness. And ultimately, just like evolution, salvation reaches far beyond just individual organisms. The goal of salvation isn't just my personal, individual salvation, but indeed the salvation and transformation of God's entire creation.

Exploring the claims of evolution, grappling with how they may or may not relate to Christianity's claim of the existence of God, and wrestling with the question of the proper way to interpret Genesis 1–11 are all valid issues Christians should take the time to investigate. I find them fascinating, and my faith has grown because I took the time to investigate them. I hope that anyone who reads this book is convinced of my arguments regarding Genesis 1–11 and evolution. Still, what is more important is that you realize that the issues of creation/evolution and the historicity of Genesis 1–11 are not fundamental tenets of the Christian faith. It is okay for Christians to have different opinions on them. They should be able to allow room for honest questioning and discussion about these things while extending grace and understanding toward those whose views may differ and not demonizing them or going to war with them. Of everything I have covered in this book, that is the most important lesson I hope everyone can learn.

I wrote *The Heresy of Ham* to warn Evangelicals about how influential and dangerously zealous YECist organizations like AiG have become within Evangelicalism. They misrepresent the historical Christian faith and attack anyone who disagrees with their interpretation of Genesis

1–11 as being some sort of anti-God liberal or "compromised Christian," and thus their enemy in the culture war. And, like I said earlier, fighting and winning the culture war is their real goal. It isn't coming to a better understanding of Scripture; it isn't about coming to a better understanding of science; it is to use them as battlefronts in the culture war.

Obviously, there are many controversial cultural and political issues facing us today. I am not suggesting Christians should be silent and not rigorously debate these issues. Christians certainly need to try to be the conscience of society, and that entails engaging with those issues. How one does so is up to that person, but what I've come to realize is that when you view everything in terms of a "culture war" and then try to tie every cultural issue to something like how to interpret Genesis 1–11, you are going to cause a great deal of harm, *and you're going to make Christianity look idiotic in the eyes of the culture you're supposedly trying to save.*

Whatever your stances on the variety of political and cultural issues might be, have well-reasoned arguments for them. But whatever you do, unless you really want to "blaspheme the name of God among the gentiles" (Romans 2:24), don't base them on the ignorant and divisive claims of YECism. Evolutionary theory and exegetical issues regarding Genesis 1–11 are not ideologically "liberal" or "conservative" stances. They are attempts to understand the natural world and the intent of the author of Genesis 1–11. Making them litmus tests for who is a true Christian and turning them into a battlefront in the culture war is to be led astray by the heresy of Ham.

Book Recommendations

Hopefully, this book has shown that when it comes to the debate regarding creation/evolution, there's a lot more to it than just science. To fully understand it, one needs to be familiar with Church history and biblical exegesis and interpretation as well. If you are interested in learning more about anything I covered in the book, let me recommend the following books. They have been extremely helpful to me.

Books Related to Church History

1. *The Triumph of Christianity,* Rodney Stark
2. *For the Glory of God,* Rodney Stark
3. *Christianity on Trial,* Vincent Carroll and David Shiflett
4. *Heresy: A History of Defending the Truth,* Alister McGrath
5. *Bad Religion: How We Became a Nation of Heretics,* Ross Douthat
6. *The Orthodox Way,* Bishop Kallistos Ware
7. *Eastern Orthodoxy Through Western Eyes,* Donald Fairbairn
8. *Eastern Orthodox Christianity: A Western Perspective,* Daniel B. Clendenin
9. *Beginnings,* Peter C. Bouteneff
10. *Early Christian Readings of Genesis One: Patristic Exegesis and Literal Interpretation,* Craig D. Allert
11. *Evangelicals: Who They Have Been, Are Now, and Could Be,* Mark A. Noll

Books Related to Biblical Interpretation

1. *How to Read the Bible for All Its Worth*, Gordon Fee and Douglas Stuart
2. *How to Read the Bible Book by Book*, Gordon Fee and Douglas Stuart
3. *The Art of Biblical Narrative*, Robert Alter
4. *The Lost World of Genesis 1*, John Walton
5. *The Lost World of Adam and Eve*, John Walton
6. *Genesis 1 as Ancient Cosmology*, John Walton
7. *The Lost World of Scripture: Ancient Literary Culture and Biblical Authority*, John Walton
8. *Saving the Original Sinner*, Karl Giberson
9. *Inspiration and Incarnation*, Peter Enns
10. *In the Beginning: A Catholic Understanding of Creation and the Fall*, Benedict XVI
11. *Judgment and Salvation*, Dustin G. Burlet

Books About the Creation/Evolution Debate

1. *Beyond the Firmament*, Gordon Glover
2. *The Language of Science and Faith*, Francis Collins
3. *Saving Darwin: How to be a Christian and Believe in Evolution*, Karl Giberson
4. *The Evolution of Adam*, Peter Enns
5. *Finding Darwin's God*, Kenneth Miller
6. *I Love Jesus and I Accept Evolution*, Denis Lamoureux
7. *From Evolution to Eden*, Greg Laughery
8. *Adam and the Genome: Reading Scripture After Genetic Evidence*, Scot McKnight and Dennis Venema
9. *The Genealogical Adam and Eve*, S. Joshua Swamidass
10. *In Quest of the Historical Adam*, William Lane Craig

11. *Since the Beginning: Interpreting Genesis 1 and 2 Through the Ages,* Kyle R. Greenwood (Editor)
12. *Science, Creation, and the Bible: Reconciling Rival Theories of Origins,* Richard F. Carlson and Tremper Longman III
13. *Four Views on Creation, Evolution, and Intelligent Design,* J. B. Stump (Editor)
14. *Ark Encounter: The Making of a Creationist Theme Park,* James S. Bielo
15. *Baby Dinosaurs on the Ark?* Janet Kellogg Ray
16. *The God of Monkey Science,* Janet Kellog Ray
17. *Friend of Science, Friend of Faith,* Gregg Davidson

Bibliography

Aquinas, Saint Thomas. *Summa Theologica: Volume 1—Part 1*. New York: Cosimo, 2007.

Bennett, Bob. "Matters of the Heart." *Matters of the Heart*. Star Song Records, 1982.

Bishop of Hippo Saint Augustine. *The Literal Meaning of Genesis*, Ancient Christian Writers, no. 41. New York: Newman, 1982.

Bouteneff, Peter. *Beginnings. Ancient Christian Readings of the Biblical Creation Narratives*. Grand Rapids: Baker Academic, 2008.

Bryan, William Jennings. *The Memoirs of William Jennings Bryan*, Vol. II. Port Washington: Kennikat, 1925.

Calvin, John. *Commentaries on the First Book of Moses Called Genesis*. Translated by John King. Grand Rapids: Eerdmans, 1948.

Carter, Humphrey. *The Inklings: C. S. Lewis, J. R. R. Tolkien, Charles Williams, and Their Friends*. HarperCollins: London, 1978.

Chaffey, Tim. "How Should We Interpret the Bible?" *Answers in Genesis*, 22 Feb 2011. Web. 16 Nov 2015.

Coffman, Elesha. "What is Darwinism?" *Christian History* 107.

Darwin, Charles. *On the Origin of Species* 2nd ed. London: John Murray, 1860.

———. *A Letter to John Fordyce, May 7, 1879*. Interdisciplinary Encyclopedia of Religion and Science, inters.org.

Davidson, Gregg. *Friend of Science, Friend of Faith: Listening to God in His Works and Word*. Grand Rapids: Kregel Academic, 2019.

Davis, Buddy. "Dinosaurs on the Ark." *Answers Magazine*, 24 Feb 2010. Web. 13 Oct 2015.

Edersheim, Alfred. *Bible History: Old Testament*. Peabody, MA: Hendrickson, 1995.

Faulkner, Danny. "The Second Law of Thermodynamics and the Curse." *Answers Research Journal*, 13 Nov 2013. Web. 14 Dec 2015.

Fee, Gordon D. and Douglas Stuart. *How to Read the Bible for All Its Worth* 4th ed. Grand Rapids: Zondervan Academic, 2014.

Foley, Avery. "Did Adam Step on an Ant Before the Fall?" *Answers in Genesis*, 4 Dec 2015. Web. 11 Dec 2015.

Giberson, Karl W. *Saving the Original Sinner*. Boston, MA: Beacon, 2015.

Griffiths, Phillip D. R. *From Calvin to Barth: A Return to Protestant Orthodoxy?* Eugene: OR: Wipf & Stock, 2014.

Ham, Ken. "Answering Claims About the Ark Project." *Answers in Genesis*, 5 June 2015. Web. 5 July 2015.

———. "What's the Core Message of the Answers in Genesis Ministry?" *Answers in Genesis*, 18 March 2013. Web. 14 Nov 2015.

———. "Was There Death Before Adam Sinned?" *New Answers Book 3*, 25 April 2014. Web. 10 Oct 2015.

———. *The Lie*. Green Forest, AR: Master, 2012.

———. "Millions of Years: Are Souls at Stake?" *Answers in Genesis*, 1 Jan 2014. Web. 6 Aug 2015.

———. "Should BioLogos be Called ContraLogos Instead?" *Answers in Genesis*, 18, Jan 2014. Web. 6 Aug 2015.

———. "The Ultimate Motivation of this Prominent Theologian?" *Answers in Genesis*, 14 Feb 2014. Web. 10 Aug 2015.

———. "Textbook Misleading Many Seminary and Bible College Students," *Answers in Genesis*, 21 May 2014. Web. 10 Aug 2015.

———. "BioLogos Targets Children and Teens with Theistic Evolution," *Answers in Genesis*, 2 July 2014. Web. 10 August 2015.

———. "We'll Find a New Earth Within 20 Years," *Answers in Genesis*, 20 July 2014. Web. 15 Aug 2015.

———. "Christian Philosopher Says Science Doesn't Oppose Faith," *Answers in Genesis*, 29 Sept 2014. Web. 17 Sept 2015.

———. "Is the Pope Right that God is Not Afraid of New Things?" *Answers in Genesis*, 29 Oct 2014. Web. 18 Sept 2015.

———. "Who's Really Raising Kids Who Can't Think?" *Answers in Genesis*, 19 Dec 2014. Web. 15 Oct 2015.

———. "Answering Claims About the Ark Project," *Answers in Genesis*, 5 June 2015. Web. 7 July 2015.

———. "What is a BDG?" *Answers in Genesis*, 19 Sept 2015. Web. 23 Sept 2015.

Ham, Ken and Britt Beemer. *Already Gone*. Green Forest AR: Master, 2009.

Ham, Ken and Tim Lovett, "Was there Really a Noah's Ark and Flood?" *New Answers Book: Answers in Genesis*, 15 Feb 2014. Web. 11 Dec 2015.

Ham, Steve. "The Lost World of Adam and Eve—A Response," *Answers in Genesis*, 29 July 2015. Web. 3 Oct 2015.

Hodge, Bodie. "Why Don't We Find Human and Dinosaur Fossils Together?" *A Pocket Guide to Dinosaurs: Is There a Biblical Explanation?* Answers in Genesis—USA, 2010.

Irenaeus of Lyons. *Proof of the Apostolic Preaching*, (Amazon Digital Services LLC, 2010).

———. *Against Heresies*, Paul Boer Sr., Ed. (Veritas Splendor Publications: Amazon Digital Services LLC, 2012).

Jaschik, Scott. "The Video that Ended a Career." *Inside Higher Ed*. 9 April 2010. Web. 15 May 2011.

Lacey, Troy. "Deceitful or Distinguishable Terms," *Answers in Genesis*, 10 June 2011. Web. 15 Sept 2015.

Lisle, Jason. "Distant Starlight: The Anisotropic Synchrony Convention," *Answers in Genesis*, 25 May 2011. Web 25 Aug 2015.

———. "Straight Answers to Common Questions," *Answers in Genesis*, 5 Dec 2007. Web. 25 Aug 2015.

Lorey, Frank. "Tree Rings and Biblical Chronology." *Institute for Creation Research*. Web. 11 April 2014.

Luther, Martin. *Luther on the Creation: A Critical and Devotional Commentary on Genesis*. Translated by John Nicholas Lenker. Minneapolis, MN: Lutherans in All Lands, 1904.

———. *Luther's Works. Vol 54. Table Talk*. Edited by Helmut T. Lehmann. Philadelphia, PA: Fortress, 1967.

McGrath, Alister. *Heresy: A History of Defending the Truth*. New York: HarperOne, 2010.

Minns, Denis. *Irenaeus*. New York: T. & T. Clark, 2010.

Mitchell, Elizabeth. "Evaluating Giberson's Book *Saving the Original Sinner* with Scripture and Science." *Answers in Genesis*, 11 Nov 2015. Web. 12 Nov 2015.

Newman, John H. *A letter to J. Walker of Scarborough, May 22, 1868*. Interdisciplinary Encyclopedia of Religion and Science, inters.org.

Nicene and Post-Nicene Fathers: Second Series. Edited by Alexander Roberts and James Donaldson. 1885–1887. 14 vols. Repr. Peabody, MA: Hendrickson, 1994.

Oard, Michael J. "Do Ice Cores Show Many of Tens of Thousands of Years?" *Answers in Genesis*, 16 Feb 2014. Web. 1 Nov 2015.

Origen, *De Principiis*, 4, 16, in *The Works of Origen*, Arthur Cleveland Cox, Ed. (Amazon Digital Services LLC: 2011).

"Public Views on Evolution." *Pew Research Center: Religion and Public Life*. 30 Dec 2013. Web. 12 June 2015.

Schneider, John R. "The Fall of 'Augustinian Adam': Original Fragility and Supralapsarian Purpose." *Zygon: Journal of Religion and Science* 47 (2012) 949–69.

Taylor, Paul F. "How did Animals Spread all Over the World from Where the Ark Landed?" *New Answers Book*, 17 Feb 2014. Web. 13 Oct 2015.

Walton, John. *The Lost World of Genesis 1*. Downers Grove, IL: Intervarsity, 2009.

Wesley, John. *Wesley's Notes on the Bible*. Grand Rapids: Francis Asbury, 1987.

"What Darwin Never Knew." *Nova*. Directors: John Rubin, Rushmore DeNooyer, Serena Davis, and Sarah Holt. 29 December 2009.

Whitcomb, John. *The Early Earth*. Grand Rapids: Baker, 1972.

"Who Was Cain's Wife?" *Answers in Genesis*. Web. 15 Nov 2015.

Wright, N. T. *Surprised by Scripture*. New York: HarperOne, 2014.

Young, Davis A. *John Calvin and the Natural World*. Lanham, MD: University Press of America, 2007.

Zimmerman, Anthony. *Evolution and the Sin in Eden*. New York: University Press of America, 1998.

About the Author

Joel Edmund Anderson is both a high school English teacher in Little Rock, Arkansas, and a former adjunct instructor in Religious Studies at the University of North Alabama, where he taught various courses on the Old Testament, New Testament, and World Religions. He taught for sixteen years at various Evangelical Christian high schools in California, Arkansas, and Alabama, teaching English Literature, Bible, Church History, and Worldview.

In addition to *The Heresy of Ham*, Anderson is the author of *Christianity and the (R)evolution in Worldviews in Western Culture*, and *The Blue-Collar Bible Scholar's Reader's Guide to the New Testament*. He has also written several articles for *Biblical Theology Bulletin*, *Journal for the Evangelical Study of the Old Testament*, and *Currents in Biblical Research*. He also maintains a blog, *resurrecting orthodoxy* (at joeledmundanderson.com), where he writes on a variety of topics, from Biblical Studies, Church History, the New Atheist Movement, Young Earth Creationism, and other topics related to Christianity.

Anderson holds a B.S. Ed. in English from Northwest Missouri State University, an M.A. in Theological Studies from Regent College, an M.A. in Old Testament Studies from Trinity Western University, and a Ph.D. in Old Testament from University of Pretoria.

www.ingramcontent.com/pod-product-compliance
Lightning Source LLC
Chambersburg PA
CBHW071229230426
43668CB00011B/1367